Greece from Junta to Crisis

Greece from Junta to Crisis

Modernization, Transition and Diversity

Dimitris Tziovas

BLOOMSBURY ACADEMIC
LONDON • NEW YORK • OXFORD • NEW DELHI • SYDNEY

BLOOMSBURY ACADEMIC
Bloomsbury Publishing Plc
50 Bedford Square, London, WC1B 3DP, UK
1385 Broadway, New York, NY 10018, USA
29 Earlsfort Terrace, Dublin 2, Ireland

BLOOMSBURY, BLOOMSBURY ACADEMIC and the Diana logo
are trademarks of Bloomsbury Publishing Plc

First published in Great Britain 2021
This paperback edition published by Bloomsbury Academic in 2023

Copyright © Dimitris Tziovas, 2021

Dimitris Tziovas has asserted his right under the Copyright,
Designs and Patents Act, 1988, to be identified as Author of this work.

Series design by Adriana Brioso
Cover image: Wall for Sale, Metaxourgeio, Athens, artwork courtesy of
Bleeps.gr, 2015, and photo courtesy of Julia Tulke, 2016

All rights reserved. No part of this publication may be reproduced or
transmitted in any form or by any means, electronic or mechanical,
including photocopying, recording, or any information storage or retrieval
system, without prior permission in writing from the publishers.

Bloomsbury Publishing Plc does not have any control over, or responsibility for,
any third-party websites referred to or in this book. All internet addresses given
in this book were correct at the time of going to press. The author and publisher
regret any inconvenience caused if addresses have changed or sites have
ceased to exist, but can accept no responsibility for any such changes.

A catalogue record for this book is available from the British Library.

A catalog record for this book is available from the Library of Congress.

ISBN: HB: 978-0-7556-1744-9
PB: 978-0-7556-4254-0
ePDF: 978-0-7556-1746-3
eBook: 978-0-7556-1745-6

Typeset by Newgen KnowledgeWorks Pvt. Ltd., Chennai, India

To find out more about our authors and books visit
www.bloomsbury.com and sign up for our newsletters.

Contents

List of Illustrations	vi
Preface	vii
Introduction	1
1 Modernization and cultural dualisms	19
2 Eurosceptics or Europhiles? The cultural dilemmas of Europeanization	43
3 Debating the nation and its contested pasts: Antiquity and mnemohistory	65
4 Identity, religion, migration: From homogeneity to embracing otherness	93
5 Language questions: From standardization to diversity	125
6 From poetry to prose: Discovering modernism and revising the canon	143
7 The challenges of deregulation: From monophonic to polyphonic media	161
8 Cinematic allegories: From history to domesticity	179
9 Youth, feminism and sexuality: From *oikos* to *demos*	199
10 The rediscoveries of Greece: From ancient ruins to the ruins of crisis	233
Conclusion	249
References	253
Index	295

Illustrations

Figures

1	German tourist in Monastiraki (Athens), 1983	34
2	PASOK poster in the Euro-elections of 1989	48
3	Graffiti on a bank branch in Athens (Summer 2011)	75
4	Are they really speaking the same language? Cartoon by Arkas	134
5	A T-shirt with a caricature of Yanis Varoufakis	176
6	An emblematic scene from Theo Angelopoulos' *Voyage to Cythera*	187
7	'*National Memory I*', a painting by Christos Bokoros	207
8	Women's Rights Demonstration in Athens (1981)	213
9	Cover of the German periodical *Der Spiegel* (11 July 2015)	239
10	A stencil on the campus of the Athens School of Fine Arts	246

Table

1	The number of novels and poetry collections published between 1999 and 2011	146

Preface

A book in English on post-junta Greece is long overdue, as has become increasingly apparent to me during my long teaching career at the University of Birmingham. After the completion of my Arts and Humanities Research Council (AHRC) project on the crisis and editing the volume *Greece in Crisis: The Cultural Politics of Austerity* (I.B. Tauris, 2017), I decided that the time had come to attempt such an interdisciplinary project, using two watershed events in Greek history, the fall of the military junta and the economic crisis, to bookend it. Analysing and mapping out cultural undercurrents has to be done in relation to an extensive time span and this accounts for the long period covered by this study. Obviously, the book does not aspire to offer comprehensive coverage of developments in Greece after 1974 but simply aims to explore certain important areas, deploying a cultural perspective and using three key concepts as connecting threads in the analysis: modernization, transition and diversity. The number of articles published in English on the crisis, as well as on post-junta Greece, over the last decade has been unprecedented and the time has come for a broader study, which can synthesize research findings, critically reflect on the accumulated material and appeal to academic and non-specialist audiences alike. The book's range may seem ambitious, but hopefully it will provide a sound basis for more extensive studies in the future.

This project was made possible, thanks to a two-year Leverhulme Research Fellowship (2018–20), for which I am most grateful to the Leverhulme Trust. I have had the opportunity to present material from this book in lectures at the Universities of Munich and Cambridge and in papers at conferences in Athens, Thessaloniki and the University of Crete. An earlier version of the first chapter has been published in the journal *Byzantine and Modern Greek Studies* (vol. 41, no. 2, 2017) and a shorter version of the last chapter in the book *Political and Cultural Aspects of Greek Exoticism*, edited by Panayis Panagiotopoulos and Dimitris P. Sotiropoulos (Palgrave Macmillan, 2020). I would like to thank those who invited me to present my work as well as all those who either helped me with research and other inquiries or have read parts of the book. These include N. C. Alivizatos, Maria Antonopoulou, Venetia Apostolidou, Maria Chalkou, Dimitris Christopoulos, Elissavet Evangelidou, Eleni Fournaraki, Gregory

Jusdanis, Vicky Kaisidou, Socrates Kabouropoulos, Eleni Kovaiou, Kostas Kostis, Katerina Krikos-Davis, Vassilis Lambropoulos, Peter Mackridge, Vassilis Makrides, Gerasimia Melissaratou, Valerie Nunn, Grigoris Paschalidis, Georgia Pateridou, Nikos Sarantakos, Erik Sjöberg, Maria Stassinopoulou, Julia Tulke, Marianna Spanaki, Yannis Tzortzis and Lina Ventura. Their assistance is very much appreciated and duly acknowledged. Special thanks are also due to the Leventis Foundation for their assistance with the production/editorial costs of the book.

September 2020

Introduction

From junta to crisis

The period following the fall of the military junta in 1974 could be seen as a time of consolidating and celebrating democracy and has been described as the 'Swiss phase' of Greek history. Known as the *Metapolitefsi* (meaning regime change), referring both to the transition from dictatorship to democracy and to the ensuing period (but with no agreement as to its duration), it changed the political landscape of Greece and led to the country's longest period of peace and prosperity.[1] It also contributed to the reconciliation of warring factions in Greek society with the legalization of the Communist Party (KKE) and the return of political refugees and paved the way to consensus on the abolition of the monarchy (1974), the language question (1976) and membership of the European club (1981). A period of high expectations, dynamism and mobility was inaugurated and Greece gradually developed into a tolerant society. The restoration of democracy challenged the post-Civil War ideological status quo by replacing anti-communism with anti-fascism as the country's foundational myth, the nation (*ethnos*) with the people (*laos*), *ethnikofrosyni* (patriotism) with *ellenikotita/romiosyni* (Greekness) and the promotion of democratic values.

Though the *Metapolitefsi* is seen primarily as a political event or turning point, we do not need yet another book about its politics. The emphasis on the political developments has obscured the cultural dynamics of the period and therefore the main aim of this book is to explore the pivotal role of culture in shaping the post-junta era. If the *Metapolitefsi* can be described in political terms as an age of democratization and reconciliation, in cultural terms it might be defined as the age of identities, since its main preoccupations, as discussed

---

[1] During the 1970s and 1980s the word 'Metapolitefsi' was used to refer primarily to the regime change in 1974, but since 1989 its meaning has been expanded to cover a wider period (Kallivretakis 2017: 215). Some people also refer to the post-junta period as the 'Third Hellenic Republic'.

in this study (Europeanization, contested pasts, religion, migration, language and gender), converge from different pathways on the notion of identity as a common denominator. And this backs up the claim that culture has always been ahead of political or institutional initiatives in rehabilitating or promoting the other, the marginal or the neglected in various cultural discourses and art forms.

How then should we define or periodize the *Metapolitefsi*? When does it end? And is it a useful term? These questions have been discussed for years and, while the term itself is still shrouded in vagueness, there are definitely two main approaches to the *Metapolitefsi*: the politico-historical one, which tends to focus on outlining its various phases or speculating about its end, and the evaluative, which is retrospective and totalizing in assessing the period as a whole. In his book *Greece of Metapolitefsi 1974–2009*, Yannis Voulgaris divides this period into two phases: 1974–89 (Greece of *Metapolitefsi*) and 1990–2009 (Greece of globalization) (2013: 13).[2] This periodization may appear confusing because the term *Metapolitefsi* is used for both a shorter and a longer period, yet it reflects the widespread uncertainty about its death throes. As with the postwar period, most historians tend to delimit the beginning but not the end of the era. And punning statements such as 'let's put an end to the *Metapolitefsi*' show an eagerness for closure. It is worth noting that similar pronouncements have been made ever since the mid-1980s. Later on historians were keen to place the end firmly in 1989, which they justified by citing the rise of individualism and the receding of the political as a social ideal (Voglis 2011), while others saw the start of the economic crisis as decisively marking its end (Pappas 2014) and the threshold to the twenty-first century (Liakos 2014: 13–14).

The *Metapolitefsi* might be seen as a break with the past or a new era, yet what is celebrated on 24 July every year is not a new beginning but a kind of continuity: the restoration of democracy after the hiatus of the dictatorship and the return to power of politicians from the 1960s. The nostalgia for earlier, better times or the fantasy of the restoration of an elusive prosperity can also be detected in some discussions about the crisis. Though there was even talk of a 'second *Metapolitefsi*' (Pretenderis 1996) and the qualifier 'perpetual'(αέναη) has occasionally been attached to the term, signalling a constant desire for a

---

[2] Christoforos Vernardakis has offered another periodization by referring to an early period (1974–81), an intermediate (1981–96) and a late *Metapolitefsi* (1996–2010) (2011: xxi). N. C. Alivizatos (2015) singles out two forward-looking and creative periods of the *Metapolitefsi* (1974–7 and 1996–2000) describing the other periods as static or even retrogressive. Membership of the eurozone (1 January 2002) has also been seen as another turning point in the history of the *Metapolitefsi*, while the two referenda of December 1974 (on the restoration/abolition of the monarchy) and July 2015 have been suggested as possible markers in the period (Avgeridis, Gazi and Kornetis 2015: 16).

symbolic new beginning, the crisis seems to have provided a definite end point for the *Metapolitefsi*. Yet it could be argued that a period reaches its end when we start reflecting back on it or speculating about its end. In this case, however, the period of reflection was rather lengthy, pointing to a *longue durée* or, for some, to an endless hangover.

On the one hand the *Metapolitefsi* has been praised as a period of prosperity, democratization, peace and improved access to health and education, while on the other it has been criticized for clientelism, failed modernization, state expansion, corruption and political violence (Kalyvas 2016: 56, 60). The crisis strengthened this dual perception of the post-1974 period both as success and failure, progress and regression. Though critical assessments can be found earlier, with the 1980s being described as either a wasted or a populist decade (Clogg 1993; cf. Vamvakas and Panagiotopoulos 2014), the crisis has fostered a rereading and retrospective criticism of the post-dictatorship transition to democracy (Zestanakis 2016). It has prompted many commentators, for instance, to regard the recent difficulties as the result of the earlier failures and 'populism as *the* most important chapter in the autobiography of Greece's *Metapolitefsi*' (Pappas 2014: 8–9). The country's post-1974 history has been turned into an interpretative framework and has often been blamed for the troubled present and the uncertain future (Liakos and Kouki 2015: 53).

According to the critical approach espoused in different ways by both the Right and the Left, the *Metapolitefsi* saw the rise of an agonistic mentality, particularly in the eyes of those who had been persecuted and marginalized in the aftermath of the Civil War. For the Left, the emergent anti-authoritarian culture was critical of institutions such as the Church, which were supportive of the post-Civil War status quo and the junta.[3] Such criticism has even been extended to more recent practices implied by the slogan 'The junta did not end in 1973', used as late as June 2013, when the government shut down the public broadcasting organization (ERT). From a right-wing perspective, the agonistic mentality cultivated a counterculture of disobedience and suspicion towards any form of political consensus, culminating in the events of December 2008 and the perception of the crisis as a form of colonization. Interestingly, Greece has had one of the most persistent problems with political violence in Europe and this has been a continuing aggravation in various manifestations since the 1970s (Kassimeris 2001 and 2013). It could be said, however, that the critical reception

---

[3] According to the historian Antonis Liakos, the Church is the only institution not to have been touched by the *Metapolitefsi* ('Ο Δεσπότης και η πλύστρα', *To Vima*, 20 March 2005).

of the post-junta period was not so much directed at its politics as its so-called 'culture', inviting us to take a cultural approach to the period.

Though the economic crisis had begun earlier, May 2010, the date of the first bailout agreement between the Greek government and the EU/IMF, has been treated as the starting point of the period of impoverishment and loss of sovereignty that saw Greece lose a quarter of its GDP.[4] The qualifier 'economic' (or 'debt') was quite quickly dropped, indicating that the crisis was a wider phenomenon than a purely financial one, which had inaugurated a period of post-democracy with decisions being taken by technocrats or unelected bodies outside the country, undermining the democratic processes. A discourse of Greek exceptionalism was also encouraged by the crisis, presenting Greece as a 'sinful' country not comparable to other EU members.[5] What characterized the Greek crisis was not just its intensity but also its duration for political and economic reasons related to the lack of consensus among politicians compared to the other countries in crisis (e.g. Portugal, Cyprus) or involving Greece's inability to devalue its currency and thus reduce the debt. Because of its financial difficulties, Greece secured the largest ever support package offered to a nation state, yet the crisis led to new social and ideological divisions and has radically altered the way of life of many Greeks.[6] For some it brought back the ghost of the Civil War and divided Greeks once again (with references to *Germanotsoliades* and *tagmatasfalites*),[7] while for others it made them more critical of the elites and the political parties.

---

[4] In October 2009 the newly elected socialist government admitted that Greece was running an unsustainably high budget deficit and public debt.

[5] Klaus Regling, ESM Managing Director, in a speech in Munich on 16 February 2017 stated, 'Greece is a special case. Nowhere the extent of the problems was as large as in Greece, and the administration as weak' https://www.esm.europa.eu/speeches-and-presentations/next-steps-make-euro-area-more-resilient. On 3 August 2018 the *Washington Post* reported that 'Greece has been one of the biggest economic failures you'll ever see short of a war or revolution ... there are only four countries that have grown less – or, more accurately, shrunk more – than Greece has in the past 10 years: Libya, Yemen, Venezuela and Equatorial Guinea' (Matt O'Brien, 'Only four economies have shrunk more than Greece's in the past 10 years. Two of them have been hit by civil wars', https://www.washingtonpost.com/business/2018/08/03/only-four-economies-have-shrunk-more-than-greeces-last-years-two-them-have-been-hit-by-civil-wars/?noredirect=on&utm_term=.286d50556909).

[6] The demographic impact of the crisis is enormous with the population of Greece shrinking and expected to decline even further in the coming years. The number of births between 2009 and 2017 went down by 29,380, a rate similar to the 1940s. See http://www.sev.org.gr/vivliothiki-tekmiriosi/evdomadiaio-deltio-gia-tin-elliniki-oikonomia/sos-o-plithysmos-tis-choras-meionetai-kai-gernaei-6-dekemvriou-2018/. The reduction in kiosks in Athens also shows the extent of the crisis. In 2011 there were 931 kiosks and in seven years (2018) these were reduced to 600, while the Municipality of Athens decided to remove 323 deserted kiosks. On the other hand, the number of pawnshops shot up during the crisis from 81 in 2010 to 274 in 2012.

[7] Meaning the Greek collaborationist security battalions formed by the puppet government of Ioannis Rallis during the Axis Occupation of Greece in order to support the German troops.

The Greek word 'κρίση' is indeed an elusive signifier with a number of possible referents, denoting also 'choice', 'judgement' and 'decision'. Crisis and critique are cognates in Greek, as Reinhart Koselleck (1988) reminds us. The word crisis can refer to an event (e.g. the Suez crisis) or a condition, whether permanent or temporary (e.g. institutions in crisis). For many it is never a descriptive designation but a framework that privileges and legitimizes narratives and interpretations. Are we constantly in a state of crisis? Have crises replaced the historical questions of the past (e.g. the Eastern Question) in the sociopolitical discourse? How is a crisis diagnosed and by whom? Who is articulating claims to crisis? Crisis compared to what? Can a crisis act as an explanatory trope or is it just a state of affairs? Does a crisis produce a tendency to retrospection, a sort of nostalgia for the happy days of the past or a forward-looking desire for reform or the politics of possibility? Is the crisis just a narrative device (Roitman 2013), an 'iterative periodic concept' or a 'concept of futurity' (Koselleck 2006)? Are crises inherent in the capitalist process (Harvey 2010)? Can we narrate a future without crisis? These are some of the general questions which can apply to different kinds of crises, including the recent Greek crisis.

The phrase a 'nation in crisis' may have been used to describe Greece in the 1940s (Iatrides 1981), indicating that the country had experienced crises before in its history, yet the big issue in the recent crisis has been whether it could be seen as just an economic phenomenon and, thus, part of the global economic meltdown of 2008 or whether it was a more localized phenomenon with traceable historical and cultural roots.[8] Though the economy tended to be the primary focus during the crisis, those who argued that the crisis was primarily social and cultural and tried to trace its origins in the past saw it more from a sociocultural perspective. As opposed to the structural and globalist interpretation of the Greek crisis, the culturalist approach, according to some analysts on the Left, moralizes austerity as a primarily transformative or disciplinary programme and shifts the focus onto culture as the deeper root of the problem (Mylonas 2014). The culturalization of politics involves explaining political developments according to a narrative that locates the roots of the crisis in inherent 'cultural flaws' and downplays the structural problems of the eurozone. Therefore, the structural/globalist and the culturalist approach came into conflict, and this might be one of the reasons that the Greek crisis

---

[8] Panayiotis Ioakimidis claimed that the crisis was 'made in Greece' and was primarily cultural (2011: 21) while Mitsopoulos and Pelagidis argued 'that the causes of this crisis were deeply rooted in the way the country had been run during the last thirty years' (2012: 211). See also Marangudakis (2019: xiv) and Danopoulos (2014).

attracted such unprecedented international interest (Tziovas 2017). There is also an ethical and spiritual framing of the crisis as a trial or even a God-given 'instructive' punishment, accompanied by an understanding of austerity as an opportunity for salvation.[9]

Just as the fall of the junta encouraged a re-examination of the post-Civil War period, the recent economic crisis has prompted a rethink of the *Metapolitefsi*, triggering self-reflection and prompting a revisiting of political and cultural trends in Greece since 1974. The country's post-war struggle focused on overcoming poverty and rebuilding the economy after the devastation of the 1940s, thus leading to the expansion of the middle class, increased social mobility and rapid improvements in living standards during the 1960s and early 1970s. This brought about a shift from economic to cultural concerns and a post-junta preoccupation with questions of identity and memory in an attempt to come to terms with otherness and diversity. Without adopting a deterministic culturalist explanation, this study revisits a range of cultural developments in order to present a more nuanced picture of the period from junta to crisis. But first it is useful to review the analytical paradigms of the *Metapolitefsi* and see how we can move beyond them.

Beyond the dependency and modernization paradigms

Dependency, (under)development and modernization were key concepts in the *Metapolitefsi* with the 'dependency' of the late 1970s and early 1980s and 'modernization' (a term loaded with meaning but often lacking in definition) from the mid-1980s onwards being the two dominant theories for explaining Greece's position in the world. The former involved either the Cold War dynamics and its political divisions, assigning Greece nominally to the West, or the neo-Marxist 'dependency narrative', placing Greece in the Third World or the capitalist periphery (echoing the theories of the American economists Paul A. Baran and Paul Sweezy and their book *Monopoly Capital* (1966)). This approach relied mainly on political oppositions and economic considerations without explaining either why Greece was prone to more economic crises than

---

[9] According to some religious fundamentalists, the crisis has to do with the adoption of a secular way of life marked by individualism and materialism. This reading of the crisis as a kind of theodicy, requiring a move away from Western-style consumption and corruption to ascesis and endurance, shifts the emphasis from the external economic conditions to the transformation of the self and the restoration of Orthodox values (Kessareas 2018).

other Organization for Economic Co-operation and Development (OECD) or EU partners or why it developed a decent parliamentary system at an early stage, joined exclusive Western clubs (OECD, NATO and EU) and was among the top forty countries in terms of its per capita income.

Earlier contributions to the modernization debate by Marxist sociologists adopted the dependency approach and focused primarily on the role of the state. In a paper on tradition and modernization, Konstantinos Tsoukalas points out that 'the "difference" between peripheral and central societies is usually experienced as "lack", "distortion" or "weakness"' (1983: 40). He also added that peripheral societies develop 'forms of articulation between society and state' completely different to Western European models. In his view, in Greece the state has not functioned according to Weberian criteria of rational bureaucracy and this constitutes the particularity of the Greek case in contrast to the 'West'. His approach was informed by the neo-Marxist dependency theory, as the title of his study *Dependency and Reproduction: The social role of educational mechanisms in Greece (1830–1922)* and the following passage from its introduction suggest: 'The dependence of Greek society on the forces of the capitalist centre has determined its political, social and economic development for one and a half centuries' (1977: 15).

Another leading sociologist, Nicos Mouzelis, used the notions of 'clientelism', 'patronage' and 'underdevelopment' to demonstrate that Greece 'deviated' from the paradigm of the capitalist Western societies. For him the state is a 'shapeless monster', unwilling and unable to react to a rapidly changing international environment, while its rigid, over-politicized and particularistic orientations 'have made it act in ways that merely consolidate Greece's semi-peripheral/peripheral status within the world economy and also within the European Union' (1996: 222). In reviewing different theories of modernization and their relevance to Greece, Mouzelis considers them unacceptably Eurocentric, but he still argues for some sort of 'catching up' in terms of democratization.

> The way for Greece to maintain its national identity within Europe is neither by turning its back on the values of Western Enlightenment nor, on the other hand, by imitating in a servile manner the commercialized syncretism of the global, postmodern culture. Instead, the way for Greece to maintain its national identity within Europe is to pursue a type of integration where 'catching up with the West' refers less to mindless consumerism and more to deep democratization – i.e., to the spread of rights from the top to the bottom of the social pyramid. (1996: 226)

Though he sees the development of Greece not as 'a question of imitating or catching up with the West' (1978: 153), he still promotes Western Enlightenment as opposed to the anti-Europeanism and fanatical obscurantism of the Orthodox Church, considering the former's achievements as 'basic prerequisites for the maintenance and revival of Greece's cultural heritage and national identity' (1996: 227).

Tsoukalas's and Mouzelis's approaches to modernization are informed, as I said, by the neo-Marxist theory of the dependency of the (semi-)periphery on the capitalist centre (Voulgaris 2019). From another Marxist perspective of the 1970s, Costis Moskov pointed to the dependency of the Greek state on the West and particularly the inadequate appropriation of its liberal ideology by the Greek bourgeois compradors. Though the 'popular Orthodox tradition' was in decline during the first decades of the new Greek state (1830–1909), he highlighted its potential for liberating Greeks from the capitalist West and forming an alliance with communism, provided that the latter relinquished its economic positivism. By combining Orthodoxy and Marxism, Moskov tried to outline a different pathway for overcoming Western dominance and securing the Greek state's autonomy (Moskov 1972/4 and 1980).

Later approaches equated modernization with Europeanization, focusing on institutional, legal or social policy reform and following EU guidelines. Their focus was not so much on Greece's economic dependency as on catching up with Europe. Modernization, coupled with Europeanization and rationalization, became the mantra of Costas Simitis's period of office (1996–2004) and for his followers (Economides 2017). As a one-way process, it involved equating the West with modernity and the efforts of a state with inadequate institutional infrastructure to catch up with the Western model. Being evolutionary, teleological and referring to a number of processes such as industrialization, secularization and democratization, modernization represented an invitation to internalize the need to strive to catch up and invited Greeks to measure themselves against European models or work towards achieving European standards and in turn shed any traces of belatedness or underdevelopment. Assessing Greece's place in comparison to the 'advanced', 'modernized' countries of the West, as well as where it should be and how it was to get there, were questions deemed crucial and pressing for most of the intellectuals of the *Metapolitefsi*.

Practices such as locating Greece in the capitalist periphery or judging its performance by European standards were accompanied by debates on cultural dualism. Greece was seen as constantly caught between tradition and modernity,

East and West, Orthodoxy and Enlightenment, Byzantium/the Romeic and Antiquity/the Hellenic and the reformist and the underdog culture. One of the best sellers of the *Metapolitefsi* was a short book by Nikos Dimou, *On the Unhappiness of Being Greek* (1975), which was first published soon after the fall of junta and has since then gone through a number of editions (thirty-eight so far) and been translated into English. An excerpt from the postscript to the 2013 edition demonstrates the resilience of the dualist perception of the Greek torn between opposing forces: 'He is divided between his glorious past and his meagre present, between his Eastern mentality and his European aspirations – torn asunder by forces of tradition (like the Orthodox Church) and modernity. His is a difficult fate' (2013: 41). The tyranny of dualism seems to trap Greeks into two incompatible identity roles: as both Western, responsible and disciplined individuals (an image on display during the first Covid-19 lockdown) and as members of a caring, traditional community, marked by cultural intimacy and family values.

Modernization in politics and economics and dualism in the area of culture emerged as the dominant analytical paradigms of post-junta Greece. While in the domain of social and economic policy or institutional reform modernization was driven by the Europeanization agenda, discussions about the cultural orientation and identity of the country were more ambivalent and open-ended. The main challenge Greece faced during the *Metapolitefsi* was to demonstrate that the country was able to complete the project of modernization, which, in turn, would have tipped the balance in the sphere of dualist oppositions by overcoming divisions and dissent and achieving some sort of synthesis or consensus. Following the crisis this still seems to be desirable for some and open to debate for others.

Relying on a comparison with the 'developed' world and an idealized picture of the 'West' (often taken as an undifferentiated entity), modernization points to a series of deviations or absences in Greek society (e.g. a middle class (Kondylis 1991/2011), civil society (Mouzelis 1978 and 1996) and individualization (Ramfos 2000)), while the narrative of modernization highlighted underdeveloped projects or frustrated reforms (e.g. education (Dimaras 1973 and 1974)). Intellectual historians asked, 'Why did the Enlightenment not lead to the development of a liberal political culture in Greece?' (Kitromilides 1996a and 2013) and economic historians enquired, 'Why was there no heavy industry in Greece?' or noted the absence of a large Greek working class comparable to those in Western European countries.[10] The

---

[10] In the preface (omitted in the second, 2016, edition) of the first edition of his book *Modern Greece* (2001: xiii), Thomas Gallant expresses his scepticism about the term but he still uses it: 'I am

country has been judged according to a Western model and has been found lacking or simply divergent, as the following quotation from a recent article by the anthropologist Renée Hirschon suggests: 'What I call a "pre-modern" approach (or a "non-Western" one) to issues of time-management continues to prevail in Greece, because Greece did not follow the path of industrialization of the developed countries of the EU' (2014: 156). By adopting a comparative or dualist approach, the modernization theory treats Greece as a story of inadequacy or belatedness.[11]

Belated compared to other Europeans and inferior in respect to their ancient ancestors, Greeks have always been measured and found wanting. In his book *Belated Modernity and Aesthetic Culture*, Gregory Jusdanis put forward the view that modernization in Greece had been judged 'imperfect' on the assumption that in non-western societies belated modernization 'remains "incomplete" not because it deviates from the supposedly correct path but because it cannot culminate in a faithful duplication of western prototypes' (1991: xiii). Peripheral societies internalize the incongruity between Western originals and local realities as a structural deficiency. Therefore, the lack of modernity is seen as a flaw, which, according to Jusdanis, 'lies not in modernity's absence but in its purposeful introduction, ignoring autochthonous exigencies' (1991: xiii).

Modernization theories based on the pattern of the Western model and its inadequate reproduction have been supported by the Western idealization of Classical Greece, which also presupposes the comparative difference between the latter and the present day as well as the Western discontent with the modern country (Gourgouris 1996: 73). This could range from disappointment, a falling short of Greece's reputation in the Western imaginary, to the consideration of the country as inadequately modern or institutionally inefficient, an image reinforced by the recent crisis. The conflicting symbiosis of these two discourses among Westerners, and even Greeks themselves, became more visible as a result of the challenges of EEC/EU membership and received additional impetus during the crisis. Notions of underdevelopment, belatedness or insufficient

---

aware that modernization is a loaded term and that in its most robust form modernization theory has come in for considerable criticism, much of which I accept. However, I would suggest that modernization theory may still provide us with a useful heuristic device for categorization or a yardstick against which we can measure developments in any specific culture. In other words, if we accept for the sake of argument that certain features of the developed western world may be labeled as "modern", then we can employ for the sake of argument the term "modernization" as a form of shorthand abbreviation for a comparison of those specified features found in the developed world and elsewhere. I employ the term in this limited sense.'

[11] The themes of 'failure', 'lack' and 'inadequacy' characterize the speaking subject of 'Indian' history (Chakrabarty 2000: 34). On modernization in the Balkans see Daskalov (1997).

modernity formed a negative and pre-modern picture of Greece. Things become further complicated by the fact that Greeks themselves might either be complicit in this blaming and self-orientalizing process or strenuously resist it by harking back to the glory of the Classical era or displaying national pride. Greeks appear to have internalized their presumed inferiority to 'Europeans', while at the same time trying to deny it using the cultural capital of antiquity, thus facing the predicament of a postcolonial subject looking for signs of rejection as much as signs of affirmation. Culture has enabled elites in postcolonial and belated societies to understand and try to overcome their 'backwardness' and has therefore figured prominently in modernization projects.

Even in a recent study it has been claimed that 'in the case of peripheral capitalist societies, like Greece, for instance, tradition and modernity emerge as conflictual trends in an antagonistic relationship' (Triandafyllidou et al. 2013: 12). Such statements confirm that up to now the narratives about Greece have been dominated by binarisms (West–East, modernity–traditionalism, modernization–populism), informed by political developments and promoting Westernizing and modernizing trends. All this suggests that the discussion of modernization in Greece has pointed to different forms of engagement with Europe: socio-economic (dependency theory), political-institutional (Europeanization) or cultural (dualisms).

Departing from this approach, my study aspires to produce a more complex and hybrid narrative by focusing on the area of culture and self-understanding. The changing patterns of migration and attitudes to the past, the roller coaster of Euroscepticism, the rehabilitation of those defeated in the Civil War (1946–9), the rediscovery of the Balkans following the end of the Cold War, the proliferation of audiences, canons and pasts, the growth of social movements, the rise of otherness and increased linguistic diversity add up to a more diverse society, whose development has to be seen as more complex. As a result, the dominant paradigm of modernization has begun to be questioned, while the practice of equating Europe with modernity began to break down, particularly during the crisis, when the discourse of 'normalization' (expressed by the slogan 'Greece should become a normal country') seems to have run parallel with that of modernization.

Despite its revitalization in the 1990s in the form of the democratization of the countries of Eastern Europe, modernization has been challenged for being a neo-colonial strategy to force 'others' onto an inescapable and not culturally specific track towards development. The critique of teleological modernization theories led to the concepts of 'multiple modernities'

(Eisenstadt 2000 and 2003), varieties of modernity (Schmidt 2006) or the ambivalences of modernity (Bauman 1991). Furthermore, the concept of reflexive modernization was introduced by Ulrich Beck in connection with the notion of 'second modernity' and the emergence of the so-called 'risk society' with its increasing reflexivity or self-criticism (Beck, Giddens and Lash 1994). The concept of reflexive modernization takes into account the contradictions and consequences of modernizing developments and is concerned with re-evaluating existing resources rather than increasing them (Mergel 2012). Modernity, as a sociopolitical concept, has not vanished, but it is becoming increasingly problematic (Beck, Bonss and Lau 2003: 2). Postcolonial studies also rejected the normative pattern of modernization modelled on the European example and defended the autochthonous intellectual traditions of non-Western societies (Chakrabatry 2000). Working with concepts such as 'glocalization' or 'hybridization' to introduce variety and a dynamic perspective into the analysis of the contemporary world, it scrutinized the evolutionary premise of modernity, thus encouraging a move from a normative notion of modernization to perceiving it as a heterogeneous, hybrid and self-reflexive process.

Modernization might be defined and measured in institutional terms as convergence with Western models; from a cultural perspective it can be seen as a period of enhanced pluralism and diversity, involving resistances and setbacks, which in turn foster further differentiation from any presumed models. Modernization theories tend to underrate existing cultural differences, whereas 'multiple modernities' or 'varieties of modernity' emphasize them. The multiple modernities theory has been applied to the countries of East Asia (Japan and Singapore) or Eastern Europe after the collapse of communism and promotes the idea of varieties of modernity in the same way as we talk about varieties of capitalism. Multiple modernities are attentive to differences and modernization seems to be 'more of a multidimensional process than was traditionally assumed' (Allardt 2005: 498). On the basis that all contemporary societies are modern, only differently modern, it might be useful to look at political, institutional and cultural development in Greece from this perspective and the multitude of ways in which modernity expresses itself.

Hitherto the models used to analyse Greek society have been permeated by theories of dependency, belatedness or absence, but gradually a shift is taking place from a comparative juxtaposition of Greece with Europe, using Western modernity as a yardstick, to a comparative consideration of Greece in postcolonial, orientalist or anti-Western terms. This has involved either exploring its semi- or crypto-colonial status and its role in the orientalist imaginative process or focusing on the world of the East/Byzantium/Orthodoxy to try and articulate Greece's cultural difference vis-à-vis the West. The efforts at EU level to establish a common cultural 'European identity', the end of the Cold War, which had encouraged the age-old lumping together of 'Eastern', 'Balkan', 'Byzantine' and 'Greek', and the perception of Orthodoxy as a hindrance to modernization heightened the focus on religion and identity. The questioning of the idea of 'Europe' as coextensive with modernity and as a symbol of cultural superiority pointed up the in-betweenness of the Balkans as a manifestation of an intra-European Orientalism and the role of Orthodoxy in the new international reality. In a period in which Europeanization and modernization were being promoted, new critical positions towards the West emerged, originating from different intellectual perspectives and challenging Eurocentric theories of adjustment. They marked the transition from conformity with European modernization to the acceptance of notions of cultural difference and otherness. The theory, which in a way prepared this transition and facilitated the shift of emphasis from politics to culture, is that of cultural dualism, which had been a popular analytical tool since the 1980s and which is critically discussed in Chapter 1.

As long as the project of modernization was thought to be incomplete (though the recent book by Yannis Voulgaris (2019) challenges this perception), the dualist dilemmas were perpetuated and the tensions between Westernized trends and pre-modern practices remained unresolved, leading to an increasing preoccupation with Greekness. Following the growing discussion about Europeanization or modernization and the proliferation of debates on Greek identity, a new space opened up in which culture started to operate alongside and even compete with politics and economics, in an attempt to give answers to some pressing questions. By analysing changing trends and problematizing the notion of modernization, this study aims to highlight the growing diversity and ambivalence of Greek society in the period between the fall of the junta and the economic crisis.

From politics to culture

The pluralism and prosperity Greece enjoyed after the fall of junta together with the fast pace of changing lifestyles and international developments (EEC/EU membership, collapse of communist regimes and the changing map of the Balkans) shifted attention from politics to issues of culture and history and from political amnesia to the recollection of marginalized historical subjects. Political conflicts subsided and were transferred to the domain of culture: debates and controversies about identities, religion, gender or minorities and disputes about history, heritage or literary canons. The story of the *Metapolitefsi* could be seen as a challenge to cultural homogenization and a growing movement towards diversity. In other words, a transition occurred from a traditional and hierarchical power structure to a more pluralistic method of governance, involving various institutions, independent monitoring authorities, consultations, digital networks and generally a shift from a centripetal to a centrifugal trend. At the same time there was a growing sense of insecurity and cultural defensiveness due to Europeanization and globalization. The paradoxical coexistence of pluralism and diversity on the one hand and insecurity and protectionism on the other increased the debates on identity and the fetishization of Greekness, in an attempt to resolve cultural dilemmas or navigate between opposing perspectives on the past. One of the hallmarks of the *Metapolitefsi* involves the subtle transition from a struggle for political power to a contest for cultural hegemony and the gradual disentanglement of cultural identities from political affiliations.

This transition has entailed a process of self-examination and reflection on the cultural dynamics of the period. Adopting a cultural perspective when looking at social changes may offer new ways of charting those changes as well as alternative paradigms by revisiting dominant models of analysis. It has been claimed that by the 1990s,

> the notion of 'society' – as it had been practiced by social historians in the twentieth century and particularly after 1945 – was swept away by the interpretative onslaught of memory and cultural studies. The notion of society, broadly speaking again, was based on a linear concept of history developing forward along one temporal timeline, and privileging social and economic topics interpreted in terms of their function and structure. The notion of 'culture', in contrast, is based on a multi-temporal concept of history where past and present commingle and coalesce, capturing simultaneously different and opposing narratives, and privileging topics of representation and memory interpreted in terms of experience, negotiation, agency, and shifting relationships. (Confino 2011: 38–9)

This emphasis on culture, being understood as both an explanation and something requiring explanation, can be seen even in the later work of Marxist intellectuals concerned with the 'cultural turn' (Jameson 1998) or who write books on culture (Eagleton 2000). The primacy of the political and economic gives way to the cultural and this necessitates a shift from collective self-definitions to personal lifestyles. Traditionally, according to Terry Eagleton, culture 'was a way in which we could sink our petty particularisms in some more capacious, all-inclusive medium ... [and] now means the affirmation of a specific identity – national, sexual, ethnic, regional – rather than the transcendence of it' (2000: 38). Yet, culture as identity or differentiation is a continuation of politics by other means. Focusing on human rights and gender, minorities and identities, biopolitics and ecology, the new cultural politics have re-accentuated the old polarities between Right and Left along these lines. The emphasis on diversity and identity politics was also fostered by the growth of the 'cultural Left' after the fall of the junta, which together with the 'social Left' promoted new social movements, human rights and tolerance of otherness. In this respect, the role of the Greek universities was instrumental. Their number increased exponentially after the junta and they evolved into vibrant cultural and political hubs with the academics assuming the role of public intellectuals, blending cultural intervention and political activism.[12] Even the crisis, according to Antonis Liakos, 'gave cultural depth to social problems and made social differences cultural' (2014: 39). Hence, this book aims to pay particular attention to Greek cultural politics from 1974 onwards but without treating the period from junta to crisis as a unified entity.

The *Metapolitefsi* has been seen primarily as a 'political turn' towards democracy and Europe, but in the long run it was also a 'cultural turn' involving the diversification of Greek society and culture and the rearticulation of collective action and the individual, of radical politics and new lifestyles. Central to the political turn and democratization studies has been the idea of transition, used in the case of countries such as Greece, Spain and Portugal to describe their smooth passage to democracy (Chilcote et al. 1990; Linz et al. 1995; Cavallaro and Kornetis 2019). Though these countries served as examples of political realism for other countries, in the age of crisis 'these "model" transitions [were] no longer regarded as transparent and exemplary processes' (Kornetis 2015: 5). Democratization, as a successful transition to democratic rule, has started to be questioned in the light of the re-evaluation of the quality of democracy itself and the 'failed' transition to European modernity.[13] Democratization and

---

[12] The same could be said about the proliferation of magazines (particularly those associated with the Left) during the post-junta period such as *Ο Πολίτης* (1976–2008), *Αντί* (1974–2008), *Σχολιαστής* (1983–90) and others.

[13] One consequence of the crisis has been the appearance of a grass-roots fascist movement in Greece (Beaton 2019: 385).

Europeanization/modernization could be considered the two major top-down transitions of the *Metapolitefsi*, but a number of other bottom-up transitions took place at a cultural level, which this book aims to explore.

These transitions are not teleological but are marked by ambiguities, complexities, regressions and uncertainties. For example, the political orientation of Greek fiction in the early post-junta period was followed by a period of 'inwardness' and 'individuation', regaining a new kind of (re)politicization in the twenty-first century as Greek society hovers between collective and individual engagement with politics and culture (Hatzivasileiou 2018). Transitions in culture tend to be long term and not always clearly demarcated whereas social and political transitions are more easily identifiable without, however, always being one-way processes. For example, in the 1990s Greece went from being a land of emigration to a country of immigration; then, with the brain drain due to the crisis, it reverted to its earlier status (notwithstanding transit migration, with the new post-2015 wave of refugees and migrants also looking to leave the country for Western and Northern Europe). Similarly, Europe was treated in the 1970s and 1980s as a source of funding, then as an agent of modernization and again during the crisis as a provider of rescue funding. It could be argued that the post-junta years are a period of transitions and cultural ambivalence, rather than a period of continuities and ruptures (Nikolakopoulos 2013 and 2015). Multidirectional transitions and uncertainties about its end suggest that the *Metapolitefsi* offers a new way of understanding temporality, abandoning the linear, causal and homogeneous conception of time characteristic of earlier regimes of historicity. This is in line with the wider changes in the conception of time.

Towards the end of the twentieth century, the dominant conception of time 'has changed from a linear, irreversible and progressivist time conception to a non-linear, reversible and non-progressivist one' (Lorenz 2014: 46). This allows for a pluralization of times and the replacement of *progress* with *crisis* as the key concept for structuring the relationship between past, present and future in Western culture (Jordheim and Wigen 2018; Tamm and Olivier 2019). The linear-cyclical dichotomy, characteristic of historicist thinking, is circumvented by the notion of multiple temporalities or 'sediments of time' (Koselleck 2018). Modernity lost its credentials and the future lost its promise of progress. This called for a renewed reflection on the notion of time, as the past had lost its safe distance from the present. A new vision of temporality, as more variable and less monolithic, offers multiple perspectives on renegotiating and reshuffling the archives of the past, one of the distinctive features of the post-junta period and the crisis.

The increased emphasis on contested pasts since 1974 has undermined any sense of homogeneity in Greek culture and raised questions of identity more intensely than before. The rise of cultural diversity and gender politics also fostered cultural ambiguity and hybridization, but these moves towards diversity and pluralism are not without setbacks. While looking ahead was characteristic of the period, the crisis encouraged a retrospective trend, reviving old divisions, revisiting past events and cultivating Eurosceptic sentiments with the affective history of the *Metapolitefsi* representing a passage from euphoria to indignation and ultimately to melancholic self-reproach or stoic resignation. The theories of inadequate or belated modernity gave way in the 2000s to cautious optimism about the achievements of Greece as a modern nation (culminating in the Athens Olympics in 2004). But the crisis reversed the elation of the Olympics and encouraged a pessimistic reading of modern Greek history, focusing on the successive economic crises (Dertilis 2016). Even in relation to living standards, we can see a similar roller coaster. From 1974, when a substantial number of households in Greece were living below the poverty line, we moved to the fake affluence of the turn of the century, ending up with the devastating crisis in 2010. Hence, a study of the post-junta period cannot look for inexorable one-way transitions but is more inclined to see them as somewhat precarious processes.

Aiming to explore different intellectual positions and informed by cultural and postcolonial theories, this book adopts transition as a trope for investigating cultural change. Whereas until now transitions have been thought of in terms of an impetus towards institutional modernization, going from the centre to the periphery, or transfers of cultural capital, we now need to approach them from the opposite end of the spectrum and see them as more complex and ambivalent phenomena. In this book transitions are not seen as deterministic or linear changes from one state or condition to another but as multidirectional and fluctuating trajectories, involving forward and backward movements, adjustments, shifts, uncertainties and blurred boundaries. They suggest the *Metapolitefsi* should be considered one of the most pluralistic and diverse periods in Greek history[14] and as a project summed up by the subtitle of this book: aspiration (modernization), process (transition) and outcome (diversity).

---

[14] Theodoros Grigoriadis offers a fictional account of the transition from junta to crisis in his novels on the 1970s (*Το Παρτάλι*, 2001), the 1980s (*Ζωή μεθόρια*, 2015), the 1990s (*Καινούργια πόλη*, 2017), the turn of the century (*Ο παλαιστής και ο δερβίσης*, 2010) and the period of the crisis

Earlier studies have focused on political and economic aspects of post-1974 Greece, but the cultural developments of the overall period do not yet seem to have received adequate attention.[15] My work aims to redress the balance and offer a cultural history of the *Metapolitefsi*, revisiting certain key trends in order to present a more subtle picture of the period and highlight its diversity. Without aspiring to be a comprehensive study of Greek culture from 'junta to crisis', this book deals with some important areas such as identity, antiquity, religion, language, literature, media, cinema, youth, gender and sexuality and addresses crucial questions in the attempt to map Greek culture in transition over the last fifty years.

(*Το μυστικό της Έλλης*, 2012). The period is also performed in Michail Marmarinos's play *Κομμώτριες/Μεταπολίτευση* (2020).

[15] See Voulgaris (2001 and 2013); Kalyvas, Pagoulatos and Tsoukas (2012); Avgeridis, Gazi and Kornetis (2015); Kalyvas (2015); Passas et al. (2016). Even those books, which include chapters or sections on culture, tend to offer surveys of specific areas rather than trying to capture and analyse more general cultural trends (Panagiotopoulos 2003). Earlier books in English on post-war Greece (Sarafis and Eve 1990; Pettifer 1993/2000; Close 2002) have also tended to concentrate on political developments, and their discussion of cultural issues is rather limited. This also applies to the histories of modern Greece by Clogg (1992/2002), Koliopoulos and Veremis (2010), Gallant (2001/16) and Kostis (2018) which all contain chapters on the post-junta period, the restoration of democracy and the crisis. Beaton (2019) makes some references to the cultural developments of the period, but they are not as extensive as those in Liakos (2019).

1

Modernization and cultural dualisms

Exploring the cultural developments that have taken place since the fall of the junta, this chapter will focus on two crucial and interconnected areas, namely the discussion of various manifestations of dualism as a method of cultural analysis and the increasing tension between humanist and consumerist cultural practices.[1] The first part of this chapter interrogates the ways in which dualism has been deployed by a range of scholars to assess the extent of Greece's modernization and how it has developed into a dominant transdisciplinary method of analysis since the 1980s. Culture in this part is discussed within a wider historical and political context. The second part looks at increasingly competing conceptions of culture in the period from junta to crisis and highlights the implications of the growing trend towards popular and material culture.[2] Although both parts deal with the coexistence of two competing cultural discourses and engage respectively with the two dreams of the *Metapolitefsi* – modernization and consumerism – the aim is not to reaffirm oppositions or reverse hierarchies but to explore hybrid tensions and cultural ambivalences.

---

[1] Consumerism means different things to different people. While consumption is an act, consumerism is a way of life (Miles 1998: 4) and often takes on negative overtones when referring to excessive preoccupation with consumption, lifestyle and material culture. People become overly concerned with their own self-interest rather than mutual and communal interests and in this way consumerism represents the triumph of economic over social value. In Greece it has been associated with postmodern ephemerality, a materialistic lifestyle and cultural superficiality. Most importantly, at the turn of the twenty-first century economic growth in Greece was based on consumption.

[2] This trend might not be particular to Greece, and it is likely to have occurred earlier or at the same time in other countries. What could be considered as making the difference in the case of Greece is the rapid pace of change, and this cannot always serve as a reliable measure of comparison due to the differing political and sociocultural conditions within each country.

Modernization, hybridization and cultural ambivalence

One of the most enduring and influential interpretations of Greek cultural and political developments advanced during the *Metapolitefsi* is that of cultural dualism, which is based on the assumption that two opposing trends or forces are vying for supremacy. Greek culture, like Greek identity, has been seen from a dualist perspective, marked by symbolic oppositions or tensions. Theories of cultural dualism, reflecting opposing views on the past and future orientation of Greek society, have been adopted in different forms by anthropologists, political scientists and historians and have framed the discussions of political and cultural developments in Greece after the fall of junta.[3]

In the 1980s, building on Patrick Leigh Fermor's schema regarding the 'Helleno-Romaic dilemma', the anthropologist Michael Herzfeld proposed the Hellenic-Romeic distinction as 'the difference between an outward-directed conformity to international expectations about the national image and an inward-looking self-critical collective appraisal' (Herzfeld 1986: 20). Although Herzfeld has been keen to challenge two-column diagrams (such as the one used by Leigh Fermor) as a European product, he introduced the concept of *disemia* to argue that Greek identity is caught between two cultural forms: the official and the vernacular. The outward-looking and Western Hellenic self-presentation inspired by classical Greece is contrasted with the introspective Romeic self-image associated with the East, Byzantium and the Ottoman past. He suggested that the Hellenic and Romeic, or 'outside' and 'inside', views of Greek culture are the two historical images informing the respective ideals of *self-presentation* and *self-knowledge* (or *self-recognition*) while Korais and Zorba compete for the Greek soul (Herzfeld 1987: 95–122). More recently the Hellenic-Romeic distinction, and its class associations, has been used to analyse stylistic differences in the Greek film musical and how these differences project two distinct types of cultural identity (Papadimitriou 2012).

In the early 1990s the political scientist Nikiforos Diamandouros explored the relationship between culture and politics in Greece and charted the evolution of two cultures, which held sway alternately according to political circumstances (Diamandouros 1993: 125, 1994 and 2000).[4] The older of these two, the

---

[3] For a review of some of the discussions, see Katsoulis (2017).
[4] With reference to the Panhellenic Socialist Movement (PASOK) and from a leftist perspective, Euclid Tsakalotos (2008) attempts a critique of Diamandouros's dualism. Sotiris Mitralexis (2017) also criticizes the same model as a kind of Greek neo-orientalism and presents it as the theory that underpinned the modernization project of the Simitis government.

underdog culture, has been seen as marked by a pronounced introversion, xenophobia, anti-Westernism and adherence to pre-capitalist practices.[5] Defined by Diamandouros in a somewhat contradictory manner as combining a potent egalitarianism with a pre-democratic mentality, this culture competes with its younger counterpart, which has its intellectual roots in the Enlightenment and liberalism. It is also claimed that this modernizing and reformist culture, 'outward-looking and less parochial than its rival', was in the ascendant in the Greek world from the second half of the nineteenth century until the early to mid-1930s. From then on, until the mid-1970s, it entered a period of decline, following the weakening of the diaspora communities and the exhaustion of the Venizelist project. However, according to Diamandouros, what might have tipped the balance in favour of this culture was Greece's increasing integration into the EU.

More than ten years later, the historians John Koliopoulos and Thanos Veremis adopted a different, but essentially similar, binary opposition, using Ernest Gellner's concept of the 'segmentary society', which refers to a pre-modern social structure intended to protect the extended family and prevent the authorities from encroaching on its power (Koliopoulos and Veremis 2010). They saw the traditional segmentary society as a deep structure, resisting the unifying impetus of the modern unitary state and the adoption of Western principles of governance. This opposition contrasts the pre-modern segmentary society, broadly associated with the East, with the civil society and Western models of administration (which in the case of Greece were championed by diaspora and modernizing elites including the statesmen Kapodistrias, Mavrokordatos, Trikoupis and Venizelos) (Veremis 2011).[6] In short, the segmentary society and the underdog culture are perceived as impediments to modernization and militate against the formation of civil society.

Cultural and political dualism, in its various forms, has emerged as the dominant model of and for the post-junta period and also for the earlier history of Greece. My aim here is to show its inadequacies as an interpretive methodology and question its evaluative implications and political uses. A cultural perspective

---

[5] Nicos Mouzelis (1995) specifies two distinct types of the underdog culture, the clientelistic, dominant in the pre-junta period, and the populist, dominant in the post-junta period.

[6] See also his lecture 'The Greek crisis: When the segmentary community meets with populism' (Hellenic Centre, London, 1 June 2013: http://www.livemedia.com/video/45135) and his articles 'Όταν η κατακερματισμένη κοινωνία συναντά τον λαϊκισμό', *Protagon*, 9 December 2011: https://www.protagon.gr/epikairotita/politiki/otan-i-katakermatismeni-koinwnia-synantaei-ton-laikismo-10772000000 and 'Η κατακερματισμένη κοινωνία μας', *To Vima*, 7 June 2020. It should be noted that Andreas Papandreou, who spent a number of years teaching in America and Europe, is not included among those whom Veremis calls 'diaspora statesmen'.

can help us to reassess the operation of this dualism from the point of view of the underdog culture rather than that of the elitist modernizing culture. This, in turn, might shift attention from demarcating the discourses of the two cultures or confirming the superiority of one over the other to highlighting the instability and hybridity involved in constructing cultural identities. Greeks, for example, may simultaneously admire and hate anything associated with modern Europe. They aspire to be Western while at the same time looking down on Northern Europeans, saying, 'When we were building the Parthenon, you were living in the trees' in the same way as they treat their 'homeland' as a 'whore' and a 'Madonna'.[7] Caught in a 'double bind', as the source of Western civilization and its belated recipient, between colonization and self-colonization, they simultaneously display cultural arrogance and parochialism (Calotychos 2013: 31–2).

Recently, the cultural dualism proposed by Diamandouros has been revisited (Diamandouros 2013) and the 'underdog' culture blamed 'for bringing the country to the verge of economic and political bankruptcy' (Triandafyllidou et al. 2013: 9, 15). This culture has been presented and understood as being at the root of Greece's debt crisis and of the country's inability to address its structural shortcomings. Despite occasional reservations, this dualism continues to inform the way Greek identity is analysed, and Greece is presented as poised between a troubled tradition and a desired modernity. Trying to demarcate the two trends, the exponents of the dualist approach aim to highlight binary oppositions while its critics tend to emphasize their fusion.[8] Instances of hybridization have been explored, a good example being the fusion of the two clashing modes of time. The 'pre-modern' mode of cyclical and ritual time embodied in the celebration of name days now coexists with an increasing awareness of the irreversible and linear time associated with birthdays. Nowadays an increasing number of people in Greece celebrate both, whereas in the past the celebration of name days was more prevalent.[9] Critiquing the rigidity of the dualist approach by highlighting cases of hybridization or demonstrating how an individual-centred culture coexists with an earlier collectivist mentality is not sufficient. What is missing here is a historical and, to some extent, a cultural perspective, although the defenders of the dualist approach will argue otherwise.

---

[7] It is interesting that *Ellinismos* (i.e. the Greek nation) is often perceived both in terms of great achievement and bare survival.
[8] On hybridity and a critique of the dualist approach, see Tziovas (2001) and Xenakis (2013).
[9] Hirschon (2014: 164–5) and Tziovas (2003b: 13–29). On the Greek notion of time, see Ramfos (2012).

The resilience of the dualist approach as a useful analytical tool has something to do with the fact that the notion of modernization, in the sense of 'catching up with Europe', has increasingly entered debates on national identity as representing a break with the vestiges of the country's 'Ottoman' and 'oriental' past.[10] Cultural dualism, as outlined above, involves a form of Eurocentrism which has been indicted by postcolonial theorists studying former colonies in south Asia. Postcolonial theory reflects a desire to avoid Eurocentrism by provincializing Europe (Chakrabarty 2000) and the need to understand the importance of local cultural categories, practices and identities. The underdog culture could be seen in terms of the 'subaltern' (the under-represented in India's history and their hidden history) and the classic question 'Can the subaltern speak?' could be applied to it.[11] As with the subaltern, whose identity is its difference, one cannot construct the underdog culture as a category with 'an effective voice clearly and unproblematically identifiable as such' (Ashcroft et al. 2007: 201). Yet, until now the emphasis by those practising cultural dualism has been on the modernizing culture and its transformative potential, while the underdog culture has been seen primarily in political and not in cultural terms and its proponents in the area of culture are not being clearly identified. What I propose to do here is to reverse the order and approach the underdogs from a cultural perspective.

The dualist approach tends to boil everything down to an underlying opposition between East and West by tacitly valorizing the West and ignoring the negative aspects of Western modernity. However, what is not acknowledged here is that the westernizing trend has always had the upper hand, not expressed in the form of a modern polity or civil society but as a centralizing state mechanism suppressing cultural diversity. In Greece the state represented an authoritarian caricature of Western modernity and kept any manifestations of the underdog culture or the segmentary society under control, both culturally and politically.[12] The unitary state exercised its power through the symbolic power of the Greek language and the classical past or through homogenizing and centralizing policies. The uniform education system has also assisted the Greek state in shaping national identity and assimilating otherness. On the other

[10] Even the recent SKAI documentary on the 1821 Greek War of Independence has been seen as popularizing the main argument of modernization theory through the lens of cultural dualism (Andriakaina 2016).
[11] In the South Asian context, the term 'subaltern' applies to all groups that are perceived as 'subordinate' in terms of class, caste, gender, office or 'in any other way'. See Spivak (1998: 271–313), Guha and Spivak (1988) and Morton (2007: 96–7).
[12] George T. Mavrogordatos points out that 'Antivenizelism typically sheltered and expressed the stubborn resistance of a variety of *particularisms* against the modern, liberal, and national state, which aspired to control, assimilate, neutralize, or even suppress them' (1983: 271).

hand, the Romeic self-image, the underdog culture and the segmentary society have invariably been associated either with the backward or the dangerous Other. This otherness threatened cultural homogeneity and the authority of the state and therefore had to be suppressed (see Chapter 4).

Although the binary oppositions outlined above are intended to facilitate the analysis of political and cultural developments in Greece since the nineteenth century and help account for them in a balanced and detached manner, they do not seem to take into account the hierarchy of power involved in those oppositions or, as Jacques Derrida has argued, that there is always a relation of power between the poles of a binary opposition (1981: 41–2). The opposing trends or self-images are simply presented as being either in constant tension or in some sort of fragile equilibrium. None of them appear to dominate or set the agenda for long. However, as mentioned above, what is not considered here is the role of the state and its contribution to tipping the balance. The dualistic interpretation, therefore, tends to overlook the state's role as a kind of hybrid space between the two poles, where an attempt is made to follow Western models at the same time as exercising oppressive regulation of the underdog culture. The cultural policy of the Greek state was to assimilate or even suppress ethnic, regional, cultural and linguistic differences while it fostered a clientelistic system, which attracted large sections of the segmentary society by promising individual benefits.

This dual role of the state can be held to justify its intermediary position between the two poles of the binary patterns proposed. Although it is often pointed out that state-building in Greece did not live up to Western expectations and standards, it is also claimed that 'Greece's state-building began with a war of independence in 1821 and continued along the lines of its Western prototypes – the twentieth-century French administration, the German legal system, and British parliamentary practices'.[13] Greece has been described as 'one of the earliest late modernizers' in the sense that it embarked unusually early on its modernization drive (Kalyvas 2015: 197). State-building, therefore, seems to have followed an ambivalent process of development by being both Western and non-Western and carving out a space between conformity to the notion of the individual rights of Western civil societies and loyalty to the extended family (segmentary society). This complicates the binary oppositions outlined above,

---

[13] Koliopoulos and Veremis (2010: 1); Voulgaris (2019: 200). Nicos Alivizatos claims that during the Greek War of Independence the most conservative strata of Greek society adopted principles contained in the most progressive constitutions in Europe (2003: 21 and 2011).

because the state is seen to act not as a modernizing but as a homogenizing and centralizing force. Although the Greek state has undergone rudimentary modernization and institutional reform over the years, its role in suppressing various manifestations of the underdog culture remained largely unchanged until the 1980s.[14]

In the past, the state was perceived more in adversarial terms and less as a source of social security or employment. This antagonistic perception has become more nuanced since 1981 and in some cases the balance has even been reversed, while EU subsidies have reinforced the perception of the state as provider.[15] A 'culture of entitlement' and a desire to extract compensation for the poverty and material deprivation that followed the Second World War developed. Complaints about state inefficiency were combined with an expectation that the state would provide jobs for life and handsome pensions. However, the expansion of the state was not accompanied by the development of a proper welfare system and in spite of its liberalization during the post-junta period, it was still treated by many people in a contradictory way – being seen as both provider and opponent.[16] Over time the Greek state, that reluctant agent of modernization, has been replaced by the EU and more recently by the so-called Troika (International Monetary Fund, European Central Bank and European Commission) with the task of reforming Greece and its economy. However, integration in Europe or the implementation of the recent economic adjustment programme may not be enough to ensure the swansong of the underdog culture.

Previous studies have emphasized the political role of the modernizing culture, while underestimating the cultural dimension of the underdog culture. The latter is not simply associated with backwardness or vested interests, but also with forms of social exclusion and cultural otherness. One of the problems with the concepts of the underdog culture and the segmentary society is that it is assumed that both remained static and undeveloped for centuries.[17] In post-junta

---

[14] P. C. Ioakimidis argues that 'Greece was rightly considered as the most centralized unitary state in Europe in the early 1980s' (2001: 78).

[15] Perhaps the perception of the state changed with the rise of PASOK to power in 1981, when state mechanisms were taken over by the party (Kostis 2018: 374–5).

[16] The following observation sums up the peculiar role of the state in Greece: 'The size of the state by conventional metrics is about average for a European country, but its influence on the incomes of private households, and especially of the middle class, is extraordinary. Whereas in northern Europe states typically provide public services for all and a safety net for the most needy, in Greece a major function of the state is to provide, or to support, the incomes of middle-class occupational groups, during their working age' (Doxiadis and Matsaganis 2012: 40). It is interesting to note that the term used in Greek is 'κρατικοποιώ' (bring (an industry) under state ownership) rather than 'εθνικοποιώ', the literal equivalent of the English verb 'to nationalize'.

[17] Nicolas Demertzis criticizes 'cultural dualism' for treating 'tradition and modernity as two pre-constituted and mutually exclusive rather than inter-constituted and interrelated cultural entities'.

Greece, however, these categories can be said to have expanded to include different, and even apparently incompatible, groups of people: intellectuals, minorities or anti-establishment activists. For the first time, for example, the anti-Western trend even found rigorous intellectual support from academics, intellectuals and philosophers, including Yorgos Karabelias, Dimitris Kitsikis, Yorgos Kontogiorgis, Costis Moskov, Kostas Zouraris and Christos Yannaras. One could also query whether the ideological supremacy of the Left after the military dictatorship or the revival of interest in the *rebetika* in the 1980s were connected to the ascendancy of the underdog culture, the legitimization of otherness and the emancipation of anti-establishment forces.[18]

After 1974 the underdog culture emerged not as a parochial culture but as an agent of the repressed other and a challenge to high culture (as seen in the second part of this chapter). The empowerment of the repressed Other (political, social, ethnic or linguistic) turned the underdog culture into a broader, and increasingly powerful, coalition of anti-systemic forces. Two popular albums by Manolis Rasoulis and Nikos Xydakis, *Η εκδίκηση της γυφτιάς* [The Revenge of the Gypsies] (1978) and *Δήθεν* [Pretentious] (1979) can be seen as an attempt to give a voice to the underdog culture through music and song. It was not until the 1970s that the centralizing culture first acknowledged the underdog culture, when, for example, the word 'decentralization' (αποκέντρωση) became de rigueur and attention was turned to the provinces. A sign of cultural decentralization was the creation in 1983 of the Municipal Regional Theatres (ΔΗΠΕΘΕ) by the then Minister of Culture Melina Mercouri. Even the culturally pejorative term 'province' (επαρχία) was avoided in favour of the rather more neutral 'region' (περιφέρεια).

Although one might have expected that otherness would find support among those who promoted the modernizing culture paradoxically, it has mostly been associated with the underdog culture, whereas the modernizing culture, relying on state authority, has sometimes been tainted with authoritarianism. After years of authoritarian practices, the unshackling of otherness created a cultural

---

Instead, he proposes 'inverted syncretism' as 'a category designed to deal more accurately with the articulation of modernity and tradition in Greek political cultures' and the ways 'modernizing patterns lost their original function while traditional ones remained intact or even became rejuvenated' (1997: 119; Stefanidis 2007: 6–11).

[18] With reference to the Greek Civil War and the return of the repressed Left/Other, G. T. Mavrogordatos has used the phrase 'the revenge (revanche) of the vanquished' to suggest that since 1981 history has been rewritten from the point of view of the defeated during the civil strife: 'Η "ρεβάνς" των ηττημένων', *To Vima*, 17 October 1999, available at http://www.tovima.gr/opinions/article/?aid=115282. Kostis Kornetis also writes about the 'triumph of the Left in the realm of memory', and particularly in the area of cinema (2014: 98).

and intellectual climate in which it was difficult for the modernizing culture (even in the form of the EU) to stage a comeback.[19] The often patronizing, top-down practices of the modernizing culture, supported by the state, created a mentality of resistance and disobedience among representatives of the underdog culture, which tends to be egalitarian.[20]

Before the crisis, Greek society relied heavily on the state for employment and for funding cultural activities and projects (e.g. films subsidized by the Greek Film Centre). As a result, the neologism κρατικοδίαιτος (state-nourished) was coined. However, in a way the crisis has contributed to the detachment of people from the anchor of the state by undermining their perception of it as a secure provider and challenging the deep-seated statist mentality. People gradually lost faith in the state's accountability and its capacity for law enforcement, while the state and its institutions went from being an authoritarian agent or job provider to being a target for attack, along with the whole political system. The growing mistrust of any government made it very hard for reform of any kind to be accepted by the public, who increasingly placed their trust in the achievements of the past and the myth of national exceptionalism.

The tension between the two cultures increased in the last quarter of the twentieth century and could be detected in a number of areas, but the outcome of this tension has been rather ambiguous. Cultural identity, according to Homi Bhabha, emerges in a contradictory and ambivalent 'Third Space of enunciation' that makes the claim to a hierarchical 'purity' of cultures untenable (Bhabha 1994: 37). As in postcolonial cultures we might have to consider the mutuality and hybridization of these two cultures in post-authoritarian Greece. It may be useful to concentrate on three case studies from different decades of the post-junta period in order to demonstrate this tension and raise some questions.

The language reform of 1976, which can serve as the first case in point, poses the question as to whether this is a victory of the modernizing or the underdog culture. On the one hand, it could be seen as a form of modernization with a beneficial impact on education. On the other hand, it could be treated as a rehabilitation of the underdog culture and the Romeic trend. It is also interesting to note that some of those who fought for the institutionalization of the demotic language resisted the introduction of the monotonic system in the

---

[19] The frequent reference to a 'colony of debt' to describe the bailout for the Greek economy suggests that the eurozone is seen by many Greeks as a colonizing power.
[20] The historian Nicos Svoronos identified resistance, primarily towards foreign intervention, as a constant feature of modern Greek history (1976: 12). In this connection, see also 'Η αντιστασιακή υφή του ελληνισμού/The resisting nature of Hellenism', Ardin (2003: 40–1).

early 1980s and agonized over the lexical poverty of the young or the general decline in linguistic standards. Secondly, the liberalization of the Greek media after 1989 could similarly be considered a sign of a modernizing pluralism, as well as offering a platform of expression to the popular, underdog culture and promoting a star system. The state media were generally viewed as being controlled by the government and their programmes were seen as boring, although this assessment was later revised to some extent when their quality came to be compared with the popular shows of the commercial media. The third case concerns religion and the controversy over identity cards in 2000–1. Although the outcome of this controversy has been hailed as a victory for the reformist and Western-oriented culture (perhaps the first in this area since the declaration of the autocephalous status of the Greek Church in 1833), at the same time the presence of the Church in the media and elsewhere has grown exponentially.[21] It has become commonplace to find bishops writing in newspapers, interviewed in the media or expressing the Church's opposition to non-traditional practices (e.g. cremation, reform of religious teaching in schools, even yoga), thus confirming the increasingly influential role of Orthodox religion in Greek society.[22] These three cases (analysed in greater detail in subsequent chapters) demonstrate that since 1974 the tension between the modernizing and the underdog culture has been more ambivalent than ever before. They also show that the underdog culture, along with otherness, gained in strength rather than losing influence, fostering some ambiguous or interstitial spaces in the syncretic encounter between the two cultures. Just as the postcolonial identity emerges in the ambivalent spaces of the colonial encounter, similarly the strengthening of the underdog culture suggests that change in post-junta Greece is not in one direction alone but rather multidirectional and transcultural, involving an increasingly fluctuating relationship, interaction and tension between the two cultures by comparison with the earlier periods.

A similar type of ambivalence can be traced in a recent study on the crisis in which modernization is defined as 'a mechanistic importation of Western models without consideration of anthropological differences', although the conventions

---

[21] On the politicization of Christian Orthodox discourse following the decision of the Greek government to exclude any reference to religion from identity cards, see Stavrakakis (2002).
[22] Although Greece elected its first professedly atheist prime minister, Alexis Tsipras, in January 2015, spectacles mixing religious sentiment and patriotic pride continued unabated. In May 2015 the remains of St Barbara, which had been kept in Venice for the last thousand years (a gift from a Byzantine emperor in 1003), were flown to Athens and met with an exuberant welcome from crowds of ordinary people. Something similar occurred two years later with the relics of St Helen, 'Equal to the Apostles' and mother of Constantine the Great. The relics arrived in Greece from Venice amid the pomp and splendour reserved for heads of state.

and values supporting the Greek economy and polity are recognized as differing from those of the West (Douzinas 2013: 36). It is argued that identities and social bonds in Greece are based on family, friends and the community, creating a non-Western 'social ethos'. This 'Greek ethos' has been considered the primary target of the austerity measures, but its status seems ambiguous, apparently coming close to the notion of the underdog culture. Douzinas claims that, although in its corrupted version this ethos promotes neo-liberalism, it is at the same time the most powerful force for resisting it. Yet there is no explanation as to how the Greek ethos, 'with its mild nationalism, secular religiosity and familial base' and its presumed resistance to westernization, performs this double act (2013: 38).

During the crisis the slogan 'Greece needs to become a "normal" country' gained ground and in turn 'modernization' was succeeded by the term 'normalization'. The interpretation of the economic crisis as being the result of insufficient modernization has often been questioned (Liakos 2014: 68–83), while its approach as a series of stalled reforms cannot easily be applied to developments in Greek culture. Alternatively, Greeks are presented as having to cope with the conflicting tensions resulting from a fusion of dated and modern practices. For example, the mass media in Greece are considered modern in form and technology but outmoded in content, while in the social sphere the Greek nuclear family embodies competing 'archaic' and modern features (Panagiotopoulos and Vamvakas 2014). Pulled in different directions, Greeks appear to walk a tightrope stretched between archaic institutions and structures and modern aspirations and lifestyles. It should be evident by now that the theory of cultural dualism tends to obscure ambivalence and hybridizations, which in turn leads to treating the state both as a source of secure employment (a survival of the earlier clientelist mentality) and as an adversary (a result of the increasingly anti-systemic discourse of the underdog culture). It seems that during the crisis this ambivalent attitude towards the state has been extended to the EU, leading to its being considered as both saviour and enemy, and thus suggesting that the crisis has simultaneously strengthened and profoundly undermined the authority of the modernizing discourse (see Chapter 2).

Despite its limitations, Diamandouros's dualist scheme is forward-looking and modernizers found in it a way of reading the past as well as a vision of the future.[23] On the other hand, left-wing intellectuals focused more on

---

[23] The antithetical juxtaposition of historical figures such as Korais-Rhigas and Mavrokordatos-Kolokotronis by modern scholars, Nikos Themelis's novels, and Stathis Kalyvas's view of Greek history as 'a succession of peculiar boom and bust cycles' (2015: 2) could also be read in connection to this dualist prism.

re-examining and rehabilitating the past than on articulating an alternative paradigm that might prove as popular as that of Diamandouros. They tended to take a reflective and critical attitude (verging on left-wing melancholy to recall Walter Benjamin's term (Traverso 2017)) rather than constructing rival national narratives about the future orientation of the country.

Having looked at cultural dualism and its limitations as an analytical tool in accounting for the belated or incomplete modernization of Greece, I will now explore how the tension between two competing notions of culture intensified in post-junta Greece and further complicated the hierarchies involved in the dualist approaches. This was partly due to the confluence of the anti-Western underdog culture and the ascendancy of a westernized consumer culture, which is bound up with materialism and the exercise of free personal choice in the private sphere of everyday life.

Greek culture between humanism and consumerism

The dualist approaches to Greek culture and politics discussed above gained additional momentum by increasingly opposing notions of culture during the post-junta period. The growing social diversity, the increased visibility of various minorities and the striking improvements in living standards in Greece at the end of the twentieth and the beginning of the twenty-first century challenged the notion of culture as an autonomous and homogeneous realm and created the conditions for cultural debates similar to those that had arisen in other Western societies, and particularly in Britain, decades earlier.

These involved F. R. Leavis and T. S. Eliot, who exemplified an idealistic and highly selective tradition of cultural criticism, and Raymond Williams and others, whose more materialistic approach envisioned culture as always 'ordinary' (Williams 1989). For Leavis and Eliot culture linked different individuals in an 'organic community', built around historical continuity and tradition. This notion of an organic national culture was seen as being threatened in the modern mass society by technology and popular entertainment, which eroded its cohesion and its high standards. Williams, on the other hand, saw culture as 'a whole way of life' and not in selective terms. During the twentieth century, the debate in England about the meaning of culture was largely informed by 'the distinction, established by nineteenth-century writers such as Matthew Arnold and John Ruskin, between culture as a realm of ideal values (nobility of purpose, beauty of forms) and the non-culture of an industrial society increasingly defined as mechanical and dehumanised' (Swingewood 1998). Culture was thought of as either ordinary or ideal and this opposition involves a variety of contrasting terms: mechanical versus organic solidarity, community versus association, use value versus exchange value (Slater 1997: 64–6).

The fact that recent Greek cultural trends present certain similarities with earlier cultural debates and transitions in England is not a matter of belatedness but of social developments leading to a more pronounced distinction between high and low culture. Over the years, high culture, associated with universalism and absolutism, has become part of the problem rather than part of the solution. The perception of culture as art and civility gave way to the perception of culture as lifestyle and identity politics, highlighting the tension between making and being made. As Terry Eagleton points out, 'culture as spirituality is eroded by culture as the commodity, to give birth to culture as identity' (Eagleton 2000: 72). Although it is hard to see cultural values as not being bound up with those of everyday life, one could argue that two broad notions of culture have driven the cultural impulse in Greece since 1974: the humanist or elitist definition of culture (the best of everything) and the anthropological or lifestyle perception of culture as primarily a way of life and identity.

The earlier humanist conception of culture presupposes canonization and hierarchy, with high culture taking precedence over popular culture or subcultures. The modern conception of culture as lifestyle involves plurality and choice, leading in turn to individualization and the challenging of the idea of society as a cohesive and collective body. In this case, society is perceived as a collection of individuals with changing personal tastes, identities and lifestyles. The humanist conception of culture promotes an allegiance to a set of spiritual values, ideas and works of art, whereas the conception of culture as diverse ways of life promotes individual lifestyles and personal choices, which often override community values and humanist principles. In Greece the development of the latter form of culture led to the rise of individualism, a feature widely recognized by analysts as being a key feature of the period since 1980 (Vamvakas 2014).

It could be said that humanist culture works top-down and tends to look to the past, whereas the conception of culture as lifestyle is more forward-looking and prone to differentiation, developing in various directions across the board. This conception also fosters a proliferation of audiences, communities of readers or spectators as the focus shifts from producers to end users.[24] Humanist culture

---

[24] It is interesting to note that until recently the Greek word for audience/public (κοινό) was hardly ever used in its plural form. Literary awards decided exclusively by the public are also a recent phenomenon in Greece.

tends to rely more on tradition, heritage and ideal standards, whereas lifestyle culture relies on conditions that can become dated or obsolete more quickly due to advances in living standards, social mobility, technology and modes of communication or entertainment. Yet, the discrepancy between what people say and what they do in their everyday lives has increased at transnational level and complicates cultural dichotomies even further. For example, people benefit from globalization as consumers but fear its consequences as employees; they support social cohesion and solidarity but practise a hedonistic and narcissistic lifestyle. This discrepancy cannot be easily resolved and often leads to confusion, but it does not render cultural distinctions invalid.

The apparent polarization in Greek culture between elitist aestheticism and hedonistic consumerism can be seen as corresponding to the disjunction between humanist/high and lifestyle/popular/consumer culture. The latter is associated with the growing privatization of leisure activities and the aestheticization of everyday life leading either to accentuating or erasing the distinction between 'high' and 'low' culture. Of course, tensions between high and popular culture can be traced even farther back, but it was at the end of the twentieth century that the representatives of high culture first felt seriously threatened by popular culture and the postmodern celebration of consumerism, hedonism and style. As a consequence of postmodernism and the fusion of styles, it became more difficult in a number of Western countries to maintain a meaningful distinction between art and popular culture. While postmodernism's 'aesthetic populism' dissolved the distinction between high and low culture, this does not seem to have been the case in Greece. Whereas the boundaries between the two were not so apparent in Greece earlier,[25] since the 1980s there has been an attempt to draw a clear line between them and, above all, high culture has felt itself to be under attack.

This was partly due to the fact that the earlier left-wing rejection of the 'American way of life', which was discarded as fake or a form of cultural imperialism, in favour of an authentic popular Greek culture, no longer held sway, resulting in a reversal of earlier taxonomies and changing the cultural landscape in Greece. The earlier, politically driven, distinction between the authentic 'Greek tradition' and the 'American way of life' gradually gave way to a depoliticized, broader opposition between high and popular culture or led to the

---

[25] Vrasidas Karalis points out that 'the dividing line between an artistic production for an educated and sophisticated middle class, or a self-conscious aristocracy, and an entertainment for the masses has not been very clear in post-war Greek history' (2012a: 138).

paradox that the folk tradition and *ithageneia* was venerated and yet at the same time anything defined as folkloric or *ethographic* (ηθογραφικό) was downplayed or even rejected.²⁶

This was evident in a book on Greek kitsch published in 1984, where the negative association of popular culture with the anti-aesthetic is made explicit (Koutsikou et al. 1984). The volume includes articles by contemporary art historians, literary critics, anthropologists, musicians and intellectuals, as well as historical texts by Periklis Yannopoulos and Dimitris Pikionis. It was richly illustrated with photographs of buildings (exteriors and interiors), cars, advertisements, social events, pages from newspapers, film stills and other pictures, which purported to show Greek bad taste. Kitsch was presented as an epidemic spreading through Greek society and signifying a decline in the quality of Greek life (Figure 1).

Conceived as an attack on the anti-aesthetic in Greece, this volume articulates a nostalgia for some sort of vanishing popular authenticity and the purity of the Greek landscape. It also represents a reflection on Greek identity, judging from the references to the 'face of Greece' and a resistance to commercialization and consumerism, as implied in the foreword written by the then Greek minister of culture Melina Mercouri and other contributions. In short, the volume tries to record a 'fake', urban or semi-urban, popular culture, as opposed to an earlier genuine folk culture, which raises the question whether the volume was merely a study of popular forms of expression or an attempt to correct and improve the aesthetics of popular culture.²⁷

Conversely, the pejorative neologism *koultouriaris*, assigned to intellectuals and artists in the 1980s, can be seen as a kind of response to this corrective aspiration and a sign of confidence in the popular, consumerist culture. It should be noted that both the Socialist Prime Minister Andreas Papandreou and the Culture Minister Melina Mercouri were not fans of high culture (Zorba 2014: 334). Also, the opposition in the same decade between the public and the private becomes evident when comparing the magazines of the Left (*O Politis*, *Anti* and to some extent *Scholiastis*) with the new lifestyle magazines. The former

---

[26] In March 1976 in the periodical *Anti* a discussion on 'What is folk/popular culture (λαϊκός πολιτισμός)', coordinated by the author Dimitris Hatzis, starts with contributions from scholars and intellectuals. It should be noted that it was in this period that the concept of 'Greek tradition' was historicized and its normative conceptualization questioned. It is also significant that the Greek Ministry of Education and Religious Affairs designated the academic year 1978–9 the 'year of Greek tradition' (Karavidas 2015; Papadogiannis 2015: 180–2).

[27] Vamvakas and Panagiotopoulos point out that 'it was in the 1980s that "kitsch" and "culture" became the two oppositional terms corresponding to new, opposed social groups' (2014: xlviii).

Figure 1 German tourist in Monastiraki (Athens), 1983, from *Kitsch – made in Greece*, courtesy of Daphni Koutsikou-Iliadi.

tend to avoid engaging with aspects of everyday life whereas the latter marked a new era for journalism, sexuality and popular culture with their narcissistic consumerism. The first Greek lifestyle magazine *Klik* (Click) was launched in 1987 (followed by others such as *Nitro, Down Town* and *Men*), while a year later Dick Hebdige's book on subculture was translated into Greek, indicating a growing interest in cultural diversity. Narcissistic individualism and the search for an 'authentic self' coexisted with new forms of social intimacy and crowd rituals (open-air concerts, beach parties, football celebrations and mass demonstrations). It could be said that during the post-junta period there has been a transition from the politicization of leisure to its aestheticization and from the classification of cultural products as 'progressive' and 'reactionary' to their hierarchical separation into 'artistic' and 'popular'.

The difference between the humanist and consumerist cultures was manifested mainly in areas which had opened up to commercialization rather belatedly, such as the book trade and the media. Music and film had become commercial much earlier, but even in those areas it was in the 1980s that the flourishing of the so-called *skyladika*,[28] new modes of entertainment (e.g. watching videos) and the frequent screenings of popular films on Greek television contributed to a further accentuation of cultural divisions. Meanwhile, under the directorship of Manos Chatzidakis from 1975 to 1981, the Greek Radio's Third Programme promoted qualitative distinctions and tried to redefine cultural boundaries. Chatzidakis's stand-off with the newspaper *Avriani* in 1987 and the so-called *Avrianismos* are indicative of the cultural polarization that was developing during the 1980s (see Chapter 9). From the early 1970s onwards, youth became a less vague cultural category; new subcultures and youth slangs developed, school uniforms were abolished and students' customary leisure activities (*frappé* and backgammon, together with a taste for *rebetika* and old partisan songs) gradually changed (Papadogiannis 2015).[29] The patterns of entertainment also changed with bars, cafeterias and whisky becoming symbols of identity and new wealth. Food and drink were no longer linked and traditional drinks (ouzo, tsipouro, brandy, etc.) started to decline in popularity. Consuming imported drinks was seen as supporting multinational capitalism, but this did not prevent whisky, as a symbol

---

[28] A derogatory term, deriving from the Greek word for dog, to describe a branch of popular music and refer to cheap or often unlicensed night clubs.

[29] The number of students in higher education increased considerably during the post-junta period. From less than 30,000 in 1960, their numbers more than doubled by 1971–2 (70,161) and continued to rise till 1981–2 (87,476) and the subsequent years (111,911 by 1991–2) (Charalambis et al. 2004: 584). It should be noted that these figures do not include those studying abroad whose numbers increased rapidly from 9,985 in 1970 to 41,086 in 1981.

of global modernity and a hedonistic lifestyle, from becoming popular in Greece. It owed part of its popularity to the fact that the former prime minister Andreas Papandreou was very fond of whisky, and the peak period of its consumption has been linked to the emergence of consumerism in Greece in the 1980s and 1990s (Bampilis 2013).

In order to better understand cultural developments in Greece, we also need to delve into the ways concepts such as the 'popular' (λαϊκό) have been used over the years. In the past, 'popular' was defined either in linguistic terms (demotic vs formal/archaic) or by the mode of production (collective/individual) or it had class connotations with reference to marginal or proletarian cultural production. After 1974, and more particularly after 1981 (with the rise of PASOK to power), the words 'people' (λαός) and 'popular' (λαϊκό) became overused, albeit in ways that their meaning was hard to pin down. The settling of the language question in 1976 and increasing social mobility made the earlier uses of the term 'popular' more or less obsolete, as we moved from the aesthetic populism of the 1930s intellectuals to the left-wing populism of the 1980s.

With the emergence of consumer culture in Greece, the popular was increasingly associated with material culture, lifestyles and light entertainment (e.g. a revival of interest in the Greek cinema of the 1950s to the early 1970s), in opposition to high culture. There has been a move away from the Marxist model of popular culture (with the focus on production) to a more Weberian model (with the focus on consumption) (Parker 2011: 158). The popular has to a large extent lost its earlier association with authenticity and has come to be judged aesthetically or ethically.[30] In a way, the popular, associated with consumerism and lifestyle, has assumed the position previously reserved for the 'other' by the elitist culture. It could be argued that the negativity associated with otherness and underdog culture has been transferred to the notion of the popular and the related phenomenon of populism, which has manifested itself primarily in the area of politics but which has wider ramifications (Sevastakis and Stavrakakis 2012). The redefinition of the popular accentuated the distinction between popular and high culture in Greece, which has become all the more evident in the area of literature.

---

[30] Adopting a Marxist perspective, Yorgos Veloudis argues that there are two kinds of 'popular' literature: the old, associated with rural communities and the demotic, and the new, associated with urbanism and so-called 'para-literature'. The former originates from the people and is a primary form of popular literature while the latter is written for the people and is a secondary form of popular literature. In the first case producer and consumer are identical, whereas in the second they are distinct ('"Λόγια" και "λαϊκή" λογοτεχνία', 1992: 57).

The novel by Alexandros Kotzias *Φανταστική περιπέτεια/Imaginary Adventure* (1985) was the first to deal with culture as a state institution and produce a grotesque caricature of literary kitsch.[31] Although the novel focuses on the events of a single day (tellingly 21 April 1983), it deals with the emergence and collapse of a literary bubble and the rise and fall of a megalomaniac narcissist, aspiring to capture the ethos of the post-junta period and chart its cultural trends. Alexandros Kapandais, the book's main character, personifies, as a writer and high-ranking civil servant, corruption, self-promotion and the abuse of power. His career also exemplifies the role of public relations in literary careers and the dominance of pompous junk literature in 1980s Greece and its connections with state institutions. The cynical Kapandais had managed to become a fake literary celebrity and has received a number of awards in Greece and abroad while making scornful remarks about established writers such as the 'pervert' Cavafy, the 'charlatan' Seferis or the 'opportunistic' Tsirkas. Thus, the novel highlights the widening gap between trash and highbrow literature due to the increasing institutionalization of culture and its exploitation by figures such as Kapandais, who even managed to have his own biographer.

The novel has been seen as a fictional caricature of the state of affairs that led Greece into the crisis and perhaps for this reason it was reprinted in 2012.[32] It also aimed to demonstrate how state machinery promoted the so-called *paralogotechnia* ('para-literature', i.e. popular or trashy literature), thus suggesting that alongside the earlier notion of the 'para-state' a similar concept emerged in the cultural arena after the junta. In this case, Kotzias was not so much concerned with literature written for a mass audience, since this was a later phenomenon in Greece, but was trying to show how opportunists could take advantage of state and party mechanisms in order to promote themselves and thus undermine values or blur aesthetic distinctions. Moreover, he suggests that para-literature is more of a cultural practice, a kind of subculture, increasingly fostered by state institutions during the 1980s.[33] It should be noted

---

[31] More recently a novel published under the nom de plume Aliki Doufexi-Pope, *Το ακατέργαστόν μου* (2013) has satirically explored the interaction and antagonism between highbrow and popular literature. The fictional author Alkis Chatzikostis – at the suggestion of his publisher – changes from being a serious and elitist writer to being a commercially successful popular fiction writer, publishing under the pen name of Aliki Doufexi-Pope (a supposed descendant of Alexander Pope) in order to subsidize publication of his highbrow fiction (a novel of 832 pages). The irony here is that Alkis easily and successfully imitates the style of the popular writers he despises. A parody of the literary community could also be found in the novels by Petros Tatsopoulos, *Τιμής Ένεκεν* (2004) and Michalis Michailidis, *Πινακοθήκη Τεράτων* (2009).

[32] More recently in April 2017, the newspaper *Το Βήμα* reprinted and distributed it to its readers, describing it as a prophetic novel that offered insights to post-junta Greek culture and the current crisis.

[33] 'Populism in literature' was the theme of a colloquium organized by the Etaireia Scholis Moraiti in 1983. For a definition of 'literary populism', see N. Vayenas, 'Οι μεταμφιέσεις του λαϊκισμού', *Το Vima* 22 October 2006, reprinted in Vayenas (2013: 170–3).

here that although a kind of popular literature in Greece could be traced back to the nineteenth century (Kassis 1983; Moullas 2007), it was at the end of the twentieth century that it was treated as a serious commercial and aesthetic threat to high culture.

From the mid-1990s the commercialization of the novel became a feature of the production of fiction, and the setting up of the National Book Centre (EKEBI) in 1994 contributed to the trend that treated literary books as products rather than artefacts, applying quantitative criteria in exploring reading patterns and readers' responses (Kotzia 2012). Greek book production increased fourfold between 1987 (2,348 books) and 2006 (10,296 books) while increasing emphasis was placed on promoting and translating them. Some saw the introduction of book supplements by newspapers (*To Vima* in 1997, *Eleftherotypia* in 1998 and *Ta Nea* in 2002) as a sign of the expansion of the reading public and others as a confirmation of the increasing commercialization of the book market, a sense reinforced by the coining of the term 'τα ευπώλητα' for bestselling books. A shift seems to have taken place in publishing from literariness and aesthetic appreciation to cultural consumerism, something which has been met with vociferous opposition from the literati.

The growth of popular culture since the 1980s has fostered an explosion in the production of popular novels in Greece, and this may have led to the decline of the short story, which had previously dominated Greek prose fiction, although it has shown signs of recovery during the crisis.[34] In the last thirty years, the term *paralogotechnia* has become increasingly familiar in academic circles, while popular culture in Greece has been associated with two types of fiction: bestselling novels primarily addressed to and enjoyed by a female audience[35] and potboilers which have been seen since the 1980s as promoting the commercialization of literature and the emerging lifestyle culture.[36] Both types of fiction, relying on simple storytelling and shunning formal experimentation,

---

[34] This recovery (published short story collections went up from 123 in 2008 to 168 in 2014) can be attributed, among other things, to economic reasons and a proliferation of creative writing courses.
[35] The much-discussed bestseller by Maira Papathanasopoulou, *Ο Ιούδας φιλούσε υπέροχα* (1998) sold around three hundred thousand copies, a considerable number for the Greek book market, was serialized on Greek television and was translated into a number of languages. Judging from the recent book by Eva Stamou (2014) resistance to trashy literature consumed primarily by women is still growing. It should be noted that one of the first studies of para-literature goes back to the early 1980s (see Martinidis 1982).
[36] Yannis Xanthoulis, one of only two writers to be given an entry in a dictionary of 1980s Greece (the other being Chronis Missios, who wrote political narratives) is listed as being the leading representative of popular Greek fiction, and his novel *Το πεθαμένο λικέρ* [The dead liqueur] (1987) is treated as a landmark in the emerging trend for bestsellers (Vamvakas and Panagiotopoulos 2014: 379–82). It should be noted that the same dictionary has an entry for fiction but not for poetry.

became increasingly associated with popular literature, while crime fiction went from being a neglected and somewhat despised genre to becoming accepted as one of the most effective methods of engaging with contemporary social problems. For many years crime fiction in Greece was considered a form of pulp fiction, but since the 1990s its reputation has been significantly enhanced and the leading crime writer, Petros Markaris, has written a number of detective novels depicting Greek society in crisis. Also, the recent rehabilitation of the crime fiction of Yannis Maris has been seen as a legitimization of popular culture in Greece (Filippou 2015; Hatzivasileiou 2018: 536–603).

Perhaps the growth of popular fiction in Greece has to do with a reversal in the trend for subordinating function, promoted by the 'popular aesthetic', to form, favoured by the 'pure' aesthetic gaze (Bourdieu 1986). High culture is about representation and contemplation; popular culture is about performance and what is represented, in other words the affirmation of the continuity between art and life. As Pierre Bourdieu has stated, 'intellectuals could be said to believe in the representation – literature, theatre, painting – more than in the things represented, whereas the people chiefly expect representations and the conventions which govern them to allow them to believe "naively" in the things represented' (1986: 5). An elective 'aesthetic distance', to use Bourdieu's term, has been developed, while at the same time the detachment of the pure gaze has been challenged. The primacy of form over function, of manner over matter, has increasingly been questioned. As a reaction to this, those who defend the autonomy of literature and the seriousness of high culture have deplored the demise of poetry or tried to rescue fiction from the perils of facile storytelling by promoting experimentation, self-referentiality or the hybridization of essay and fiction (Giannopoulou and Tramboulis 2012–13).

In cinema the distinction between elitist and popular culture can be understood by comparing the aesthetic, existential and eclectic approach to the Balkans in Theo Angelopoulos's *Ulysses' Gaze* (1995) with the popular and stereotypical perception of the area portrayed in the road movie *Balkanisateur* (1997) by Sotiris Gkoritsas. The elegiac and highbrow pessimism of Angelopoulos contrasts with the cheeky, jocular tone of Gkoritsas's film. In *Ulysses' Gaze* the characters are crossing the Balkans, searching for the meaning of history and identity, whereas in the *Balkanisateur* they are driven by the desire to make easy money through a currency scam. The distinction between elite and popular culture is also translated into performances of antiquity and modernity, as was the case with the opening and closing ceremonies of the 2004 Olympic Games. The opening ceremony highlighted antiquity by projecting cultural and historical continuity and playing to the expectations of foreign audiences. The closing ceremony celebrated traditional music and dance and showcased popular culture.

Although the distinction between a humanist and a lifestyle conception of culture might offer useful insights into recent cultural trends, there are some areas in which this dualistic pattern seems to break down.[37] Music and song, where the distinction between popular (λαϊκό) and high popular (έντεχνο λαϊκό) has been highlighted and debated for a long time (following the rehabilitation of *rebetika* and the setting of poetry to music), could be considered as such an area in which this kind of distinction is challenged by the extensive hybridization of styles and the number of established poets who have written lyrics for popular songs.[38] It is not only earlier poets such as Nikos Gatsos and Tasos Leivaditis who have made their mark (and living) by writing popular lyrics, but contemporary ones as well (e.g. Manos Eleftheriou and Michalis Ganas). It should also be noted that during the crisis, street and hip-hop artists have increasingly blended elements from popular and elite culture.

More than other artists, poets faced the predicament of choosing elitist isolation or opening up to the wider public, thus acknowledging the incommensurability of the humanist and popular culture and at the same time trying to bridge the gap. Kiki Dimoula (1931–2020), a poet who is popular with the public, has been disparagingly described as the Harry Potter of Greek poetry[39] and a media phenomenon,[40] while other poets such as Ganas have managed to transcend poetry's isolation and lack of rapport with the public by reconciling the elitism of poetry with the popularity of song, the urban with the regional and individual lyricism with collective memories (Koutsourelis 2013b). In the last twenty years some poets and critics have lamented the mass production of unsophisticated poetry and its relegation to the status of a self-indulgent hobby (Koutsourelis

---

[37] Panagiotis Kondylis has argued that 'in Greece the "popular" song, from its narration of the sadness of the hash smoker to the setting of serious poetry to music, has helped a great deal to transcend the old basic distinction between the "urban" or "high" and "popular" culture and produced something considered desirable by theorists of postmodern culture' (1991/2011: 59).

[38] Blending the popular and the grotesque, performance and music in a carnivalesque fashion, Dionysis Savvopoulos mixed Greek folk music and *rebetiko* with rock sounds in his songs (e.g. 'Black Sea' and 'Zeibekiko') on the album Βρώμικο ψωμί [Dirty bread] (1972) and elsewhere (Papanikolaou 2007). Similar musical hybridity is promoted by groups such as *Fatme*, who reflected on the first generation of the *Metapolitefsi* in the song Ὑπάρχει λόγος σοβαρός/There is a serious reason' (1985).

[39] Topali (2005); see also the reaction of K. Georgousopoulos 'Η αλεπού και τα σταφύλια' (*Ta Nea*, 25–6 February 2006) and Topali's response ('Απάντηση στον Κώστα Γεωργουσόπουλο', *Ta Nea*, 13 March 2006).

[40] Garantoudis (2014); see also the rejoinder from Margellou Inglessi (2014).

2012). They seem to hark back to the times when poetry in Greece was more engaged with the public and aesthetically accountable. The crisis seems to have reversed this downward trend and led to an efflorescence of a new kind of poetry (see Chapter 6).

It could be argued that a gradual transition towards cultural materiality is one of the main features of the period following the fall of the junta. This can be seen in the proliferation of food programmes on Greek television, the growing number of publications on cooking (including novels on the theme of cooking and food), the increasing emphasis on body care, the first gossipy lifestyle tabloids and the attempt to promote Greek culture not only in terms of its past but also its material present. A characteristic example of this trend is a video entitled 'Be one of us' (2013) by the students of the 'Tabula Rasa' School of Arts, which aims to promote Greece and its culture.[41] In this video, images of Zorba and the Acropolis are replaced by sensory experience, food and the communal way of life.

Yet the crisis has spawned a new kind of humanism, based on the axiom that people matter more than numbers and statistics, calling for a rediscovery of human solidarity against consumerist individualism and neo-liberal austerity (Rakopoulos 2014). There is now a growing emphasis on the role of local communities and public space in an attempt to revive the sense of a spirit of human interaction among ordinary people that has been to some extent lost. The crisis has questioned the individualistic narcissism and the lifestyle culture of recent years, making the cultural ambivalence even more intense by inviting a rethink of the two dreams of *Metapolitefsi*: modernization and consumerism.

Conclusion

Between the fall of the junta and the onset of the crisis, Greece enjoyed its longest period of democracy and prosperity, and many institutional reforms have come primarily from the EU following a top-down approach. What I hope to have shown in this chapter is that by contrast, in the area of culture, we can see a bottom-up approach with an increasing prominence of materiality, diversity, otherness, popular culture and anti-systemic forces. This has meant that cultural differences are now more widely tolerated and accepted than ever before, thus

---

[41] '"Be one of us: Hellas" by Tabula Rasa' (2013), available at https://www.youtube.com/watch?v=w9bKe0KwEEA.

calling into question the notion of a homogeneous national culture. For Greece this has been particularly challenging, as for many years it had endeavoured to promote national homogenization and cultural assimilation.[42]

Although modernization and Europeanization were valorized by dualist approaches, the ascendancy of a diverse underdog culture, fostered by the undermining of the hierarchical distinctions between high and low, has not received proper attention despite its earlier vociferous manifestations and despite the fact that it has become a culture of resistance during the crisis.[43] The period from junta to crisis can be read as the story of two cultures and an era of increasing cultural tension and diversity, making it a testing ground for established models of analysis and one of the most dynamic periods of Greek culture. Interestingly, however, the underdog culture has been seen as largely anti-Western, whereas consumerist culture is seen as westernized, thus challenging neat oppositions and highlighting once again hybridizations and tensions in Greek culture. Interrogating dualist interpretations and analysing cultural oppositions offer an opportunity to revisit the two main features of the culture of *Metapolitefsi* (modernization and consumerism) and ask probing questions in the light of the recent crisis.

---

[42] It should be noted that debates over competing definitions of the nation in terms of ethnic descent or civic society have also increased in the last thirty years and have contributed to raising awareness about ethnic and cultural diversity (see Chapter 4).

[43] The manifestations of this culture range from toleration of various forms of violence or the non-payment of toll road charges to Greece's failure until recently to enforce a smoking ban.

2

Eurosceptics or Europhiles? The cultural dilemmas of Europeanization

Greece's relationship with Europe has been somewhat tense and contradictory involving both pride and angst. This entanglement has been further complicated by the Greeks claiming the 'copyright' on both Europe's name and cultural heritage. Attitudes to Europe are central to the culture of post-junta Greece and reflect its ambivalence, ranging from Euroscepticism to fervent Europeanism. In the early 1970s Andreas Papandreou claimed that 'Greece itself belongs to the Third World, even though it is part of the European continent and the western European community' (1973: 376), but since then a reluctant romance with Europe has developed which, with the formal accession of Greece to the EEC/EU in 1981, ended up in marriage. Greeks seemed only too happy to embrace the idea of belonging to Europe while talking about 'going to Europe', as if their country were not part of it and thus inviting the comment that Greeks are either pro- or anti-European but not Europeans. But having internalized their presumed inferiority vis-à-vis Western Europeans, Greeks also tried to deny it using the cultural capital of antiquity. On the one hand, economic and institutional Europeanization/integration have led to a preoccupation with identity and, on the other, the increasing fixation with national identity has been seen as a biopolitical form of resistance to Europeanization, as a result of Greeks being invited to internalize the austerity norms of Europe, particularly during the crisis.

In this chapter Greece's changing perceptions of Europe will be analysed alongside how the increasing demand for Europeanization led to people becoming more preoccupied with national identity. The term 'Europeanization' has acquired greater currency since the 1980s and has been used to gauge legal asymmetries or institutional inefficiencies. It highlights the 'mismatch' between the EU and Greek domestic policies and has featured in the titles of a number of studies (Lavdas 1997; Featherstone 1998; Ioakimidis 2000;

Economides 2005), while modernization has been associated with 'intended' rather than 'responsive' Europeanization. As we have seen in Chapter 1, in the post-junta period oppositions have taken different forms with the most prominent being that between a reformist and an underdog culture, contrasting Europeanization with Euroscepticism.[1] Here is a passage from an academic study, demonstrating in a rather awkward and schematic way the historical lineage of attitudes to Europe:

> This dualism has deep roots, reflecting split identities and interests between 'modernizers' and 'traditionalists' in the path of development. In the nineteenth century, leaders such as Adamantios Korais preached the need for Greece to imitate Europe and study Europe. Europe was modernization, as it has been again more recently for Premier Simitis. However, not all Greek leaders welcomed 'Europeanization' or 'Europeanism'. Some saw the Western culture as alien and decadent and believed that an imitation of it would prove fatal for Greece. Anti-Europeanism went with national independence and Greek irredentism. Such attitudes find partial resonance in the recent campaigns of Archbishop Christodoulos and the LAOS party. (Featherstone and Papadimitriou 2008: 41)

Though some argue that Europeanization 'portrays a complex dynamic through which Europe and the nation-state interact', they also accept that it 'is nearly always portrayed as a top-down process, with the causal arrows pointing from EU institutions and policies to the nation-state' (Checkel and Katzenstein 2009: 9–10). The dominance of the term 'Europeanization' in the political discourse raises the question as to whether we can talk about the Europeanization of Greek culture in the same way as many analysts talk about institutional or political Europeanization.[2] Anti-Europeanism has often been associated with populism and been represented as defying rationalism and modernization but, most importantly, culturally isolationist and unproductive. In spite of its positive connotations, Europeanization is an ambiguous and problematic term, given that in the minds of many Greeks Europe can be associated with different things: a repository of values, the rule of law, modernization of institutions, encroachment of Greek independence and identity or simply a source of subsidies. Gradually, however, the debate on Europe has shifted from what it 'is' to what it 'does' and

---

[1] Euroscepticism is a rather recent and malleable term and in today's political and academic discourse 'has come to be equated with different forms of opposition to European integration' (Leconte 2010: 5; Vasilopoulou 2013). However, here the term is used in a broader political and cultural sense since anti-Europeanism is often conflated with anti-Westernism.

[2] In foreign policy since the 1980s the dualist discourse has been translated as an ideological contrast between 'Europeanism' and 'nationalist populism' (Kalpadakis and Sotiropoulos 2007).

ethics has become intrinsic to the identity of the EU. Hence, it will be useful to review the fluctuations in and tensions over Greece's relations with Europe (and by extension its modernization) in the post-junta period.

From anti-Americanism to Euroscepticism

For almost three decades after the end of the Second World War, the 'European factor' in Greek foreign policy was negligible and of secondary importance in the face of US predominance (Economides 2014: 62–3).[3] The widespread belief that the United States facilitated and supported the military dictatorship (1967–1974) in Greece led to increasing scepticism about the role of the United States in Greek politics. In the late 1970s it fuelled anti-Americanism, turning it into a Greek national narrative and the angle through which the problems and tribulations of Greece were explained. Though for the Left anti-Americanism was a potent and emotive rallying point, it cut through ideological and party divides and became a national discourse. Americanocracy was often perceived as the continuation of the German occupation with Nazism and American imperialism converging in the left-wing discourse. A myth of national resistance, with the focus on the 1940s, was cultivated and lent support to anti-Americanism, idealizing the people (*laos*) and valorizing their *leventia* and the authentic Greek tradition.[4] Occupation and national resistance were removed from their historical context and deployed as anti-American metaphors (Lialiouti 2015: 204 and 2016; Stefanidis 2007). On the other hand, American pop culture has fascinated a number of writers (Lefteris Poulios, Panos Koutroumbousis, Spyros Meimaris) since the 1960s through its Beat movement, science fiction and rock music and corresponding translations featured in some short-lived magazines. Having become associated with the ritual celebration of the Polytechnic uprising in 1973 and the march to the American embassy every anniversary since 1974, popular anti-Americanism 'fanned Europeanism in the hope that it would be a substitute frame for security within the region and the pursuit of key national interests' (Featherstone 2014: 4). The European club was also seen as having a more ethical foreign policy, treating member countries as partners and not satellites.

---

[3] Greece became a NATO member in 1952, and the following year an agreement was reached whereby American bases would be installed in the country.
[4] In the late 1970s the Communist Youth (KNE) claimed that, in pursuing their goal of Greek membership of the EEC, the government had contributed to the increasing influence of the 'American way of life'.

After the fall of the junta, though Konstantinos Karamanlis may have committed Greece to the West, insisting that the country belonged there, his policy marked a departure from US pre-eminence and a move towards European security and its 'ethical power' (Aggestam 2008). The West started to be associated more with Europe and democracy and not so much with its Cold-War identification with anti-communism.[5] Though politicians of Europeanist orientation led the two main parties (New Democracy (ND) and PASOK) after 1974, both parties sought to accommodate anti-Western trends. In the late 1970s and early 1980s anti-Western-leaning socialists had behaved towards Europe as 'reluctant partners'. They perceived the EEC as the underwriter of Greece's fragile democracy and at the same time as a symbolic 'other', associated with NATO and Western imperialism. On the one hand, Greeks prided themselves on the fact that their country was the birthplace of European civilization and democracy, while on the other they adopted an instrumental, if not positively exploitative, approach towards Europe, taking advantage of its economic benefits. European norms and values were often treated with reservation or even hostility.

The desire to stabilize the recently restored democracy in Greece and combat Turkish aggression were the pressing political reasons for accession to the EEC, though the country was not ready yet for full immersion in the European sea (Karamouzi 2014). Full Greek entry to the EEC, in 1981, was followed ten months later by the formation of the first socialist government, led by PASOK, which had earlier adopted a hardline anti-EEC stance and classified Greece as a country on the periphery of capitalism. PASOK has been described as a party with a Western mind and a Third World heart. After the 1981 election, it became clear 'that PASOK had no intention of reversing the status quo of accession' (Verney 1993: 136), and the vehemence of its earlier opposition to EEC membership subsided. Its anti-imperialist rhetoric gradually gave way to plans for a Mediterranean European Community, while membership of the EEC was distinguished from membership of NATO, the Community's alleged alter ego.

The passage of time made any withdrawal from the EEC unthinkable, and the PASOK government focused more on greater redistribution of resources within the Community with the help of the integrated Mediterranean programmes. Greece no longer sought special status but made demands for more funding.

---

[5] Tony Judt argued that 'Spain, Portugal and Greece were able to enter or re-enter the "West" with such little difficulty, despite their self-imposed political isolation, because their foreign policies had always been compatible – indeed aligned – with those of NATO or the EEC states' (2010: 525).

According to Tony Judt, 'for Athens, EC membership amounted to a second Marshall Plan: in the years 1985–1989 alone, Greece received $7.9 billion from EC funds' (2010: 528). Yet, the PASOK government continued to see European political integration with suspicion as a threat to national sovereignty and maintained good relations with Eastern Europe, the Arab World and non-aligned countries (Argentina, India, Mexico, Sweden and Tanzania). All of this and its reluctance to condemn the shooting down of a Korean civilian aircraft by the Soviet Union in September 1983 created an image of Greece as an unreliable partner within the EEC. PASOK's intransigence boosted the patriotic sentiments of many Greeks who felt humiliated after the invasion of Cyprus by Turkey and like citizens of a weak state on the margins of a 'two-speed Europe'. PASOK's slogan 'Greece belongs to the Greeks' might have boosted national pride but made Greeks feel that they belonged to a hostile alien body and were not equally Europeans. In its second term in office from June 1985 to June 1989, PASOK developed a more accommodating policy towards the EEC, reflected in the poster of the Euro-elections of 1989 (Figure 2), as a result of the economic difficulties facing the country.

The designation of Athens as the first European Capital of Culture in 1985 signalled the consolidation of the European orientation of the country, and this was accompanied by the gradual transformation of PASOK from a national liberation movement to a Western European socialist party by its becoming a member of the Confederation of Socialist Parties of the EEC. In the same period ND was keen to display its Europeanism, while the KKE demanded withdrawal from the EEC, though the Communist Party of the Interior (KKE Esoterikou) had a more friendly and sophisticated attitude towards Europe. Europe in the 1980s was part of either an ideological debate about national sovereignty or a competition for getting more funds out of the Community, instead of responding constructively to the challenges arising from the integration process. In the meantime, the benefits and subsidies received from the EEC, partly gained due to PASOK's hard bargaining, started to turn people's Euroscepticism into a love affair with Europe.

From Euroscepticism to integration

After an initial period of ambivalence, the Socialists accepted EEC membership as a fait accompli, and by the third Greek Euro-election in June 1989 'it seemed that Greece's EEC orientation was finally becoming a matter of national

Figure 2 PASOK poster in the Euro-elections of 1989. Courtesy of PASOK's press office.

consensus' (Featherstone and Verney 1990: 96). Yet, Greece, still wavering between 'integration' and 'marginalization', was not ready to face the redrawing of the map of Europe after 1989, and the controversy over the name of the former Yugoslav Republic of Macedonia further alienated the country from its European partners. While the Cold War had resolved the country's identity crisis by anchoring it decisively in the West, the post-communist Balkan implosion reawakened dormant Eastern Orthodox cultural allegiances and brought to the surface nationalist undercurrents (Pagoulatos and Yataganas 2010: 185). The question 'Is Greece a Balkan country?' was raised once again, inviting people to consider the European, Mediterranean or Balkan orientation of the country. Since the nineteenth century, Greek identity had been constructed in opposition to the Slavs, first due to Jacob Philipp Fallmerayer's (1790–1861) theory about the Slavicization of the Greeks, then on account of the fear of pan-Slavism and the expansion of Bulgaria and finally during the Cold War due to fear of communism. After 1989 Greeks hoped that EU membership would help them dominate the Balkans economically and return to the eighteenth-century status quo when Greek was the lingua franca of the region, and Greek merchants could be found everywhere in the Balkans.

The rediscovery of the Balkans, following the collapse of the communist regimes and the war in the former Yugoslavia, replaced political divisions with cultural ones and brought to the fore the notion of 'Balkanism' and comparisons with Orientalism. In this respect the book by Maria Todorova was very influential, showing how the Balkans had been constructed by the West,[6] while during the same period Greece had started to be considered by academics in the West as a semi- or crypto-colony and no longer an exotic country. A number of scholars outside Greece have posited that the West exercised a kind of cultural colonialism over Greece, in the form of the 'colonization of the ideal', claiming that eighteenth-century Greece was an ideological construct of colonialist Europe without ever having been, strictly speaking, colonized.[7]

The earlier polarization over Europe and the brief interlude of coalition rule in 1989–90 was succeeded by a period when two Europhile parties alternated in power (ND, 1990–3; PASOK, 1993–2004; ND, 2004–9), while Euroscepticism became the exclusive preserve of the minor parties. With the advent of the post-Cold War era, the question was no longer 'whether Europe' but 'what

---

[6] Todorova (1997), Goldsworthy (1998), Bjelić and Savić (2002) and Mishkova (2008).
[7] Gourgouris (1996), Fleming (2000), Herzfeld (2002) and Calotychos (2003).

kind of Europe' the Greek political forces wanted (Verney and Michalaki 2014: 134). In the 1990s Europe was identified with the modernization of Greece, and the election of Costas Simitis in 1996 as leader of PASOK marked a new era in Greek-EU relations (Voulgaris 2013: 412). Europe and his modernization project defined Simitis's period in office, and the country's inclusion in the eurozone from 1 January 2002 was not just an economic accomplishment but also a symbolic referent of Greece's belonging to the 'core' of Europe. The defensive nationalism of the 1990s gradually gave way to a new confidence and openness towards Europe. On the whole, the Europeanization process had an impact on the territorial distribution of power by shifting the emphasis to the regions and being a formidable factor in rebalancing relations between the state and society in favour of the latter. The EU was regarded as the exporter of democratic governance and a force for building a pluralistic society (Ioakimidis 2001).

Earlier Euroscepticism was developed in opposition to market integration but, after the difficult process of ratifying the Maastricht Treaty (signed on 7 February 1992), it took the form of national identity politics due to the emergence of globalization and the exploitation by right-wing populist parties of anxieties concerning the loss of national identity in a denationalizing world (Hooghe 2007: 7; Kriesi 2009: 224). Europe was also associated with the conception of the nation not in terms of ethnic descent but as a civic community, promoting the idea of equal rights and respecting diversity. Greeks treated Europe either as their natural habitat of freedom, justice and democracy and a return to their roots or as a capitalist jungle which threatened national sovereignty under the combined pressure of globalization and massive migration.

The NATO bombing of the former Yugoslavia in 1999 was extremely unpopular in Greece and reignited old positions of anti-Westernism and Euroscepticism. Moreover, the public rebuffs by the Danes and the Irish of the European treaties exposed the democratic deficit and the popular disaffection with European decision-making. Notwithstanding reservations about the limits of integration and federalism, in the period after Maastricht and before the crisis almost all political parties 'saw Greece's future within the framework of European integration' (Verney and Michalaki 2014: 155). Though Greeks gradually developed into staunch Europhiles, following Greece's membership of the eurozone, some argued that they loved the Europe of subsidies, treating it as a fund rather than as a cultural ideal of greater integration. It has even been argued that, although EU membership may have brought Greece politically closer to the European institutions, it further distanced the country from Europe in cultural terms (Theodoropoulos et al. 2010: 56).

Anti-Westernism and the religious-cultural divide

Western Europe (a term often interchangeable with the West) has been identified with the Enlightenment and modernity, and Greece has constantly been measured against this European canon. The Greek identity from Korais to Seferis has also been seen as built on a dialogue with Europe[8] and the debate over Europe included for the first-time writers such as Alexandros Papadiamantis (1851–1911), who in the past had been considered as encapsulating the Orthodox Christian tradition. By the end of the twentieth century, he began to be seen as a Western writer and in dialogue with the founders of the European novel. A Paris-based Greek critic presented Papadiamantis conversing with leading European writers such as Cervantes and Rabelais in his novel Γυφτοπούλα/*Gypsy Girl* (Proguidis 1997, 2002; cf. Papagiorgis 1997). Another indicator of this cultural extroversion at the turn of the twenty-first century was the fact that 35 per cent of all new book titles were translations, while many Greek novels of the 1990s displayed an unprecedented cosmopolitanism.

However, this extrovert and westernizing trend was accompanied by suspicions that Greece did not belong to the West or that it had been its cultural victim or even its enemy for centuries. These feelings were communicated or cultivated in different ways by Greeks and Westerners. For example, a one-volume history of Europe by a distinguished French historian Jean-Baptiste Duroselle (1917–1994) was not received favourably by the Greeks. Though it aims to present the history of the continent from a European perspective rather than from one particular national viewpoint, *L'Europe: histoire de ses peuples/Europe: A History of Its Peoples* (1990) has been criticized as a history of Europe without Greece. A product of the belief in the idea of Europe as a coherent entity, it was aiming to trace the historical pedigree of this construct and highlight shared paths of development and cultural outlook. The book was intended for the general public and was more about the project of European unification and its historical roots than a history of Europe as such.

Yet, it implicitly raised the question of the making of Europe's borders and how far back the history of Europe as a sociocultural entity could be traced. Many Greeks criticized the book, often without reading it, for limiting Europe to the Western

---

[8] Takis Theodoropoulos, 'Άόμματο παρόν και εθνική ταυτότητα', *I Kathimerini*, 12 July 2015. He has published a number of articles in the same paper on the relationship between Greece and the West/Europe and on Greek identity (e.g. 22 February, 17 and 26 April, 28 June 2015, 6 March, 17 and 24 April 2016).

Europe of Latin Christendom or of the Cold War and for using the ninth-century Carolingian empire as a precursor of the idea of European unity. Even leading Greek historians criticized the book for its limited conception of the common bases of European culture and for neglecting the contribution of Greek culture to the creation of the European intellectual tradition. As Paschalis Kitromilides pointed out in his review, 'it is indeed somewhat curious to stress the Viking contribution to the creation of common European values by noting the Vikings' dedication to equality and freedom (120), and to omit any substantive reference to the profound explorations in [of] the meaning of these principles in Greek political thought and their practical testing in the democratic institutions of the Greek *polis*' (1994: 125–6; also Davies 1997: 43–4).

Geographical Europe has always had to compete with notions of Europe as a cultural community with one of its major markers being religion (Davies 1997: 9). During the Cold War the East–West divide was clear and convenient, but the end of the Cold War blurred the dividing lines in Europe and brought to the fore 'the most durable' division, that is, that between Catholic (Latin) Christianity and Orthodox (Greek) Christianity (Davies 1997: 27), thus questioning Greece's classification as European. In his popular book *Balkan Ghosts* (1993) Robert Kaplan described the friction between Catholicism and Orthodoxy as like that between capitalism and communism, while for a number of scholars religious culture has been crucial in shaping the main approaches to European integration. Brent Nelsen and James Guth 'contend that the Reformation and subsequent wars of religion divide Europe over the value of *political fragmentation*. Catholics rejected fragmentation and remained committed to a united Europe – Latin Christendom – while Protestants found refuge in the separate and new European nation-states' (2015: 4). This might explain why Britain and the Nordics are often the odd countries out but overlooks the role of Orthodoxy in the European integration process. Particularly in the post-Maastricht period, when efforts towards a common 'European identity' increased, Orthodoxy has been perceived as a barrier between Greece and EU, leading to the 'orientalization' of the former. As an Orthodox country Greece was deemed non-European and non-Western, relegated to a different cultural club from its EU partners, though with the subsequent accession of other Orthodox countries (Bulgaria, Romania) things started to change.[9] By presenting itself as part of Christendom in relation to the Islamic Orient, but as rooted in the Byzantine East and distinct from Western Christianity (both Roman Catholic

---

[9] Turkey's prospects of joining the EU also intensified the religious divide, between Islam and Christianity, and the perception of Europe as a Christian club.

and Protestant), Orthodoxy occupies an 'in-between' position, which is often projected onto Greece's relationship with Europe.

And it was not just Western commentators who questioned the Greeks' allegiance to Europe. A self-orientalizing discourse was developing among Greek cultural critics, such as Nikos Dimou, who pointed out that the only time Greeks felt entirely European was when outsiders challenged their European credentials (Dimou 2011 and 2014). Others argued that Greeks were happy to 'consume' Europe but were not really engaged in the European integration project or in shaping a common European identity (Xydakis 2014). Modernization and Europeanization have been related to the idea of 'cultural deficiency', in other words that Greece is not modern enough, not European enough, not 'enlightened' enough or – during the crisis – not responsible enough (see the Introduction).

The philosopher Stelios Ramfos, for example, argues that the individual has been insufficiently developed in Greece, and he links this underdevelopment to the 'immaturity' of Byzantium and the failure of the Orthodox tradition to develop the notion of individuality. Instead, communal ties (family, friends) are always stronger than civic obligations and this fosters corruption, preventing the development of stable institutions. In contrast, the West has managed to develop the notions of individuation and civic responsibility. Promoted by Orthodox mystics, the notion of cyclical, and in turn immutable, time, favoured the timeless or static present of the community, protecting it from the blasphemous egotism and forward-looking Western individuality (Ramfos 2000/11 and 2012).

Though Ramfos started off as one of the so-called neo-Orthodox intellectuals of the 1980s (Christos Yannaras, Kostis Moskov, Kostas Zouraris, Panagiotis Nellas and Dionysis Savvopoulos), whose emphasis on the community as a counterweight to Western individualism tallied with PASOK's slogan that 'Greece belongs to the Greeks' and underpinned Moskov's pronouncement 'We are communists and not Marxists', later on (around 1996 and after a brief stint in the United States) he subscribed to the deficiency camp and saw the Orthodox tradition as an impediment to modernization.[10] However, most of the neo-Orthodox intellectuals continued to question the theory of cultural deficiency and stressed the cultural superiority of the Greek-Orthodox tradition vis-à-vis the West. Being an intellectual and elitist trend with little wider social

---

[10] Though some of these intellectuals defined themselves as 'new theologians', the term neo-Orthodox was first introduced in an article by Yannis Milios in the journal *Scholiastis* in September 1983, entitled 'Ο "νέο-ορθόδοξος" σκοταδισμός'. In the same journal there are related interviews with Kostis Moskov (no. 5, August 1983) and Dionysis Savvopoulos (no. 6, September 1983) as well as with Sakis Karagiorgas (no. 6) regarding the controversial appointment of Christos Yannaras as Professor of Philosophy at Panteion University. Mitralexis points out that the so-called

appeal, the neo-Orthodox 'movement' was not a religious revival but a quest for an authentic Greek way of life and reassessing the spiritual legacy of Greek Orthodoxy by highlighting its distinctiveness from the religious traditions of the West (Makrides 1998).

Since the 1960s Greek theologians have challenged Augustinian scholasticism and tried to recapture the spirit of Orthodox patristic theology by highlighting the extent to which Orthodox thinking has been the prisoner of Western ideas. I will focus here above all on the ideas of Christos Yannaras because, apart from being a prolific writer, he is one of the most widely read public intellectuals in Greece and his views have attracted international attention.[11] Building on the work of George Florovsky (1893–1979), Vladimir Lossky (1903–1958) and J. S. Romanides (1927–2001),[12] Yannaras (b. 1935) criticized the West for reducing human beings to an abstract individuality and for overlooking their fundamentally *relational* nature. For him the Western politics of 'individual right', presupposing a politics of contest and conflict, is incompatible with the Orthodox relational ontology, which prioritizes community and the notion of the Church as a gathering of people in an organic living 'body' and not as an institution (Cole 2017). Drawing a distinction between 'Orthodoxy' and the 'West' based on the primacy of 'relation' over 'substance', he saw the West as individualistic, rationalist and essentialist. He argued that the Greek world had been alienated from a mode of life centred on human relations by adopting the legalistic ideas of the West, introduced with the translation into Greek of the writings of Thomas Aquinas in the late Byzantine period.

Yannaras views the modern world as the product of the Western Middle Ages and his negative assessment of the West relies on references to Augustine, Anselm and Aquinas as well as to Martin Heidegger's critique of Western metaphysics and technology. Homi Bhabha's concept of mimicry (1990: 85–92), intrinsic to all discourse between colonizer and colonized, could apply to some neo-Orthodox thinkers and the ways they 'employ academic tools of the Western

---

neo-Orthodox themselves never gave their 'movement' a label, thus casting doubt on its identity and coherence (2019: 298). It should be noted that the appearance of the neo-Orthodox 'movement' coincides with the original publication of General Makryannis's manuscript *Οράματα και Θάματα/Visions and Wonders* (1983), which, with its religious overtones, undermined his earlier image based on his *Memoirs* (1907).

[11] Yannaras belongs to the theologians from the generation of the 1960s and is seen as continuing the views on Greek identity of the literary Generation of the 1930s (Kalaitzidis 2009: 485–6).

[12] Nicolas Prevelakis argues that 'Romanides condemns the very creation of the modern Greek state, which he sees as a protectorate of foreign powers' (2012). It is interesting to note that Romanides was a candidate for the far right in the 1977 parliamentary elections in Greece and some of his early anti-Western theses can be found in a speech by the then Metropolitan of Dimitrias, Christodoulos, who later became Archbishop of Athens (Kalaitzidis 2010: 410–12).

intellectual tradition for the very purpose of narrating an eastern Christianity that was inherently free of Western pollution' (Demacopoulos and Papanikolaou 2013: 20). By challenging the Western depersonalization of God and relying on the writings of the Greek Church fathers, Yannaras's discourse is anti-Western but at the same time in dialogue with certain Western thinkers. This suggests that the Greek cultural dependence on the West is reflected as much in the endorsement of enlightened modernity as in its rejection.

In his many books and articles Yannaras defines Hellenism as a way of life and condemns individualism as both an epistemological and moral fallacy. Emphasizing the authenticity of communal life, which for him lies at the heart of the Greek Orthodox tradition, he links the individualistic conception of personhood in the West to legalistic views of sin and punishment. He often ends up criticizing 'western legalism' and has provided a critique of the overrationalizing influence of Augustine on Western thought and his equation of the Greek concept of *logos* with *ratio*, making Christianity a religion of the mind rather than the heart. Yannaras seems to have transformed a theological argument into cultural identity warfare by emphasizing Hellenism's presumed cultural sovereignty over the Church and popularizing his views through his regular column, first in the newspaper *To Vima* and since 1994 in *Kathimerini* (Kalaitzidis 2013). The eschatological deficit in his work explains his understanding of Orthodoxy in cultural rather than theological terms and his adoption of a hardened anti-Westernism with pronounced cultural underpinnings. He emphasizes the cultural disparity between the Greek East and the Latin West, but ignores the blatant discontinuity between antiquity and the Christian era (Kalaitzidis 2010: 404–5).

Defining the 'West' as a 'spiritual failure', Yannaras contrasts it with Orthodoxy, which he identifies with Hellenism. As Brandon Gallaher points out in reviewing Yannaras's book *Orthodoxy and the West* (2006, Greek edition 1992), in asserting its Eastern identity Orthodox theology 'needs someone who can fulfil the role of barbarian, whom it can define itself against' (2009: 539). There is a kind of self-affirmation through the negation of the Other and this binarism veils the dependence of the subject on the Other. Yannaras has contributed to anti-Westernism by arguing that, as a creation of Western intervention since its inception in the 1820s, the Greek state had no opportunity to reconnect with the authentic Eastern tradition associated with Byzantium and Orthodoxy, trying unsuccessfully instead to imitate Western individualistic models, which had eventually led to the current prevalence of consumerism and corruption (Yannaras 2014). His anti-Westernism belongs to a long tradition of communitarianism that can be traced from Konstantinos Karavidas to Costis Moskov in Greece and to which the poet Odysseas Elytis subscribed in 1990 with his anti-individualistic statement: 'Significance in this life lies beyond the individual' (1999: 66).[13] Interweaving theological doctrine and historiographical critique, Yannaras reads modern Greek history as a struggle between authentic Orthodoxy, found mostly in local traditions and popular religion, and the 'West', represented by the state institutions as well as the Church of Greece. Basically, he aspires to place Greece at the centre of the world's attention and to promote its cultural message as representing the transcendence of both capitalism and socialism, treated as by-products of Western metaphysics (Prevelakis 2012).

Some neo-Orthodox intellectuals oppose both capitalism and materialism and manifest their resistance to modernity by voicing their nostalgia for a return to a more communitarian ethos. Their ideas converge with those of left-wing nationalists, who argue that Greece is Europe but a Europe different from that of the West, based on the tradition of the community and far removed from Western rationalism or individualism (Karabelias 1996). By expressing their disillusionment with the nation state they articulate a kind of national romanticism and make references to the nationalist Ion Dragoumis (1878–1920), who contrasted the Helladic state with all-encompassing Hellenism. National romanticism is closer to reactionary modernism, a kind of *kulturkritik* advocating a return to the metaphysics of an authentic community. It represents a peculiar ethnocentrism or post-nationalism and identifies nationalism with modernity's suppression of the nation by the 'centripetal' state, thus entailing the suppression of the cultural diversity of Greek life and culture. National romanticism rejects the artificial and the constructed in favour of the genuine and the authentic. The cultural malaise of Europe can be overcome by its 'Hellenization', in other words its authentic Christianization and not by the westernization of Hellenism (Sevastakis 2004: 129).

During the post-junta period, according to Efstathios Kessareas (2015), there have been two conflicting trends within Greek theology: an activist, reformist and socially oriented one, represented by Savvas Agouridis and Thanasis Papathanasiou, and an inward-oriented, mystical theology which rejected both the demands for social change and ecclesiastical reform. Represented by leading

---

[13] Dionysis Savvopoulos's lines 'και μια φωνή με προφορά απ' των Σερρών την Πρώτη/ρωτάει άμα συμφωνώ να γίνουμε Ευρώπη' ('Οι εκλογές μαντινάδα') from his album *Η Ρεζέρβα* (1979) and his song 'Ας κρατήσουν οι χοροί' from *Τραπεζάκια έξω* (1983) can be included in this trend.

Greek theologians with divergent views such as Vassileios Gondikakis, Georgios Metallinos, the Metropolitan of Nafpaktos Hierotheos and Christos Yannaras, this trend often shifted from a theological to a cultural/historical discourse, leading to ethnocentrism and the equation of Greekness with anti-Westernism. Criticizing both the socio-economic systems of Western capitalism (market economy, individualism, consumerism) and Soviet communism (state control, planned economy, communal organization of work), these religious intellectuals regard Orthodox communalism as the highest form of social organization and respond to calls for modernization within the European context by highlighting the Orthodox foundations of Greek identity. Instead of seeing Greece aligning with Europe, they try to reverse the order, hoping for a European rediscovery of the ecumenical spirit of Orthodoxy.

Thinking along similar lines, another leading theologian, the Metropolitan of Pergamon Ioannis Zizioulas, has argued that Europe helps Greeks rediscover Orthodoxy and understand how it has managed to transcend Western nihilism and the preoccupation with the self (Zizioulas 1985a). For him Orthodoxy should not be afraid of the West because the latter needs the former to help it overcome problems such as its extreme individualism and human disharmony with the natural environment. Some Greek theologians claim that the Orthodox identity contains otherness within it and aspires to unity and universality, pointing to the fundamental difference between Orthodoxy's traditional universalism and modern Hellenism's ethnocentrism (Kalaitzidis 2003 and 2004). They see a clash between the nation state, associated with the European Enlightenment and the classical past, and the revival of the Christian *oecumene*, represented by the transnational ideal of the Byzantine Empire. According to this view, the Church succumbed to Greek nationalism and was transformed from a defender of the Christian *oecumene* to a propagator and supporter of the Greek national idea and this explains why there had been no serious anticlericalism in the country (Kalaitzidis 2003: 61–2). It is pointed out that the biblical and ecclesiastical meaning of terms such as *genos* and *ethnos* are completely different from their secular and national appropriation. Despite the nationalization of the Church, the debates about identity, multiculturalism and the Orthodox heritage proliferated at the turn of the twenty-first century (see Chapter 4). However, this religious revival seems to be a revival of nationalism identified with Orthodoxy. And this has been true in other Orthodox countries such as Serbia and Russia, since Eastern nationalism 'was based to a great extent on religious–cultural differences' (Merdjanova 2000: 234; Mavrogordatos 2003: 130).

The religious-cultural divide within Europe first resurfaced after the end of the Cold War with Samuel Huntington and his theory of a clash of civilizations. In his controversial article 'The Clash of Civilizations?' published in 1993, he argued that 'the fault lines between civilizations will be the battle lines of the future' (1993: 22) and identified seven or eight major civilizations, two of which were in Europe ('Western' and 'Slavic-Orthodox'). A few years later (1996) he developed the article into a book, with the same title but without a question mark, where he expanded his theory. In his view the European community rests on the shared foundation of European culture and Western Christianity and thus sanctions placing Greece on the non-Western side of the European fault line.[14] He claims that 'Greece is not part of Western civilization', describing the country as 'an anomaly, the Orthodox outsider in Western organizations' (2002: 162).[15]

What annoyed Greeks in this book was being placed outside Western civilization (despite the country being a member of NATO and the EU) and in the realm of the Slav-Orthodox, which includes Russia and other Eastern European countries. The paradox here is that this argument raises objections only when it is made by Westerners and not by the Greeks themselves. For Huntington, one of the pillars of Western civilization is classical Greece, but modern Greeks are placed outside its remit because they have been formed by Orthodoxy and Byzantium. Similarly, Robert Kaplan argued that 'Greece is geographically equidistant between Brussels and Moscow, and is as close to Russia culturally as it is to Europe, by virtue of its Eastern Orthodox Christianity, in turn a legacy of Byzantium' (Kaplan 2012: 152). The 'clash of civilizations' theory shifted the emphasis from politics to culture, and particularly religion, a shift which Greek intellectuals promoting Europeanization and the separation of the state from the church were not prepared to accept easily.[16] Basically Huntington introduced

---

[14] Huntington was not the first to raise the issue of civilizational conflict between the Western and Orthodox Christian worlds. Leading intellectuals in Russia (the Slavophiles) from the mid-nineteenth century and the historian Arnold Toynbee in the early twentieth century raised similar questions.

[15] With reference to Greece's accession to the EU/the eurozone, the former president of France Valéry Giscard d'Estaing, generally thought of as a friend of Greece, remarked in September 2012: 'To be perfectly frank, it was a mistake to accept Greece. Greece simply wasn't ready. Greece is basically an Oriental country' (Kalyvas 2015: 5).

[16] Huntington's views have received particular attention in Greece since the publication of his article. See the articles by Nicos Alivizatos, 'Ορθοδοξία, Ελληνισμός και Δύση', To Vima, 30 April 1994; Dimitris Konstas, '"Η σύγκρουση των πολιτισμών" και η Ελλάδα', To Vima, 2 October 1994; and Yannaras (1997). A year later (1994) a statement allegedly made by Henry Kissinger to the effect that Greeks were uncontrollable and could only be tamed by attacking their cultural roots was circulated widely on social media and provoked angry responses. Similar objections were raised to Martin Bernal's book *Black Athena: The Afroasiatic Roots of Classical Civilization* (three volumes first published in 1987, 1991 and 2006, respectively).

another broader dualism and sanctioned the 'conflict between the Orthodox understanding of the identity of the human person deriving from the collective and the western liberal understanding of the human person as an autonomous individual' (Payne 2003: 261). He also reinforced a reading of ethnic conflict in the Balkans in cultural terms (Islamic versus Orthodox versus Western) and claimed that civilizational conflicts will be the most significant feature of the post-communist 'new world order'.

Critics of Huntington's theory argued that the ethnic conflict is not due to a clash of civilizations but to the prioritization of nationhood over citizenship in the process of adopting the Western-European model of the nation state (Roudometof 1999). The Balkan peoples struggled between the two options of citizenship and nationhood, with the former being associated with rights and duties and the latter with historical genealogies in which cultural markers (religion, language) were elevated to determinants of the relevant national membership. The triumph of nationhood implies the politicization of cultural life and could explain recent developments in the Balkans and attitudes to Europe. In the midst of the war in former Yugoslavia, French literary scholar, feminist and psychoanalyst, Julia Kristeva, originally from Bulgaria, argued that the key to understanding Serbian violence was the country's Orthodox legacy. Europe, according to her, was 'facing a difference of cultures' and the conflict in the former Yugoslavia showed divisions going back to the Great Schism of 1054 between Byzantium and Rome and Orthodoxy and Catholicism (Kristeva 1999 and 2000).

Until a few years ago Greece was the only Orthodox country in the EU and some people argued that the Orthodox faith could act as a barrier between Greece and its European partners. The perception of the EU and the West as a threat to Greek national identity was aggravated by theories such as Huntington's, while the connection between religion and European identity has frequently been made in books on Europe (Delanty 1995: 66–9). Father Georgios Metallinos, professor of theology at Athens University, questioned the place Greece could have in a 'spiritual geography' dominated by Roman Catholicism and Protestantism and argued in 1992 that 'the problem for Greece is not primarily economic or political ... the problem is chiefly spiritual and cultural' (quoted in Fokas 2000: 289). European modernity and unification had to be resisted in the name of Orthodoxy, as happened with the ratification of the EU's new Charter of Fundamental Rights (December 2000), which gave the Greek Church the opportunity to come out publicly against homosexuality and the EU. Perceived as a manifestation of a globalizing and homogenizing Western culture, the EU was considered by most Greek Christians as a threat to Orthodoxy and the Greek identity.[17]

The Orthodox faith has often been presented as incompatible with Western or European norms (secularism, individuality, liberalism) and the following question has been posed: Is Orthodoxy resistant or adapting to the secularization coming from Western Europe? However, secularization can mean different things: for example, a decline in religious belief and practices, the privatization of those beliefs and practices or institutional secularization (Fokas 2013: 186). It could also take the form of EU directives as in the case of identity cards or religious symbols, prompting Greek clerics to complain about Europe's secularizing influence and the late Archbishop Christodoulos to declare, 'Europe may fill our pockets, but it can empty our souls.' As long as religion continues to provide resources for defending national culture and identity, European secularization is unlikely to be contagious and will not spread eastwards following EU enlargement.

Despite high levels of secularization in some European countries, attitudes to Europe can have their roots in religious differences. Contrary to the Western Christian tradition, in Orthodoxy sin is not understood as an illegitimate transgression but a misdirection; God is seen as a source of love rather than an authoritarian avenger. On the other hand, Protestantism's adherence to rules and avoidance of moral hazard echoes a long tradition of sociological thought going back to Max Weber's influential *The Protestant Ethic and the Spirit of Capitalism* (1905). Due to different constructions of notions of sin, debt and punishment, religion also becomes part of the 'clash of narratives' over the future of Europe. In this respect Chadi and Krapf argue that 'cultural differences between different religious denominators are a possible explanation for the euro crisis' (2017: 1825). In short, the East/West divide is narrated both in terms of a clash of civilizations as well as in terms of specific doctrinal positions and their multiple transformations.

---

[17] It could be said that Greek Orthodoxy has been involved in two confrontations. The first with Western modernity and its achievements such as the Enlightenment or its new practices like the ordination of women, officially rejected as a dangerous innovation stemming from the West. The second conflict is between traditional Eastern Orthodox universalism and Greek-centred nationalist particularism, reflected in the 2003–4 dispute between the Church of Greece and the Ecumenical Patriarchate of Constantinople concerning the latter's jurisdiction over various dioceses in northern Greece that had not been incorporated into the Greek state until the early twentieth century (Roudometof and Makrides 2010).

Crisis and disillusionment

The economic crisis disturbed comfortable assumptions about Greek Europeanism and raised awkward questions about the commitment of Greeks to Europe. The 'rescue' package of 2010 designed by the EU/IMF and its austerity measures caused a popular backlash and upset the balance of Greek public attitudes towards the EU and the euro. For Greeks the EU could no longer promise prosperity and economic growth and now was inextricably linked to a loss of sovereignty. The economic crisis and the possibility of expulsion from the eurozone exacerbated cultural suspicion towards the West, making Greeks increasingly anti-Western and perpetuating their emotional approach to international diplomacy. It also increased the tension between the resurgent nationalism that presents Greeks as the victims of Europe and particularly of the Germans and the new cosmopolitanism of the last thirty years. At the same time many Greeks have been keen to demonstrate that the crisis was a wider structural European phenomenon and not due to mismanagement on the part of the Greeks, thus shifting the blame to global capitalism.

Earlier Euroscepticism seemed incompatible with the exercise of power in government and had previously been the preserve of minor opposition parties. Yet the European Parliament elections in 2014 marked a Eurosceptic turn in Greece and a tectonic shift unthinkable in the previous European elections (2009) when the two major parties (PASOK and ND), firm supporters of European integration, together won over three-quarters of the popular vote. These elections also marked a meteoric increase, from 0.29 per cent to 9.4 per cent of the vote for the neo-Nazi and staunchly Eurosceptic party Golden Dawn (Verney 2015). Though the pro-/anti-EU divide tends to follow the division between parties of power and parties of protest, the economic crisis and the austerity policies adopted to combat it could be seen as potential game changers in the rise of Euroscepticism in Greece and elsewhere. Indeed, the crisis has shown that there was something extremely tenuous and fragile in the European orientation of Greek society (something not observed in other countries in crisis such as Portugal, Ireland or even Spain). In the maelstrom of the crisis Greeks adopted a 'pragmatic approach', displaying intensely Eurosceptic sentiments, while recognizing that remaining in the eurozone and the EU was their only realistic choice (Balampanidis 2019: 115).

During the crisis some Westerners presented Greeks as children (using Plato's metaphor), who refused to grow up, and themselves as mentors or parents with the avuncular former president of the European Commission Jean-Claude Juncker assuming the role of the father figure. For other Westerners Greece represented a fantasy of resistance, revealing a revolutionary spirit lost in the West (see Chapter 10). Immaturity and irrationalism coupled with idealism and the spirit of resistance suggest a suspension of time, an inability to grow or progress. In both cases Greece is treated as an aberration to the European norm and the modernization project.[18] It could be said that the crisis has increased cultural ambivalence among Greeks and contributed to the somewhat surprising situation in which 'the decline in general EU support is accompanied by an increase in support for the euro' (Clements et al. 2014: 263). Even the referendum of 5 July 2015 on the bailout agreement was seen by many as a test of the country's European identity and was turned into a referendum on Europe by the 'We stay in Europe' campaign, which got 38.6 per cent of the vote as against the 61.36 per cent of the rival 'No' side. This once again intensified debates about Europe and the commitment of the country to the EU and the eurozone. As Yanis Varoufakis aptly observed, Europe is like the Hotel California: it is easier to check in than to leave.

Germany's status as one of Greece's main creditors reawakened the ghost of the German occupation with crisis-stricken Greece being perceived as undergoing a modern-style occupation, stirring up widespread anti-German feelings among ordinary Greeks.[19] In 2011 the annual celebration of OXI day (commemorating Greece's rejection of Mussolini's demand that his troops be given free passage into Greece in 1940) turned into anti-German protests with participants shouting 'No to the Fourth Reich', 'Down with the new Occupation' and some rioters burning German flags. In Thessaloniki the scheduled parade was cancelled after the president of the Hellenic Republic was branded a traitor and booed, while in several other cities the parades were turned into anti-German protests. The anti-German hysteria was given further impetus after the re-emergence of the issue of Germany's unpaid wartime debts and

---

[18] See Palash Ghosh, 'Are Greeks really European?', *International Business Times*, 9 November 2011, available at http://www.ibtimes.com/are-greeks-really-european-212891 (accessed 20 July 2019); and David Patrikarakos, 'The Greeks are not "Western"', *Politico*, 22 April 2015, available at http://www.politico.eu/article/the-greeks-are-not-western/ (accessed 20 July 2019). The Introduction of a recent study is entitled 'Is Greece a modern European country?' (Triandafyllidou et al. 2013).

[19] The phrase 'The Germans strike again', originating from the 1948 film *Οι Γερμανοί ξανάρχονται/The Germans Strike Again*, became popular among Greeks during the crisis and has been used to sum up the fear of the Germans and their imminent threat (Lialiouti and Bithymitris 2013). According to Spyros Plakoudas, this anti-German hysteria reached its peak in 2011–13 as Greeks vividly 'relived' the memories of the Second World War (2016: 312). In a 2012 public survey approximately one-third (32.4 per cent) of Greek respondents associated the word 'Germany' with Hitler, Nazism or the Third Reich (Michailidou 2017: 98).

reparations to Greece (Tziovas 2017: 27–9). The mass media in particular played an instrumental role in exacerbating anti-German sentiments among crisis-stricken Greeks and reviving old stereotypes about the heartless and humourless Germans or recalling images of fearsome Nazi conquerors.[20] Chancellor Angela Merkel and former Finance Minister Wolfgang Schäuble became frequent targets of media populism and facile anti-German outbursts.[21] Seeking to capitalize on the widespread anti-German sentiment, almost all parties invested in the anti-German discourse and exploited the memories of wartime German oppression in various ways. The hostility towards the Germans demonstrates the internal divisions within Europe and raised doubts about the future cohesion of the EU. It also exposed the orientalizing trends within Europe itself with four countries (Portugal, Italy, Greece and Spain) given the acronym PIGS, arguably confirming the patronizing attitude of North Europeans towards the South. Their plight was far from unique. Europe's periphery was playing out a script already performed many times in the postcolonial world. Perhaps what was needed was not the provincialization of European experiences but the globalization of the postcolonial predicament.

Conclusion

In this chapter, I have charted the various manifestations of the 'idea' of Europe. Following the fall of the junta, Europe was associated with geopolitical security, the consolidation of democracy and the promise of economic prosperity. The bailouts, on the other hand, turned Greece into a democracy without choices and locked into an austerity programme largely 'made in the EU'. Attitudes to Europe in Greece could be described as swinging like a pendulum between scepticism and enthusiasm for European integration and the modernization project, with the recurrent Euroscepticism during the crisis cutting across party lines and more solid and widespread than ever before. The EU/IMF bailout agreements radically redefined the meaning of 'Europe' and during the crisis Greece ably

---

[20] For the role of the Greek media in the perpetuation of anti-German stereotypes, see Capelos and Exadaktylos (2015). Also, Spyros Vletsas, 'Ο αντιγερμανισμός και οι μύθοι που τον τροφοδοτούν', tvxs, 17 March 2012, available at https://tvxs.gr/news/apopseis/o-antigermanismos-kai-oi-mythoi-poy-ton-trofodotoyn-toy-spyroy-bletsa.

[21] The anti-German rhetoric reached a new low when a popular Greek TV comedian attacked Wolfgang Schäuble (who is confined to a wheelchair) for his strict stance on the Greek debt issue, adding that 'the longer a person is stuck in a chair, the more his mind gets stuck on an idea'. Excerpt available at https://www.youtube.com/watch?v=-LcIpCyt0L8.

demonstrated that 'Europe remains a truly ambitious work in progress' (Kaplan 2012: 153). From being at the forefront of Europeanism in the 1990s and 2000s, in the years of crisis Greece turned into a country of Eurosceptics with anti-German sentiments seeming to have replaced the anti-Americanism of the 1970s. Though Greek public opinion may have been at odds with the EU's current direction, the country still preferred to remain within the safe haven of the eurozone, thus confirming that it had moved in a Euro-critical rather than Euro-rejectionist direction. The end of the Cold War, the revival of religion in the Balkans and the anti-Westernism of neo-Orthodox and other intellectuals also noticeably affected attitudes towards Europe while institutional reforms imposed by the European integration process revived questions of identity and cultural orientation. But ultimately it was the crisis which 'resulted in one of the most pro-European societies in the EU being transformed into one of the most Eurosceptic' (Verney 2015: 292). Nowadays there is demand for more concerted European action in the areas of the economy, foreign policy and migration as 'Europe' remains the destination of choice for migrants from Asia and Africa.

3

Debating the nation and its contested pasts: Antiquity and mnemohistory

All communities, including nations, are based on the 'stories we live by' and as Homi Bhabha has put it the nation is a 'narrative strategy' (1990: 292). National identities are based on narrative templates, which give coherence to a nation's past. In the framework of these templates various historical events acquire meaning, though some events may call this coherence into question. The three fundamental questions that preoccupied the Greeks during the post-junta period were: how the nation is defined; who owns the past; and how the past is remembered. These questions will be discussed below with reference to the ancient past and the crucial decade of the 1940s, one of the most contested periods of modern Greek history. Constituted in narrative, the past is always under construction, contention and negotiation with historically disparate 'agents', each bringing different frames of reference. Disputes about the meaning of the past raise questions about the present; a premise informing the approaches (classical reception studies and memory studies) adopted in the corresponding sections of this chapter and which features in George Orwell's novel *1984*: 'Who controls the past controls the future; who controls the present controls the past.'

From Hellenism to Hellenisms: Contesting, claiming and performing antiquity

The odd thing about modern nation states is that it can help their attempts to demonstrate their modernity and secure a deserving place in the company of other modern states, if they can prove their ancient past. Modernity is often predicated on antiquity and then the role of the past is to serve as a sign of the modern. For Greece the concern has been to present itself as a modern, Western nation; and the premise that the West's own origins could be traced back to Greece was thought to bolster its credentials in this respect. Yet, modernity and archaeolatry coexist and clash in other areas, such as the construction of major infrastructure projects (the 2004 Olympics, the Athens and Thessaloniki metros, redevelopment projects) where the desire for modern facilities confronts the sanctity of the ancient ruins. Ancestral pride, the traces of classical material and the trauma of unbridged temporalities inform and complicate the national imaginary.

One of the hallmarks of the post-junta period is the more critical, and often irreverent, attitude towards antiquity and at the same time its overwhelming presence in the public sphere (from marketing tourism to national politics). As Greeks emerged from the seven-year dictatorship, they developed a somewhat critical attitude towards antiquity as a result of its misappropriation by the colonels for ideological purposes and their promotion of their own cultural agenda with the slogan 'Greece of Greek Christians'. In a way this continued the cultural policy of the earlier Metaxas dictatorship (1936–41) and built on a long-standing obsession with cultural continuity. In an earlier essay I have outlined four ways in which Greek intellectuals have approached the country's past and particularly ancient Greece over the last two centuries: symbolic or archaeological, holistic and romantic, aesthetic or modernist and ironic, critical or postmodernist (Tziovas 2008). The last approach became more pronounced after 1974, when the idea of continuity between ancient and modern Greece was increasingly challenged.

Earlier the most explicit questioning of the notion of continuity had come from some prominent figures on the Left. On the recommendation of its leader Nikos Zachariadis, the Communist Party in its seventh congress (1945) tried to dissociate antiquity from modern popular culture by locating the emergence of a modern Greek consciousness in the late Byzantine and Ottoman period (Zachariadis 1953: 202–3, 262). The most eloquent exponent of this cultural discontinuity was the left-wing writer and intellectual Dimitris Hatzis (1913–1981). While in exile in Eastern Europe in 1954 he put forward the following argument:

> In the domain of literary production, and of intellectual life generally the modern Greek world remains completely cut off from its ancient Greek cultural heritage. ... No trace of its survival or memory could be found anywhere. Continuity

here is deeply, radically and completely broken. Modern Greek literature is the literature of a completely new world. (Hatzis 2005: 83–4)

Following the fall of the junta, Hatzis, who had returned to Greece from his political exile, revisited the issue of continuity. His views were now more refined, but he still continued to talk about ruptures, discontinuities and new beginnings, imagining the Greek nation as striving to combine its two medieval traditions (the learned and the popular) in a new synthesis, informed by European ideas, but never succeeding (Apostolidou 2003: 329). His Marxist background and his opposition to the nationalist Great Idea formed the basis of his alternative perspective on the historical past and the relationship between the different phases of Greek literature. Determining the beginnings of modern Greek literature and the point at which it separated from the late Byzantine tradition was an issue which preoccupied Hatzis in the late 1970s and was also the subject of a conference held in Venice in 1991 (Panagiotakis 1993).

The beginnings of modern Hellenism continued to be debated and the posthumous publication in 2004 of an essay written in the mid-1960s, *The Greek Nation: Genesis and Formation of Modern Hellenism*, by another Marxist and exile in France, Nicos Svoronos (1911–1989), offered another opportunity to continue the discussion. Like Hatzis, he rejected crude social determinism and the nationalist certainties about the historical continuity of Hellenism, focusing on the late Byzantine period rather on antiquity. Following the earlier pattern of Greek history proposed by K. Paparrigopoulos, he talked about a 'national awakening' and tried to shift the emphasis from the nation to society and economic structures. Yet he traced a latent cultural, and to some extent ethnic, continuity, arguing that from the sixth to the eleventh century the Greeks had subconsciously maintained some sense of a Greek identity, which gradually became a more conscious awareness between the twelfth and the early nineteenth century by which time Greek nation building was almost complete. According to Svoronos, the evolving Greek language was the most decisive factor in maintaining this cultural continuity and recovering a sense of Greekness.

This essay by Svoronos, a leading and respected historian of the Left, led to a debate about nationalism and the formation of the Greek nation. According to one scholar it anticipated the ethnosymbolist theories of nationalism, developed by A. D. Smith and others, and challenged constructionist and postmodernist approaches to nation-building (Vayenas 2005). The ensuing debate in a leading Greek newspaper, labelled as a 'dialogue for the nation', involved exponents of modernist/constructionist and primordialist/perennialist conceptions of the nation. In other words, it revolved around the question of whether nationalism constructs nations or vice versa and could be considered as part of the wider debate about theories of nationalism and the impact of postmodernism on historiography.[1] Nations are no longer considered primordial but products of modernity and this debate indicated a shift from a romantic perception of the Greek nation to the processes of its making.

This emphasis on the constructedness of the nation and not on its timeless continuity has meant highlighting cultural syncretism and cross-pollination. On an academic level this shift is reflected in the wider debates about Greek historiography and the postmodernist approaches to history (see Chapter 4). It also facilitated the transition from the ethnocentric *laografia* (folklore studies) to social anthropology with the establishment of the first university departments of social anthropology at the University of the Aegean (1984) and Panteion University (1989) and the controversial renaming of the corresponding department at the University of Thessaly (2000–1). Apart from historiography and folklore studies, particular attention was also paid to archaeology and the conscription of that discipline in the process of nation-building and promoting Hellenization (Voutsaki 2017).

Archaeology has indeed been involved in the building of the nation since the nineteenth century, but remained in the background, and only after the excavations in Vergina in 1977 did it start to receive more attention or become explicitly acknowledged. Until then, the major archaeological projects (including those of the foreign archaeological schools) were concentrated in the south and Macedonia was ignored, becoming southern Greece's Other: an area of later colonization without comparable cultural production (Andreou, Fotiadis and Kotsakis 1996). As the second city of the Empire, the city of Thessaloniki was the main focus of Byzantine archaeology, and the Byzantine past was instrumental in promoting the Hellenization of Macedonia. But ever since the Greek archaeologist Manolis Andronikos excavated the tumulus in Vergina, associated with Philip II, in 1977 more excavations have been funded in Macedonia with the aim of refuting any ethnogenetic claims advanced by neighbouring states. The centre of archaeological research shifted from the south to the north of Greece and 'for the first time, the finds of archaeologists acquired a prominent

---

[1] This debate was conducted in the newspaper *To Vima* from early February to early April 2005 and involved primarily Antonis Liakos and Nasos Vayenas as well as Nikos Demertzis, Yorgos Veloudis and Dimosthenis Kourtovic with a review of the book in the newspaper *Ta Nea* on 26 March 2005. See also Nasos Vayenas, 'Θεωρητικές χρήσεις της ιστορίας' *To Vima* 24 August 2003 and 'Ο Σβορώνος και η διαμάχη των ιστορικών', *To Vima*, 19 June 2011.

place in the popular press and the media' (Kotsakis 1998: 53). The discovery of Vergina grabbed the public's imagination and put archaeology in the spotlight.

This heightened public awareness of the political role of archaeology in shaping Greek identity (Plantzos 2008), and its association with nationalism or state patronage, led to the demythologization of Andronikos and his description as a shaman by Hamilakis (2007). It has increasingly become accepted that archaeology cannot offer historical 'facts' but only interpretations of the past. Interestingly, it was the archaeologists of prehistory, with anthropological or theoretical interests, and not so much the classical archaeologists, who interrogated the ethnocentric role of archaeology and exposed the way in which the prehistoric period had been Hellenized by archaeologists such as Christos Tsountas (1857–1934), who 'clearly anticipates an idea that we usually attribute to Arthur Evans and Gordon Childe: that the prehistoric Aegean was the cradle of European civilization' (Voutsaki 2002: 120; 2017). The pre-Hellenic and prehistoric past raised the problem of the provenance of the Classical civilization and therefore had to be assimilated into an evolutionary narrative about Greek ethnic origins by presenting the prehistoric Aegean as the cradle of European civilization and denying Eastern influences.

The tendency to Hellenize the Bronze Age or Minoan era is also evident in the choice of the official mascot of the 2004 Athens games, a pair of prehistoric early seventh-century BCE terracotta figurines, or the adoption of a Minoan swallow fresco, discovered on the island of Santorini (Thera), as the official logo of Greece's presidency of the EU in the first semester of 2003. The semantically abstract term 'Hellenism', as a timeless and powerful organism, able to assimilate influences or resist threats, became synonymous with continuity. In trying to overcome the problematic notion of continuity and emphasize historical and cultural diversity, some scholars pointed to a plurality of Hellenisms (Zacharia 2008) or acknowledged a plurality of pasts (ancient, Byzantine, Ottoman, Venetian) and their interaction, construction and reimagination in the present.[2] In the 1980s the notion of continuity came under scrutiny from historians, but a new surge of nationalism in the following decade revived its popularity and widened the gap between historians and the public (Liakos 2004a: 62 and 2001b: 86). A growing number of historians, archaeologists and other scholars no longer supported hegemonic discourses; instead, they questioned established

---

[2] A number of studies on the uses, reinventions or retellings of the past in Greece have been published since the turn of the century: Brown and Hamilakis (2003), Hokwerda (2003), Epistimoniko Symposio (2003), Tziovas (2014a), Papadimitriou and Anagnostopoulos (2017) and Willert and Katsan (2019).

views and practices, and this often brought them into conflict not only with state policies but also with the general public. The discrepancy between the attitudes to the past of intellectual elites and the state or the public seems to have been exacerbated and has often led to tensions as in the cases of Anastasia Karakasidou[3] and Maria Repoussi (see Chapter 4).

While the grand historical schemes of continuity and Hellenism receded in the domain of historical studies or became limited to older historians, they continued to be powerful on a symbolic, popular and performative level. The Macedonian question and the Parthenon sculptures/Elgin Marbles brought the ancient past into the public sphere and made it, more than ever before, a question of identity for ordinary people, who acted out the 'antiquity fever' by demonstrating, signing petitions, blogging or visiting museums. These two issues discouraged Greeks from distancing themselves from earlier nationalist myths and developing a more critical stance towards their past. For many years Greeks had been preoccupied with demonstrating the continuity between ancient and modern Greek culture, and this eventually resulted in an additional concern, the question of who owns the past and, particularly, antiquity.

Before that there had been lectures and articles challenging the continuity of Greek culture, but now – for the first time since Jakob Fallmerayer – Greek claims to antiquity began to receive considerable international publicity. These two issues, with their long history and international implications, came back with a vengeance, challenging the notion of a homogeneous, continuous and unique national culture (the Macedonian question) or the unity and ownership of the national heritage (Parthenon sculptures/Elgin Marbles). In both cases the public was mobilized and involved in vociferous demonstrations, campaigns and debates. Thus, antiquity became public and Greeks were made aware that any claims to antiquity were not straightforward or uncontested. These two issues caused 'global cultural wars' or involved 'heritage restitution' campaigns. The International Association for the Reunification of the Parthenon Sculptures was formed in November 2005 by twelve national associations from around the

---

[3] The book by Anastasia N. Karakasidou, *Fields of Wheat, Hills of Blood: Passages to Nationhood in Greek Macedonia, 1870–1990* (University of Chicago Press, 1997) caused controversy both in and outside Greece. Cambridge University Press (CUP) considered the manuscript for publication but did not accept it, notwithstanding two favourable peer reviews, fearing repercussions against the Press in Greece. CUP claimed that their decision was made on the advice of the British Embassy in Athens. After a brief controversy involving newspapers, such as the *New York Times*, Chicago University Press stepped in and published the book. A Greek anthropologist working in the United States, Karakasidou had also been the target of a campaign waged in the Greek media by nationalists, who protested that her unpicking of Greek identity in twentieth-century Macedonia was heretical and even treasonous.

world for the return of all the alienated Parthenon sculptures, while the first international congress on Macedonian Studies was held in February 1988 at La Trobe University in Melbourne.

The Macedonian issue dominated Greek politics in the 1990s, and erupted once again in 2018, redefining relations with Europe and causing splits among the Greeks themselves. The dispute goes back to the late nineteenth century, but it flared up again in 1991 when the former Yugoslav Republic of Macedonia declared itself an independent state, taking the name 'Republic of Macedonia'. For many Greeks, the use of the name 'Macedonia' by the new state and the 'Slavs of Skopje' constituted an 'act of falsification or plagiarism' vis-à-vis the Greek people and their history. Greeks claimed exclusive rights to the term 'Macedonian' on the grounds that they could demonstrate the strongest historical ties to ancient Macedonia. Yet, the Greekness of ancient Macedonians was not undisputed and, in some people's eyes, they had not been Greek anyway.

The long dispute over the historical legacy of ancient Macedonia involved arguments from both sides, such as that ancient history should not be the basis for determining national identities in the present or that the Macedonian nation was not an invention of Marshal Tito and no one has the right to monopolize the term 'Macedonian'. The Macedonian question challenged the notion that nations are natural phenomena of great antiquity and reinforced the idea put forward by a number of theorists of nationalism (e.g. E. Gellner, B. Anderson) that they are socially and culturally constructed. Competition developed over historical patrimony, as the Greek slogan used in demonstrations, 'Macedonia is and always will be Greek', suggests and the title of a book by Greek historians and archaeologists published in 1983, *Macedonia: 4000 Years of Greek History and Civilization*, further illustrates. The essentialist approach to ethnic or national identity adopted by the contributors to the volume clashed with the perception of identity as situational, contextual and socially constructed, supported by anthropologists and others. As Loring M. Danforth puts it 'historical and cultural patrimony is especially important to nations whose ancient past is much more glorious than their more recent past' (2010: 579).

The Macedonian question was kept alive in Canada and Australia where rival diaspora communities organized demonstrations and this antagonism was exacerbated by the policies of multiculturalism and ethnic diversity promoted by both countries. Many Macedonians, who after the Greek Civil War had migrated to those countries, were encouraged by the multicultural policies of their host countries to cherish their ethnic heritage and identity, including their language, and thus the distant diaspora communities contributed to the intensity of the

Balkan conflict (Jeffreys 1995 and 1997). Even Greek migrants to Australia gradually developed a Slav Macedonian national identity, and this 'conversion experience' often led to their estrangement from family members, who retained their Greek identity (Danforth 1995). This suggests that the Macedonian conflict in the diaspora was more about identity than politics.

The battle of symbols revolved around Alexander the Great and the star or sun of Vergina associated with the Macedonian dynasty. The airport of Kavala was renamed 'Alexander the Great Airport' in 1992 and Skopje international airport was renamed in similar fashion in December 2006.[4] In early 2018, as a gesture of goodwill towards Greece in light of the negotiations over the name, the airport and the main highway, both hitherto named after Alexander the Great, were renamed 'International Airport of Skopje' and 'Friendship Motorway', respectively. A statue of Alexander riding his horse, Bucephalus, was also taken down at Skopje airport. The statue had been set up in the arrivals hall in 2011 and was a gift from the Turkish company TAV, which has been managing the airport since 2010. On the Greek side, environmentalists and archaeologists blocked the ambitious plan by a group of Greek Americans to carve a seven-metre-high bust of Alexander into a mountain top overlooking the Aegean Sea in Greek Macedonia. The policy of 'antiquitization' and the rival claims to the glorious legacy of Alexander the Great even involved two indigenous groups in Pakistan, the Hunzakuts (also known as Hunza) and the Kalasha (or Kalash), whom nationalists from both sides presented as living descendants of the soldiers Alexander left behind after his campaign in India (Danforth 2010: 584).

Discovered in 1977 by Manolis Andronikos, the sixteen-ray sun or star of Vergina adorned a gold larnax (or small burial chest), said to contain the ashes of Philip of Macedon, the father of Alexander the Great. In the late 1980s nationalists from both sides turned it into a powerful national symbol that could be found on T-shirts, medals and other memorabilia. Most importantly it became the 'state symbol' of the newly independent state in August 1992 when the North Macedonian parliament voted to place the sun/star at the centre of the Republic's new flag. The Macedonian question shows how heavily national cultures and their contested patrimonies rely on claiming an ancient legacy. The Greek claim about the 'falsification of history' was met with scepticism by the international community and made Greeks feel isolated and victimized, while

---

[4] A massive rebuilding project called Skopje 2014, inspired by classical architecture, started in 2014 and was reminiscent of the neoclassical building programme in Athens during the nineteenth century. On nationalism and the use of cultural heritage in Northern Macedonia, see Trpeski (2013).

studies by archaeologists, historians and anthropologists challenged the way many Greeks read their past and understood the role of heritage.

Like the Macedonian Question, the issue of the Parthenon sculptures is not a new one. Lord Byron and others called for their return within a few years of their removal by Lord Elgin from the Parthenon in Athens, their transfer to London and subsequent acquisition by the British Museum in 1816. The use of different terms to describe the exhibits in the British Museum ('Elgin Marbles', named after the person who oversaw their removal to Britain, and 'Parthenon sculptures' shifting the emphasis to the monument in Athens) is indicative of the different approaches and readings of the past. Similarly, a variety of terms, with different connotations, have been used to refer to the 'return' of the marbles to Athens: repatriation, restitution, recovery or reunification. The cumbersome nomenclature reflects the potency of the issue, which has been the subject of many books and articles, turning the marbles into the urtext of similar claims for the repatriation of cultural heritage.

In June 1986 in a speech to the Oxford Union about the return of the marbles, the then Greek minister for culture, Melina Mercouri, stated, 'The very name of our country is immediately associated with the Parthenon' (Jenkins 2016: 90). The controversy over the sculptures brought the Parthenon to the fore, not simply as a political monument or a temple to demonstrate the wealth and pride of Athens in the age of Pericles, but also as a building that had been subject to transformations over the ages, having been converted to a church, a mosque, a living space, an ammunition store and finally a 'purified monument of the Greek genius' (Beard 2002; Neils 2005). The 'cleansing' of the Parthenon of later accretions could also be seen as symbolic of the effacement of Greece's medieval and post-medieval history and culture. Like the Greek language, culture and identity, the Parthenon has come to be seen by Greeks in an ahistorical way as something eternal and unchanging (Mackridge 2008: 307). However, in the last twenty years or so the post-classical history of the Parthenon has received particular attention from authors, filmmakers and scholars as part of a critical approach to Greek antiquity.[5] The Parthenon has been turned from an 'eternal monument' into a 'historical palimpsest'.

Whereas for literature or music questions such as who owns the works of Shakespeare or Mozart do not arise, for monuments or artifacts the following

---

[5] Some novels (e.g. Vasilis Gourogiannis, *Βέβηλη Πτήση/Sacrilegious Flight* (2003); and Christos Chrysopoulos, *Ο Βομβιστής του Παρθενώνα /The Bomber of the Parthenon* (2010)) and short films (Eva Stefani, *Acropolis* (2001); and Costa-Gavras's video on the history of the Parthenon) have been considered irreverent and even subversive.

questions are often posed: Do they belong to those who live in the place where they were first made? To what extent can they be owned by international organizations (e.g. UNESCO or the EU) or 'global' museums? Can we enjoy a work of art as a fragment or only in its aesthetic totality? The discussion over 'global' museums (where national art can be seen in the context of other cultures) and national ones replicates to some extent the debates about globalization and nationalism or protectionism.

The Macedonian Question and the Parthenon sculptures placed Greek antiquity at the centre of international debates and raised questions of more general interest by contrasting nationalist and internationalist approaches to cultural heritage. Though cultural internationalism appears to be winning the argument, it has been criticized for relying 'on market-based principles and as apologetic for the wide-scale looting of archaeological sites' (Gerstenblith 2001: 200). This approach has often been associated with cultural imperialism, while retentionists are criticized for condemning 'the parochial nationalism of their opponents, but rarely question[ing] their own more imperial nationalism, which they mask in the name of internationalism' (Handler 1991: 71).

In exploring attitudes towards antiquity in contemporary Greece, there seems to have been a shift from the notion of cultural continuity to contesting, claiming and performing antiquity. The idea of continuity may have come under fire by academics and intellectuals (Danforth 1984), yet it can be found embedded in debates about heritage ownership and performances such as the opening ceremony of the Athens Olympic Games in 2004 or indeed on the inside pages of Greek passports with their images of mostly ancient and medieval monuments.

This notion of continuity has also remained dominant in the Greek tourist industry's advertising along with the idea of Greece being 'the cradle of Western civilization'. The role of the Greek National Tourist Organization has been decisive in shaping the country's brand image (nation branding) and cultivating the alleged Greek exceptionalism. Though it has tried to promote a more diversified and modern image of the country as a tourist destination, antiquity has conferred the aura of the 'West's secular Eden' on Greece (Hanink 2017: 35) and reinforced earlier stereotypes and values such as authenticity and hospitality, forcing today's Greeks to be measured against an idealized past. Even ancient theatres, promoted in tourism advertising as bringing together festivals of antiquity and modern drama performances, have become the symbols of an 'eternal' Greekness.

The 2005 tourist campaign 'Live your Myth in Greece' followed the country's successes in organizing the Olympic Games (2004) and winning the UEFA

European Championship (2004) and the European song contest with Helena Paparizou's 'My Number One' (2005). The use of the word 'myth' alluded both to Classical mythology as well as to the legendary sensuality of the country, promising a personal dreamlike experience (González-Vaquerizo 2017: 265). Redolent of the years of prosperity and self-confidence after the Olympics, the sea-sun-marble myth of this campaign was shattered in the subsequent years of the crisis, when the slogan was remembered with anger and bitter irony. During the demonstrations in the summer of 2011, 'Live your Greece in Myth' graffiti appeared on the streets of Athens, critically revisiting the earlier tourist illusion and inviting foreigners and Greeks alike to exchange the fantasy of the classical past for the dystopia of crisis-stricken Greece (Figure 3).

From tracing continuities and developing grand narratives of the Greek nation, the focus has shifted to uses of or claims to the past, its inventions, articulations and performances. This also entailed a shift from exploring the genealogy of the nation to how the past is embedded in present-day experiences. In the twenty-first century we have moved from an aesthetic Hellenism based on revelation and appreciation to critical Hellenism(s) and the concomitant notions of demythologization and construction.

Figure 3 Graffiti on a bank branch in Syntagma Square (Athens, Summer 2011) Photo courtesy of Aris Messinis.

Debating and narrativizing the Civil War

The 1940s, when Greece experienced the harsh consequences of the Axis occupation (1941–4) and a devastating civil war (1946–9), began to receive more attention after 1974 and constitutes a crucial period for studying the relationship between history and memory in Greece. These years impacted decisively on post-war Greek society and became the arena in which the clash of memory narratives and discourses played out (Voglis 2008: 63). With the 'epic of resistance' followed by the 'tragedy of civil war', scholars have described it as an 'era of confusion' (Antoniou and Marantzidis 2008) and a 'troubled decade' (Kastrinaki 2005). It is interesting that the multivolume *History of the Greek Nation* (Ιστορία του Ελληνικού Έθνους), published in the 1970s and seen as an outcome of the post-junta consensus, did not include the 1940s. We had to wait until 2000 for the publication of the sixteenth volume, covering this period and beyond. Like the Greco-Turkish War of 1922 and its aftermath, the Civil War was an event with a long-standing impact on Greek society and its collective memory. Using the Civil War as a case in point, David Close points out that 'in no other country, perhaps, has manipulation of the past been more ruthless and ingenious than in Greece, where it has continued until quite recently' (2004: 258).

Paradoxically Greece does not officially commemorate the end of the Second World War or the liberation from the Axis occupation; instead, it commemorates the outbreak of the Greek-Italian War on 28 October 1940. Similarly the legacy of the Civil War is not as visible as in Spain, where there is a monumental memorial Valley of the Fallen (*Valle de los Caldos*), conceived by Franco, to honour those who died in the Spanish Civil War.[6] Though the winners of the Greek Civil War commemorated the event on a local level, and the day of the national army's victory against the guerrillas (29 August 1949) was designated a day of celebration in 1959, the commemoration of the Civil War was intended to honour the 'military prowess of the Greeks' and was integrated into the historical chain of Hellenism's 'heroic struggles'. As soon as PASOK came to power in 1981, they suspended these so-called 'celebrations of hatred' and banned the participation of state officials in them (Antoniou 2013). In Greece there was no Truth and Reconciliation Committee, like in other countries such as Ireland or South Africa, and for successive generations the perception of the

---

[6] References to the Spanish Civil War (1936–9) were avoided during the years of the *Transición*, the transition from the Francoist regime to democracy (1975–82) (Paloma Aguilar 2002).

period of the Axis occupation and the Resistance were filtered through attitudes to the Civil War.

It has been claimed that until 1974 the Civil War was not narratable or simply did not exist for the opposing camps (Vervenioti 2002: 164). For the Right it was a war against 'bandits' (συμμορίτες) aided by foreigners, who wanted to detach Macedonia from Greece, and for the Left it was a second resistance, this time against the British and the Americans, following on from the one against the Axis powers. Left and Right formed rival interpretive frameworks for the events of the 1940s in their attempts to control the collective memory and influence the public debate. Their rivalry centred on the relationship between the Resistance and the Civil War.[7] Demarcating the period of resistance clearly, the Left insisted that the Civil War began in 1946 and focused on the Truman doctrine and the British and US intervention during and after the Civil War. The resistance by the Left was considered patriotic, whereas the right-wing resistance was treated as pseudo-patriotic, trying to undermine the popular forces and displaying collaborationist tendencies.

The official right-wing discourse, on the other hand, played down the significance of the 1940s and saw the Resistance as a prelude to the Civil War and not as the foundational narrative of post-war democracy in Greece (like in France or Italy). It traced the early stages of the civil conflict back to the clashes between the resistance groups during the last years (1943–4) of the Axis occupation, adopting the so-called theory of 'three rounds' and the argument that the intention of the Greek Communist Party all along was to seize power. Interpreting the events of the 1940s through a Cold War perspective, the right-wing victors denied the patriotism of the left-wing resistance and identified communism with the Russian threat. The contributions of non-Greeks (such as the British conservative politician and historian C. M. Woodhouse (1917–2001)) to the discussion of the events in the 1940s were also significant and sometimes caused controversy inside Greece.

After the fall of the Junta, the splits that had occurred during the dictatorship within the ranks of the Right and the Left encouraged revisionist trends, while a number of Greeks, particularly the young, reacted against the prevailing values of the post-Civil War period and developed romanticized views of the Resistance

---

[7] It should be noted that the terms 'Resistance' or 'National Resistance' were not commonly used in Greek left-wing writings during the 1940s. They were more common in Greek liberal newspapers and in books written by non-communists such as Komninos Pyromaglou, the former political leader of the second largest resistance group the National Republican Greek League (EDES) (Avgeridis 2017: 17).

(including its songs, the so-called *andartika*). The left-wing tradition of the 1940s resurfaced as a powerful force in the party politics, and political allegiances were based on attitudes to the Civil War. The elections of 1981 and 1984 were fought on appeals to the past and parties manipulated its memory, thus making it more difficult for the media or educational institutions to promote a dispassionate public understanding of it. In the meantime, memories of the 1940s were kept alive by veterans' associations for whose votes PASOK and KKE competed.

The competing claims on the past and the collective memory of the Civil War were explored by anthropologists who 'found that national divisions in the 1940s had interacted with personal and family feuds so that they were experienced with intense emotions' (Close 2004: 261; Collard 1990 and 1993). Gradually the period of resistance against the Axis occupation emerged as the past with the potential to unite rather than divide Greek society. Emphasizing the patriotism and heroism of almost all Greeks (excluding collaborators) and shedding any revolutionary or political baggage, the Resistance emerged as the inclusive narrative that could bring Greeks together. Thus, attention shifted away from the Civil War and 'in the 1980s the commemoration of the National Resistance gained a conspicuous position in Greece's historical culture and public history' (Voglis and Nioutsikos 2017: 321).

After its recognition by the PASOK government in 1982, the Resistance became 'nationalized' and was no longer identified with or claimed by the Left. Its commemoration began to occupy a prominent position in Greek collective memory and public history. It became a unifying symbolic national reference that transcended the divisions of the Civil War and thus the focus shifted from Grammos (the mountain where the last battles of the Civil War were fought) to Gorgopotamos (an early success for the partisans) (Voulgaris 2001: 29).[8] Described as 'united', 'national and liberating', the memory of the resistance to the occupation offered the opportunity for reconciliation, while leaving behind internecine conflict and earlier political divisions. The Resistance was presented as the shining light and the most unimpeachable aspect of the 1940s while the Civil War was seen as its dark and controversial side.

By avoiding references to the armed struggle during the Civil War, what was now being highlighted was the struggle during the Axis occupation (with Aris Velouchiotis, the Greek People's Liberation Army (ELAS) guerrilla leader, as its most emblematic figure) and the subsequent suffering of the supporters of

---

[8] On 25 November 1942 Greek partisans, assisted by a group of British Special Operations Executive (SOE) officers, blew up the railway bridge over the Gorgopotamos river.

the Left (with the emphasis on the islands to which they were exiled, such as Makronisos) (Voglis 2008: 78). This shift of emphasis to the Resistance signalled an attempt by the Left to present itself as a patriotic force and not a violent and divisive one. The PASOK government did not simply officially recognize the National Resistance, it also offered pensions to the veterans of all the resistance organizations. The partisans became the new national heroes. The war was no longer referred to as a 'bandit war' (συμμοριτοπόλεμος), but as a civil war (εμφύλιος), and PASOK emerged as the third pole between the communist Left and the Right. The return of political refugees exiled in Eastern Europe after the Civil War, the renaming of streets and the removal of some of the symbols of anti-communism contributed to the revision of the collective memory of the Civil War.[9]

Apart from the different approaches to the Civil War and the attempts at reconciliation following official recognition of the Resistance, there were memory wars going on as can be witnessed in the memoirs of some 1940s veterans. According to Marantzidis and Antoniou 'almost half of the right-wing production [of memoirs] was published in the first ten years after the end of World War II and related to state activities and goals' (2004: 225), but after the end of the Civil War they lost momentum and never recovered. Their aims were mainly political and not to construct an individual identity or project a cultural agenda. Left-wing memoirs were rare immediately after the war, while the image of the leaders (*Kapetanioi*) of resistance fighters as patriotic and popular figures achieved greater prominence, thanks to studies written outside Greece (Eudes 1970).

Until 1974 the political subjects of the period (former guerrillas, prisoners and exiles) were 'written' and constructed by hegemonic discourses and anti-communist propaganda. Since the 1980s these subjects have been attempting to rewrite themselves and narrate their life stories, blending autobiographical account with historical essay. Following the legalization of the Communist Party of Greece in 1974 (banned since 1947) and with burgeoning interest in the 1940s, it was the country's first socialist government (1981-9) that fostered the proliferation of left-wing memoir publications.[10] Out of a sample of 918 personal

---

[9] According to David Close 'by 1988 about 45,000 refugees or their children had returned to settle, of whom only 7,872 had returned before 1975; and those repatriated were given some advice and financial help by the government' (2004: 265-6).

[10] The first conferences on the 1940s were organized outside Greece (Washington and London 1978; see Iatrides 1981 and Sarafis 1980), while the first conference in Greece was held in 1984 but stopped short of dealing with the Civil War (Fleischer and Svoronos 1989). The first conference exclusively dedicated to the Civil War took place in 1984 in Denmark (Baerentzen, Iatrides and Smith 1987) and the first to be held in Athens covering the period 1936-49 was held in 1995. As Antonis Liakos has

narratives about the 1940s, published between 1945 and 2001, more than half were published after 1981 and the majority of these (over 80 per cent) came from the Left (Antoniou and Marantzidis 2003).[11] In the anti-communist period of 1945–74 almost two in every three books published were anti-Left, whereas in the period 1974–2003 four out of every five books published were by left-wing authors (Marantzidis and Antoniou 2004: 224). Perhaps due to the limited access to archives, the role of memoirs and testimonies has been more important for the 1940s than for any other period, so much so that it could perhaps be described as the decade of narratives.

The collapse of the communist regimes and the sharing of power between the conservative *Nea Dimokratia* and the Communist Party in 1989 laid the ground for reconciliation but did not discourage the continuing publication of memoirs. According to the oral historian Tasoula Vervenioti, it was the coalition government and not the collapse of the USSR which made the Civil War narratable and encouraged oral testimonies (2002: 163). However, the decision of the coalition government to destroy the files on left-wingers kept by the police led to new divisions between those who viewed the files as a valuable historical source and those who treated them as an unwelcome reminder of a painful past (Karamanolakis 2019). Thus, the *Metapolitefsi* emerged as a theatre where memory and oblivion were in competition, a kind of remembering to forget (Demertzis 2011: 147), and 1989 is now seen as a turning point, which led to a boom in Greek historiography. The establishment in 1992 of the Contemporary Social History Archives (ASKI), consisting mainly of left-wing records, and the release of classified archives after the collapse of the communist regimes promoted the study of the 1940s. And from the 1990s (after its existential crisis following the collapse of the USSR) the Greek Communist Party focused on the study of the Civil War in order to defend its revolutionary past, rehabilitate some of its members and demarcate its position in opposition to the political establishment.[12]

---

pointed out, none of the papers of the 1995 conference had in fact dealt with either the internecine conflicts of the 1943–4 years, the *Dekemvriana* or the events of the full-scale Civil War in 1947–9 (2003a: 33).

[11] From 1945 to 2003 around 1,800 books were published on the 1940s, most of them (1,600) non-academic. More than 50 per cent of them were published after 1981. It should be noted that until 1991, books in other languages on the 1940s outnumbered those published in Greek (Antoniou and Marantzidis 2008: 28–32)

[12] Dionysis Charitopoulos's two-volume biography (or – according to some – his hagiography) of Aris Velouchiotis (1997 and 2001) became a bestseller while in the same year (1997) as the publication of the first volume the state-owned ERT aired Roviros Manthoulis's documentary on the Greek Civil War. The programme was a huge success and was shown again three days later in response to some two thousand requests from viewers.

This explosion of memoirs had other significant parameters. Their authors were at first predominantly men (particularly party members and guerrilla leaders), who tended to combine a memory narrative with a historical essay. But from 1990 onwards women and some less fiercely partisan people started publishing their own stories, with the autobiographical book by Pagona Stefanou Των Αφανών/*For the Invisible* (1998), marking the transition from heroic collectivity to gendered subjectivity (Voglis 2008: 70; Vervenioti 2008). The hard-line oppositions of the past gradually receded and the focus shifted to selfhood, which led to identity crises and a re-examination of collective memories and their variations among those who had fought in the Civil War, been imprisoned or exiled in Eastern Europe or experienced the war from a distance. We should not forget that the Civil War was fought primarily in the countryside and not so much in the cities or the islands (e.g. the Dodecanese belonged to Italy until 1947) and therefore it was a multifaceted and complex event with substantial regional differences of varying intensity.

The fiftieth anniversary of its cessation in 1999 turned attention once again to the Civil War (with a number of conferences and the publication of sixteen volumes of army archives) and how society was involved or affected by it during the internecine war or in its aftermath.[13] On the occasion of this anniversary it was argued that the left-wing rewriting of history had ultimately triumphed, leading to the victorious return and ideological hegemony of those defeated in the Civil War (Mavrogordatos 1999). According to this view, the 'generation of the *Metapolitefsi*' had projected its own imagined utopia and its unfulfilled revolutionary fantasies onto a romantic construction of the 1940s. While the Right was burdened by guilt on account of the post-Civil War authoritarian state, the Left laid claim to the innocence of the defeated. This theory of the ideological supremacy of the Left, which emerged as a result of the romanticization of the defeated, met with opposition for its use as a spurious explanatory tool for the widespread defiance of the law and for defending the role of the state in contemporary Greece (Fytili 2013; Zenakos and Natsis 2017). Yet, this reaction did not stop a revisionist approach developing that focused on the role of violence on a local level in the civil strife and revived the idea of a long Civil War between 1943 and 1949, based on the alleged plans of the communists to seize power at an early stage.[14] In March 2004 two political scientists Stathis Kalyvas

---

[13] The establishment in the summer of 2000 of the Network for the Study of Civil Wars, an informal group of scholars from different disciplines with common research interests in the Civil War and its legacies, promoted research and discussion on the 1940s in Greece.

[14] According to G. Antoniou the public debate about the 1940s and 'revisionism' in the Second World War historiography emerged relatively recently in Greece, not following the Western historiographic

and Nikos Marantzidis, leading representatives of this revisionist or 'new wave' trend, published their article 'New trends in the study of the Civil War' in a leading Greek newspaper (*Ta Nea*) and initiated a vigorous debate, a kind of *Historikerstreit*, that lasted for some months in the same paper (Kalyvas and Marantzidis 2004).

Their approach highlighted the issue of the moral responsibility of the Left and challenged the role of ideology as the partisans' primary motive. Pointing out that polarization and demonization, mythology and martyrology had up till then dominated approaches to the 1940s, the revisionist historiography favoured what might be called micro approaches over the earlier grand narratives and tried to shift attention from the role of the leaders to the identities of ordinary people (Kalyvas 2000 and 2003; Kalyvas and Marantzidis 2015). The old question 'Whose fault was it?' gave way to a new one: 'How did the civil war happen?' encouraging interdisciplinary research and fostering the exploration of memory narratives, ethnic allegiances, local identities and the part women played in the warfare. Moreover, the oral stories of those who had left Greece as political refugees and ended up in Eastern Europe and the memories of the 'children of the Civil War' now received attention alongside other things that had been covered up by the Communist Party. Following an international trend associated with the growth of memory studies, the word 'memory' has featured in the titles of a number of publications dealing with the 1940s from the last twenty years or so (van Boeschoten 2000). Memory, according to Paul Ricoeur (2004), has an intrinsic capacity to crystallize into narrative, and this transformative process accounts for the proliferation of narratives and the paradigm shift in the treatment of the Civil War during the later post-junta period, involving a change of emphasis from the macro- to the micro-level and from the fetishization of written documents and foreign archival material to local communities and oral (hi)stories. This, according to some historians, often leads to the de-ideologization and fragmentation of the Civil War and the undermining of attempts to study it holistically (Margaritis 2000–1 and 2002). Thus, the 1940s has developed into both a conciliatory myth and the contested ground of the post-junta period (see also Chapter 8).

---

paradigm developed in the late 1970s and 1980s but that of Eastern Europe after the collapse of communism (2007: 99).

From history to mnemohistory

According to Viet Thanh Nguyen, 'All wars are fought twice, the first time on the battlefield, the second time in memory' (2016: 4), and this could easily apply to the Greek Civil War as the post-junta narratives about the 1940s signal a transition from history to mnemohistory, or in other words from a study of the events of the past to that of their later impact and meaning. The term 'mnemohistory' (*Gedächtnisgeschichte*) was coined by Jan Assmann who defined it as follows:

> Unlike history proper, mnemohistory is concerned not with the past as such, but only with the past as it is remembered. ... Mnemohistory is reception theory applied to history. But 'reception' is not to be understood here merely in the narrow sense of transmitting and receiving. The past is not simply 'received' by the present. The present is 'haunted' by the past and the past is modeled, invented, reinvented, and reconstructed by the present. (1998: 8–9)

Favouring research into the actuality, not the factuality of the past, mnemohistory relinquishes the positivist investigation of the past (Tamm 2008: 501). Earlier, traditional historians presupposed that the hot present 'cools off' and transforms into a cold past by itself while scholars, like Maurice Halbwachs, viewed history as a science and separated it from memory. Now, approaches to both history and memory converge and commingle in the notion of a malleable understanding of the past, though some still believe that history is governed to various degrees by rules of evidence and verification (Confino 2011: 43). The notion of mnemohistory, with its theoretical foundations in hermeneutics and primarily the work of Hans-Georg Gadamer, 'allows one to move beyond the otherwise often unresolvable questions of "what really happened" to questions of how particular ways of constructing the past enable later communities to constitute and sustain themselves' (Tamm 2013: 464). Using the notion of effective history (*Wirkungsgeschichte*), Gadamer claims that the interpretations of an event are not external to the event but constitute the self-unfolding of the event itself (Gadamer 1989; Gorner 2000: 146–7). And this notion could be applied to interpretations of the Greek Civil War and its effective history.

One could argue that the approaches to and the discussion of the Civil War in post-1974 Greece went through different phases: the earlier emphasis on the involvement of external powers was succeeded around the 1990s by the study of the social conditions and more recently by the traumatic memories and the public history of the war, reflecting the international 'memory boom'.

This transition suggests that the controversies regarding the explosive 1940s are not just confined to academia but extend into the public sphere. Photographic exhibitions, films, city walks, debates, public talks, blogs and literary texts have aroused public interest, leading to a growth in public history and to many studies on how this explosive decade is remembered.[15] Memory emerges as 'haunting history' and a kind of Derridean 'hauntology' has developed with commentators referring to the fact that the Civil War is still haunting Greece (Derrida 1994; Pournara 2011; Hatzivasileiou 2010).

Historians are no longer considered the leaders in research into the 1940s, while anthropologists, political scientists, fiction writers, filmmakers, cultural and oral historians are becoming increasingly involved. In the post-Cold War era the study of politics and ideology inspired by Marxist determinism has been challenged by memory studies and the epistemological question as to how the past is remembered and narrated in the present. Concerned with representation and the present, rather than facts and the past, the concept of memory as provisional and subjective 'suggests a way out of the impasse into which historiography might have been driven by the poststructuralist assault on truth' (Hodgkin and Radstone 2003: 2). This transition has been assisted by the fictional representations of the Greek Civil War and its aftermath, which contributed to a shift from an ideologically or politically driven reading of the Civil War to a more anthropocentric and societal perspective. By focusing on everyday life, the struggle for survival, individual motives or the role of (post) memory and often overlooking the primacy of the ideological and political issues of the period, fictional texts have begun to construct a more complex image of the Civil War and its aftermath and pose moral questions.

Fiction was ahead of historiography in attempting to demythologize the Civil War and reflecting on historical relativity and the ethics of memory.[16] The 1980s and 1990s would become a kind of Herodotean period of literary experimentation in historical writing and extended thinking about history as a literary form. As a consequence of the 'linguistic turn', the past started to be perceived as having no 'determinable meaning' outside language and always

---

[15] After 1999 multivolume histories were published, devoting numerous pages to the 1940s. These include the *History of Greece in the Twentieth Century*/Ιστορία της Ελλάδας του 20ου αιώνα (1999–2010, ed. Hristos Hatziiosif), *The History of Modern Hellenism*/Ιστορία του Νέου Ελληνισμού (2003, ed. Vasilis Panagiotopoulos), *The History of Greeks* /Ιστορία των Ελλήνων (2006, ed. Nikos Vardiampasis). It should be noted that the last two were commissioned and printed by leading Greek newspapers, indicative of the growth of public history.

[16] The publication of *Eleni* (1983), an autobiographical memoir by the Greek-born American writer and investigative journalist Nicholas Gage, and its subsequent screen adaptation (1985) caused the first public debate on the Civil War in Greece.

needing some sort of 'emplotment' to use Hayden White's celebrated term. It was not only White with his influential essays (1978 and 1987) who pointed to the treatment of history as a literary-narrative genre, but other 'historians were becoming increasingly interested in finding new ways of writing – especially micro-narratives, multiple points of view, and also fragmentation, montage, and genre-crossing' (Curthoys and Docker 2005: 201–2). In his celebrated essay 'History of events and the revival of narrative' (1991) Peter Burke encouraged further experimentation in form and technique, arguing that if historians 'are looking for models of narratives which juxtapose the structures of ordinary life to extraordinary events, and the view from below to the view from above … [they] might be well advised to turn to twentieth-century fiction, including cinema' (2001: 296). Like the novelist, the historian needs to practice *heteroglossia* and such a 'device would allow an interpretation of conflict in terms of a conflict of interpretations' (Burke 2001: 289). Historians have come to see their sources as stories told by particular people rather than as objective reflections of the past, and this reduction in scale suggests that historians have turned to micronarratives as a means of illuminating structures. The debate on the 1940s in Greece could be seen as part of the wider opposition in historiography between structures and narratives and as Burke points out 'it might be possible to make civil wars and other conflicts more intelligible by following the model of the novelists who tell their stories from more than one viewpoint' (2001: 289).

It could be said that literature, particularly fiction, engaged with the Civil War before historiography began to take it seriously. Though some Greek writers tried to distance themselves from the 1940s in-fighting, most of the pre-1974 fictional narratives either adopt the discourse of left-wing victimhood or lean towards an anti-communist stance (Nikolopoulou 2008a). Following the fall of the junta, things moved on and it could be argued that Greek fiction contributed to the transition from structures to narratives and the narrativization of the history of the period by introducing new approaches to the Civil War based on the destabilization of traditional historical narratives and a reconsideration of established methods of inquiry. Three fictional texts, Aris Alexandrou's *To Κιβώτιο/Mission Box* (1974), Alexandros Kotzias's *Ιαγουάρος/Jaguar* (1987) Thanassis Valtinos's *Ορθοκωστά/Orthokosta* (1994), published in three different decades and all dealing with the Civil War and its aftermath, shifted the emphasis from seeking an objective investigation of the events to the remembering or reading subject, experimenting with evidence from 'below' and its interpretation.

All three texts share a preoccupation with the validity of narrative either in terms of testimony (*The Mission Box*), memory (*Jaguar*) or oral history

(*Orthokosta*) and demythologize the Civil War by focusing on human motives and self-interest. They are based on the modalities of recollection, inviting readers to ponder the question of how the Civil War and its aftermath have been reconstructed, mediated and legitimized. They move from the objectivity of history to the subjectivity of memory and from testimonial authenticity to the narrative appropriation or manipulation of the past, relying on 'memory's capacity to destabilise the authority of the "grand narratives" with which History has become associated' (Radstone and Hodgkin 2007: 10). Memory has been valorized as possessing the potential to contest the public 'regimes' of history and run counter to universalizing and monolithic generalities. While history is negatively associated with 'objectivity', memory is positively linked with the subjective, the local and the embedded. It even bears traces of what cannot enter discourse or representation.

The most celebrated novel about the Civil War, enjoying emblematic status in the Greek literary canon, is Aris Alexandrou's *The Mission Box*. With its allegorical narrative and deceptive realism, it inaugurated a self-reflexive approach to the Civil War and invited the Greek Left to rethink its role in the period by questioning historical objectivity and ideological correctness. While in prison the narrator supposedly confesses what he knows about a secret mission during the Civil War involving carrying a box, which turns out in the end to be empty, emphasizing the unreliability of meaning and the meaninglessness of the civil conflict. The other novel that challenged the traditional self-image of the Left as the 'pious victim' of the civil conflict by reversing the roles of victims and victimizers was Valtinos's *Orthokosta*, which anticipated the debates over the Civil War. The fierceness of those debates clearly showed that Greek society in the early 1990s was not yet ready to take all of its Civil War skeletons out of the closet.

Orthokosta is a classic example of the sort of Civil War fiction which, according to Venetia Apostolidou, has served as an 'intermediate public space' (2010: 21), a testing ground for different memories and interpretations that later passed into the spheres of historiography and the public domain. Caught in the crossfire between historiographic and political agendas and mixing 'unmediated' oral testimonies with personal memories, it raised questions about historical memorialization and the ethics of representation. Those who denounced the novel's depiction of the events of the Civil War missed the crucial point, which is that the novel does not so much represent the facts of the past as constitute a discourse about those facts. From this perspective, *Orthokosta* drew 'attention to the new legitimacy of oral history and anthropological fieldwork in historical scholarship on the Civil War' (Papailias 2005: 150). It highlighted the dark side of the Greek Resistance and how its violence led to the vicious Civil War, offering an anthropological and regional account (centred on the villages of Kynouria in the Peloponnese) and reinforcing the argument that the beginnings of the internecine conflict should be dated earlier in the 1940s.

Yet, the text which showed the transition from history to mnemohistory most vividly and moved the focus onto the realm of memory and the aftermath of the Civil War is Alexandros Kotzias's Ιαγουάρος/*Jaguar* (1987/1991). While the other two novels deal with 'what happened' during the Civil War, Kotzias's novella transfers the internecine conflict to within the Greek family, pointing to its lasting impact on Greek society. This rather neglected novella did not achieve the emblematic status of Alexandrou's and Valtinos's novels, but it represents a skilful handling of the memories of the Civil War and its aftermath. It narrates the meeting of Dimitra and her sister-in-law Filio, who both lay claim to the family house, on the basis of what happened during the Occupation and the Civil War regarding the death of Fanis, Dimitra's brother and Filio's husband. Filio had left Greece with her small son during the Civil War and settled in the United States with her second husband, returning to Greece some years later to claim her son's share of his father's property. Dimitra had stayed in Greece and, as a member of the Left, was persecuted, jailed and then experienced job insecurity after being released from prison. The narrative consists of her monologue, which also incorporates and reproduces Filio's views. Filio was a secondary character in Πολιορκία/*Siege* (1953), an earlier novel by Kotzias, in which she helped to ambush and murder a member of the Security Battalions called Sarantis. This event had an impact on her relationship with her husband Fanis, who had forced her into this role, which had haunted her ever since, so that, even in America, she had difficulty sleeping.

The encounter between the two women takes place on 20 May 1958 in the middle of the period that Kotzias himself called the 'Modern Greek Thirty-Year War' (1943–73) and a week after the (EDA) elections of 1958 that were very successful for the Greek Left. This seems to have been a turning point in the post-Civil War years, giving the Left an opportunity to promote its own narrative about the previous decade. In the *Jaguar* the trauma of the Civil War is re-enacted at a mnemonic level, since the text thematizes the role of memory and how it is shaped by the competing claims of the present (Anastasiadis 2011; Nikolopoulou 2008b).

The clash between Dimitra and Filio highlights the central role of memory in constructing the events of the past. For the left-wing Dimitra, her memory of the

Civil War is part of her identity. Her narrative is driven by ideological conviction and displays a deceptive certainty about events. It sounds resentful, calculating and selective, excluding anything that does not support a heroic version of the past. Dimitra tries to undermine Filio's narrative because, by involving her brother Fanis in the ambush and murder of Sarantis, it mars his image. She seeks vindication and the family property on moral grounds and as a victim of political circumstances.

Filio, on the other hand, is deeply traumatized and cannot articulate a coherent narrative of the past. Yet she cannot let go of it: 'I haven't forgotten either, Dimitra. I've forgotten nothing! ... I wish I could forget, yes, I wish I could ... then I'd get my sleep back. It's nearly fifteen years since...' (Kotzias 1991: 50 and 1987: 44). Revisiting places associated with the past triggers her recollections and a therapeutic process that involves stripping her husband Fanis of any aura of heroism. The memory of the past is a burden for her, and therefore she seeks peace and redemption, while Dimitra relentlessly continues to adhere to a divisive hard line, showing how her recollection of the past serves her self-interest in the present. She cannot distance herself from the role of victim, and her ideological rigidity prevents her from developing a critical stance to the past. Her husband Elias challenges her and encourages Filio not to compromise, thus tipping the balance towards the resolution of the argument going in her favour and encouraging the reader to side with Filio.

The reader is invited to assess the symbolic claims of the past and the moral consequences of the Civil War: 'Dreadful things, dreadful things have happened in this land. And nobody has repented. It's awful ... no one has done any of it' (1991: 132 and 1987: 117). Kotzias appears to suggest that the memories and the moral burden of the Civil War still haunt Greek society, thus offering a commentary on the policy of reconciliation and forgetting promoted by the PASOK government in the 1980s. A policy of forgetting simply cannot conceal the intolerance, the selfishness and the ideological use of memory that still marked Greek society. The Civil War appears to be an event indelibly stamped on the subconscious of the Greeks, and even when they make an effort to forget these traumatic memories, as in the case of Filio, they keep coming back. The dispute between Dimitra and Filio about the inheritance and the heroism of Fanis represents a continuation of the internecine conflict as a memory war and as a question of moral responsibility.

The texts discussed here challenge the conventional notions of history based on the search for 'facts' or 'justifications for past actions' and instead focus on the traumas of war, the meaningless violence, the absence of victories or the elliptical and unreliable testimonies. Due to the 'extensive Holocaust scholarship, notions such as the witness, victim, and survivor became important to the way scholars understand modern history overall' (Confino 2011: 40). Just as the Holocaust contributed to the increasing intensity of discussions about memory, mediation and authenticity, the Greek Civil War generated lively debates among historians, while the proliferation of memoirs and fictional texts since 1974 has elevated their readers into the role of historian, complicated the relationship between memory and historical actuality and encouraged the reading of history 'as the symptom of the past, rather than simply its triumphant record' (Radstone 2000: 84). The three novels mentioned above, written by writers who had lived through the Civil War and published in the first three decades after the fall of the Junta, were not the only ones of their kind. The turn towards oral (hi)stories, memoirs and new topics for fictional narratives such as children of the war, the persecution of the Greek Jews, the events of December 1944, the Polk case, etc. further contributed to the narrativization of the turbulent decade of the 1940s.

As we have seen above, the upsurge in academic and the general public's interest in the 1940s and the Civil War continued unabated into the new millennium. Since the 2000s there has been a boom in novels on different aspects of the Civil War from younger writers, who had not lived through the 1940s, such as Marlena Politopoulou (1950–), Thomas Skassis (1953–), Nikos Davvetas (1960–), Sophia Nikolaidou (1968–) and others.[17] In them, characters–researchers delve into historical and private archives as repositories of testimonies, memories, diaries, letters and photographs, trying to understand how the traumas of the civil strife resonate with the present. In their search for fragmented evidence to reconstruct the untold stories, the narrators in these novels display archive fever and approach the events through a post-generational perspective, defined by Marianne Hirsch as 'postmemory'. With reference to the descendants of Holocaust survivors, postmemory describes the relationship that the 'generation after' has to the personal, collective and cultural trauma of those who went before and suggests a connection to the past not mediated by recall but by imaginative investment, projection and creation (Hirsch 2012: 5). In this sense the post-generational narratives become investigative and creative acts of memory, contributing to the diversity of fictional engagements with the

---

[17] Their novels include *Η μνήμη της πολαρόιντ* (2009) by Marlena Politopoulou, *Ελληνικό Σταυρόλεξο* (2000) by Thomas Skassis, Nikos Davvetas's so-called 'Trilogy of Memory', consisting of *Το Θήραμα* (2004), *Λευκή πετσέτα στο ρινγκ* (2006) and the award-winning *Η Εβραία Νύφη* (2009) and Sophia Nikolaidou's trilogy *Απόψε δεν έχουμε φίλους* (2010) *Χορεύουν οι ελέφαντες* (2012) and *Στο τέλος νικάω εγώ* (2017). See Hatzivasileiou (2018: 751–802).

Civil War and confirming the claim that, for all that the 1940s may have been the most devastating decade in the twentieth century for Greece, yet it offered the most fruitful interaction between history and fiction, leading to a transition from history to mnemohistory.

By the end of 2008, engagement with the traumatic past of the 1940s was enjoying a widespread revival that extended well beyond lecture halls, the pages of novels or special features in mass-circulation newspapers. It had begun to take over the streets of Athens, the same streets that had become part of the urban battlefields during the *Dekemvriana* sixty-four years earlier. It all started on the night of 6 December when fifteen-year-old student Alexis Grigoropoulos was killed in cold blood by an armed police officer in the neighbourhood of Exarchia in central Athens. What ensued was three weeks of civil unrest and mass demonstrations that soon escalated into violent clashes between protesters and the police, nation-wide occupations of universities and school buildings, and large-scale destruction of private and public property.

Almost from the outbreak of the riots, the use of the term *Dekemvriana* became standardized in the mass media and comparisons with the events of December 1944 became commonplace. Despite their initial refusal to adhere to a specific ideological heritage, the young December activists also made explicit references to the events of December 1944, associating the traumas of the past with present grievances. Slogans like 'In these December events we shall win', 'The *Dekemvriana* of our generation', 'We are in a Civil War' or 'Varkiza is over' started to appear on flyers, stickers and other widely distributed literature as well as on the walls of a number of Athenian buildings (Kornetis 2010: 179). And although the situation had begun to de-escalate by early 2009, the memory of the once repressed past was reignited with a vengeance (see also Chapter 9).

Conclusion

Since the turn of the century a number of books dealing with the Greek past have been published, demonstrating its invention, reimagination or retelling as well as a growing understanding of the constructedness of the nation. The 'postmodern turn' in Western historiography played a role in the debates about the Greek nation's pasts and showed that a number of Greek academics were aware of the wider theoretical shifts and ensuing epistemological changes. Earlier the dominant social history paradigm viewed perceptions of the past as a 'natural' corollary of social and political developments. By contrast, present-day memory studies view representations of the past as shapers of political and social developments (Confino 2011: 45). Greek fiction has been more involved in the historiographical debates and the public history surrounding the 1940s than for any other period, because, like memory, fiction lays bare the process of construction of the past and the myths associated with it.

4

Identity, religion, migration: From homogeneity to embracing otherness

Who is Greek? Coming to terms with otherness

To understand cultural developments in Greece or to pinpoint what marks them out, it is necessary to consider some changes that have occurred in the last few decades. One of these is a transition from cultural homogeneity to diversity, involving a reconsideration of otherness in a variety of areas and primarily in linguistic, ethnic or religious terms. To assess the implications of this we have to look back at the ways in which monoculturalism has been designed and imposed from above over the last two centuries. Since independence, the Greek state has concentrated on consolidating its authority and has built national cohesion through cultural assimilation, suppression of minorities, eradication of *heteroglossia* and centripetal institutional organization. In 1836 George Finlay observed, 'The Greek rarely speaks of his nation, yet he speaks continually, and with enthusiasm, of his country – an epithet which he applies to his native village' (1836: 34). Since then, there has been a concerted effort to turn villagers into national subjects. The state has tried to enforce the assimilation of regional particularities into a homogenous national culture in which society was conceptualized as an entity to be surveyed, regulated and sanitized. Though the differences, both of opinion and of culture, persisted, suppression of cultural difference could be seen as one of the main features of the period since Greece won its independence. Reviewing Greek constitutional history, Nicos Alivizatos has argued that there has been a long-standing preference for egalitarianism (in the sense of levelling differences) at the expense of individual freedom and self-determination, which has led to a deficit of liberalism and state prejudice against various forms of otherness or minority rights. Hence minorities were treated as an obstacle to the constitutionally enshrined egalitarianism rather than as a form of cultural enrichment (2011: 669–71).

Definitions of who could be Greek in the early nineteenth century may have been broad and all-embracing, leading to the linguistic Hellenization of many Albanian, Vlach or Slav speakers, yet suppressing otherness in the form of localism or regionalism, ethnic or religious minorities and political dissent proved the key mechanism to establishing a unitary and monocultural state (Kitromilides 1989). According to the nationalist discourse, otherness was absorbed by the assimilationist power of Hellenism, based on the superiority of Greek culture. Nationhood, not citizenship, was elevated into the foundational principle of the Balkan nation states and this led to discrimination against minorities, legitimized by reference to cultural differences. Minorities were not treated as equal citizens and their inclusion in the national body was not feasible. Given that the ties connecting the Balkan Orthodox populations were predominantly religious, it is not surprising that for Balkan nationalists the first step was to manipulate religious institutions so as to transform those ties into national ones. Belonging to a church became equivalent to membership of a nation.

After the exchange of populations, based on religion, following the Greco-Turkish war of 1919–22, the aim of the Greek authorities was to construct a culturally and ethnically homogeneous country. After the population exchange, a voluntaristic definition of the Greek nation gave way to an organic one. There was less tolerance of cultural and linguistic diversity and this had an impact on the treatment of linguistic and ethnic minorities. The last census to include data about the language and religion of those residing in Greece was that of 7 April 1951. Subsequent censuses did not include such data, suggesting that the Greek state was trying to promote the image of a country with no linguistic or ethnic minorities. Out of a total population of 7,632,801 inhabitants recorded in the census of 1951, 7,297,827 declared Greek as their native language (95.6 per cent) and 179,895 Turkish (of whom 87,654 identified as Christians of all denominations and 92,219 as Muslims). According to the census there were 41,017 Slav native speakers, 39,885 Vlach speakers, 22,736 Albanian speakers/ Arvanites and 18,671 Pomak speakers. The majority of the population declared themselves to be Christians (whether Orthodox, Catholics or Protestants) and 112,665 Muslims (1.5 per cent), while there were just 6,325 Greek Jews compared to 72,791 in the pre-war census of 1928 (Rozakis 1996; Embirikos et al. 2001; Baltsiotis 2016).[1]

---

[1] On the different language groups currently in Greece, see Sella-Mazi (1997) and Baltsiotis (1997).

Article 19 of the Nationality Code, established in 1955, stated that any Greek citizen of non-Greek descent (*allogenis*) who leaves Greek territory with no intention of returning may be declared as having lost his Greek citizenship. The article explicitly divided Greek citizens on the basis of their ethnicity and those of 'non-Greek descent' risked losing their citizenship, as happened to thousands of members of Greece's minorities. Though the Article was revoked in 1998, after pressure from the high commissioner on National Minorities of the Organization for Security and Co-operation in Europe (OSCE) and from the Parliamentary Assembly of the Council of Europe, the abolition did not have retroactive effect and this meant that approximately 60,000 Greek citizens lost their citizenship as a result of its enactment (Grigoriadis 2011: 171).

The fear of linguistic and religious otherness in Greece was deeply rooted and any discussion about minorities remained taboo, since it involved languages spoken in neighbouring countries. For example, the existence of a Slavophone population in Greece was a well-kept secret until the end of the 1980s. In 1982, when the PASOK government allowed back political refugees who had left during the Civil War, it denied the right of return to all those Slavophones who were 'not Greek by origin'. Discriminatory laws such as the ban on access to the Muslim minority's mountain region (lifted in 1995) and administrative harassment radicalized the Muslim minority on the issue of their identity. With the deterioration in relations with Turkey and the emergence of the former Yugoslav Republic of Macedonia as an independent state in 1991 (see Chapter 3), the Turkophone and Slavophone minorities became more visible and demanded proper recognition. In the European elections of 1994, the Macedonian Rainbow Party won at least seven thousand votes, but it was prosecuted for putting up a sign in Macedonian outside its offices in Florina in 1995 (and subsequently acquitted in 1998). In June 2000, KEMO (the Minority Groups Research Centre) organized a conference to discuss the Council of Europe's Charter of Minority and Regional Languages, but it was subsequently cancelled due to backstage interventions by officials of the Greek Ministry of Foreign Affairs. Interestingly, Greece has signed but not ratified (as other Balkan countries, including North Macedonia and Albania, have done) the Framework Convention for the Protection of National Minorities.[2]

Despite Greece's historical suspicion of its non-Greek speaking and non-Orthodox citizens, since the late 1980s it has been forced to acknowledge the issue of minorities and witness the country's gradual transformation into a

---

[2] For more details visit the Convention's website: https://www.coe.int/en/web/minorities/home.

multicultural society due to the influx of migrants. An attempt was made to open up space for the Other in the face of earlier totalizing and homogenizing trends and, as Roderick Beaton points out, 'for the first time in its history, Greece in the 1990s was rapidly becoming "multi-cultural"' (2019: 362). European bodies such as the OSCE or the European Convention on Human Rights promoted the recognition and protection of minorities in Greece as well as the rest of Europe. The resurgence of otherness in Greek society is attested, inter alia, by the number of studies dealing with the Other(s) in Greece published in the last thirty years. There have also been an increasing number of conferences on otherness, perceptions of the ethnic other in literature and textbooks, books on migration and definitions of Greek citizenship as well as studies on Jews in Greece and other minorities.[3] Some of the most critically acclaimed Greek films of the 1990s and 2000s such as *From the Snow* (1993), *Ulysses' Gaze* (1995), *Mirupafshim* (1997), *From the Edge of the City* (1998), *A Touch of Spice* (2003), *Hostage* (2004) and *Xenia* (2014) deal with otherness, identity or border-crossing (Calotychos 2013). Though recent statistics indicate that racism in Greece is still on the increase, the growing academic and cultural engagement with otherness suggests that culture is showing society the way.

This explosion of interest in otherness was unprecedented and led to the view that, if Greek modernity was characterized by a totalizing and homogenizing impulse, postmodernity has highlighted difference, heterogeneity and diversity, while modern Greece itself has often been seen in postcolonial terms as the discursive product of Europe's 'othering' process. Otherness, according to postcolonial theory, is constructed by the dominant discourse in an ambivalent manner. Whilst it attempts to construct the Other as radically different from itself, it ascribes to it an element of its identity in order to justify the control it exerts. In turn, the Other becomes recognizable 'as a subject of a difference that is almost the same, but not quite' (Bhabha 1994: 86).

In Greece, urbanization did not involve the same transformation of *Gemeinschaft* into *Gesellschaft* as in Germany or Britain (Fukuyama 2012). Instead of the breakdown of traditional kin and village networks and their replacement by a modern division of labour, there was a wholesale transfer

---

[3] I can only give a small sample of the wide range of books and studies on otherness in Greece here: e.g. Christopoulos (1999 and 2019); Fais (1999); Politou-Marmarinou and Denissi (2000); Millas (2001); Clogg (2002); Papataxiarchis (2006); Fleming (2008); Androusou and Askouni (2011); Tsibiridou and Palantzas (2013); Lemos and Yannakakis (2015); Tabaki and Polycandrioti (2016). As Vassilis Lambropoulos has pointed out, 'Modern Greek has been dramatically transformed into the study of Greek margins and aliens (linguistic, ethnic, religious, sexual, and other), documenting a long record of human rights abuses' (1997: 200).

of the *Gemeinschaft* into an urban environment with the consequent survival of traditional patron–client relationships. This transition had been completed by the fall of the junta in 1974, while the increasing urbanization of villagers entailed a process of cultural homogenization and some loss of local accents. Towards the end of the twentieth century, however, this process started to be questioned from below by an explosion of cultural difference and regional diversity, which seriously undermined the notion of monoculturalism and the idea of a dominant monolithic high culture.[4] First, after 1981 and the rise of the socialists to power, it involved the empowerment of rural or previously unprivileged social strata, who for the first time felt that they had a voice and could exercise some influence, thanks to political and cultural changes. Secondly, the influx of migrants, various public debates and controversies over minorities in Greece as well as the revisiting of the Balkan and Ottoman pasts led to changing attitudes towards otherness.[5] Greece did not simply open up to Europe but also to the areas north and east of its borders. The collapse of the communist regimes forced Greece to confront its position in the Balkans and to accept that the old political divisions had been replaced by competing religious spheres of influence. In this way religion re-entered the identity and otherness agendas in a more active fashion.

It has also been claimed that globalization and the weakening of the traditional notion of the nation state has led to a reaction against cultural homogenization and the revival of locality (Mackridge and Yannakakis 2004: 9). This renewed and flourishing sense of localism has meant that local differences in language, culture, religion, race and gender are now tolerated and accepted more than ever before, thus questioning the notion of a homogenous national culture. This has been particularly challenging for Greece, which for years had endeavoured to promote national homogenization and cultural assimilation. Debates over competing definitions of the nation in terms of ethnic descent or civic society have increased in Greece over the last thirty years and have contributed to raising awareness about ethnic and linguistic otherness.

Apart from the issue of minorities, another vexing question, which exposed a number of prejudices, was, Who can claim to be Greek? Are you born Greek or do you become Greek? This question, related to the essentialist or constructivist

---

[4] It should be noted that since 1974, cultural associations (πολιτιστικοί/μορφωτικοί σύλλογοι) have mushroomed in Greece and their main aim has been to preserve and promote local distinctiveness and regional culture.

[5] In the 1990s, following the dissolution of Yugoslavia and the collapse of the communist regimes, Greece discovered its repressed Balkanness without abandoning the notion of Greek exceptionality (Kitromilides 1996b and 1999; Roudometof 2001; Tziovas 2003a).

perception of identity, was raised more frequently when recent migrants appeared to be in a position to apply to become Greek citizens and were thus perceived as a threat to Greek purity. Having been an ethnically homogenous country in the past, Greece had not often faced the question of who could make a case to be Greek and on what grounds. The influx of migrants of Pontic origin from the former Soviet Union, who claimed to be Greek but had never lived in or even visited Greece before, and the settlement of migrants from neighbouring countries, particularly Albania, after the collapse of their communist regimes raised the question as to whether those who were not Greeks by birth could become Greeks. Pontic migrants were granted citizenship regardless of whether or not they spoke the language or were familiar with Greek culture, but the children of non-Greek parents, born and bred in Greece, were considered aliens because they could not demonstrate Greek ancestry. The *jus sanguinis* principle was deeply embedded in Greek legislation on nationality and thus Greek law considered only persons born of a Greek man or woman to be Greeks (Tsitselikis 2006).

Greece was not alone in basing its citizenship laws on the *jus sanguinis*, but its refusal to recognize ethnic minorities and the emphasis on racial purity has been particularly marked until recently and therefore integration through naturalization has not been an easy option. Though dual (or multiple) citizenship is allowed, Greek law still permits differential treatment on the basis of *genos*. Greeks are those of Greek genealogy and not those who live in the country (Triantafyllidou 2014: 128). The end of the Cold War and mass migration rekindled the discussion about what it meant to be Greek and how Greek national identity should be understood (Christopoulos 2006 and 2019). A genealogical and ethnic conception of the nation competed with a civic and voluntaristic one, while European integration questioned Greek national identity from a supranational perspective.

Though football players from Argentina or athletes from Georgia could be fast-tracked to Greek citizenship in order to play in Greek clubs or represent Greece in international athletic competitions, others were denied any such privilege. In 2000 the prospect of an Albanian student (Odysseas Tsenai-Odhise Qenaj) holding the Greek flag and leading the parade for the national celebration of 28 October caused a great deal of controversy. Because he was the top student in his class, his teachers were prepared to allow Qenaj to carry the flag, but this contravened a Ministry of Education circular (a relic of the Metaxas era) restricting this right to Greek nationals or those of Greek descent. Due to public and media reaction, he decided to forfeit his right to bear the Greek flag, while the slogan 'Albanian, you will never become Greek' appeared once again on the walls in various parts of Greece. This incident sparked a debate about the assimilation versus integration policy on migrants and the definition of Greekness with reference to Isocrates's saying that a Greek is anyone who participates in Greek *paideia*.

Contrary to the Ottoman *millet* legacy and the earlier voluntary integration of Balkan Christians into the Greek nation, Qenaj's success in the Greek school system, his conversion to Orthodoxy and his knowledge of Greek language and culture did not prove sufficient to challenge organic notions of national identity. Eventually Qenaj left Greece to study in the United States and was followed in 2009 by another Albanian, the acclaimed writer Gazmend Kaplani, who, after 25 years of living and working in Greece, felt that he was not welcome in Greece any longer.[6] On the other hand, National Basketball Association (NBA) star player Giannis Antetokounmpo, the son of undocumented immigrants from Nigeria who arrived in 1991, became an iconic figure in Greece and was assigned the role of Greek tourism ambassador by the Ministry of Tourism. However, most children of migrants in Greece have not shared Antetokounmpo's good fortune and have lived in Greece for many years without any hope of naturalization.[7]

Even allowing for lack of data and the unreliability of Greek statistics, there is evidence to suggest that the number of migrants of non-Greek descent who were naturalized in the period 1995–2004 doubled (to over ten thousand) compared to the five thousand in the period 1980–94 (Christopoulos 2019: 214). This is a paradox because during this period Greek legislation made it harder to acquire Greek citizenship and, according to the Citizenship Policy Index (CPI), Greece (after Austria and Denmark) had one of the toughest citizenship policies, sliding back from a CPI score of 1.25 in the 1980s to 1.0 in 2008 (Howard 2012: 111). From the end of the Greek Civil War onwards the issue of citizenship has been considered 'nationally sensitive' and a 'no-go' area for public debate, while until the 1990s far more people had been deprived of their citizenship by the Greek state than were being granted Greek citizenship. This changed just before the signing of the bailout memorandum in 2010 when the Greek Citizenship

---

[6] The critically acclaimed film Ακαδημία Πλάτωνος/*Plato's Academy* (2009) by Filippos Tsitos raises issues of xenophobia, identity and the hostile reception of migrants in Greece. The film tells the story of Stavros, a kiosk owner, and his middle-aged friends who idly pass the time watching passers-by and criticizing foreign workers who, in contrast, are always on the move. One day his dying mother unexpectedly tells him that he has an Albanian brother and he is forced to examine his life, his identity and his values (Phillis 2017).

[7] One of the greatest American divers and LGBTQI+ activist, Greg Louganis (b. 1960), of Samoan and Swedish descent, never wished to be Greek, but the Greeks claimed him because his adoptive father was of Greek descent.

Act (Law 3138/2010) was passed by the Parliament and hailed as a major breakthrough. However, two changes introduced by the Act were considered unconstitutional: the acquisition of Greek nationality by second-generation migrants through a declaration and the migrants' right to vote and run for office in municipal elections. In the ensuing discussions in the Greek Council of State, the majority of its members argued that nations and people 'are not spineless organisms and ephemeral creations but represent a diachronic unity ... with a long tradition, passed from generation to generation' (Christopoulos 2017: 489). While the country was still in the midst of the financial crisis and facing increasing waves of refugees, the revised Act was finally adopted in 2015 (Law 4332/2015), a sign of the relative autonomy of institutions from the economy and the pressures of migration. The adoption of the Act was a step towards superseding the *jus sangunis* and understanding Greek nationality in legal terms.

The exposure to different manifestations of otherness, its representation or rehabilitation in various media and the demands from the EU and other international bodies that Greece should provide legal protection for its minorities has raised issues of identity and attempts to allay the instinctive fear of the 'Other' associated with the increased numbers of migrants. It has also intensified cultural dilemmas and reinforced a deep-seated sense of insecurity among Greeks, tainting attitudes to Europe and encouraging Greeks to side with people deemed at times to be enemies of the West (e.g. Serbs, Arabs, even Russians). For years many Greeks perceived themselves as the economic victims or the pawns of western diplomacy and approached international relations in emotional terms by continuing to employ dated terms such as 'philhellenes'. In the early years of the *Metapolitefsi* the journalist and amateur historian Kyriakos Simopoulos (1921–2001) published a number of books on historic foreign travellers to Greece and on how foreigners saw the Greece of 1821. These were followed by his *Ξενοκρατία, μισελληνισμός και υποτέλεια/Foreignocracy, Hellenism-Hating and Subjugation* (1990, reprinted in 1999) where he claimed that 'from the Romans to the EEC, Greece has always been alone in a hostile world', thus presenting Greece as a constant victim of foreign powers.

Interestingly, the notion of victimization gained new ground towards the end of the twentieth century when the idea of European integration acquired increased momentum, culminating in the economic crisis (Tziovas 2017). Perceiving the crisis in terms of a national humiliation has made national exceptionalism and victimization the default reflexes of both Left and Right. Issues of sovereignty can unite people at a visceral level and cultivate a fear of the

'Other', whether in the form of the westerner or the migrant. Though migrants are the main target of the politics of hate, since the outbreak of the crisis phobic discourses have been levelled at various other social groups (Dalakoglou 2013).

Images of the others and the history wars

Constructions and conceptualizations of ethnic otherness in literary texts and history textbooks have received particular attention during the last thirty years or so. Silences, contradictions and ethnic stereotypes have been revisited and studied in Greek texts as well as in those originating from neighbouring countries. It has been claimed that the Turks are portrayed negatively in abstract or generalized representations, but positively when they are presented as concrete or everyday characters (Millas 2006). This binary image of the Turk, as either abstract or concrete ethnic Other, was often connected with a negative representation of the period of Ottoman rule over the Greeks (the *Tourkokratia*) or the identification of the Ottoman Empire with barbarism.[8] The Turks of the *Tourkokratia* tend to be presented as unappealing, middle-aged men or, in their rare appearances in literary texts, women, who could be part of a harem but are never presented as mothers. The main feature of Greek and Turkish school textbooks appears to be the belittling of each other with the Greeks claiming to be the founders of world civilization and the Turks associating themselves with the ancient Aegean civilization (Millas 1991: 24, 29). A series of past conflicts and national historical narratives have exacerbated each nation's perception of itself as the innocent victim of the other.

The Turk is the most salient 'Other' for Greeks, a blank space that can be loaded with additional properties but instrumental in shaping the worldviews of Greeks and Cypriots (Theodossopoulos 2007). Like other ethnic or religious conflicts (Palestinians and Israelis, Catholics and Protestants in Northern Ireland), the Greco-Turkish hostility, despite some shared humanity or 'cultural intimacy' between the two peoples, is naturalized and reproduced as primordial. Central to the othering mechanism between Greeks and Turks is the question of who is civilized and who is not, with toleration of the other being a sign of civilization and in turn a challenge to the nationalist perceptions of the Ottoman Empire. The Greeks, as self-defined 'Europeans' and descendants of the 'original

---

[8] As Vangelis Calotychos notes, 'The Balkans are organized as much around their Ottoman legacy as by its negation' (2013: 124).

civilizers' of the classical period, presented the Turks as 'uncivilized' barbarians in order to boost their own self-image and identity as modern, progressive and democratic (Heraclides 2012). This self-presentation of Greece as a country of 'civilization and history' breeds cultural arrogance and megalomania but also conceals an 'existential insecurity', leading to defensive nationalism and 'continuous perennialism', the view that 'a particular nation has existed for centuries, if not millennia' (Smith 2000: 5). Similarly, the Turks demonized the Greeks and returned the compliment as regards backwardness, while promoting the view of a tolerant Ottoman Empire.

However, from the 1980s onwards this nationalistic approach to history began to be studied and questioned, while the state of diplomatic relations between the two countries has alternately encouraged or halted such initiatives. The Greek-Turkish Friendship Committee (established in 1986) has repeatedly called for improvements in the textbooks, while conferences, convoked either by UNESCO in Istanbul (1986) or by the Friedrich-Naumann-Stiftung (Athens 1988), were designed to discuss the textbooks of neighbouring countries and suggest amendments. Since 1989, the politics of history teaching in the Balkans and the construction of otherness has also been the focus of a number of research projects (Vouri 1992/2010; Koulouri 2002). This signalled a revisiting of repressed national traumas, namely the Ottoman legacy, ethnic conflicts and forced displacements. A shift from the negatively charged concept of the *Tourkokratia* to a growing interest in the multi-ethnic Ottoman Empire and its heritage led, among other things, to the development of Ottoman studies in Greece. Interestingly, the comparative study of Greece and Turkey has in recent years been boosted by studies focusing on nationalism, modernity and religion.[9] Moreover, the EU's enlargement policy in respect of Turkey, considered a vital ally for stability and peace in South-Eastern Europe, blurred the East-West demarcation and complicated the practice of treating Turkey as a threatening Other.

With the so-called earthquake diplomacy of 1999, when Greeks and Turks each rushed to the aid of the other's earthquake victims, and the relative political stability that ensued, attitudes changed. This is reflected in two novels: *Innocent and Guilty/Αθώοι και Φταίχτες* (2004) by Maro Douka and the bestselling *Imaret/ Ιμαρέτ* (2008) by Yannis Kalpouzos. Blurring fact and fiction and bringing together revisionist historiography and the historical novel in the spirit of New

---

[9] Frangoudaki and Keyder (2007), Özkırımlı and Sofos (2008), Anastasakis et al. (2009), Grigoriadis (2012) and Lytra (2014).

Historicism, these novels attempt to rehabilitate Greece's Ottoman legacy by including it in the national narrative and treating their Muslim protagonists with empathy. Encouraging readers to view their national past from the perspective of non-Greek characters, the novels challenge prejudices against Muslims and ethnocentric approaches to the Ottoman Empire. Taking place in Greek lands, the novels by Douka and Kalpouzos lend a voice to the non-Greek Other and revisit the past nostalgically, highlighting what was lost with the dissolution of the Ottoman Empire and the ending of an era when different religions coexisted side by side. These novels either attempt to include Muslims/Turks in the European Enlightenment discourse (*Innocent and Guilty*) or tap into an Orientalizing fascination with the past (*Imaret*), reflected in the popularity of Turkish TV series like *Suleiman the Magnificent*, screened in Greece in 2012–13 (Willert 2019a and 2019b). The growing interest in Ottoman monuments and their restoration in Greece (e.g. Fethiye and Tzisdarakis mosques in Athens) is another sign of the reappraisal of the Ottoman legacy. This has also involved debunking the myth of the 'secret schools' of the Ottoman 'dark ages' (Angelou 1997) and highlighting the multiculturalism of the Empire, as explored in the documentary by Maria Iliou, *Smyrna: The Destruction of a Cosmopolitan City* (2011), or in Milton's book on pre-national Smyrna as a 'lost paradise' (2009). A rediscovery of Ottoman music and greater familiarization with traditional Eastern musical instruments has also been noted in Greece since the 1980s.

Yet, the years of Ottoman occupation were underplayed in the linear and seamless representation of Greek history during the opening ceremony of the 2004 Olympiad in Athens, while the increased interest in Thessaloniki's Ottoman heritage promoted by the city's former mayor Yannis Boutaris and historians such as Mark Mazower with his book on Salonica (2004) has incited nationalistic rejoinders (Tachopoulos 2012). Moreover, school history textbooks perpetuated stereotypically hostile images of Turks and myths of national exceptionalism, remaining impervious to the historiographical developments in Greece since 1974. The teaching of history in Greece, still centred around a single compulsory textbook following official curriculum guidelines, was based on an ethnocentric and event-driven narrative. As comparative studies suggest, controversies over history textbooks, which according to Jacques Le Goff offer privileged access to the historical mentality of a period (1992: 127–8), are more likely to arise in centralized education systems than in those where textbooks are authorized at a regional or local level (Popp 2008/2009; Sjöberg 2011).

In September 2006 a new history textbook for the sixth grade of primary school challenged these established assumptions and caused a good deal of controversy (Repoussi et al. 2006). The textbook dealt with the history of the modern world and was part of an overhaul of the teaching books that were published and distributed free to Greek and Cypriot schools. It was condemned by a number of institutions and groups ranging from the Greek Church to the Greek Communist Party, which criticized the textbook as a manifestation of the spirit of European integration and globalization. The polemic against the book focused on three points: the representation of Ottoman rule, the role of the Orthodox Church in this period and the myth of its secret schools maintaining ethnic identity and the expulsion of the Greek population from Asia Minor after the end of the Greco-Turkish War 1919–22. The book challenged traditional narratives of modern Greek history and some cornerstones of Greek identity based on the 'us and them' dichotomy (Athanasiadis 2015: 45–99; Kechriotis 2013; Meselidis 2010).

The opponents of the book demanded its withdrawal for doubting the continuity of the Greek nation and not properly recording the suffering of the Greeks at the hands of the Turks during the evacuation of Smyrna.[10] A copy of the book was even burnt publicly in Constitution Square by the neo-Nazi party Golden Dawn. The vehement and unprecedented reactions against the textbook were fuelled by the polarized atmosphere of the upcoming elections of 16 September 2007 and the involvement of social media in spreading conspiracy theories. Social media turned the controversy into a confrontation between identity and national pride on the one hand and historical interpretation on the other. Despite the fact that around five hundred academic historians and teachers supported the book and its first print run of 175,000 copies sold out, the Ministry of Education eventually withdrew it after the elections, when the minister who had supported the book failed to be re-elected (Repoussi 2009). This incident exposed the gaps between collective memory and academic history and encouraged people to confront different versions of the past and come to terms with otherness.[11]

From 1974 onwards history teaching has turned into a hot issue and its own historiography gradually became a separate academic discipline (Avdela 2000). The didactics of history also emerged as a new field and

---

[10] The book was criticized for using the arguably neutral and unsentimental phrase 'waterfront crowding' (*synostismos*) in relation to the Greeks who gathered in the harbour of Smyrna/Izmir after the defeat of the Greek Army in August 1922.

[11] In the 1980s the books by the Greek-Canadian historian Leften Stavrianos (1913–2004) were withdrawn from classrooms following intense reaction from nationalist and religious groups. On this and other withdrawals of textbooks in Greece and Cyprus, see Repoussi (2007) and Kechriotis (2013).

the foundation of university pedagogical departments in 1984 led to the recognition of history didactics as a discipline involving the study of the methods used for the acquisition of knowledge and the educational function of history (Repoussi 2011). The controversies regarding the renegotiation of the ways history was taught in Greek schools suggest that history became the main vehicle for the reaffirmation of national identity, while globalization seems to have played a role in the turn towards the past. The amnesia of globalization was contrasted to the historical memory of the nation (Liakos 2008/9).

Though there has never been a historical association in Greece, after 1974 historiography flourished under the influence of leading historians trained in France, such as K. Th. Dimaras, Nicos Svoronos, Spyros Asdrachas, Filippos Iliou and Vassilis Panagiotopoulos. They practised a kind of 'new history', the equivalent of the French 'nouvelle histoire', and saw it more as a social science than part of the humanities. Also a number of new historical periodicals began to be published, such as *Mnimon* (1971), *Historika* (1983), *Histor* (1990), *Historein* (1999 with English as its main language) and *Archeiotaxio* (1999), testifying to the renewal of discourse on history and its increasing role in the debates on Greek identity (Liakos 2004b and 2019: 668–9). Greek historiography has begun to challenge Greek exceptionalism and emancipate itself from the legacy of Paparrigopoulos. And this attempt to debunk the 'ideological myths' of Greek history and its conceptualization as the 'biography' of the nation often led to history wars, while the preoccupation with national identity could explain the proliferation of history supplements in the Greek press and the popularization of public history. The question 'Who owns history?' could easily turn into 'Who owns the nation?' More than ever before, history has turned into a cultural battleground where versions of the past clash, vying with literature for centre stage in the national imaginary and the discussions on national identity.

One of the history wars involved the debate about postmodernism, connected to wider debates on historiography, nationalism and epistemology. The discussion was primarily between left-wing historians and was sparked off by a conference on the historiography of modern and contemporary Greece (1833–2002) held in Athens in 2002. Traditional historians saw the turn towards historiography as a shift away from the objectivity of history and the importance of archival research. The crisis of the *Annales* school in the 1990s was attributed to increased Anglo-Saxon influence in Greek academia and indicated a paradigm shift, which in the eyes of many traditional historians was associated with postmodernism and the undermining of rationalism (Kremmydas 2004: 739). Postmodernism was perceived as a cultural by-product of Americanization, a sign of the hegemony of the English language and the Anglo-Saxon academic system promoted by the EU in Greek higher education (the 'Bologna process'). This turn posed a threat to academics following the Marxist tradition and trained in the intellectual traditions of other European countries (e.g. Vassilis Kremmydas, Yorgos Margaritis, Nikos Theotokas in France, Kosmas Psychopedis and Christos Hatziiosif in Germany).

The fall of the Berlin wall in 1989, according to Kremmydas, did not just crush the so-called existing socialism, it also crushed Marxism and unleashed all kinds of anti-Enlightenment and irrational forces (Kremmydas 2002). Though Marxism continued to be a force to be reckoned within Greek historiography, there were a number of historians who flirted with postmodern relativism (Exertzoglou 2002; Gazi 2003; Liakos 2003b), identified by its opponents with anti-Enlightenment and a general hostility to reason. Supporters of postmodernism were also criticized for assigning a secondary role to the analysis of social structures and classes in history. By ascribing equal importance to all categories (class, gender, race, etc.) and by rejecting totalizing interpretative patterns (what is usually referred to in Lyotard's terms as 'grand narratives'), they promoted a depoliticization of history by emphasizing personal experiences and memories. Contrasting Enlightenment to relativism, totality to fragmentation and archives to memories, Marxist historians put the role and the definition of history at the heart of the Left's identity, arguing that history is not just narratives (Theotokas 2002a and 2002b).

No longer seen as a space for open dialogue and constructive disagreement, the Greek Left was divided by postmodernism. It was claimed that earlier historiographical approaches represented the authentic Left while the latest trends had abandoned its radical political identity and given in to 'neoliberal eclecticism' (Theotokas 2003: 22). For the opponents of postmodernism, the problem was not epistemological but political and, therefore, they felt the need to defend Marxism, perceived as under attack from postmodernism. The history wars at the turn of the twenty-first century signalled another reluctant transition from Marxist history to postmodern historiography and from the hegemony of French cultural influence to Anglo-American epistemological and theoretical paradigms.

Anti-Semitism and genocides

In the 1980s the memory of the Holocaust in Western Europe came to the fore and the term was consolidated alongside its Hebrew equivalent 'Shoah'.[12] For some in the West the Holocaust was a Central and Eastern European atrocity and, due to the Sephardic origin of Greek Jews, their genocide has been underplayed (Varon-Vassard 2008: 330). The fact that Greek identity is so intertwined with Orthodoxy (and the junta with its slogan 'Greece of Greek Christians' offered a constant reminder of this) contributed to the way the genocide of the Greek Jews was treated as an event involving 'others', not Greeks. Though in the early post-dictatorship period the subject of the Holocaust was not discussed, and it was only in the 1980s that some testimonies of those who survived the concentration camps started appearing, the explosion of interest in the Holocaust comes in the next decade.[13]

In the 1990s, memoirs, testimonies and studies about the Greek Jews were published with literary scholars leading the way and historians following in their footsteps (Ambatzopoulou 1993, 1995, 1998). It was in 1990 that the Society for the Study of Greek Hebraism was set up in Thessaloniki, the special issue (52–3) of the periodical *Synchrona Themata* on 'The Jews in Greece' was published in 1994, and monuments to mark the Jewish suffering also started to be erected in public spaces by local authorities (Varon-Vassard 2019).[14] Conferences, translations, films and various publications on Greek Jewry proliferated, while for the first time in the autumn of 2007 school textbooks included references to the Holocaust. Holocaust Remembrance Day (27 January) was officially adopted in Greece in 2004, and a chair in Jewish studies was established at the University of Thessaloniki in 2014. The documentary by Vassilis Loules, *Φιλιά εις τα παιδιά/ Kisses to the Children* (2011), telling the stories of five elderly Greek Jews saved by Christian families during the German occupation, attracted national and international interest.

Despite this growing interest in the plight of the Greek Jews, anti-Semitism continued unabated.[15] The Jewish cemeteries in Athens, Thessaloniki, Larissa and Ioannina were vandalized and the synagogue in Chania suffered two

---

[12] Varon-Vassard prefers the term 'genocide' to 'Holocaust' (2013:158–60). Cf. Antoniou and Moses (2018).
[13] It should be noted that in the periodical *Nea Estia*'s 1985 special issue (1403) on Thessaloniki, on the occasion of the city becoming European Capital of Culture, there are scant references to the Jews of the city.
[14] Cities like Thessaloniki were reconciled with their multiethnic and multicultural past and saw tourism as a way out of the crisis.
[15] For a list of anti-Semitic attacks in Greece since 2000, see Panagiotis Dimitras, 'Πρωτιές Ελλάδας σε αντισημιτισμό και ατιμωρησία δραστών', *The Books' Journal*, 30 December 2014, available at

arson attacks. The Greek Church has never issued an explicit condemnation of manifestations of anti-Semitism, while there was an irruption of anti-Semitic views from bishops and other clergy in the public arena (Zoumboulakis 2013: 147–9). In 2014 the Anti-Defamation League (ADL) in the United States published the results of a survey that examined attitudes towards the Jews around the world. According to the survey anti-Semitic prejudices, resentments and stereotypes registered an average 69 per cent in Greece (compared to 24 per cent in Western Europe and 34 per cent in Eastern Europe)[16] and, according to an Israeli newspaper, the country could claim 'the ignominious title of [the] most anti-Semitic country in Europe'.[17]

In Greece itself the findings of the survey were called into question but a new survey commissioned by the Heinrich Böll Foundation and conducted by Greek academics from the University of Macedonia in Thessaloniki and the University of Oxford reached similar conclusions.[18] However, in their study the researchers also found that anti-Semitism has been combated more proactively in Greece in recent years with the Holocaust being part of the school curriculum, and the number of Greek students visiting Auschwitz or Jewish museums in Greece having risen sharply.[19] Perhaps the catalyst for this change in Greece was the rise of the neo-Nazi party Golden Dawn and the improved relations with Israel (recognized by Greece only in 1990). Greece has traditionally cultivated close relations with the Arab world, but recently relations between Israel and Greece have become increasingly close and this has been reflected in the changing attitudes towards the Holocaust, as outlined above.

The Holocaust, as a new form of 'cosmopolitan memory' that transcends national boundaries, shifted the emphasis away from the original historical context to the public remembrance of the event, making it a transnational concern beyond the Jewish victims and the German perpetrators. The trauma of the Holocaust provided the template for activists of all kinds to register their own historical or cultural trauma. The growing attention paid to human rights

http://booksjournal.gr/slideshow/item/776-πρωτιές-ελλάδας-σε-αντισημιτισμό-και-ατιμωρησία-δραστών.

[16] For more details about the survey visit http://global100.adl.org/#country/greece/2014.
[17] 'Why is Greece the most anti-Semitic country in Europe?', *Haaretz*, 20 May 2014, available at https://www.haaretz.com/jewish/how-anti-semitic-is-greece-really-1.5248999.
[18] The survey is available in Greek on this website: https://gr.boell.org/en/2017/05/17/anti-semitism-greece-today and the report was written by Yorgos Antoniou, Spyros Kosmidis, Elias Dinas and Leon Saltiel (Thessaloniki 2017).
[19] In the local elections of May 2019 Moses Elisaf, a descendant of Holocaust survivors and head of the tiny Jewish community in the north-western Greek city of Ioannina, was elected the first-ever Jewish mayor of a Greek city in modern memory.

issues enabled local experiences or ethnic memories to become global concerns. This emerging transnational culture of remembrance encouraged Greeks not only to commemorate the 'genocide of the Greeks of Pontus' but to press for its transnational recognition following the example of the Armenian genocide.

Since the 1980s there has been cultural and political reinvestment in the Pontic community, ranging from the growing demands for recognition of its genocide to the addition of its traditional costume to the sartorial options of the Presidential Guard. From being local and peripheral, Pontic culture has become central to the Greek national imaginary and the narrative of victimhood (Baltsiotis 2013). Erik Sjöberg locates the birth of the new Pontic trauma drama in September 1986 and the manifesto by Michalis Charalambidis *Pontians: Right to Memory* (2017: 64–5). A founder member of the PASOK central committee and the creator of a Centre for Pontic Studies, Charalambidis portrayed the struggle for recognition as having 'liberating dynamics' and assisting the Kurds and the Armenians in their own struggles.

By claiming the right to be remembered, the Pontic genocide has generated debates inside and outside Greece since February 1994, when the Greek state first officially recognized the mass persecution and uprooting of the Pontic Greeks from Turkey. In 1919, on the fringes of the Paris Peace Conference, Metropolitan Chrysanthos proposed the establishment of a fully independent Republic of Pontus, but neither Greece nor the other delegations supported this. His plea for international protection was further thwarted by Mustafa Kemal, primarily concerned with the possibility of Armenian independence, who had landed in Samsun on 19 May. This date has acquired symbolic significance and has been designated as Remembrance Day for the Genocide of the Greeks of Pontus and as an opportunity for the Pontic communities across the world to strengthen their bonds.

The issue of the 'genocide' had not been raised before on the part of the Greeks for a number of reasons. First, the Treaty of Lausanne in 1923 and the subsequent peace treaty of friendship signed in June 1930 make no reference to this issue. Secondly, the context of the Cold War, in which Greece and Turkey were allies against the common communist threat, was not conducive to any references to the genocide. Thirdly, a kind of intra-Greek 'racism' classified Pontians as underdogs and denied them a proper Hellenic identity. The Turkish nationalists, on the other hand, claim that the reference to a Pontic genocide is an effort to mar the image of Turkey, and 'May 19, 1919, will always be remembered as the war that the Greeks and the Imperial states badly lost'.[20] In Turkey, this date

---

[20] Ferhat Küçük, 'Historical background to the Pontic genocide allegations', *Daily Sabah*, 18 April 2019, available at https://www.dailysabah.com/op-ed/2019/04/18/historical-background-to-the-pontic-genocide-allegations.

marks the first step on the road to a Turkish Republic, while for the descendants of Ottoman Greeks and Greece it marks the end of the centuries-long Pontic Greek presence on the shores of the Black Sea.

Demand for the recognition of the Pontic genocide gained momentum in the final decades of the twentieth century, following pressure from the survivors and their descendants and the publicity surrounding the arrival in Greece of the so-called 'Russo-Pontians' after the break-up of the Soviet Union. There were also calls for recognition of the genocide perpetrated against the Greeks of Anatolia as a whole, and in 1998 the Greek Parliament voted unanimously to designate 14 September as a national day commemorating the 'Genocide of the Greeks of Asia Minor'. However, a presidential decree enforcing the parliamentary vote, issued in 2001, was revoked a few days later, as a result of doubts regarding the recognition of two 'genocides' (Sjöberg 2017).

The term 'genocide' was coined and included in international law in 1948 to describe in legal terms the mass crimes of ruling authorities that were systematically planned and intended to partially or completely exterminate any ethnic, racial, religious or other minorities. Some claim that the Pontic Greeks, not being a separate ethnic, racial or religious group, would get in the way of international recognition of the Greek genocide perpetrated on a much grander scale in Anatolia. Others have raised doubts as to whether the terms 'genocide' or 'ethnic cleansing' should be applied to the plight of the Pontic Greeks.[21] But the annual commemorations of the event (particularly in its centenary year in 2019) have added further impetus to demands that the Pontic genocide be officially recognized.

Supplementing the narrative of the lost homelands, the genocide discourse reinforced traditional stereotypes about the Turks as the national Other and transcended dividing lines between Left and Right, indigenous Greeks and Anatolian refugees, activists and historians. Though remembrance of the Pontic genocide was in danger of being hijacked by the neofascists and denying it risked becoming a criminal offence or a hostage to memory politics, it was quietly turning into an international concern. In 2007 the International Association of Genocide Scholars took an interest in the case, thus marking the transition from an ethnic/national to a cosmopolitan memory. This was also evinced by the success of Thea Halo's book *Not Even My Name* (2000), which gave a voice to the

---

[21] In November 2015, the then Minister of Education Nikos Filis caused controversy and political opponents instituted legal proceedings against him for doubting whether the term 'genocide' could be applied to the Pontic Greeks (Petsini and Christopoulos 2018: 329–2).

anonymous victims of the Pontic tragedy and ensured their genocide narrative reached a global audience. Gradually the notion of a 'Christian Holocaust' emerged, stressing unity in suffering with other Christians (Armenians and Assyrians), emphasizing religious affiliation over ethnicity and thus framing transnational suffering in religious terms.

Orthodoxy revisited: Challenges and transitions

The role of religion in Greece could be categorized roughly in three successive periods. The first involves the transformation of the Orthodox Balkan commonwealth in the late Ottoman period and the reinterpretation of Orthodoxy as a national religion and a central feature of the building of nation states. The second period, covering the nineteenth and most of the twentieth century, is characterized by a synthesis of religion and national identity (*ellinochristianismos*), while the third period (from the last quarter of the twentieth century until now) features confrontation between religion and secular modernity, church and state, leading to the increasing privatization of faith in the post-junta period.

Similar confrontation could also be observed on the international scene. Popular books such as Richard Dawkins's *The God Delusion* might voice hardline secularism, but this has not prevented religion from making a comeback in the public sphere in Europe (Habermas 2006), judging from France's *l'affaire de Mandil*, the publication of cartoons of the prophet Mohammed in Denmark or the decision to ban the building of a mosque in Switzerland (Roudometof 2011: 96). In Greece the decline in the rates of regular church attendance may be deceptive and a visitor to the country quickly forms the impression that the Orthodox Church is everywhere. Paradoxically, though the Greeks might not be devout Christians, they are deeply Orthodox. Moreover, for many Greeks the Church appears to be a more reliable institution than institutions such as the parliament or the political parties. However, respect for the freedom of religious identity is compromised by the non-differentiation between Greek ethnicity and Orthodox religion and the clause in the Greek constitution stating that 'education is a basic mission of the state aiming at the development of the national and religious consciousness' of Greek citizens.

Until 2007, Law 1566/1985, regulating Greek education and passed by the socialist government of Andreas Papandreou, stated that schools should encourage 'the student's loyalty to the country and faithfulness to the authentic elements of the Orthodox Christian tradition'. By fostering Greek nationalism, religion has never divided Greeks even during the Civil War and this might explain the absence of any hard-line anti-clericalism unlike in other countries such as Spain or France. Due to the liturgical and ceremonial richness of its religious life, Orthodox Greece presents a distinctive picture by comparison with the rest of Catholic and Protestant Europe and does not follow the example of Spain, Sweden or Norway where the relationship between Church and state has been settled in a different way.

Yet the official ties between church and state do not substantially differentiate Greece from other countries. What is distinctive is the manifestation of those ties in everyday life and politics. For example, Article 3 of the Greek Constitution (adopted in 1975) states that the 'prevailing religion of Greece' is that of the Eastern Orthodox Church and that for Greek residents of other faiths the exercise of their religious freedom shall not be actively impeded. Though Article 13 of the constitution forbids proselytism of any kind, Orthodox doctrines are taught in schools (Alivizatos 1999). The European Court even condemned the Greek state for infringing the right of a Jehovah's Witness to religious freedom (Kokkinakis v. Greece 1993 case) without, however, declaring the Greek law on proselytism incompatible with the European Convention, since it was seen as protecting the rights and freedoms of others (Fokas 2008). Harassment of conscientious objectors, including Jehovah's Witnesses, continued for years under many guises, though the latter have acquired the right to alternative military service since 1998. It should be noted that all major changes regarding the rights of minorities in Greece were the result of litigation in the Greek courts and particularly at the European Court of Human Rights.

Greek resistance to implementing religious freedom stems from the way nationalism has been fused with religion and the conception of Greekness 'as an organic whole in which Greek Orthodoxy, the *ethnos*, and the state are a unity' (Pollis 1992a: 171). In Adamantia Pollis's view, for Greece to meet European norms of respect for religious minorities it would require a transformation of the current notion of Greekness. Individualization of a person is alien to Eastern Orthodoxy, since it holds that believers must strive for loss of self in the organic spiritual community of the *ekklisia*. Thus, the modern belief in individual rights is not compatible with the Church's doctrines (Pollis 1993).

The Orthodox Church does not differentiate its institutional structure from the community of the faithful and this in turn militates against the separation of Self and Other. Its value system does not fully recognize the Other as an autonomous agent, which goes some way to explaining its ambivalence to modernity. Orthodox theologians have focused primarily on the Orthodox Church fathers, and comparatively few of the works of the great Western theologians have been translated into modern Greek by analogy with translations of texts from other cultural fields. The so-called 'neo-Orthodox' intellectuals, and particularly Christos Yannaras, have emphasized the anti-westernism of Orthodoxy by juxtaposing Greek *logos* and *koinonia* to western *ratio* and *societas* (see Chapter 2).

In contrast to the western philosophical tradition with its Aristotelian roots, it has been claimed that the Orthodox tradition's roots are in Plato and that it understands the human being ecclesiastically rather than individualistically (Zizioulas 1985b: 49–65). Therefore, the concept of individual human rights is lacking in the ethos of the Orthodox political culture due to its understanding of human beings not as autonomous individuals but as part of a larger community. Rather than emphasizing the 'rights' of the individual, the Orthodox philosophy highlights each person's responsibility to a social group (church, nation) from which she/he has received recognition and identity (Payne 2003).

Since the foundation of the Greek state, the Greek Orthodox Church has acted as a political power and a trustee of Hellenism, while neglecting its social mission apart from the charitable work of distributing food and clothing. Its involvement in national conflicts meant that the Church often became a vehicle of nationalism and anti-communism, due to the persecution of religion in communist countries. Though the church leadership under Archbishop Seraphim (1974–98), following the forced resignation of Ieronymos I (1967–73), almost seemed to act in opposition to the junta, Seraphim himself was installed by the most hard-line group of the junta. The cooperation between the Church hierarchy and the junta damaged the former's reputation and delegitimized its ideology of 'Greek Christianity'. As a result, the first post-junta prime minister, Konstantinos Karamanlis, tried to disassociate the state from the church administration through its new Constitutional Charter (1977), which abolished the government's representation at the Holy Synod.

However, the Church remained impervious to the democratizing spirit of the post-dictatorship years and resisted any legal reforms (e.g. with regard to the decriminalization of adultery, cohabitation law, conscientious objectors, the abolition of confession for pupils, etc.). Church–state relations were seriously tested in the post-junta period when the then Socialist Minister of Education and Religious Affairs Antonis Tritsis introduced Laws 1700/1988 on 'the regulation of church estates' and 1811/1988 on 'the yielding of forest and agricultural estates of the monasteries of the Church of Greece to the public'. The plans provoked adverse reaction from the church hierarchy and the laws were never implemented, leading to the resignation of Tritsis. The other point of contention was civil marriage with the state ultimately compromising under pressure from the church and making a civil marriage optional. The state's financing of the Church's running expenses and the question of its property remain unresolved issues, demonstrating the political influence wielded by the Orthodox Church and the important place of religion in the Greek public sphere.

Separation of church and state was merely a pipe dream, while the appointment of Seraphim's successor Christodoulos (1998–2008) meant that the Church resumed its political and nationalist role within the context of growing globalization.[22] Defending the nation against the 'threat' of globalization and mixing religion and nationalism, the Church still voices its opposition to any form of modernization. It also encourages the political use of Orthodoxy, something that was made explicit with the formation in 2000 of a new far-right political party: *Popular Orthodox Rally* (Laikos Orthodoxos Synagermos or LAOS), a Eurosceptic, nationalist and anti-migrant movement. The waves of immigrants coming from Muslim countries that have entered Greece since the early 1990s have highlighted the lack of provision of formal space for their worship, which until recently had to be conducted in basements and other spaces not legally constituted as places of worship. A project to build a mosque in Athens became a protracted issue of political and diplomatic controversy involving Muslim countries, which offered to finance its construction. It also became part of a larger security debate related to Islamic fundamentalism and the threat perceived to be posed by Turkey. The construction of the mosque 'exemplified the difficulty of coming to terms with religious diversity in Greece' and the obstacles posed by outdated legislation, particularly a 1939 law requiring (at least until recently) the approval of the local Orthodox bishop in order to construct places of worship for minority faiths (Triandafyllidou and Gropas 2009: 963). Due to the recent influx of migrants and refugees, Greece has – for the first time since 1922 – seen an increase in its Muslim population.

It should also be noted that until recently Greece was the only country in Europe where Islamic (Sharia) law has been applied to family and inheritance issues. In January 2018 the power of Islamic courts was limited and the application of Sharia law became optional, but a few months later the European

---

[22] As George Mavrogordatos aptly points out: 'The impression of immutable traditionalism usually associated with Orthodoxy may mask its malleability. Over the centuries, there is not a single issue on which the church has absolutely refused to compromise with the state, except one: their separation' (2003: 15).

Court of Human Rights ruled against this option and gave priority to civil courts. Interestingly, of the forty-seven member countries of the European Court of Human Rights, Greece is the worst offender as regards convictions for violations of religious freedom (mostly in respect of the Muslim minority in Thrace). On the other hand, the project for Reform of the Education of Muslim Minority Children launched in 1997 improved the educational prospects of the Muslims in Thrace and offered a measure of positive discrimination by allowing a 0.5 per cent quota of the total annual admissions to enter Greek universities by sitting special exams (Dragona 2014: 143). Such measures helped the predominantly agricultural Muslim minority to overcome its isolation and attenuate its exclusive attachment to Muslim traditions.

Though there has been constant talk about their separation, state and Church coexist in a paradoxical symbiosis: 'the state used the clout of the Church to foster its nation-building efforts while the Church hierarchy used the state in order to maintain its hegemony in society but also to guarantee its fiscal sources – through state salaries paid to priests' (Roudometof 2011: 103).[23] The close connection between Church and state is illustrated by the way in which the Holy Light, sent from Jerusalem, is welcomed as for a head of state at Athens airport every Easter.[24] Separation of Church and state, following the example of Western European countries, may not yet have been achieved, but civil marriage was instituted in 1982 and affirmation (rather than swearing on the Bible) is now possible for government ministers being sworn in. The Greek Church experienced a major setback in 2000 when the socialist government of Costas Simitis decided to remove any mention of religious affiliation from identity cards, following EU regulations and a ruling of the Greek Authority for the Protection of Personal Data, which outlawed the mention of religion on identity cards. At Sunday services, and also in public demonstrations, the clergy mobilized Orthodox congregations against this decision by emphasizing the threats to national identity. The Church and Orthodox fundamentalist groups, under the leadership of Archbishop Christodoulos, launched an ideological and political campaign against the government's decision, but lost.

This episode was not just a turning point in Church–state relations but contributed to the negative image of the Orthodox Church as an anti-modern institution set against any Europeanizing trends. On the other hand, the Church

---

[23] On the relationship between Church and state and issues of religious freedom, see Manitakis (2000) and Christopoulos (1999).
[24] In April 2018 the Archbishop interrupted the Resurrection liturgy at Athens Cathedral to sing the national anthem.

and its followers continued to maintain considerable voting power and some issues took a long time to be resolved (e.g. the building of a mosque or the lack of an Islamic cemetery in Athens) or remain unresolved, such as cremation and the availability of crematoria (it was not until 2019 that one became available in Euboea/Evia). Religious instruction in schools has also remained a thorny issue because of its catechetical and compulsory nature, though since 2008 students of other religions or denominations and from 2019 all students have been exempted from such classes. There have been proposals for classes in comparative religion, but the Greek Church and the majority of theologians insist on keeping the subject strictly denominational (Zoumboulakis 2013: 147).

The collapse of the communist regimes in Eastern Europe offered an opportunity to the Church of Greece to reassert its cultural role beyond national borders with the revival of Orthodoxy in the former communist countries of the Balkans and Eastern Europe. Following public support for their Serb brethren, the Orthodox Church of Greece publicly sided with the Serbs during the Yugoslav war in the early 1990s with the hope of forming a Balkan-wide Orthodox alliance against Muslim/Turkish 'threats'. Yet the Greek Church has faced multiple challenges in trying to maintain its traditional privileged legal, social and cultural status. For example, the documentary series '1821' about Greece's War of Independence (1821–7), broadcast by SKAI TV in the first half of 2011, challenged the 'national role' of the Church and presented it as an institution that had been incorporated into the Ottoman administration. As a response to these challenges, and as part of the Greek ecclesiastical hierarchy's long-term struggle to preserve the symbiotic relationship between Church and state, high-ranking clerics increased their visibility in the media, at various demonstrations and in the public sphere generally. At times they even continued to use the threat of excommunication to silence their critics, inducing the latter to say that the 'black robes of the clergy are like a piece of coal, which – if touched – either blackens or burns'.

The Greek Orthodox Church has been characterized by its insularity and occasional hostility to other churches. For example, the 2001 visit to Greece by John Paul II, the first pope to visit the country, stirred up controversy. The then Archbishop of Athens and all Greece, Christodoulos, read a list of '13 offences' committed by the Roman Catholic Church against the Eastern Orthodox Church, including the plundering of Constantinople by the crusaders in 1204, and deplored the lack of any apology from the Vatican. This reaction reinforced the image of a nationalist and politicized church, incompatible with the norms of European secular neutrality.

Particularly during the period of office of the late Archbishop Christodoulos (1998–2008) and his fervent support for the 'national mission of the Church', certain ecclesiastical circles resisted the emerging multiculturalism of Greek society and objected to granting Greek citizenship to the children of immigrants. On the other hand, younger theologians criticized the Church's national rhetoric and argued for a return to the authentic Eucharistic tradition.[25] Thus followers of Greek Orthodoxy in the twenty-first century face the dilemma as to whether to be 'children of Abraham', following the patriarch's example of estrangement from his 'heritage', or 'children of Plato', reducing Orthodoxy to the realm of ancestral heritage and ethnocultural identity (Kalaitzidis 2010: 417–19).

From *omogenia* to brain drain: The changing patterns of diaspora and migration

Traditionally Greece has been a country of emigrants with waves of migration to North America from the nineteenth century onwards or to Australia and Europe, particularly Germany, after the Second World War. Due to the political persecution following the Civil War and rising unemployment in the 1950s and early 1960s, emigration increased and Greece signed migration agreements with many Western European countries. However, the oil crisis in 1973 halted the demand for foreign workers in Western Europe and increased the rate of repatriation among Greek migrants. Moreover, most of the political exiles who fled to Eastern Europe after the Civil War were allowed back after the fall of junta. The role of the Greek lobby in shaping American policy on Cyprus after the Turkish invasion in 1974, the Greek state's growing interest in the education of the children of Greek migrants with the creation of a number of all Greek schools in Germany after 1981 and the provision made for the transfer of social security and pension rights of repatriates demonstrated the growing interest of the Greek state from 1974 onwards in the political influence of the Greek diaspora and the economic and social problems of emigrants to Europe.[26] Since the 1980s the term 'diaspora' has been less strongly associated with a traumatic

---

[25] This new attitude is, for example, reflected in the special issue of the leading Greek theological journal *Synaxis* with the indicative title 'Church and nation: Ties and shackles' (no. 79, 2001).
[26] There has been interest in the Greek diaspora since the 1970s and the *Journal of the Hellenic Diaspora* began publication in 1974 in the United States. Partly influenced by Marxist historiography, a shift of emphasis has also been noted from the history of the Greek state to the history of Greek expatriate communities before the Greek War of Independence.

experience and has started to signify something positive in terms of its historical and cultural contribution.

A turning point in government policy on expatriates and returnees was the setting up in 1982 of a General Secretariat for Greeks Abroad and the organization of the First World Congress for Greeks Abroad in 1985, which prepared the ground for the creation of a World Council of Hellenism Abroad (SAE) in ten years' time (Venturas 2009). In 2001 the SAE was even enshrined in the constitution and triggered the establishment of a number of centres and diaspora networks, including the Centre for Research and Development of Hellenic Culture in the Black Sea, the World Inter-Parliamentary Union of Hellenism and the Federation of Greek Diaspora Journalists.

With the end of the Cold War, Greece turned from a country of emigrants into a destination for immigrants, as it found itself in the frontline of migration flows from Eastern Europe and the former Soviet Union as well as from other Asian and African countries. Between the 1991 and the 2001 national census, the immigrant population grew exponentially from less than two per cent of the total population to about seven per cent. By the 1991 census there were 10,260,000 residents in Greece of whom 167,000 were foreigners and, according to the 2001 census, out of Greece's 10,964,020 inhabitants 797,091 were foreigners, most of whom had entered the country illegally (Gropas and Triandafyllidou 2005). The number of foreigners in the 2011 census was 911,929 or about 9 per cent of the total population (10,815,197) with Balkan immigrants being the largest single group.[27] A strikingly high proportion for a country that a few years earlier had been sending out rather than receiving migrants.

The momentous events in Eastern Europe and the Balkans in the years 1989–91 resulted in an influx of immigrants from former socialist countries, including around 155,000 Pontic Greeks from the former Soviet Union and 185,000 members of the Greek minority from Albania (Triandafyllidou and Maroufof 2008: 12). These developments highlighted the distinction between 'omogeneis' (co-ethnics) and 'allogeneis' (of non-Greek lineage) and shaped policies towards the incomers. Greek policy towards these categories of migrants was rather ambivalent. On the one hand, Greece helped some of the *omogeneis* repatriate and settle in the country, while, on the other, it encouraged others to remain in their countries of origin to facilitate the soft diplomacy of the 'national centre'

---

[27] Announcement of the demographic and social characteristics of the Resident Population of Greece according to the 2011 Population-Housing Census. Available at https://web.archive.org/web/20131225192921/http://www.statistics.gr/portal/page/portal/ESYE/BUCKET/General/nws_SAM01_EN.PDF.

from afar and encourage economic expansion in the Balkans and the Black Sea. Therefore, citizenship was not granted equally to all *omogeneis* but meted out according to the extent to which it promoted the 'national interest'. Greek law awkwardly tried to accommodate two opposing policies: conferring citizenship on some *omogeneis* while limiting the naturalization of *allogeneis* as far as possible. In 2003 there were 98,241 *allogeneis* and 31,837 *omogeneis* students in Greek schools, but the so-called 'intercultural education' is more of a one-way process since there is no teaching in the migrants' native languages or culture (Tsitselikis 2006).

Until 1991 Greece lacked a legislative framework for the control and management of immigration and the first immigrant regularization programme took place only in spring 1998, with 371,641 immigrants applying for a white card, the first step towards a temporary stay permit or green card. The naturalization procedure was rather cumbersome and Law 2130/1994 required that immigrants who applied to become Greek citizens had to have been resident in Greece for more than ten of the previous twelve years. The preferential treatment given to immigrants of Greek descent in the naturalization process raised additional legal problems and discouraged the integration of 'other' immigrants. Immigration posed an important challenge to the Greek nationalist discourse and led to the de facto recognition of Greek society as multiethnic. The influx of migrants in the 1990s, whether of Greek or non-Greek descent, may have made Greece a more multicultural society and contributed substantially to the Greek economy, yet it increased xenophobia and hostility to otherness.

The 1990s could be described as the decade of the Greek diaspora, since Greek populations were 'discovered' in some former socialist countries and the SAE assumed the role of providing the link between them and the 'national centre'. The diaspora was also used to promote Greece's views on 'national issues' and to expand Greece's economic, cultural and political agendas in international fora. It was deployed to build economic bridges with the Balkans and the former Soviet Union countries and secure privileged access as a potential intermediary to the EU.[28] Particular emphasis was also given to Greek-language teaching abroad, though a new law in 1996 on Greek schooling abroad criticized the all-Greek teaching in these schools.

---

[28] The SAE and its first Greek-American president, with the backing of US and Greek governments and business, organized a medical relief programme (sending medicine and opening medical centres) for the 'omogeneis' of the former Soviet Union and Albania.

At the end of the twentieth century the figure for the number of 'Hellenes abroad' tended to be inflated and references to 'Global Hellenism' proliferated, contributing to the country's projected self-image as a global player and the powerhouse of South-Eastern Europe.[29] The earlier proletarian image of the migrant Greek gave way to the presentation of '*omogenia*' as dynamic, entrepreneurial and prosperous, like the flourishing pre-1821 merchant diaspora. Diaspora and migration could point to a post-national condition, yet diasporic Hellenism has emerged as a new cultural 'Great Idea' accompanied by a growing interest in foreign artists and writers of Greek origin in recent decades (Tziovas 2009: 7). Terms such as '*apodimoi*/expatriates' or '*metanastes*/ migrants' receded in favour of more positive terms such as '*omogenia*', 'diaspora' or 'ecumenical Hellenism', thus emphasizing the deterritorialization of the Greek nation.[30] Diaspora Greeks were often keen to anchor their identity or ethnic pride to the abstract notion of Hellenism and dissociate themselves from the inefficient Helladic state.

The most widely proposed models for the Greek diaspora are those of the tree and the galaxy. The former symbolically illustrates the vital interconnectedness of the metropolitan centre (the trunk) with its diaspora communities (the branches) while the latter, though not abandoning the existing relationship with the national centre, emphasizes the autonomous existence of the diaspora communities, thus promoting the notion of ecumenical Hellenism (Kanarakis 2012: 297). The policy of granting Greek citizenship to ever widening categories of '*omogeneis*' continued apace in the 1990s and an imaginary transterritorial national community emerged without diminishing the paternalistic role of the 'national centre' (i.e. the state) and the mobilization of the diaspora in promoting its interests. For the first time since 1922 the Greek nation felt as if it was expanding in symbolic terms and transcending its territorial boundaries.

However, from 2010 onwards the economic crisis shattered hopes that the domestic market would continue to expand and the number of foreigners in Greece gradually started to decline (excluding the mainly transitory migration of refugees and migrants arriving for the most part through Turkey from 2015 onwards). In the second quarter of 2015, according to the OECD, they numbered 647,700 (of which 547,300 were non-EU citizens legally in

---

[29] Publications on Greek diaspora and migration proliferated and all recent general histories of Greece include chapters on Hellenism abroad. For a review of the historiography of Greek diaspora and migration see Korma (2017).

[30] See 'The puzzle of global Hellenism', *Odyssey*, March–April 1995, 27–31 and 76 and Kanarakis (2012).

the country), accounting for 6 per cent of the total population, while many recent non-Greek migrants had left the country (49 per cent of all emigrants in 2016) and only strong economic incentives or growth will entice them to return.[31] The global aspirations of the Greek nation since the 1990s changed dramatically during the crisis when Greece became once again a country of emigration, this time not of manual workers and *Gastarbeiter* but of young professionals seeking skilled employment abroad. Though a steep increase has been noted in levels of emigration among the unemployed, who account for 51 per cent of the total emigration outflow during the crisis compared to 27 per cent in the 2000s and 17 per cent in the 1990s, the old Fordist labour migration has been replaced by new and different types of migration. More than 350,000 young Greeks have emigrated – mainly to other EU countries (Germany 150,000 and the UK 60,000) – during the crisis. The average age of these emigrants is 30.7, while their counterparts in previous decades have on average been younger. In contrast to earlier migration flows, more than two-thirds are university graduates and many have postgraduate qualifications. Though this 'brain drain' will be difficult to reverse, in 2016 net emigration of Greek nationals fell to its lowest point since 2010. According to a 2018 survey the lack of meritocracy and the prevalence of corruption (44 per cent), or the economic crisis and uncertainty in Greece (36 per cent) were the main reasons for seeking employment abroad.[32] The same survey indicates that the main cultural bonds that tied the recent expatriates to Greece were above all music (58 per cent) and then a mixture of Church, tradition and customs (41 per cent).[33]

The brain drain, on the one hand, is considered a waste of the public funds invested in the education of these migrants and – together with austerity – likely to lead in the long run to a cycle of underdevelopment. On the other hand, people understood that the country could benefit from the knowledge transfer, remittances and circulation of skills that come through the operation of

---

[31] OECD International Migration Outlook 2016, available at https://read.oecd-ilibrary.org/social-issues-migration-health/international-migration-outlook-2016_migr_outlook-2016-en#page264.

[32] The ICAP survey was conducted electronically with 1,068 participants from sixty-one countries. Details of the survey are available at https://dir.icap.gr/mailimages/icap.gr/Posts/HCS18_Brain Drain_Draft presentation_June 7th.pdf.

[33] A survey entitled 'Hellenism in the world', carried out across five continents between 2016–18 by Kapa Research and the Center for Hellenic Studies (Harvard University), suggests that their cultural heritage, national pride and Orthodox faith seems to unite Greeks around the world. According to the survey 69 per cent believe that speaking Greek is a key factor for maintaining their Greek identity and 65 per cent are disappointed and concerned about the current situation in Greece. Available at https://kaparesearch.com/en/hellenism-in-the-world-a-survey-across-five-continents-presentation-of-key-findings/.

transnational networks. Despite many reports in the Greek and international press about the negative impact of the brain drain on the country's prospects for recovery and Greek demographics, it has been argued that the public debate on the new migration is characterized by two misconceptions.[34] First, the emigration of the highly skilled is presented as a new phenomenon and the result of the crisis, and not as a more widespread phenomenon with deeper roots. Second, crisis-driven emigration is presented as the preserve of the young and educated, while older, less skilled migrants are often overlooked (Labrianidis and Pratsinakis 2017; Pratsinakis, Hatziprokopiou, Grammatikas and Labrianidis 2017).

As a result of the new migration, new diaspora communities have emerged that are not like the old ones but based on professional organizations and formed in countries (e.g. Dubai) where no expatriate communities existed in the past. Technology and social media help to maintain closer links with Greece, while there is increased demand from expatriate Greeks for the right to vote in Greek elections. In Greece itself there is growing discussion about the need to reverse the brain drain and minimize the economic impact of so many young professionals leaving the country.[35] Divesting Greece of its 'best and the brightest' will have long-term consequences for its economy, development and demographics. From the political lobbies of the 1970s we have moved to the economics of the brain drain and the changing patterns of the Greek diaspora with new diasporic subjects emerging in the form of nomadic professionals. Many hope that the new Greek diaspora, through initiatives such as 'Reload Greece' in London, will help Greece to recover and stimulate its economy.[36]

Conclusion

Despite the substantial legislative and other advances in protecting different forms of otherness or promoting tolerance and multiculturalism in Greece,

---

[34] Kerin Hope, 'Greece brain drain hampers recovery from economic crisis', *Financial Times*, 16 August 2018, available at https://www.ft.com/content/24866436-9f9f-11e8-85da-eeb7a9ce36e4 and Yannis Palaiologos, 'Επιταχύνεται η διαρροή εγκεφάλων', *I Kathimerini*, 8 November 2015, available at http://www.kathimerini.gr/837966/article/epikairothta/ellada/epitaxynetai-h-diarroh-egkefalwn.

[35] Certain Greek newspapers (e.g. *I Kathimerini* http://www.kathimerini.gr/1005439/gallery/epikairothta/ellada/istories-epityxias-ellhnwn-sto-hnwmeno-vasileio) regularly run success stories of Greeks who have left the country recently.

[36] 'Reload Greece' (https://www.reloadgreece.com/about-us/who-is-it-for/) was the initiative of a few young people, who wanted to reverse the negative publicity that Greece was receiving by showcasing the productive and creative side of the country, in a bid to inspire other young people to develop their own innovative ideas.

prejudices persist and the recent findings of a series of surveys conducted by the Pew Research Center between 2015 and 2017 involving nearly fifty-six thousand adults (aged 18 and above) in thirty-four Western, Central and Eastern European countries confirm this. In these surveys Greece with 76 per cent is in fourth place (behind Armenia, Georgia and Serbia) as regards seeing religion as a key component of their national identity.[37] In Western Europe, by contrast, most people do not feel that religion is a major part of their national identity. In France (32 per cent) and the UK (34 per cent), for example, most people say it is not important to be Christian to be truly French or truly British, and in countries such as Latvia (11 per cent), Sweden (15 per cent) and Belgium (19 per cent) the proportion is even lower. According to the same surveys only 31 per cent of Greeks would welcome Muslims into their family and only 35 per cent Jews. It is also indicative with regard to attitudes to otherness that 89 per cent of Greeks regard their culture as being superior to that of others and 85 per cent believe that ancestry is important to national identity. The above findings indicate an East–West European divide, with high levels of religious nationalism in the East and more openness toward multiculturalism in the West. Recalling the views of Samuel Huntington, the report points out that 'although Greece was *not* part of the Eastern bloc, it is categorized in Central and Eastern Europe because of both its geographical location and its public attitudes, which are more in line with Eastern than Western Europe on the issues covered in this report'. Therefore, though the transition from homogeneity to embracing otherness may have made considerable progress in the post-junta period, there is still some way to go in transforming the national imaginary, especially now that migration is becoming a vexed issue for many European societies.

---

[37] The findings of the surveys are available at http://www.pewforum.org/2018/10/29/eastern-and-western-europeans-differ-on-importance-of-religion-views-of-minorities-and-key-social-issues/.

5

Language questions: From standardization to diversity

Diglossia, standardization and political correctness

Since the foundation of the modern Greek state in the 1830s, the 'language question' has troubled Greek public life despite, or perhaps partly because of, the establishment of *katharevousa* (literally 'purifying') as the official language of the state and its institutions at the expense of the vernacular. The institutionalization of *katharevousa* was intended to provide a standard national language in an effort to overcome regional variations and communication problems among speakers of divergent dialects and above all as a compromise between the spoken language and the archaizing form(s) of Greek used by the state, scholars, the Church hierarchy and others. Though Greeks often made reference to *diglossia*, the application of Ferguson's definition of this term is rather dubious since from the early nineteenth century there had been substantial interpenetration and intra-lingual convergence between the 'high' (*katharevousa*) and 'low' (demotic) forms of Greek (Holton 2002).[1] The language question was never simply an issue about language alone but had social, cultural, ideological, political and educational aspects too, confirming Pierre Bourdieu's view that 'authority comes to language from outside' (2003: 109). It was about the ways Greeks tried to control and manipulate language to achieve cultural dominance, construct their own identity and shape attitudes to their past.

Apart from a few short-lived reforms, swiftly reversed by conservative governments, the dominance of *katharevousa* continued until the fall of the junta[2] when for the first time the new constitution of 1975 made no mention

---

[1] Charles Ferguson defined *diglossia* as 'one particular kind of standardization where two varieties of a language exist side by side throughout the community, with each having a definite role to play' (1959: 325).

[2] The obsessive promotion of *katharevousa* as a 'national language' by the junta and its misuse by the dictators themselves contributed to its discrediting. *Εθνική Γλώσσα/National Language* was the title

of an 'official' language.³ Technically the following year marks the settlement of the language question in Greece with the institution of demotic (νεοελληνική/ δημοτική) as the language of education and administration. Law 309/1976 introduced *Neoelliniki*/modern Greek as 'the language of teaching, the object of teaching and the language of all textbooks at all levels of General Education' and defined modern Greek as 'the demotic devoid of regionalisms and excesses'. Following this change, the state invited civil servants to attend language seminars in order to familiarize themselves with the new register and introduced a textbook entitled *Modern Greek Grammar* (*Νεοελληνική Γραμματική*) into schools. This was an adaptation of the *Concise Grammar of Demotic* (*Μικρή Νεοελληνική Γραμματική (της Δημοτικής)*) prepared by Manolis Triantafyllidis in 1949, which was in its turn an abridged version of his more comprehensive grammar, which had been published in 1941. In the 1970s Demoticism (the movement supporting spoken/demotic Greek from the nineteenth century onward) was seen as an integral part of the long and incomplete process of modernization and educational reform going back to the eighteenth-century Greek Enlightenment. Hence, the official recognition of the demotic led to a number of studies about the history of the movement, providing relevant sources and engaging with the question as to whether the earlier demoticists were liberal bourgeois intellectuals (Dimaras 1973 and 1974; Frangoudaki 1977 and 1978) or a disorganized group of nationalists and socialists (Stavridi-Patrikiou 1976).

Following the 1976 language reform, pressure mounted to abolish the polytonic system of diacritics (involving three accents and two breathings) and introduce the 'monotonic' (single-accent) system. In 1977 the Centre for Educational Research and Training (KEME) of the Ministry of Education proposed to the government that the monotonic system be introduced into schools. Though this proposal was rejected, by 1979 a consensus in favour of introducing the monotonic system had gradually emerged among the political parties. The prolonged pre-election period may have delayed the resolution of this issue, but the use of a dot instead of accents and breathings by some newspapers (others used an inverted triangle instead) contributed to the adoption of the new system in January 1982. The newspaper *Eleftherotypia* had started using the dot

---

of a booklet, inveighing against the demotic, published by the Greek Army and circulated to all Greek schools in 1972.

³ The constitution of 1975 was written in *katharevousa* and the Greek Parliament had to wait until 1986 to ratify its first demotic translation without, however, granting it legal precedence over its original version.

in January 1978 and only its headlines employed the polytonic system.[4] Other newspapers followed suit, but, surprisingly, the newspapers of the Left adopted it later. The Communist Party newspaper *Rizospastis* started using the monotonic from 6 June 1982 and *Avgi* from 29 January 1984, two years after its official introduction (Sarantakos 2013).

Although it was cheaper to use the monotonic system, a number of established and new publishers (Estia, Ikaros, Agra, Kichli), periodicals (*Poitiki*) and authors continue using the polytonic as a symbol of intellectual elitism in order to display their distinctive, elegant style vis-à-vis cheap books and commercial publishers (Kouzeli 2014). Generally speaking, the abolition of the polytonic system met with more sustained resistance than the introduction of the demotic, to judge from the exchanges in newspapers and continuing references to linguistic fascism more than fifteen years after the reform.[5] Supporters of the polytonic were concerned as to whether children would be in a position to appreciate earlier forms of writing and asked, where will all this simplification end? The monotonic was perceived as undermining the long tradition of writing in Greek or even as a step towards Latinization, though no one seems to have noticed the tacit abolition of the grave accent by the new school grammar of 1976.

The replacement of the polytonic system in 1982 shifted the debate about language to anxieties about the loss of its historical identity and prestige due to the trend towards simplification. In the same year as the introduction of the monotonic system, seven leading public figures (Odysseas Elytis, Georgios Babiniotis, Aristotelis Nikolaidis, Yannis Negrepontis, Aristoxenos Skiadas, Nikos Hadjikyriakos-Ghikas and Yorgos Heimonas) formed the Greek Language Society (Ellinikos Glossikos Omilos) and issued a declaration defending the Greek language, emphasizing its transhistorical character and thus questioning the boundaries between demotic, *katharevousa* and ancient Greek (Ellinikos Glossikos Omilos 1984). Subscribing to the theory that the Greek language was now in decline or had been somehow impoverished, they argued that it had been cut off from its historical roots.

The metaphor of the tree is most commonly used by Greeks to demonstrate the conflation of the diachronic with the synchronic and promote the ideas of a 'unitary Greek language' and the 'diachronicity of Greek'. The tree metaphor challenges the boundaries between different historical periods and implies that

---

[4] The first newspaper to adopt the system of a dot (on 23 February 1964), was *Macedonia* published in Thessaloniki.
[5] See Kriaras (1997 and 2000); Paratiritis (1997); and Kambris (2000).

the Greek language is incapable of flourishing unless it is constantly nourished through its ancient roots. It also suggests that it is impossible to learn modern Greek properly without knowing ancient Greek (Mackridge 2009b). The perception of a language as a tree questions the idea of evolution and proposes going back to the past. Coupled with connotations of decline, the notion of 'uninterrupted linguistic continuity' leads to a denial of history and suggests a negatively valued present and a positively valued past. The allegations of linguistic decline encouraged the belief that ancient and modern Greek are identical and increased concerns regarding national identity.

Historically, the great prestige accorded by Europeans to ancient Greece had encouraged modern Greeks to undervalue their society's present culture and language and, by returning to an idealized ancient form, they sought to share in the high value put upon ancient Greece (Frangoudaki 1997). The fact that, unlike Latin, ancient Greek did not split into distinct modern languages allowed Greeks to claim it as their exclusive cultural capital and as something needing protection from any devaluation, corruption or dualisms (ancient–popular, learned–popular), which might challenge its diachronic value. In turn, the settlement of the 'language question' encouraged a number of speakers and writers to espouse freedom from standardization and argue that the rich reservoir of a 'diachronic Greek' should be creatively exploited.

A further step in the direction of transcending diglossia was to agree the term to be used for the Greek language: *Demotiki, Nea Elliniki/Neoelliniki* or *Koini Nea Elliniki/Koini Neoelliniki*.[6] Demotic was a historic term, ideologically charged but, for some, no longer relevant since *Katharevousa* was no longer its active opponent. Using the term in the present day would arguably perpetuate historical oppositions and memories no longer meaningful for younger generations. Lexicographers, such as the veteran demoticist Emmanouil Kriaras, argued that the time had not yet come to replace 'demotic' with '*neoelliniki*/modern Greek' and that those who did this tended to ignore or downplay the importance of the demoticist movement (Kriaras 1999). He even kept the word demotic in the title of his dictionary while Georgios Babiniotis, who was professor of linguistics and later rector of Athens University, preferred the term 'Neoelliniki' for his dictionary, thus suggesting the conflation of demotic and *katharevousa* and the transition from the turmoil of the language question to a kind of linguistic neutrality or indifference (Maronitis 1999). Based on the idea that the language

---

[6] *Koini* here means 'common' or standard and should not be confused with *Koine Greek* used as a *lingua franca* during the Hellenistic and Roman periods.

could be separated into distinct periods (ancient, medieval and modern), the term stresses the historical dimension of the Greek language, while the term *koini Neoelliniki*, preferred by the Triantafyllidis Foundation's dictionary, was used in the sense of standard modern Greek. Others, however, like Babiniotis, use the term *koini* to refer to an urban, demotic discourse which had to a large degree assimilated learned elements (mainly lexical but also phonological, morphological and syntactical) (Babiniotis 1999).

The resolution of the language question in 1976 turned the spotlight on the demotic itself and inaugurated a period in which other language questions emerged (Moschonas 2004). Despite being heavily criticized for its artificial character by the early demoticists, in the 1970s *katharevousa* started to be considered once again as representing the triumph of Enlightenment intellectuals over those who, in the first half of the nineteenth century, planned a revival of ancient Greek (Frangoudaki 1978 and 1992: 367). Demotic might have won the battle of the language question, but it lost the war against *katharevousa*. The latter's long dominance had influenced the use of language in a number of areas such as law, science and public administration and with hindsight its enriching contribution to written (and to some extent spoken) Greek was acknowledged. The spoken language had been much influenced by its rival over a long period and had absorbed a number of archaic words and grammatical features without adjusting them to the phonological or morphological system of the demotic. In other words, purism undermined the demotic from within since the vocabulary and the structure of spoken Greek became almost identical to basic *katharevousa* and differed only in terms of endings and some forms (Mackridge 2000: 66). In the early post-junta years, the zeal to 'demoticize' the language was demonstrated by avoiding puristic endings or archaic words and using demotic forms. Puristic words and phrases were reserved for purposes of irony, self-mockery or to fill gaps in the demotic register. Later on, there was a backlash against this over demoticization, seen as a new kind of linguistic engineering, replicating the rigid formalism of purism. Non-Greek scholars compiling Greek grammars pointed out the linguistic anarchy and the chaos of spoken Greek. They argued that lexical inflation and not richness of vocabulary characterizes modern Greek with vernacular words used for literal meanings and *katharevousa* words for figurative meanings (Makridge 2009a: 328).

The 1990s was the decade in which efforts to promote and standardize the Greek language culminated. The Centre for the Greek Language, administered and financed by the Ministry of Education, Research and Religious Affairs, came into being in 1994 in Thessaloniki with the aim of promoting Greek language and culture. The first volume of a structural, functional and communicative *Grammar of Modern Greek* (1996) by Christos Klairis and Georgios Babiniotis and the first *Comprehensive Grammar of the Modern Language* (1997, Gr. trans. 1999) by David Holton, Peter Mackridge and Irene Philippaki-Warburton were published, followed by histories of the Greek language, two written by Henri Tonnet (1993) and Geoffrey Horrocks (1997) respectively and another two edited respectively by M. Z. Kopidakis (1999) and A. F. Christidis (2001, chiefly a history of ancient Greek). It was also the decade that saw new and up-to-date dictionaries, which aspired to record the new linguistic reality. First, Emmanouil Kriaras published his own dictionary of the demotic in 1995 and this was followed by the dictionaries of Georgios Babiniotis and the Triantafyllidis Foundation both published in 1998.[7] None of these dictionaries relies on a corpus of texts or a database like the COBUILD of the Collins English dictionaries and this might explain the absence or presence of certain words. Even in their titles, as indicated above, the dictionaries reflect different approaches to the Greek language. And the dictionary by Babiniotis sparked a controversy.

As soon as it was published, a member of the Thessaloniki local council went to court to have the dictionary banned because it included the slang meaning of the word 'Bulgar', which he deemed insulting. A 'Bulgar', according to the dictionary, is not just someone who lives in Bulgaria; he may also be a fan of the Thessaloniki football club PAOK (cf. the recent controversy over the *Oxford English Dictionary*'s decision to include the information that 'yid' is used to mean a supporter of Tottenham Hotspur). A court in July 1998 temporarily banned sales of the dictionary, asked for the slang use of the word 'Bulgar' to be removed from any future editions of the dictionary and threatened Babiniotis with a fine and imprisonment if he did not comply. It is interesting that the court ruling stated that 'a good dictionary does not simply record the linguistic reality, but its mission is also to teach' (Hatsios 1998). On the back of this court ruling, Thessaloniki's Pontic Greeks, whose ancestors came from the area around the Black Sea, sued Babiniotis because his dictionary included a slang definition of Pontians (often the focus of jokes in the equally deplorable 'thick Irishman' tradition) as 'dopey'.[8] Finally, the Supreme Court annulled the lower

---

[7] Emmanouil Kriaras, *Νέο λεξικό της σύγχρονης δημοτικής γλώσσας/Modern Greek Dictionary of the Contemporary Demotic Language* (1995); Tegopoulos-Fytrakis, *Μείζον Ελληνικό Λεξικό/Magnum Greek Dictionary* (1997); Georgios Babiniotis, *Λεξικό της Νέας Ελληνικής/Dictionary of the Modern Greek Language* (1998); Triantafyllidis Foundation, *Λεξικό της Κοινής Νεοελληνικής/Dictionary of the Standard Modern Greek Language* (1998). For a comparison of these dictionaries see Iordanidou (2000) and Tseronis and Iordanidou (2009).

[8] For his response to his critics, see Babiniotis (1998) and on what has been written in the press about the dictionary, see Koutsombolis (2005).

court's decision, but the controversial entry had already been removed from subsequent editions of the dictionary. The dictionary managed to get enormous publicity in the media and was distributed in exchange for coupons by a leading newspaper *To Vima*; evidence that linguistic issues in Greece continued to attract public attention and compiling dictionaries does not simply involve issues of standardization and prescriptiveness, but also ways of controlling the linguistic behaviour of a whole community. As Deborah Cameron has argued 'there is no language without normativity' (2012: 163).

However, the northern critics of the dictionary seemed untroubled by other derogatory terms, deemed insulting to southerners, in the dictionary. Under 'γαύροι/anchovies', for instance, it was noted that, besides its fishy meaning, the word is a term of abuse for fans of Olympiakos, a football team based in the port of Piraeus. The dictionary also omitted to mention that 'Vaseline boys' is a nickname of Panathinaikos's supporters or that another Athens football club, AEK, is known as 'the harem girls', because it was founded by Greeks from Istanbul. The paradox here is that a linguist with rather conservative and ethnocentric views (particularly on the issue of the Macedonian language) was criticized for an 'anti-national' entry. Academics and intellectuals rallied in support of Babiniotis, though some pointed out that in the past he himself had promoted theories of linguistic purity (Christidis 1998 and 1999:103–9). His dictionary was also criticized for presenting the Vlachs/Aromanians (a group that traditionally spoke a Romance language closely related to Romanian) as Greeks by descent and consciousness, thus claiming to have established the truth and refuting what foreign interests and political expediencies have tried to impose in the past.

The attack on the Babiniotis dictionary was treated as a challenge to a basic principle of lexicography: the accurate and faithful recording of all the current meanings and uses of words. Interestingly, scholars representing the Lexicography Section of the Centre for the Greek Language argued that the dictionary was not descriptive, that is, just recording words as they appear in oral or textual form, but rather prescriptive and addressed to the general public and schools. Its prescriptive character is also highlighted by its subtitle: 'With notes on the correct use of words'. Therefore, the way the word 'Bulgar' had been used by a small group of fans should not have been listed, since similar derogatory words for other fans were not (Kazazis 1998).[9] Moreover, the scholarly impartiality

---

[9] The controversy regarding the Babiniotis dictionary led once again to a confrontation between academics from the University of Thessaloniki (Maronitis, Kazazis, Christidis), associated with the

of the dictionary was compromised by the ethnocentric comments by the lexicographer on the entries for Vlachs and the language of the Slav-speaking Pomaks (Karantzola 1998). The debate over the dictionary, similar to the earlier ones in the Western world that focused on racism (concerning the word 'nigger') and feminism, developed into a North–South divide and a test of political correctness, indicative of the nationalist hysteria and defensiveness surrounding the Greek language (Fleischer 2014). The notion of linguistic purity returned, accompanied by patriotic protectionism, censorship and intolerance of freedom of speech. The earlier oppositional discourse of *diglossia* was succeeded by the invocation of various ethnocentric 'myths' to delegitimize linguistic positions and oppose the mythical and the ideological to the historical and scientific.[10] In the early days the language controversy was more about choices, but since 1976 the focus has shifted to internal and external challenges, which are perceived to threaten the integrity and prestige of the Greek language.

While in the past literary writers of the 'Generation of 1930' such as Seferis, Terzakis or Theotokas were considered models of the demotic style, no younger writers assumed this role in the post-junta period. Literature was no longer seen as contributing to the promotion of linguistic standardization but rather to the celebration of an idiomatic, idiosyncratic or distinctive style. In the last quarter of the twentieth century, Greek was neither the language of the militant demoticists nor the idealized demotic of Triantafyllidis, founded on folk songs and literature. It was closer to the hybrid language of Costas Tachtsis's novel *The Third Wedding* (1963), which had by then started to be appreciated for its orality and linguistic boldness.

Protectionism, diversity and language politics

After the end of *diglossia*, Greek faced the challenges of standardization, while warnings about its decline or its vulnerability to foreign influences proliferated. In a book with the telling title, *Ο Γλωσσικός Αφελληνισμός/Linguistic de-Hellenization* (1984/1993), Yannis Kalioris warned against such dangers. The euphoria resulting from the resolution of the language question was followed by disappointment at the decline in linguistic standards, the impoverished

---

Centre for Greek Language, and Babiniotis himself at the University of Athens (see the exchanges in the newspaper *To Vima*, 28 June, 19, 26 July and 2 August 1998).

[10] The language decline was one of the ten myths about the Greek language discussed by ten academics in the newspaper *Ta Nea* in 2000. See Haris (2001b) and Goutsos (2009).

vocabulary of the young or the use of the Latin alphabet in commercial signs, advertising and graffiti. The increase in the use of computers in Greece contributed both to the use of English terms untranslated and the invention of neologisms for their translation. As Peter Mackridge has pointed out, 'the "language controversy" has been replaced by a widespread perception among Greeks that the Greek language is in crisis' (2009a: 330).

It could be argued that in the post-junta period the divisions and conflicts of the language question were replaced by anxiety among some Greeks that their language was under threat. One of these threats was the increasing use of Greeklish (Greek written in Latin characters) in email and texting technologies in the 1990s, which brought back memories of the so-called *Frangolevantinika* and *Frangochiotika*[11] or early Greek texts written in Latin characters. It also recalled the attempt in the early 1930s to replace the Greek with the Latin script, which was supported by men of letters such as Kostas Karthaios, Fotos Yofyllis, Menos Filintas and few others (Androutsopoulos 1999; Bernal 2007). Unlike these historical precedents for Latin-alphabet Greek, Greeklish emerged as a response to a technology-induced necessity, marking a transition from *diglossia* to *digraphia* (the use of two different scripts for the representation of the same language) (Figure 4). Greek script has been viewed as a national symbol and Greeklish in computer-mediated communication caused a 'moral panic', even though it was the default choice in a number of diaspora networks and newsgroups. Objections to *digraphia* fall into three categories: technology-related (e.g. readability, impeding keyword search), aesthetic ('deformation' of Greek by visual and not phonetic transliteration) and identity-related (Androutsopoulos 2009).

Greeklish has been approached as a 'glocal' social practice and three main trends have been identified. The retrospective trend considers Greeklish as a threat to the Greek language and aligns with the Latinization phobia; the prospective trend challenges this approach and views Greeklish as a transitory phenomenon which would disappear due to technological advances and the resistive trend which points to the negative homogenizing effects of globalization and relates Greeklish to other communication and sociocultural practices. It has also been suggested that these trends are reminiscent of earlier debates on the 'language question', with the retrospective trend being reminiscent of arguments supporting *katharevousa* and the other two reflecting ideas used in support of demotic (Koutsogiannis and Mitsikopoulou 2003).

---

[11] Latinized Greek used by Levantine (Christian but ethnically non-Greek) traders from Smyrna and Catholic Greek traders from the island of Chios, respectively.

Figure 4 Are they really speaking the same language? © Arkas and S. Patakis S.A. (Patakis Publishers), Athens 2019.
Note: Translation: (above) What makes you think you're in any way related to the ancient Greeks? [written in the Greek alphabet] (below) In the first place we have kept the same language! [written in the Latin alphabet].

On 6 January 2001 a manifesto signed by forty members of the Academy of Athens highlighted the danger to the Greek language in the use of 'Greeklish' and the widespread use of Latin script, which was seen as the demon that threatened to demolish what Greeks believe to be Europe's oldest civilized tongue. Though Greek is now available as an option on almost all computers and therefore the use of Greeklish is no longer necessary (apart from website addresses), this manifesto voiced Greek anxieties, mixed with technophobia, over threats to the Greek language by the Latin script or the influence of English, echoing similar

French anxieties over 'Franglais'.[12] Yet, the use of the Greek alphabet presents problems in other areas such as car registration plates. For years now, the letters on Greek car number plates have been limited to the Euro-acceptable 'fourteen' – in other words, the letters the Greek alphabet shares with the Latin.

In the same year anxiety over the future of the Greek language was intensified by the proposal from the then Greek commissioner to the EU Anna Diamantopoulou that English be introduced as the second official language of the Greek state. In an interview in the newspaper *Kathimerini* (18 November 2001) she argued that with the future expansion of the EU and its more than twenty languages it would be difficult to use all of them as working languages in the EU or in a European network of academic exchanges. The EU would end up as a modern babel of languages and would be forced to adopt English as its working language. She argued that Greece could forestall a linguistic exclusion by adopting English as a 'second official language'. This proposal provoked widespread reaction, and Diamantopoulou clarified that by 'official' she meant that the state needed to ensure its citizens were sufficiently proficient in English for it to become an instrument of communication, learning and working in Greece. Her idea might have been related to the designation of 2001 as the European Year of Languages by the EU and the Council of Europe, yet it was treated as a threat to Greek identity rather than a way of improving the economic competitiveness of Greece and the employability of its citizens.[13] The prospect of an anglophone Europe was also seen as a threat to cultural equality, promoting a Europe of powerful nations rather than a people's Europe (Frangoudaki 2001). The controversy surrounding Diamantopoulou's suggestion gave some Greeks the opportunity to stress the richness, history and exceptional status of the Greek language. It should be noted that in December 1994 a French proposal (later withdrawn) to reduce the number of working languages in the European Parliament and other EU organizations to five was perceived by some Greeks as an orchestrated attempt to devalue their language.

In the past French words and phrases had tended to be introduced into Greek, but after the fall of the junta English assumed a hegemonic cultural role and many English words and terms have entered into Greek through popular culture (song lyrics, film and television subtitles) or more recently the internet. Print culture

---

[12] The manifesto of the academics caused a good deal of debate in the press. See, for example, Babiniotis (2001), Haris (2001a), Liakos (2001a) and Xydakis (2001).

[13] The controversy also highlighted that foreign language teaching was a lucrative business in Greece, and Greeks were spending 152 billion drachmas a year for their children to learn English (*Ta Nea*, 20 November 2001).

continued to contribute to the linguistic convergence of Greek with English and other major European languages through the huge volume of translations into Greek in the fields of literature, law, administration, technology and commerce (especially since Greece joined the EEC/EU in 1981). It has been argued that the widespread contempt for the spoken language over the long period when the language question was being debated and the lack of confidence in modern Greek as an autonomous system 'has left Modern Greek fragile and vulnerable to the influence of languages that are perceived to be more modern, more prestigious or, in contemporary parlance, "smarter' or "cooler"' (Mackridge 2016: 475). Some see the Anglicization of the Greek language as an inevitable process of modernization, westernization and globalization, while others feel that loan words or phrases threaten the unique identity of the language and lead to a lamentable decline in the quality of contemporary Greek.[14] The regulation of language and the practice of 'verbal hygiene', to use Deborah Cameron's term, represent a symbolic attempt to impose order on the social world.

The supremacy of the Greek language was deemed to be threatened by the growing awareness of linguistic diversity and the existence of minorities in a territory thought to be linguistically unified. Until the 1930s the salient marker of Greek national identity was religious affiliation with language playing a smaller role. The concept of an Orthodox 'nation', derived from the Ottoman practice of dividing their subjects into *millets* (religious communities), was used to claim Orthodox non-Greek speakers for the new nation and raised obstacles to embracing Greek citizens who were Roman Catholics, let alone Jews or Muslims. The first constitution of Greece defined as Greeks those natives who believed in Christ, and the exchange of populations between Greece and Turkey in 1923 was on the basis of religion, not ethnicity or language. As Renée Hirschon pointed out, 'for a long period the Greek language was a less important factor than religion in defining national identity' (1999: 161). Though no Greek census after 1951 has included a question about language (see Chapter 4), since the early 1990s, due to the Macedonian question, linguistic minorities have received particular attention while language and national identity became ever more closely related. The European Bureau for Lesser-Used Languages (1982–2010) organized two visits to Greece in 1987 and 1990 and produced a report about linguistic minorities, including Turkish and Slav speakers, Pomaks, Aromanians (Vlachs) and Arvanites (a bilingual group who traditionally speak Arvanitika,

---

[14] They often try to replace English words with Greek neologisms (e.g. βραχυμηνύματα/twitter, αυτοφωτογράφηση/selfie) which, due to their pedestrian literalism, stand no chance of catching on.

a dialectal variant of Albanian).¹⁵ The greater visibility of linguistic minorities increased Greece's historical suspicion of its non-Greek speaking citizens. This suspicion has been exacerbated since 1991 with the discussion over the language of North Macedonia and whether it should be recognized as a genuine language (Macedonian) or as a Bulgarian dialect. In addition to patriotic speeches and protests, there were publications on ancient Macedonian Greek and the so-called 'language of Skopje' (Babiniotis 1992).

Part of this growing linguistic nationalism drew on the earlier myth that Greek narrowly missed becoming the language of the United States after the American declaration of independence in 1776 and theories about the uniqueness of the Greek language (the only one to have two words for life – ζωή and βίος – and love – αγάπη and έρωτας) or attempts to make it international. There is also a belief that all languages are crypto-Greek (with English having borrowed 41,615 of its 490,000 words from Greek).¹⁶ In 1985 the Organization for the Promotion of Greek Language was established with the aim of promoting Greek language and culture all over the world. In 1990 the organization started publishing a magazine called *Ελληνική Διεθνής Γλώσσα/Greek [an] International Language*, which since 2013 has been published online.¹⁷ There was also a growing interest in the promotion and teaching of Greek outside the country, dialects such as Greco in Southern Italy or Cypriot Greek.

To the old fears about the Greek language, new ones were added concerning the allegedly limited vocabulary of young people.¹⁸ In the 1985 national entrance exams to higher education, many students appeared not to understand two words: αρωγή (succour) and ευδοκίμηση (prosperity), causing national concern about young people's apparently poor vocabulary, which was attributed to the abolition of the teaching of ancient Greek in the first stage of secondary school (*gymnasio*). The apparent failure of the students to understand the meaning of two 'learned' words was treated as an alarming indicator of Greek teenagers' growing λεξιπενία (vocabulary deficiency). The prominence of this issue led the

---

[15] Attempts to revive *Arvanitika* were hampered by its speakers wanting to distance themselves from the Albanian immigrants, who had been arriving in Greece since the fall of the Communist regime in their country in 1991.

[16] The talks given in 1957 and 1959 by the leading economist and banker Xenophon Zolotas to the IMF and the World Bank in Washington, DC, using almost exclusively English words of Greek origin, are still mentioned proudly by a number of Greeks. They also take pride in the fact that the Greek word 'pandemic' had become the universal buzzword word in 2020.

[17] Since 2017 the Greek state has designated 9 February as International Greek Language Day which coincides with the commemoration of the death of the national poet Dionysios Solomos.

[18] Alexandra Patrikiou points out that 'after 1974, the focus of the public discussions regarding the language shifted towards the so-called decline of modern Greek' (2017: 112).

Minister of Education Antonis Tritsis to announce in 1986 the reintroduction of the compulsory teaching of ancient Greek to the *gymnasio*, that is starting from the age of twelve rather than fifteen. This decision split Greek linguists and educationalists into two camps with one side arguing for the unbroken continuity of the Greek language and the other claiming modern Greek was distinct from ancient Greek.[19] The reintroduction of ancient Greek at an early stage was intended to stop any further impoverishment, and in 1992 a textbook entitled *Η Ελληνική Γλώσσα μέσα από κείμενα Αρχαία, Βυζαντινά και Λόγια/The Greek Language through Ancient, Byzantine and Learned Texts* was introduced in schools.

The customary complaint of the Greeks that young people's vocabulary was deficient was reinforced by the spread of youth slang in the 1980s, also judged to be 'poor' or 'vulgar' and a symptom of a wider linguistic decay. As in other European countries, and following international trends, 'youth language' emerged as an umbrella term in Greece towards the end of the twentieth century to refer to the linguistic features that characterize the verbal behaviour of young people.[20] Youth slang is seen as an 'act of identity', demonstrating the speaker's affiliation to particular networks and youth subcultures. Borrowing English words and expressions morphologically assimilated, it also demonstrates an awareness of difference and a playful use of language for cryptic purposes.[21]

The campaign to 'depauperize' the vocabulary of young Greeks and to initiate them into the riches of 'older forms of Greek' could also be linked to attitudes towards intra-lingual translation, particularly of literary texts written in *katharevousa*. In 1997 Menis Koumandareas 'translated' Alexandros Papadiamantis's story Έρωτας στα χιόνια/Love in the snow' into demotic Greek and this provoked a debate about the purpose of such 'translations' and whether they indeed helped young readers to appreciate Greek fiction written in puristic Greek.[22] A few years later the translations into the demotic of Emmanuil Roidis's *Pope Joan* by Dimitris Kalokyris (2005), A. Papadiamantis's *The Murderess* by Yorgos Aristinos (2006) and Dionysios Solomos's *The Woman of Zaky[n]thos* by

---

[19] A leading Greek newspaper, *Eleftherotypia*, conducted a debate about the teaching of ancient Greek in secondary education by publishing a number of letters on a daily basis from 24 November 1986 to 1 June 1987 (Koutsou 2004).

[20] Iordanidou and Androutsopoulos (2001), Chambers (2003) and Romaine (1984).

[21] Samples of the youth slang of the 1980s and 1990s can be found in Katsikis and Spyropoulos (1999). In 1984 a conference on 'Youth and language' was organized in Athens by the Ministry of Youth and Sports.

[22] The translation was published in the newspaper *To Vima* (27 July 1997) and attracted responses (mostly negative) in the same newspaper from Yorgis Yatromanolakis (10 August 1997), Dimitris Nollas and Kostas Akrivos (31 August 1997) and Takis Theodoropoulos (*Ta Nea*, 22 August 1997).

Aris Maragkopoulos (2006) caused further controversies. A similar discussion was provoked by the decision of the Greek Church and its Holy Synod in September 2004 that passages from the New Testament in demotic translation should be read (in parallel with the original text) to congregations as part of a pilot scheme. It should be noted that the Greek Constitution (even in the revisions of 1986, 2001, 2008 and 2019) retained the clause (3.3) from the 1911 Constitution, which stipulates that an official intra-lingual translation of the 'holy texts' requires permission from the Church of Greece and the Ecumenical Patriarchate.[23] The central point of these debates concerns the accessibility of older texts to young or poorly educated people, whereas critics of these 'translations' argue that the stylistic richness of the texts and knowledge of earlier forms of Greek are lost.[24] This controversy is another version of the modernization debate between those who emphasize the importance of communicating the message of those texts to a wider audience and the proponents of their original spirit and style; the latter even argue that the abolition of the use of Latin in Catholic masses by the Vatican in 1965 did nothing to bring more people to the churches.

The theory of linguistic decline was linked with nationalist positions and cut across groups with different ideological orientations. A case in point was the former president of the Hellenic Republic (1985–90) Christos Sartzetakis, who became famous as a judge in the court case that dealt with the assassination of Grigoris Lambrakis, brought to the screen by Costa-Gavras in the film *Z*. He made constant references to the 'four-thousand-year unity' of the Greek language and expressed his concern about its decline. This concern led to TV programmes and quizzes on the Greek language on the state television (ERT) while most of the private TV channels set up during the same period had Latinized Greek names (MEGA, ALPHA) or foreign ones (STAR, SKAI).[25] The fear of Latinization increased calls for restrictions on the use of Latin characters in public signs. The fact that Greek is an *Abstand* language (i.e. radically different from all the languages spoken around it) is often treated as something precious (a 'national treasure') to the detriment of the practical needs of its users.

During the economic crisis the highly polarized discourses and their ethical dimensions were served by intricate linguistic realizations and rhetorical

---

[23] See differing views on this issue in the newspapers *To Vima* (12 September 2004) and *Ta Nea* (18 September 2004).
[24] Orthographic harmonization or printing classic literary texts in the monotonic system have also preoccupied scholars and publishers (Ricks 2009).
[25] The programme 'Omileite ellinika' (Do you speak Greek?) was shown from 1986 to 1989 with Liana Kanelli as its presenter and resumed in 2002–3 and again in 2008 with Maria Houkli as the new presenter.

mechanisms. For example, the junta metaphor of the 'plaster cast' ('the state is a patient in a plaster cast') resurfaced in the Greek press in statements such as 'Greece in IMF's plaster cast' and 'salaries in a plaster cast', while the medico-pharmacological rhetoric (e.g. Greek virus, contagion effect) in the foreign press received particular attention in the context of blame attribution. Some dictionaries even appeared that either explained economic terms related to the crisis (Varoufakis 2011b) or exposed linguistic engineering by recording the neologisms, euphemisms or the 'double language' invented during the crisis (ιδιωτικοποίηση/privatization replaced by αξιοποίηση/development or αποκρατικοποίηση/denationalization) (Vlastaris 2018). The discourse of the protagonists of the Greek crisis and the responses from political parties, protesters, social media and other social actors have been analysed using keyword analysis and lexical clusters (Goutsos and Hatzidaki 2017a and 2017b). Linguistic research focused on the 'sense making' mechanisms and the discursive construction of the crisis in order to unpack how it was enacted in discourse and negotiated in various micro contexts (Angouri and Wodak 2014; Bickes et al. 2014). We have come a long way from the politics of the language question to the politics of language use and its legitimization mechanisms.[26]

Conclusion

Since the official end of *diglossia* in 1976 the Greek language has been admired more as 'a national monument' than as an instrument of communication, while the tools for its study and use (dictionaries, grammars, electronic resources) have proliferated. Linguistic diversity (e.g. varieties of registers, the use of abundant loanwords, acknowledgment of minorities) may have gained momentum, but the number of books on the correct use of Greek has also increased. It seems that we have moved from the earlier polarization to linguistic hybridization, assisted by computer-mediated communication and 'glocalization' (Robertson 1995). This retreat from a rigid linguistic division between learned and popular forms has offered Greeks the opportunity to enjoy a rich stylistic repertoire, combining features of both demotic and *katharevousa*. As Peter

---

[26] By starting from the premise that identity is viewed as the effect (rather than the origin) of practices of signification and reformulating questions about gay and lesbian languages in terms of language and desire, linguists have, since the 1990s, developed a new field of inquiry focusing on sexuality (Cameron and Kulick 2003). On Greek language and sexuality, see Canakis, Kantsa and Yannakopoulos (2010).

Mackridge has pointed out 'Greek language debates no longer take the form of battles between the supporters of two varieties of Greek that are perceived to be in contrast but among people who promote different nuances within a unified language' (2009a: 334). However, it has been claimed that since 1976 there was no clear language policy on or vision of the role of Greek in the new globalized conditions of communication. In the absence of any policy, language protectionism by various interested parties has been allowed to grow, and Greek has been presented as being under constant threat from English, technology, various forms of slang or deficiencies in vocabulary that have been attributed at least in part to young Greeks no longer studying ancient Greek. Language issues became headline news, led to debates and petitions while the general public was regularly invited to join a crusade to 'save' Greek. We may have put the old *diglossia* behind us, but new questions about the state of the written and spoken language have arisen and different challenges have surfaced.

6

From poetry to prose: Discovering modernism and revising the canon

Literature as a commodity and the vicissitudes of poetry

Traditionally Greece has been a country of poetry and it was proud of its poets, who have given the country two Nobel Prizes (Seferis and Elytis) or, in the case of Cavafy, achieved a truly global reputation. Once poetry had been set to music, it helped popularize the genre and attracted crowds to the open-air concerts of the early years of the *Metapolitefsi*. During the dictatorship the relative lack of new fiction allowed poetry, and particularly song lyrics, to play a more visible role in resistance to the regime. There were three important discussions on Greek fiction during or just after the dictatorship and in all three there was broad agreement that the Greek novel lagged behind poetry (Beaton 1999: 275).[1] However, the close relationship between poetry and the public started to break down in the 1990s when readers and publishers turned their attention to fiction. Even in the previous decade leading poets had turned to prose, as, for example, Yannis Ritsos with his *Iconostasis of Anonymous Saints* (1982–6), while women poets such as Rhea Galanaki started writing novels (*The Life of Ismail Ferik Pasha*, 1989).

The emergence of new audiences and the increasing commercialization of the book market also contributed to this turn. The Greek book market grew to over 10,000 new titles a year for the first time in 2006, compared to 2,348 titles in 1987, while the number of literary books almost trebled, rising to 2,260 in 2007 from 728 in 1987, before starting to decline due to the crisis.[2] It was

---

[1] The three discussions are: Germanacos (1973), Argyriou et al. (1973), Argyriou et al. (1976/7).
[2] For more details, see the periodical *Ιχνευτής*, 8 (Spring–Summer 2004) and the following websites: http://ekebi.gr/appdata/documents/BookMarketInGreece2011-8.pdf, http://www.ekebi.gr/appdata/documents/vivlio2008.pdf. It should be noted that the data cited in *Ιχνευτής*, which refers to the 1980s, includes reprints and is not always reliable.

not just the number of books published that increased, but also the number of copies sold. For example, *Achilles' Fiancée* (1987), the first adult novel by Alki Zei, who had already achieved an international reputation for children's fiction, sold over one hundred thousand copies in its first three years in print. The words 'commercial' and 'market' shed their negative connotations and began to be acceptable in the literary arena (Kotzia 2009 and 2012: 381). The notions of 'literary' and 'bestselling' texts became blurred and at the same time were disentangled, particularly in the domain of the novel (see Chapter 1). Not having a tradition of well-crafted novels on which to rely, Greek writers felt more at home writing short stories and developed a respected tradition in that genre. But the commodification of the book market in the 1990s increased the demand for popular novels, and as a consequence the production of short stories declined, only to recover later on in the period of crisis.

During the same period more state funding became available for the promotion of Greek literature both at home and abroad either through special events or translations.[3] Communication between Greek writers and the rest of Europe increased due to Greek authors' participation in conferences or book fairs (e.g. Greece was the guest of honour at the Frankfurt book fair in 2001), the financing of translations into other languages and the general promotion of Greek literature abroad (Spyropoulou and Tsimpouki 2002). Greek writers became more outward-looking and familiar with the work of many foreign writers either in the original or through the increasing number of translations into Greek. Hence, the notion of national literature has gradually been eroded by the spread of popular global genres (e.g. noir, fantasy) and the emphasis on individual writers rather than on countries.

From the 1980s on and particularly during the 1990s the Greek novel was turned into a commodity and the logic of the bestseller entered the literary and critical discourse. Bestseller lists first appeared in magazines (*Diavazo*, January 1979) and later in newspapers. The desire to sell more copies and capture a larger audience dictated aesthetic compromises for some popular writers and encouraged titillating or melodramatic plots, eschewing narrative experimentation. Greek literature entered its commercial phase and this led to the upstaging of poetry and the short story by page-turner novels popular with women readers. Fiction also received more critical attention, judging from the

---

[3] It has already been pointed out that the funding for cultural activities and institutions has increased enormously since the 1970s and the situation cannot be compared to the earlier so-called 'culture of poverty' (Theodoropoulos et al. 2010: 217–21).

discussions in periodicals, the conferences on Greek prose[4] and the number of post-junta critics focusing more on fiction than poetry (D. Kourtovic, E. Kotzia, Y. Perantonakis, L. Pantaleon). It should be noted that, if we examine book production during the period (1999–2011), when reliable data exists, it will be seen that the number of poetry collections published occasionally exceed the novels (Table 1). This is often due to the fact that most of these poets paid to have their poems published.

In the 1990s it was not only poetry but also the notion of 'generation' that seemed to lose ground. With the exception of the well-established 'generation of the 1970s', the dominant genealogical pattern of literary periodization recedes and this suggests that the perception of developments in collective or evolutionary terms starts to be questioned, moving from a centripetal to a centrifugal understanding of cultural activity and from the linearity of succession to intertwined temporalities. The break-up of the generation pattern is another sign of the movement towards acknowledging diversity at the end of twentieth century. The fact that the term 'generation' becomes gradually obsolete is confirmed by Vasilis Amanatidis, a poet of the 1990s himself, who remarked, 'Particularly for the decade of the '90s in Greece it is indeed impossible to talk about a "generation", not only for lack of a common focus and a shared perspective among the younger poets ... but primarily because these poets seem to be few in number or, more generally, obscure' (2001: 49). In another anthology the same generation is described as 'αθέατη/invisible' (Kostavara 2002). Amanatidis concludes his essay by criticizing poetry for its 'complacent isolationism' compared to the other arts in Greece, which tend to be more outward-looking and communicate among themselves. Despite the use of poetry in public spaces, Greek poets lament its alienation from the general public and try to identify the stages in this separation from Romanticism to Modernism. In the context of the general devaluation of poetry, they ultimately blame the poets for this divorce and for turning an entertaining art form into a crossword puzzle (Koutsourelis 2013a and 2019). As Dimosthenis Kourtovik has argued 'poetry in Greece was shaken more than fiction by the collapse of grand collective myths and the weakening of tradition' (2002: 321).

Seeking a new orientation and a role for poetry, poets tended either to carve out an inner space for their work, thus marking a shift from a collective to a

---

[4] Epistimoniko Symposio (1997), Dimitroulia et al. (2009), *To Dentro* (60–1, March–April 1991 and 86–7, March–April 1995). Also, on 12–13 February 2014 the Etaireia Spoudon Scholis Moraiti organized a colloquium on the fiction of the *Metapolitefsi* and the public sphere.

Table 1 Numbers of novels and poetry collections published between 1999–2011

Greek novels (Source: Biblionet/EKEVI)													
1999	2000	2001	2002	2003	2004	2005	2006	2007	2008	2009	2010	2011
233	244	302	305	304	297	340	345	332	435	417	442	533
Greek poetry collections (Source: Biblionet/EKEVI)												
1999	2000	2001	2002	2003	2004	2005	2006	2007	2008	2009	2010	2011
230	235	286	285	306	347	313	330	390	441	495	539	553

private vision or demonstrated renewed anxiety about form.⁵ In an attempt to revitalize the faltering appeal of poetry and to reconnect with the wider public, some poets returned to traditional versification, abandoning free verse. Though metrical forms can be found in post-war poetry, it was in the early 1990s that poets tried to overcome the crisis of free verse by returning to metrical forms as a way of reinvigorating the enchantment of poetry.⁶ The manifesto of this return was a collection of three ballads, *Τριώδιον/Three-Way Crossroads* (1991), by the poets Dionysis Kapsalis, Yorgos Koropoulis and Ilias Lagios, which was followed two years later by another collection of 'poems and songs for one night', *Ανθοδέσμη/Bouquet* (1993), with the addition of a contribution from Michalis Ganas. This was a symbolic gesture intended to make traditional versification less of a taboo for young poets. Their example was followed by Orestis Alexakis (*Αγαθά παιγνίδια/Innocent Games*, 1994), Nasos Vayenas (*Σκοτεινές μπαλάντες/ Dark Ballads*, 2001) and much younger poets, such as Yannis Doukas, *Στα μέσα σύνορα/The Inner Borders* (2011) and *Το σύνδρομο Σταντάλ/Stendhal's Syndrome* (2013), or others publishing their poems online.⁷ Parody and satire also relied on metrical forms (e.g. Manolis Anagnostakis) and some leading non-Greek poets have been translated in verse (Ovid by Theodoros Papagelis (2000) and Calderon by Nikos Hatzopoulos (2003)). Was this playful experimentation, a reaction to poets being freed from any formal constraints or a defence of poetry against solipsism and its social devaluation by the proliferation of poetic idioms? At more or less the same time this trend can also be found in other countries, as the anthology edited by Philip Dacey and David Jauss, *Strong Measures: Contemporary American Poetry in Traditional Forms* (New York, 1986) suggests and the American poet Barton Sutter confirms with his statement that 'the most radical poem a poet can write today is a sonnet'. On the other hand, this new formalism has been seen as part of a wider trend involving the return to representation in painting and sculpture, narrative in historiography and a new humanism in classical studies (Koutsourelis 2008).

Interestingly, the return to traditional forms coincided with the publication of the journal *Ποίηση/Poetry* (1993), which, in an attempt to revitalize the Greek

---

⁵ The use of the term 'private vision' in relation to the poets of the 1980s caused a good deal of discussion. See Kefalas (1987), Kassos (1989) and Anagnostopoulos (1993).
⁶ At the same time scholars also showed renewed interest in metrical forms and their use by both earlier and contemporary poets. See Garantoudis (1991) and Vayenas (1991). Vayenas, in particular, argued for a 'metricalization' of free verse rather than a revival of the traditional versification (Vayenas 2001).
⁷ For an anthology of contemporary poetry in traditional forms visit https://pampalaionero.wordpress.com/about/.

poetic landscape, moved in the opposite direction by focusing on the translation of anglophone poetry and essays. This trend provoked a hostile reaction from a critic in her review of the twentieth issue of the journal, on the occasion of its tenth anniversary, for being too Anglocentric and not promoting earlier modern Greek poetry (Theodossopoulou 2003). In the 1990s poetry lost faith in its social mission due to the collapse of the leftist utopia following the fall of the Berlin Wall and was 'overshadowed by the Greek postmodern novel of the postcolonial condition' (Lambropoulos 2016a: 405 and 2016b).

With the arrival of the new millennium, poetry production showed signs of recovery, thanks (at least in part) to the internet enabling poets to publish online. New poetry magazines appeared in print (φρμκ (2013–), Τα Ποιητικά (2011–)) or online (poeticanet (2006–), e-poema (2006–), Lexima) alongside the continuation of long-established ones such as Ποίηση/Ποιητική, while the diversity of poetic voices made the notion of generation redundant. Translations of foreign poets (particularly women) and anthologies of poetry also proliferated.[8]

The crisis reignited international interest in Greek poetry, as is evinced by the two anthologies in English by Theodoros Chiotis, *Futures: Poetry of the Greek Crisis* (2015) and Karen van Dyck, *Austerity Measures: The New Greek Poetry* (2016) (on its reception see Chapter 10). Readers were keen to find out how the impact of political turmoil, social precarity and fiscal austerity might be conveyed through poetic idioms. Both anthologies, whose titles make allusions to the economy, include work by poets who, though not native Greeks, have some connections with Greece. Communication technologies, transnational conversations, performative poetry and intermedial experimentation have altered the cultural landscape and helped poetry make a significant comeback. As Vassilis Lambropoulos notes 'of all the arts, poetry has been identified as the most representative of the current national crisis. It constitutes the major cultural domain where the Greek emergency and/or exception are being negotiated' (2016a: 404). Poetry seems to have captured the crisis well, because it went through its own crisis and emerged with a sceptical mood known in political and literary theory as Left-Wing Melancholy. In short, the crisis made poetry relevant again in a rapidly changing world.[9]

---

[8] I mention here only the ones in English by Peter Bien et al. (2004) and Valaoritis and Maskaleris (2003) and in Greek by Garantoudis (2008), Papageorgiou and Hatzivasileiou (2007–13). It has to be acknowledged that the turn of the century contributed to the compilation of anthologies of works from the previous century. On the anthologies of work by young poets in the early twenty-first century, see Dimitroulia (2012: 404).

[9] The poet Panayotis Ioannidis has summed up recent developments in poetry thus: 'Since the 1960s, literature historians and critics have tended to assign a poetic "generation" to each decade: thus, there are poets of the 1960s, the 1970s, the 1980s. But in the 1990s, Greek poetry seems to have dropped

From political engagement to the crisis of representation

In discussions and essays on Greek fiction the word 'reality' features prominently. This was the case with the discussion in the periodical *Synechia* in 1973 and another one in the periodical *Diavazo* in 1976/7 where a consensus seems to emerge among the participants that novelists have a duty to portray the reality of their time and not to follow the writers of the 1930s, who turned their backs on the political realities or failed to grasp them. In the latter discussion, political engagement appears more important than the craft of fiction. Two years later in a brief article entitled 'The end of our small literature?', alluding to Dimitris Hatzis's collection of stories, Periklis Korovesis discussed the recently published novels by Aris Alexandrou, *Το κιβώτιο/The Mission Box* (1974), Stratis Tsirkas, *Χαμένη Άνοιξη/The Lost Spring* (1976), and Dimitris Hatzis, *Το Διπλό Βιβλίο/The Double Book* (1976). He concluded that only the first of these signalled 'a break with the traditional style of representation' and promised 'a new form of writing going against representation' (1978: 30). According to Korovesis, the novels of Hatzis and Tsirkas tend to identify fiction with realism, seeking verisimilitude and resembling a Madame Tussauds with characters like dummies. Making reference to the Russian formalists, he argued that literature is above all a linguistic creation and, therefore, realism, the emblematic style of the bourgeoisie, 'looks like an unburied corpse'. The discussion in *Diavazo* and the article by Korovesis set out the agenda of post-1974 fiction and mapped out the crossroads it had reached between sociopolitical awareness and self-referentiality. Since then, modernist self-referentiality seems to be increasingly displacing realism and politics in the critical approaches to fiction employed even by the older left-wing critics (Raftopoulos 1999).

Three writers (Maro Douka, Dimitris Nollas and Alexis Panselinos), all born in the 1940s and who started publishing in the 1970s and 1980s, seem to stand at the crossroads and have been seen as connecting the political orientation of the earlier fiction with the fragmentation, introversion and narrative sophistication of the post-junta period (Kotzia and Hatzivasileiou 2003: 188). The preoccupation with politics and reality in the early 1970s gradually gave way to the transcendence of reality and the emphasis on form (as demonstrated

---

off the radar: its centuries-old, traditionally unquestioned supremacy yielded for the first time to that of prose – and more specifically to the long and, more often than not, mainstream novel. Critics and readers focused back on poetry with the advent of the "crisis" in 2008. And it is this same "crisis" that seems to have re-kindled international interest in contemporary Greek poetry, with anthologies appearing in several languages' (http://und-athens.com/journal/und-poetry-2019).

in Thanassis Valtinos's essay 'Πέρα από την πραγματικότητα'/'Beyond reality' (1995/2009)), thus marking the epistemological shift in critical vocabulary from reality to modernity.

In discussions of post-junta fiction there seems to be a consensus that there are two dominant trends: increased introspection/self-absorption and archival poetics, involving explorations of the past through oral narratives, photographs, diaries, emails or other written material. It has been claimed that between these trends any engagement with the current social reality is missing, though this is partly covered by the revival of crime fiction (Dimitroulia et al. 2009: 51). It seems that 'social reality' is perceived in this case in a rather narrow and parochial way, ignoring the new issues, both global and Greek, tackled by post-junta fiction: gender and identity, migration and otherness, political violence and ecology. It has to be said that the crisis of representation in post-1974 fiction shifted the emphasis from social reality or experience to mediation. Authors no longer lay claim to the raw and authentic representation of their experience but rather tend to highlight how this experience is mediated and relativized through secondary (written or oral) devices and documents such as letters, personal accounts or newspaper extracts. Yet this increasing reliance on textual/documentary or archival evidence is contested by building up an illusion of realism and subsequently dispelling it through some metafictional strategy. Hence the proliferation of metafictional techniques in Greek fiction since the early 1990s entails the representation of reality being problematized and questioned. As I have argued elsewhere this produces a kind of documentary or archival metafiction where the boundaries between fiction and reality, history and invention are blurred (Tziovas 2004).

Another argument that claims post-junta writers, as compared to earlier generations, do not display any sense of collective vision or moral responsibility in relation to Greek society in their writings and instead give in to individualistic navel-gazing and focusing on issues of a personal or private nature requires careful rethinking (Kotzia 2000; Mackridge and Yannakakis 2004: 11). This opposition might be convenient, but it shows that critical approaches are still hostage to earlier expectations and do not seem capable of acknowledging that Greek society has become gradually more pluralistic, multicultural and diverse and therefore this is reflected in the fiction. Diversity inevitably thwarts any attempt to have collective missions or ideals. In an age of globalization, lifestyles and digital communication, it would be unusual not to expect individual responses and diverse handling of issues such as identity, gender, otherness and history. This diversity is also reflected in the language of fiction, which includes different kinds of discourse from idiolects and colloquialisms to journalistic clichés and foreign words.

The gradual transformation of Greek fiction since the fall of junta has gone through various stages. First we can see the erosion of the political by the subjective critical perspectives in some novels of the 1970s such as the *Mission Box* (1975) by Aris Alexandrou and *Αρχαία Σκουριά/Fool's Gold* (1979) by Maro Douka, then the erosion of the national by highlighting the Other and the suppressed or the critical revisiting of the historical past. This overlaps with an expansive transformation of the social by the emphasis on the cultural, the transnational or the cosmopolitan and the proliferation of women writers. Over the years there has been a gradual shift from the earlier political concerns to historical and cultural questions and this has meant shunning collective visions or social prescriptions. Fiction followed the transition in Greek society towards diversity and the creation of space for the inclusion of the Other more closely than poetry did. In this respect, the themes which have preoccupied fiction writers since the early 1990s can be classified under three broad and overlapping categories: identity and otherness, the historical past and the validity of its representation, and cultural metaphors and cosmopolitanism. I shall outline each category briefly below and list some illustrative examples.

The novels on identity and otherness deal with characters of complex ethnic or religious backgrounds such as the protagonist of Rhea Galanaki's *Ο Βίος του Ισμαήλ Φερίκ Πασά/The Life of Ismail Ferik Pasha* (1989). This narrative involves an encounter between the world of Crete, where Ismail was born a Christian, and that of Egypt, where he was taken captive and became Minister of War. Although Ismail finally returns to Crete where he dies, the novel contrasts these two worlds associated with different narrative modes, history and myth, and ponders on the ambiguities of ethnic and cultural identities. Another novel by Galanaki *Ελένη ή ο κανένας/Eleni, or Nobody* (1998), which follows the life of a minor female painter, Eleni Boukoura-Altamoura, who pretended to be a man in order to study painting in a foreign country, falls into the same category. In the same vein, Theodoros Grigoriadis's novel *Τα Νερά της Χερσονήσου/The Waters of the Peninsula* (1998) highlights the bonds among people in the Balkans of different religions and with different perspectives on life (British Orientalism, Greek patriotism and Muslim mysticism) at the beginning of the twentieth century and projects them into the present day as an antidote to war and violence. The increasing flow of migrants to Greece after 1989 and growing awareness about minorities increased the number of novels on otherness and identity. In this category the novels by Vasilis Gourogiannis, *Το ασημόχορτο* ανθίζει/*The Silver-Grass Is Blooming* (1992), Sotiris Dimitriou, Ν' ακούω καλά τ' όνομά σου/*May Your Name Be Blessed* (1993), Maro Douka, Αθώοι και Φταίχτες/ *Innocent and Guilty* (2004), and stories by Dimitris Nollas, Tilemachos Kotsias (born in Albania) and others could be included. Gender identity features in the novels of Angela Dimitrakaki such as Μέσα σ' ένα κορίτσι σαν κι εσένα/*Inside a Girl Like You* (2009), while Christos Oikonomou, focusing on working-class areas in his award-winning collection of stories Κάτι θα γίνει, θα δεις/*Something Will Happen, You'll See* (2010), 'was the first writer to highlight the Others of the economic crisis' (Chartoulari 2015: 67).

Novels with a historical theme, which do not aim to recreate the past, but rather to reinvent it and produce a more contemporary reading of it, belong in the second category. These novels challenged the modalities of historiography, the truth-seeking involvement with the past, and, in turn, questioned the grand national narratives promoted once upon a time through poetry. They blend an archival sense of history with the idea of its contestation and fabrication. A number of novels can be included in this category such as Yannis Panou, … *από το στόμα της παλιάς Remington* … /…*from the mouth of the old Remington* … (1981), Thanassis Valtinos, *Στοιχεία για τη δεκαετία του'60?/Data from the Decade of the Sixties* (1989), Michel Fais, *Αυτοβιογραφία ενός Βιβλίου/ Autobiography of a Book* (1994), Diamantis Axiotis, *Το ελάχιστον της ζωής του/The Least Measure of His Life* (1999), Dimosthenis Kourtovik, *Τι ζητούν οι βάρβαροι/What the Barbarians Are Asking for* (2008), Elena Houzouri, *Πατρίδα από βαμβάκι/Homeland Made Out of Cotton* (2009) and others which have been discussed in Chapter 3.[10] Maro Douka sums up in a note at the end of her novel *Ένας σκούφος από πορφύρα/Come Forth, King* (1995) the contemporary resonances of her Byzantine historiographic metafiction: 'So, having decided to write a book about the life and work of Alexios Komnenos, I was to write a book about our own time, by way of this present that keeps us and defines us.'

The third category (cultural metaphors and cosmopolitanism) also brings together novelists from different backgrounds but all reflecting on cultural identity and sharing some common features. Their narratives take place (partly or entirely) outside Greece, involve travel or migration and non-Greek characters. I mention here some examples, which could easily form part of the first or the second category. In his novel *Ζαΐδα ή Η καμήλα στα χιόνια/Zaida or The Camel in the Snow* (1996), Alexis Panselinos recounts the visit of a Viennese musician

---

[10] This category could also include writers (e.g. Stavros Kritiotis) who embark on playful inquiries into textual archives and intertextual constructions.

to Greek lands where he meets an exiled poet and revolutionary from Lefkada. The implicit association of the musician with Mozart and the poet with the Greek poet Dionysios Solomos (1798–1857) points to the allegorical character of the novel and suggests a dialogue between East and West. Setting the novel in the period when Greece was about to emerge as an independent nation state, Panselinos turns the novel into a cultural metaphor, with the Viennese musician trying to graft elements from the local music onto his own, thus highlighting the role of music in articulating tensions in European culture. Nikos Themelis in his *Η Ανατροπή/The Overthrow* (2000) fictionalizes Greeks' migratory tendencies and highlights the porous ethnic, linguistic and commercial boundaries in south-east Europe prior to the twentieth century. Mimika Kranaki (*Φιλέλληνες/ Philhellenes* 1992) and Vasilis Alexakis (*Η Μητρική Γλώσσα/Mother Tongue*, 1995 and *Οι Ξένες Λέξεις/Foreign Words*, 2003) thematize the cultural adjustment and identity problems of Greeks living in France, while a number of such novels by other novelists (Soti Triantafyllou, Yiannis Kiourtsakis, Michalis Modinos, Christos Chrysopoulos, Christos Asteriou) also take place outside Greece.[11] These novels point to the increasing centrality of space, the growing role of technology, the increased circulation of ideas and fluidity of identities as a result of the interaction between global and local, home and abroad. The tapestry of the post-junta novel is further enriched by other kinds of narrative deploying parody, fantasy, noir, mathematics or graphics and an increasing emphasis on the architectonics of writing and the hybridization of genres (Hatzivasileiou 2018).

From tradition to canons: (Post)modernism and critical discourse

Without ignoring linguistic or ideological differences, Greek critics and writers over the years have emphasized the organic coherence of the Greek literary tradition, while the concept of the canon (despite the Greek provenance of the word) was absent from the Greek critical discourse. The notion of tradition highlights continuity and treats the past as monumental or even unchanged, whereas the canon relies on selection and hierarchy. Tradition is presented as something natural and non-ideological while the canon is seen as constructed

---

[11] A number of Greek prose writers live outside Greece (Eleni Yannakakis, Angela Dimitrakaki, Dimitra Kolliakou) or write their fiction in English (Panos Karnezis).

and prone to revision (Tziovas 2014c: 201–15).[12] The singularity of tradition is often contrasted with the potential multiplicity of canons. Notwithstanding the series entitled *Our Prose Tradition* (Nefeli), published from 1987 to the present day, the notion of the canon has been introduced into the Greek critical vocabulary in the last thirty years or so as a result of growing familiarity with critical theory, the general trend in Greek society towards diversity and changing attitudes to language.

The settlement of the language question in 1976 (see Chapter 5) led to a reassessment of some forgotten nineteenth-century novels written in puristic Greek and their connections with European literary trends such as the picaresque (e.g. Grigorios Palaiologos, *Πολυπαθής/The Polypath* (1939)). There was also a revival of the nineteenth-century fiction of Alexandros Papadiamantis, Emmanouil Roidis and Yeorgios Vizyinos. All of them were reprinted (sometimes more than once) and re-evaluated from the 1980s onwards. In the area of poetry avant-garde trends together with the settlement of the language question brought to the fore the surrealists (particularly Andreas Empeirikos and Nikos Engonopoulos) and the literary resistance to the demotic (Vayenas 1999). Their poems and other texts have been reprinted from the 1970s onwards and have enjoyed popularity and scholarly attention. Andreas Empeirikos's voluminous erotic novel *Ο Μέγας Ανατολικός/The Great Eastern* was published posthumously in 1991–2 and is set on a transatlantic liner in the Victorian era. In this novel, written in *katharevousa*, 'a significant amount of humour is generated by the incongruity between the traditionally straitlaced and euphemistic nature of *katharévousa* and the explicit nature of the sexual descriptions' (Mackridge 2009a: 323). It has to be said that the language aspect, which contributed to the obscurity of a number of nineteenth-century narrative texts, has resurfaced in a different form and encouraged the rehabilitation of stylistically unconventional twentieth-century texts (e.g. Yannis Skarimbas's novels, surrealist poems).

The official recognition of the Communist Party and the rehabilitation of the Left after the restoration of democracy helped Yannis Ritsos and other left-wing poets take centre stage. Their approach was no longer exclusively ideological or political but their use of myth has been highlighted (Ritsos) and the existential aspects of their poetry were pronounced (Anagnostakis). Also, the popularity of reception theory in Greece made critics and readers more aware of how a writer's reputation was built up or changed. On the other hand, the increase in

---

[12] The Greek translation of Harold Bloom's *The Western Canon* (1994) generated discussion (because it does not include any Greek writers) and suggestions for a Greek canon.

the number of books being published before the crisis required publishers and editors to be more selective and justify any reprinting of forgotten texts.

New texts and writers may have been rediscovered by and for different audiences (women, queer, (post)modernist, diaspora and non-Greek scholars), but this has not led to canon wars, as in other countries, but rather to an expansion of the literary tradition (and to including Greek Cypriot literature). This might be due to the way literature is taught in Greek schools (i.e. using comprehensive anthologies of extracts rather than a selection of a few whole novels or poems). Despite its increasing social diversity, Greece lacked an imperial past and therefore writers and readers with diverse racial or religious backgrounds who could claim Greek heritage. Instead, the growing anti-realist tendencies of the Greek critics and their fascination with literary modernity coupled with anxiety about belatedness played an instrumental role in reshaping the Greek literary and critical landscape.

Following the death of leading critics such as Vasos Varikas (1912–1971), Aimilios Chourmouzios (1904–1973) and Yannis Chatzinis (1900–1975) and the withdrawal after the fall of the junta of Antreas Karantonis (1910–1982) as one of its alleged supporters, by the mid-1970s a space had opened up for younger left-wing critics such as Alexandros Argyriou (1921–2009), Spyros Tsaknias (1929–1999), Dimitris Maronitis (1929–2016), Alexis Ziras (1945–) and others to dominate the field of literary criticism. Though they adopted an approach, highlighting the interaction between literature and society, their critical discourse was rather idiosyncratic or dated and this is partly evinced by the absence of the concept of 'modernism' from their vocabulary. Critics and scholars used terms such as 'πρωτοπορία' (not, however, in the sense of European avant-garde) or 'ανανέωση' (renewal) without defining them adequately or making explicit references to international movements. Even Mario Vitti in his influential study on the Generation of the 1930s in 1977 does not have a chapter on modernism. In his 1996 article on modernism in Greek literature, Alexandros Argyriou blends a historical review of futurism, dadaism and surrealism with modernism without displaying a sound grasp of the latter. For example, he does not make any reference to Greek modernist fiction writers with the exception of the novels by Melpo Axioti, whom he described as a surrealist rather than a modernist (1996: 267). He acknowledged that the term 'modernism' had recently been introduced by young scholars, who had studied outside Greece, but seemed to prefer the term 'νεοτερικός', pointing to renewal and reform, and first used by Daniel Philippidis and Grigorios Konstantas in their book Γεωγραφία Νεωτερική/*Modern Geography* (1791).[13] Interestingly, the term 'ηθογραφία', used above all for nineteenth- and early-twentieth-century fiction, is still deployed to refer to the contemporary 'anti-modernist' mode of writing (Yannopoulou and Tramboulis 2012–13).

The concept of 'modernism' in its Anglo-Saxon sense gradually started to be introduced into Greek criticism and two edited volumes in English were instrumental in this respect (Layoun 1990 and Tziovas 1997). This could be seen in the context of a growing realignment with western literary and critical terms, and as a result of the development of courses on comparative literature, critical theory and translation in Greek universities with academics starting to renew their critical approaches and be more involved in studying current literary production. Following the student revolt in 1973 and the proliferation of universities in Greece after the junta, academics began to have an increasingly high-profile role, assuming institutional positions or enjoying the status of public intellectuals and maintaining regular columns in newspapers. Increased visibility of academics is one of the features of the culture of the *Metapolitefsi*.

Until the 1980s scholars with French academic training and intellectual pedigree dominated Greek academic and cultural life, while Greek intellectuals living in France and writing in French such as Nicos Poulantzas (1936–1979), Cornelius Castoriadis (1922–1997) and Kostas Axelos (1924–2010) enjoyed considerable popularity. French structuralism and semiotics found followers among Greek academics and the Greek Semiotic Society was established in 1978. Yet from the 1980s onwards the paradigm began to change and academics with an Anglo-Saxon education started to challenge the Greek critical discourse. Academics from the anglophone world once again raised the issue of modernization in the literary field by presenting Greece as not 'modern enough' to participate in western literary or cultural developments due to the lack of a significant modernist or avant-garde movement.

In 1987 Gregory Jusdanis examined the possibility of postmodernism in Greece and argued that 'if modernism did not establish itself securely, a postmodernism would probably not arise as a reaction to it' (1987: 71). According to him the appearance of postmodernism presupposed the existence of high modernism (against which it reacted) and a distinction between high and popular art. Our assumptions, he argued, about literature, art, modernism, the avant-garde and postmodernism, do not necessarily hold true for Greece. As

---

[13] The term 'neoteriki' (modern) poetry is also used in the anthology edited by Alexandros Argyriou (1979).

long as modernism and the avant-garde developed along different pathways and Greek culture had not bifurcated into high and low, the necessary conditions for the emergence of postmodernism were not in place.

A year later Vassilis Lambropoulos compared two texts, one of Greek and one of non-Greek fiction (Renos Apostolidis's 'Ο Γιάννης της ζωής μου/The John of my life' and Italo Calvino's *Se una notte d'inverno un viaggiatore/If on a Winter's Night a Traveller*) to show that what made Greek postmodernism so paradoxical was the lack of a modernist tradition and of an avant-gardist understanding of literature (1988: 139). For him the tradition of twentieth-century Greek literature has been fiercely anti-modernist and this makes postmodernism 'the impossible paradox of contemporary Greek literature – a deviation, an aberration, a scandal' (1988: 156). As in the modernization debate, the approach here was Eurocentric and aimed to expose absences or belated developments. Treated as an indigenous or even ethnocentric project, Greek modernism has been caught up in the discussions about Greek identity through its identification with the so-called Generation of the 1930s, perceived by some as modernist or European-oriented and by others as Hellenocentric or as having reinvented Greekness. Thus, Greek modernism became part of an identity and cultural debate during the post-junta period rather than part of a western aesthetic movement (Vayenas 1997; Vayenas et al. 1997; Tziovas 2011).

There was also an attempt to reread earlier Greek fiction from a modernist perspective and this has led to the reassessment of writers such as Melpo Axioti, Yannis Skarimbas, Nikos Gavriil Pentzikis, Yannis Beratis, Nikos Kachtitsis and Dimosthenis Voutyras during the post-junta period.[14] Their texts have been reprinted and formed an alternative modernist canon, upstaging the writers of the 1930s (such as Myrivilis, Terzakis, and Theotokas), who managed to retain some of their past popularity by their novels being serialized on television (a new phenomenon beginning in the last quarter of the twentieth century as discussed in Chapter 7). Of the old guard only Kosmas Politis, treated as a cosmopolitan modernist, survived unscathed (Kallinis 2001) and to some extent M. Karagatsis with his *Ο Κίτρινος Φάκελλος/The Yellow File* (1956). Nicolas Kalas also received special attention as an eccentric diasporic and avant-garde writer.

The effort to create a modernist or even a (post)modernist canon extended to cover nineteenth-century and even earlier writing, as the anthologies by Yorgos

---

[14] Skarimbas's *Mariambas* (1935) has also been described as 'precociously postmodern' and N. G. Pentzikis's novel *Το μυθιστόρημα της κυρίας Έρσης/The Novel of Mrs Ersi* (1966) as heralding postmodernism in Greece (Papargyriou 2011: 72, 93).

Aristinos, *Narcissus and Janus* (2007) and Kostas Voulgaris on Greek metafiction (2017) suggest. Aristinos compiled an anthology of seventy-two writers, going as far back as the *Anonymous of 1789* and Dionysios Solomos (1798–1857), describing their prose as νεωτερική (which could be rendered both as modern and (post)modern).[15] It seems that he was not just trying to construct a canon of modernist texts but to include all those resisting realistic representation. The same applies to Voulgaris's book which, though it concentrates for the most part on post-1974 (post)modernist texts, goes back to the nineteenth century and beyond. The desire to construct a genealogy of a (post)modernist Greek tradition is evident in both projects. We have gone from having no concept of modernism in the 1970s, to considering many post-1974 writers as modernists or even postmodernists (Dimitroulia et al. 2009: 64), while younger writers have been keen to flaunt their elaborate narrative constructions and allusions to foreign literature (Hatzivasileiou 2018).

Whereas modernism maintained the distinction between 'high' and 'low' culture, postmodernism questioned, hybridized or parodied such a distinction. It problematized the relationship between 'facts' and fiction and forced writers and readers to confront the ways in which the past can be known. By exploding the notion of an 'objective truth', postmodernism 'denaturalizes' history in the form of historiographic metafiction (Hutcheon 1988 and 2003). Since until recently in Greece the distinction between elitist and popular culture has not been very pronounced (see Chapter 1), the impact of postmodernism has been primarily on the 'rewriting' of history and challenging the essentialism of the national identity. In this respect the role of fiction has been instrumental, as the case of the writer Thanassis Valtinos demonstrates.

In January 2014 the online magazine bookpress.gr and the bookshop Politeia invited 120 writers to vote for the best one hundred books in Greek literature of the last two centuries (1813–2013).[16] Of the sixty writers on the list, only Valtinos and Nikos Kazantzakis had four books cited while the poets George Seferis and Odysseas Elytis had a similar number but their individual collections overlapped with their collected poems. What does it take to make Valtinos the most popular living writer of Greece and the *Metapolitefsi*? I think it is the combination of postmodern relativity with the seeming objectivity of his disparate documentary material (oral accounts, extracts from newspapers or radio programmes,

---

[15] Critics have treated it as a modernist anthology (Elisavet Kotzia, *I Kathimerini*, 21 October 2007 and Vangelis Hatzivasileiou, *Eleftherotypia*, 14 March 2008).

[16] For more details, see https://www.bookpress.gr/politismos/teleutaia-nea/ 100-kalitera-vivlia-apotelesmata.

sound recordings); in other words, his exploration of historical periods and events from various perspectives and his deceptive archival poetics, which spawned a number of followers. He allows readers to synthesize his fragmented narratives and construct their own meanings. Despite the reservations of Greek intellectuals, who argue that postmodernism promotes an 'anything goes' approach, Valtinos's reputation owes a good deal to postmodern negotiation of historical events and other narrative material. The solidity of the past and our inability to 'know' it through objective and verifiable sources is questioned in his fiction by bringing together documentation and self-doubt, an anxiety about history and a preoccupation with language and form. An engagement with the past and the relativity of historical understanding, rather than endless irony, playfulness or fusion of styles, has been the hallmark of Greek postmodernism and explains the popularity of Valtinos in Greece.

Postmodernism in Greece allowed the exploration of alternative choices as to how Greek identity is constructed and provided strategies for negotiating narratives, histories and myths. Awareness of metafictional techniques also offered Greek writers ways to speak about the crisis by making connections between the present and the past. A characteristic example is Sophia Nikolaidou's novel *Χορεύουν οι Ελέφαντες* (2012) (translated into English with the title *The Scapegoat*, 2015), which moves back and forth between the time of the economic crisis and that of the Greek Civil War, and more specifically the murder of the American journalist George Polk in 1948, signalling the start of the Cold War. What links the two periods is the sense that Greek people have been powerless and their lives have been determined elsewhere, somewhere higher up, as the Greek title of the novel suggests.[17] Greek postmodernism is not so much a critique of western capitalism and its cultural hegemony as a questioning of ethnocentrism and the discourse of exceptionalism.

Conclusion

During the post-junta period there was a pendulum-like swing between the relative popularity of poetry and prose, with prose predominating in the 1990s and early 2000s, due to the commodification of literature, and poetry showing signs of recovery just before the onset of and during the crisis. After

---

[17] The title uses the first words of a Greek saying which can be roughly translated as 'The mighty call the tune and the little man pays for it'.

its 'painful transition to politicization', to recall the title of the 1976/7 discussion mentioned earlier, Greek fiction moved to new territories, opened up by the crisis of representation, documentary metafiction and its preoccupation with the increasing diversity of Greek society. The illusion of realist transparency was irrevocably lost and novels became opaque, multilayered and multivocal, thus resolving the tension between experimental writing and storytelling, literary and popular fiction. The fictionalization of the past redefined and shaped historiographic and public agendas by adopting a bottom-up approach (private archives and oral testimonies) and challenging hegemonic versions of history. The years between the fall of the junta and the crisis could also be described as a period of fascination with modernity and of the transition from the holistic notion of a literary tradition to the construction of an eclectic canon along (post) modernist lines. It is a period of divergent aesthetic visions, with no literary or critical manifestos.

7

The challenges of deregulation: From monophonic to polyphonic media

Comparing international media systems and trying to classify them, Daniel Hallin and Paolo Mancini propose three models: the Liberal Model, which prevails across North America, Britain and Ireland; the Democratic Corporatist Model dominant in northern continental Europe; and the Polarized Pluralist Model of the Mediterranean countries of Southern Europe. The first model is characterized by the relative dominance of market mechanisms and commercial media, strong development of print media and journalistic professionalism, and weak government intervention; the second by the historical coexistence of commercial media and media tied to organized social and political groups, with the state playing a relatively active but legally limited role; while the third model is characterized by integration of the media into party politics, late development of commercial media, intense and antagonistic political pluralism, weak professionalism and the state playing a dominant role (2004: 11). Hallin and Mancini see Greece as an example of their third model, though they caution that these models are ideal types, neither static nor homogenous, with the media systems of individual countries only approximately conforming to them while differentiation between nations is ever diminishing.

The centrality of the state in the Mediterranean media has limited the latter's capacity to play the 'watchdog' role or practise the investigative reporting so widely valued in the prevailing liberal media theory. The existence of a strong tradition of regarding the media as a means of ideological expression and of being involved in the political conflicts that mark the history of Mediterranean countries often leads to their instrumentalization by the state, political parties or tycoons with political aspirations. Yet, the impact of globalization and the common legal framework of the EU on media systems may mitigate this sort of instrumentalization and weaken the close relationship between the media and domestic politics (Harcourt 2002). As the media are changing under the impact of globalization and digital technology, the main question to be addressed in this chapter is whether commercialization leads to independent media and cultural diversity.

From state monopoly to broadcasting deregulation

Since the fall of the junta, the press and the media have undergone major changes, followed by the rapid and haphazard deregulation of Greek broadcasting in the 1990s. More than any other area, Greece's communications sector has been transformed and expanded exponentially from two state TV channels to an overcrowded and, until recently, unregulated media universe with 135 private TV channels, 890 private radio stations, 23 national and 135 local newspapers as well as 800 magazines (Papathanassopoulos 2010: 222). Compared to other European countries, the advent of television in Greece was significantly delayed due to bickering in the 1950s and early 1960s as to whether the country could afford it and whether its development should be a state initiative or privately financed, involving foreign companies or broadcasting corporations (Tsimas 2014). Partly due to the fear of propaganda from neighbouring countries to the north, who had television networks up and running earlier than Greece, television was often treated as a threat, and even importing television sets into the country required special permission. Eventually the setting up of a television network coincided with the dynamic 1960s and the growing industrialization and urbanization of the country. Promoting a more introvert entertainment pattern, television had to compete with cinema, which was very popular in the 1960s (around six hundred cinemas in Athens alone) and the powerful press lobby. Modernization theories have also been applied to the discussion of the Greek mediascape, with the country, like other Southern European states, considered to have entered 'modernity' late and the Greek media, particularly television, was seen as having delayed this process.

Greece's troubled political history ensured that Greek broadcasting came under state rather than public control. Coincidentally radio and television each took their first steps in the 1930s under the Metaxas dictatorship and the 1960s under the colonels respectively so that both were regarded as 'arms of the state' thereafter (Alivizatos 1986; Vovou 2010). What differentiates the history of broadcasting in Greece from other Western European countries is that radio and television emerged and were formed under authoritarian regimes. The armed forces also played a crucial role in the early stages of the development of Greek television. Since 1951 they had been allowed to operate radio and television stations to boost the nation's morale in wartime and this legal framework provided the ground for the armed forces to operate their own station (Armed Forces Information Services (YENED), formed in November 1970). Greece was the only European country to allow the army to operate its own radio and television network in peace time, without any government or parliamentary control, and hence the military regime (1967–74) could not ignore a medium with such mass appeal and completely under its control. This unique set of circumstances in the recent history of European broadcasting ceased to exist in 1982 when YENED came under civilian control and was renamed ERT 2.

Television in Greece developed slowly and experimentally in the 1960s and the first station started broadcasting on 23 February 1966. In 1970 the National Foundation of Radio and Television (EIRT), which operated the first nationwide television channel, was set up, and in 1975 it was turned into a state-controlled company called Greek Radio and Television (ERT).[1] The history of television in Greece involves three phases: the experimental (1960–6), the state monopoly (1967–89) and the deregulated period (1989–). From 1969 to 1974 the number of television sets in Greece increased eight times (eight hundred thousand) along with the percentage of households owning a set (81 sets per 1,000 people) and in 1988 these figures more than doubled (1,950,000 sets or 194 sets per 1,000 people) (Paschalidis 2005: 176, 179).

The main issue in the early post-junta period was the emancipation of Greek television from government control and this was the focus of the first Greek conference on Radio and Television (Athens, 6–10 June 1983). Even the 1975 constitution stated that 'radio and television will be under the direct control of the state', which did not necessarily mean a 'state monopoly'.[2] The fact that the state was the sole agent of broadcasting was justified on the grounds that there was limited availability of radio frequencies and that the state needed to provide full coverage in remote islands or mountain villages. Therefore, the state became the sole broadcasting provider and established a kind of monopoly. It has also been posited that the absence of civil society and the lack of self-regulation allowed the state to have a strong interventionist role in the media (Papathanassopoulos 1997: 352–3). And this tight and paternalistic state control

---

[1] Colour television in Greece was introduced in 1979 and now all Greek newspapers have colour on most of their pages.
[2] The first post-junta government of Konstantinos Karamanlis invited Sir Hugh Greene to make a feasibility study on the structure of Greek broadcasting but his proposals (modelled on the BBC) were not adopted.

led to even the most capable executives at the state broadcaster (ERT) having only a brief period in office.[3]

The growth of television meant, among other things, the appearance of television reviewers. In 1975 the newspapers *I Kathimerini* and *Ta Nea* introduced television reviews with Minas Christidis and Maria Papadopoulou, respectively, followed by Christos Vakalopoulos writing in the newspaper *Avgi* (March 1976–August 1977), whose approach was a combination of Althusserian Marxism, Lacanian psychoanalysis and influences from the leading English journal *Screen*. The study of the ideological mechanisms and the manipulation of the media, following Althusser's theory, was succeeded in the 1980s by a focus on the audiences, the reception of popular programmes and the role of television in everyday life (Paschalidis 2018).

The 1980s was the era of broadcasting deregulation in many European countries and therefore the deregulation of the media in Greece was due to EU regulations as well as to global developments. When, for example, the Greek Broadcasting Corporation (ERT) took the mayor of Thessaloniki to court for illegally operating a TV station, the court ruled that a state media monopoly was against the Treaty of Rome. This triggered radio deregulation and after the municipal elections of 1986 the mayors of Athens, Thessaloniki and Piraeus launched their own radio stations (Athens 98.4 FM, Kanali 1 FM and Thessaloniki 100). Their example was swiftly followed by other cities. The following year, Law 1730 allowed the proliferation of radio stations, stating that they could be owned either by local authorities or by companies with Greek citizens as shareholders. Hence, Greece ended up with three categories of radio stations: state owned, municipal and private.

In November 1989, private TV stations were allowed to operate (Law 1860) and as a result the broadcasting landscape altered radically. The race was led by the MEGA Channel, owned by a group of powerful publishers and entrepreneurs, followed by Antenna TV, owned by a shipowner. At the same time a regulatory body, the National Council for Radio and Television/Εθνικό Συμβούλιο Ραδιοτηλεόρασης (NCRT/ESR), was set up to oversee the industry, though it remained inactive for some years. The emergence of commercial broadcasting, as noted by Papathanassopoulos (2010: 225), was disastrous for ERT in terms of ratings and the decline in advertising revenues. In the meantime, industrialists with interests in shipping, construction and the oil industry became powerful

---

[3] Between 1981 and 1989, ERT had thirteen chairmen and director generals and sixteen news directors with an average term of about eight months each.

media magnates and used their media presence for political ends. The fact that the motives of the new TV magnates were political rather than commercial inevitably raised questions about media ownership.

The speed with which private broadcasters moved into the media arena was remarkable, while politicians seemed unwilling or unable, until recently, to establish order in an overcrowded sector. The incestuous relationship between media and politics was challenged by the shift away from political parties towards the media consumer. The consumer-driven mediascape opened up new opportunities and focused attention on new generic audiences outside the political arena (Paraschos 1995: 263). Since deregulation Greek television output has been dominated by entertainment programmes such as sitcoms, soap operas, game or talent shows as well as movies. Fierce rivalry for viewers and advertising revenues turned Greek television into a highly competitive market and led to a decline in audience numbers for ERT.

Until 1989 the debate centred around government control of the media and the disappointing quality of the programmes on public television. After 1989 the debate shifted to the issue of private television; in no other European country with a mixed system of public and private broadcasting was there such a spectacular shift of the audience from public to private television channels as in Greece (Paschalidis 2018: 28). The study of Greek television up to 1989 has been mainly about exploring its role as a propaganda tool and its relationship with political power. Greater emphasis has been placed on the coding of the 'hegemonic ideology' than on its decoding by audiences. With the end of the state monopoly in broadcasting, the focus was on private television as an *éminence grise*, thus completing the political story of Greek television (Tsimas 2014). Also, three-quarters of the books published in the period 1974–98 on the subject of television were printed in the 1990s, though, compared to other areas, the number of studies that were translations from other languages was rather limited. It should be noted that it was only in 1991 that the influential book by Marshall McLuhan *Understanding Media: The Extensions of Man* (1964) was translated into Greek.

In the years 1991–2 three University Departments of Media Studies were launched, at Athens, Thessaloniki and Panteion universities, and in July 1994, the government decided to establish a Ministry for Press and Mass Media, a sign of the growing importance of the media in Greek political and cultural life.[4] Since the mid-1990s there have been attempts by the Greek state to regulate

---

[4] For a review of academic research into Greek television, see Aitaki (2018a).

the media sector and bring it into line with the EU's regulations regarding advertising time, programme quotas and media ownership. The government also permitted ERT to rebroadcast satellite channels such as CNN, Euronews, TV5 Europe and others, thus connecting Greek audiences with American and European programmes. It was also decided that all digital television services in Greece had to use the same national digital platform.

Thanks to substantial increases in TV advertising revenues, both the number of imported TV programmes and domestic production soared. Pluralism and polyphony, a consequence of media deregulation, did not result in quality and wide-ranging programmes but in greater emphasis on entertainment provided by importing popular serials from other countries. Deregulation and commercialization of Greek television have also led to changes in the format of television news with the pace becoming faster and each story being accompanied by video images. More emphasis has also been given to ordinary people speaking about their personal problems, shifting the agenda from official statements to vox pops. Yet the main preoccupation of news bulletins has been to achieve high ratings and as a consequence live coverage and sensationalism have increased.[5] Commercial television promoted infotainment (with soap operas being repeated – sometimes more than once – only a few years after their first airing) and as a result the number of educational and documentary programmes declined. In October 1994, FilmNet, the first pay TV service in Greece was launched, while ERT and Antenna TV developed satellite programmes aimed at diaspora Greeks.[6] The emergence of commercial television meant that the audience for the public ERT plummeted and in October 1997 public television was relaunched in order to attract larger audiences. Its new profile included ET1, an entertainment channel, NET, an information-led channel, while ET3, based in Thessaloniki, remained a regional and culture-led channel.

Since 1989, the broadcasting regulatory framework has been ad hoc and the main TV channels have been operating with temporary licences provided by the Greek Parliament and extended either by law or by ministerial decisions. The deregulation of Greek television had led to an unregulated mediascape; private channels operated without permanent licences and this had an impact on their transparency and impartiality. The absence of regulations and licences also allowed political parties like LAOS and the Communist Party to have their own

---

[5] Mirca Madianou argues that 'news broadcasts are very popular in Greece and this is reflected in their proportion in the overall television programme' (2005: 51).
[6] For the role of the Greek media in the construction of identities or the promotion of nationalism, see Kontochristou (2007) and Demertzis, Papathanassopoulos and Armenakis (1999).

television stations. Since 1990 the Church had also been planning to set up its own television station, but it never materialized. Yet it entered the media world with a bang when Christodoulos became Archbishop of Athens and all Greece and the media exploited his charismatic personality.[7]

In autumn 2015, the Greek parliament approved a new media bill to sort out the licensing anomaly, but after an unsuccessful attempt to convene the National Council for Radio and Television (NCRT/ESR), it was stipulated that Parliament would decide on the number of licences to be issued. In 2016 the governmental majority limited the number of these licences to four, a decision that raised questions about pluralism in the media. The restricting of the TV licenses to four (while eight national private TV channels were then operating in the country) was justified on the basis of financial sustainability and the need to avoid back scratching between politicians and TV proprietors.

Intervening in this dispute, the European Commissioner for Digital Economy and Society indicated that the TV licensing procedure in Greece violated EU legislation on media pluralism and press freedom. After much debate, the outcome of a government-organized auction for TV licences in 2016 was annulled by the supreme administrative Greek court (the Council of State), which ruled that the controversial television licensing law was against the Greek constitution and that NCRT/ESR must oversee the competition. Indeed in 2018 NCRT/ESR selected five licence holders (the television channels Epilson TV, SKAI, ANT1, Alpha TV and Star) in a tender process, and they were ordered to pay the licence fee in ten instalments (Valoukos 2018). This meant that MEGA, one of the most popular channels and the first private channel to broadcast in Greece, went off air and out of business (though it reopened under new management in 2020). Thus, Greek television moved from state monopoly to deregulation and finally to a new kind of regulation.[8] Yet on-demand services and changing viewing habits among young people has put public service broadcasting in many countries (including Greece) under pressure and brought media consumption to a critical juncture by challenging the celebrity culture.

---

[7] On the presence of the Greek Church in the media and how some local bishops managed to operate or support their own stations, see Vlasidis and Karekla (2018).
[8] In July 2003, 135 regional and local TV stations were operating of which 116 broadcast continuously and 19 intermittently (Paschalidis 2005: 185). Despite the large number of stations, the regional and local mediascape is still unregulated.

The Greek press in the digital age

A country's press reflects to a large extent the strengths and weaknesses of the political and cultural context in which it operates. The development of the Greek press has always been closely connected to Greek politics, but, since the fall of the junta, it has undergone gradual change with advertising starting to play an important role in media revenues. In the mid-1980s there was rapid growth in the newspaper market and shipowners and other businessmen emerged as the new press barons.[9] They played a significant role behind the scenes in Greek politics and they were primarily after political influence and not profit. Media moguls used their newspapers as mouthpieces to promote political agendas, to put pressure on governments or political parties and to do business with the state (Stangos 1991). In Greece, like in other Mediterranean countries, there has been a strong tradition of advocacy journalism, promoting commentary from a distinct political perspective (Zaharopoulos and Paraschos 1993).

As purely partisan press in Greece continued to decline and market-orientated newspapers started dominating the scene, the growth of commercial television put newspaper advertising and readership under pressure. It is indicative that in 1979 there were twelve morning and afternoon dailies published in Athens with an average daily combined circulation of 713,000 copies. In 1989 there were twenty-two titles with a total average circulation of 1,128,589 copies while in 1998 there were twenty-three titles with a total average circulation of 500,893 copies (less than half of the circulation of 1989) (Papathanassopoulos 2001: 120). Declining sales continued in subsequent years and particularly during the crisis when in 2019 the total average circulation of the dailies dropped to around sixty thousand and the Sunday editions to around two hundred thousand.[10] On the other hand, the number of pages in Athenian newspapers was going in the opposite direction; in 1980 the dailies ranged from 16 to 32 pages, increasing to 48 pages for Sunday editions. Twenty years later the average number of pages had risen to between 32 and 64 for dailies and 120 for Sunday editions (Papathanassopoulos 2002).

In a highly centralized country like Greece, the Athenian press dominates the market with the regional press not being as strong as it is, for example,

---

[9] George Koskotas, a Greek American entrepreneur who managed to go from being a bank employee to a bank owner and publishing tycoon in five years, became the protagonist of the most notorious chapter in the history of the Greek press.

[10] Newspapers in Greece and other Mediterranean countries are far more dependent on news-stand sales than subscriptions (Hallin and Mancini 2004: 96).

in Germany. Since 1993 Athenian newspapers have tried to reverse the downward trend in sales by offering add-on services (books, coupons and other supplements), transforming their Sunday editions into a hybrid that is something between a newspaper and a periodical. The tabloid format was introduced for the first time in September 1981 with the publication of *Ethnos*, which also marked the invasion of the Greek press by big business. The tabloid sensationalist press has been growing in Greece since the 1980s, following the example of other European countries such as Britain (*The Sun*) and Germany (*Bild*), but its circulation has been limited.

The advent of the internet, the free press[11] and later the economic crisis led to the closure of leading papers such as the emblematic post-junta newspaper *Eleftherotypia* (1975–2014), while others in financial difficulties (*To Vima, Ta Nea, Ethnos*) were bought up in public auctions by wealthy businessmen, and new dailies sprang up such as *Efimerida ton Syntakton, Kontra News, Nea Selida* along with some new Sunday papers (e.g. *Documento*). Although Greece has a high literacy level (1.5 in ten have a university degree), its newspaper readership is one of the lowest in the developed world (fifty-three in one thousand in 2010) (Papathanassopoulos 2019).

The state provided indirect financial aid to the press, obliging, for example, state institutions to make announcements through the newspapers; but this does not explain how Greek newspapers with very low circulation have managed to survive. The financial benefits provided by the state were in theory aimed at helping the press, but in practice they kept it a prisoner of successive governments.[12] The same could be said about ESIEA, the union of journalists in Greece. Until the fall of the junta, it functioned as a private club, but since then it has opened its doors to many journalists who had once been excluded because of their political beliefs. Although ESIEA became more inclusive, it still did not function as a union for journalists, but rather as a guild, applying several screening processes aimed at keeping its membership as low as possible in order to preserve the considerable benefits enjoyed by its members (Stangos 1991: 279–80). This may not have enhanced the reputation of the journalists, but the rapid development of the Greek media market has increased their social and professional status. Traditional journalism, associated with print media, has

---

[11] The first free daily *Metrorama* (renamed *Metro*) began circulation in November 2000, followed by *City Press* in 2003.

[12] In order to create a powerful national news agency, the Athens News Agency, founded in 1895 and the Macedonian News Agency, founded in 1991 in Thessaloniki by the state, were merged in 2006 (Kontochristou and Terzis 2007: 230).

been upstaged by a more-market-oriented journalism related to television and electronic media. In particular television journalists have become public figures and often entered into politics.[13] Yet the public does not trust either politicians or journalists, and thus, disillusionment with politics has been transferred to the media.

The old paternalistic rhetoric of the traditional mass media has been challenged by the rise of blogs and social networks and this has led to a radical restructuring of the Greek media culture. The press has lost its monopoly with regard to news, but still manages to compete with the electronic media, which, in turn, have served as an alternative to the country's highly concentrated conventional media.[14] Greek indifference to politics had an effect on sales, and newspapers tried to halt the decline and attract more readers with their online editions and a proliferation of news portals run by journalists. However, Greek users tend to visit and trust alternative digital news outlets or blogs and not the mainstream established media. As in other countries, the content of major Athenian newspaper articles was structured in such a way as to optimize their web visibility and were enhanced with embedded videos to facilitate consumption. Technological progress has also increased the speed of news transmission. In an age of globalization and with an instant flow of information through the social media, the press has had to redefine its role. Newspapers all over the world are an endangered species and struggle to attract younger readers. The onslaught of digital communications has changed the ways in which the public acquires news and thus has exacerbated the crisis in the press.[15] The Greek media market is characterized more by supply than consumer demand and the country has more newspapers than such a small market can support.

Greek identity and the cultural power of television

While in the 1950s and 1960s cinema was the dominant form of entertainment in Greece, in the post-junta period television has increasingly assumed this

---

[13] An increasing number of journalists have stood as parliamentary candidates for different parties in recent years and it should be noted that in the elections of July 2019 at least seventeen journalists stood as candidates for the *New Democracy* party.
[14] Television and social media have emerged as the dominant source of information and therefore newspapers have mimicked television journalism with which they cannot easily compete.
[15] According to Eurostat data from the end of 2013, Greece was twenty-sixth out of the twenty-eight EU member-states in terms of internet access, with 36 percent of Greek citizens having no access to the internet.

role with frequent showings of Greek popular films or by contributing to the production of new films and thus becoming the main culture industry (Adorno 1991). A gradual shift occurred from a social (i.e. cinema) to a more housebound (i.e. television) form of entertainment (see Chapter 8). In its early stages Greek television had an important cultural and educational role, at first by offering many Greeks in rural areas a glimpse of the outside world and later with the introduction of educational programmes in 1977 (Vovou 2010: 108). This was particularly true in the first few years after the junta when some important cultural programmes were added to ERT's schedules under the aegis of the deputy director Roviros Manthoulis (1975–January 1977), such as *Monday Theatre* (from 8 March 1976, ending in 1995), *Cinema Nights* and *Paraskinio* (by Lakis Papastathis and Takis Hatzopoulos), a programme about leading figures in Greek cultural life. These cultural programmes had to compete with some popular American serials such as *Dallas* and *Dynasty*, which provoked references to American cultural imperialism (Vamvakas and Gazi 2017).[16] Even after the introduction of private television in Greece in 1989, imports from the United States continued to be the main source of programming, but gradually the share of foreign programmes decreased as the Greek stations increased their local production, raising issues of cultural consumption and identity (Zaharopoulos 2002: 45).

Another example of the cultural role of television was the popularization of a number of Greek novels by adapting them for the screen in the same way as musicians had popularized Greek poems by setting them to music. Greek fiction received a commercial boost through the serialization of novels, starting with Alexandros Papadiamantis's *Οι έμποροι των εθνών/The Merchants of the Nations* in 1973 and *Γυφτοπούλα/The Gypsy Girl* in 1974. The following year Kostas Ferris directed *Η Μενεξεδένια Πολιτεία/The Purple City* by Angelos Terzakis, and Vassilis Georgiadis directed the novel *Ο Χριστός ξανασταυρώνεται/Christ Recrucified* by Nikos Kazantzakis. These were followed by Dionysios Romas's *Περίπλους/Periplus* (1975), Elias Venezis's *Γαλήνη/Tranquility* (1976), M. Karagatsis's *Γιούγκερμαν/Jungermann* (1976), Grigorios Xenopoulos's *Η Αναδυομένη/The Emerging One* (1978), Antonis Travlantonis's *Λεηλασία μιας ζωής/The Ravaging of a Life* (1978), Kosmas Politis's *Το Λεμονοδάσος/The Lemon*

---

[16] In the early 1980s *Dallas* was withdrawn from Greek television as part of the anti-imperialist campaign and during the same period there were some incidents of censorship (Tsimas 2014: 382–3). It should be noted that until 1976 live programmes were avoided on Greek television to prevent any anti-government views being aired. Even the most emblematic cultural programme of ERT 'Paraskinio' was subjected to censorship in the 1970s and 1980s (Petsini and Christopoulos 2018: 449–53).

Grove (1978), Stratis Myrivilis's *Η δασκάλα με τα χρυσά μάτια/The Schoolmistress with the Golden Eyes* (1979) and many others during the 1980s and 1990s. At least nine popular novels by Grigorios Xenopoulos were serialized during the 1970s and 1980s, demonstrating the role of television in popularizing Greek fiction (Vidos 2014). With the advent of commercial television, new TV dramas were produced, though the serialization of novels such as *The Island* by Victoria Hislop (2005, aired by MEGA channel from October 2010) proved very popular.

The emergence of commercial television in Greece might not have promoted art and cultural programmes – which represented only 1 per cent of its programmes compared to 10 per cent of public television (Paschalidis 2005: 193) – yet it marked a transition from literary to TV fiction and one of the earliest and most popular programmes was *Οι Αυθαίρετοι/Without Consent* (MEGA channel, 1989–91), which encapsulated what it meant to be Greek in that period. It premiered only two days after the channel's official launch (22 November 1989) and involved the rivalry between two families living on different floors of the same block of flats who loathe one another. Though not related, they share the same surname, behave like nouveaux riches and disregard moral and legal requirements. The programme acquired iconic status in Greek popular culture and has been singled out as offering insights into Greek society in the late 1980s and early 1990s (Aitaki 2019).

Without Consent dissects Greek transgressive behavioural patterns, highlighting negative features such as antagonism, opportunism, deceit and lack of respect for the law. As the title alludes to buildings constructed without planning permission, a perennial problem in contemporary Greece, the programme seems to expose a cultural identity constructed in an unorthodox way. It also makes frequent references to Greece's EEC/EU membership and closely reflects contemporary Greek politics. It has been suggested that the antagonism between the two families resembles the political rivalry between Andreas Papandreou (then leader of the socialist PASOK) and Konstantinos Mitsotakis (then leader of the conservative New Democracy) (Valoukos 1998: 70).

Through their fictional stories such programmes articulated identity-related anxieties and encouraged viewers to laugh at satirical takes on 'flawed' Greek characteristics, internalizing rather than challenging them. It seems that commercial TV reinforced Greek stereotypes through humour and repetition instead of prompting viewers to debunk those stereotypes. Making fun of the behavioural patterns of the *Neohellene* (modern Greek) did not foster a critical or unsettling presentation of the national self but demonstrated (or perhaps only aped) a condescending attitude to a problematic Greekness. Greek television fiction often explores what it means to be Greek in a changing society, reflecting on a number of issues such as xenophobia, family crisis, sexual relations or the contrast between town and country. It represents the 'private life of the nation state' and offers a rich resource for analyzing national self-imaginings and tropes of othering. Cinema, according to John Ellis, has a highly integrated international aspect, while television is an essentially national activity for the vast majority of its audience (1992: 5). As well as minimizing costs the frequent reruns of some popular Greek TV serials have demonstrated the cultural power of television by probing certain aspects of the Greek identity and holding up a 'mirror' to Greek society. If, according to Billig's theory of banal nationalism, national identity embraces all those forgotten reminders to be found in the embodied habits of social life (1995: 8), then similarly in some TV serials there is a continual flagging up of certain identity features which are so familiar that they are not consciously registered as reminders.

Commercialization has made Greek TV more Hellenocentric with some Greek serials casting an (often satirical) eye on Greek society and its cultural conventions. This kind of nativism was also fostered by the promotion of Greek serials to the prime-time slots and transferring American serials/soap operas, particularly after 2007, to the internet or subscription TV (Vamvakas 2018: 218). Hybridizing the American drama pattern 'wealth, beauty, power' and the melodramatic formula of Latin American *telenovelas*, Greek television fiction has been treated as a framing mechanism, affecting public perceptions of social issues and becoming an arena for moral evaluations. Its study offers insights into Greek popular culture, the ideological role of media discourse and how Greek television serials adopt international screen conventions.

The media and the crisis

The crisis has increasingly brought to the fore the interconnections between media, politics and economics and the interweaving of the media with social life. A kind of vernacularization of the public sphere, brought about by the rise of social media, has produced arenas of crisis contestation in which public anger and disappointment with the political system can be expressed. The constant interest shown by the world's media in the Greek crisis can be attributed to its potential impact on the euro and its possible spread to other countries. With the American, British and German press being more hostile than the French and Italian, Greece was stigmatized more heavily than the other countries in crisis

(Portugal and Ireland) (Tzogopoulos 2013: 129). This may have contributed to the country's credibility deficit, but it also led to the internationalization of the crisis. The impact of the crisis on the media can be seen at various levels: institutional, cultural and transnational. I will start with the institutional.

For years the public broadcaster (ERT) was seen as lacking independence and slavishly toeing the government line. However, it was valued for its documentaries and films not shown by commercial channels and for sponsoring cultural events and films. On 11 June 2013 the Greek government decided to shut it down, claiming that this measure was inevitable due to public spending cuts and Greece's bailout terms. One month later the new interim Greek Public Television (DT and later NERIT) began broadcasting on the three channels formerly allocated to ERT. Meanwhile ERT's premises had been occupied by some of its former employees with the support of the opposition parties and had become the symbol of free speech and the 'voice of democracy'. The abrupt closure of ERT caused a heated debate in the Greek public sphere and was treated as a blow to democracy and journalism. ERT, which had supported two orchestras, was seen as a bastion of quality programming in a media landscape dominated by private stations. On the other hand, it has been claimed that for decades ERT had been overstaffed and a 'state' rather than a politically independent 'public service' broadcaster. It could be said that the only positive outcome of this controversy was the reinforcement of the view that Greece needed a public rather than a state broadcasting organization. As promised in its election manifesto, in July 2015 the SYRIZA-led coalition government reopened ERT, but its audience ratings remained low (Valoukos 2018).

Due to the crisis advertising revenue collapsed and the number of serials on domestic television shrank (Skamnakis 2018). TV channels started looking for alternative options to fill the gaps in their programming. One of these options was to import Turkish TV serials, which are less expensive than Greek productions. Turkish soap operas, such as the popular *Suleiman the Magnificent*, dominated prime-time Greek television during the crisis, achieving high ratings but causing adverse reactions and protests about the screening of a Turkish TV soap opera by the MEGA Channel on the anniversary of Greek Independence Day. This trend towards showing Turkish TV serials mirrored what had happened some years earlier with Brazilian and Mexican soap operas, but the airing of Turkish TV programmes touched national sensitivities and made some people talk about a new *Tourkokratia* ('Turkocracy' or Turkish occupation). It is interesting to note that before the crisis, Greek-Cypriot productions were not screened on Greek TV, but since the crisis they have started to compete with Turkish programmes.

The impact of the crisis can also be seen in the popularity of other programmes. For example, the reality show *The Survivor* (2017), in which a group of contestants are stranded in a remote location and have to try to survive (relying on their own resources), was rated top of the most highly rated shows since 1989. Its unprecedented success has been attributed partly to the economic crisis, on the basis that the show makes viewers feel better about their own circumstances when seeing other people living in worse conditions and fighting for food. Greek TV fiction (*Πίσω στο σπίτι/Back Home*, MEGA Channel, 2011–12 and 2012–13) also thematized the Greek crisis and offered a comic commentary on its effects by presenting a half-German character lending money to a Greek family to save their home from the banks, while demanding in exchange total control of the household (Aitaki 2018b).[17] Featuring a family living beyond their means, the series places Greece's bailout agreement in a domestic context with the family home becoming the target of austerity measures and acting as a metonymy of the dysfunctional Greek society and its cultural flaws. The contrast the series makes between the feckless but warm-hearted Greeks and the austere, disciplined Germans, suggests that even Greek TV has contributed to the reproduction of narratives and stereotypes of the crisis which dominated the public sphere. TV fiction offered a platform for the representation or interpretation of crisis as a discursively constructed event.

The intensive and value-laden coverage of the Greek crisis by the international media contributed to the downward spiral in the level of confidence among foreign investors and has attracted scholarly scrutiny.[18] The use of sensational language or alarming headlines such as 'Shockwave from Athens', 'Time bomb for the euro', 'Greek drama' or 'Greek tragedy' have reinforced negative cultural stereotypes and created the sense of a looming Armageddon. The sensationalist presentation of the crisis often contributed to its 'spectacularization' and 'tabloidization', while the explosive rise in media output on the Greek crisis played an important role in constructing Greece's exceptionalism as the 'problem child' of Europe (see Chapter 10). Foreign, and even Greek, media were seen as instrumental in legitimizing the austerity management of the crisis (Mylonas 2014: 310).

Yanis Varoufakis, the former Greek finance minister (January–June 2015), emerged as an emblematic figure in the Western media (including YouTube

---

[17] Other TV series which touch upon crisis-related themes are, *Το Κάτω Παρτάλι/To Kato Partali* (MEGA Channel, 2014–15) and *Εθνική Ελλάδος/National Team of Greece* (MEGA Channel, 2015).
[18] Juko (2010), Mylonas (2012 and 2014), Echtler (2013), Tzogopoulos (2013), Bickes et al. (2014), Papathanassopoulos (2015).

and Twitter) and his showbiz style earned him pop celebrity status, as attested by the popular video 'V for Varoufakis' produced in 2015 by the controversial German comedian and TV personality Jan Böhmermann (Georgakopoulou and Giaxoglou 2018). The mediatized iconography of Varoufakis across different media involved tweets depicting him as Hercules, rescripting emblematic quotes (e.g. 'you just killed the Troika'), YouTube satirical videos, images of him motorbike-riding, and even T-shirts (Figure 5). At times the coverage of the Greek crisis in the European media was hostile and unflattering, reinforcing a negative image of Greece and massively increasing the visibility of the country on the international scene, with its touristic images being replaced by the words 'rousfeti' (special favours/nepotism) and 'fakelaki' (backhanders) in the media discourse. The international media perpetuated crisis clichés, promoted the

Figure 5 A T-shirt with a caricature of Yanis Varoufakis. Artwork copyright © Rob Art | illustration 2020, https://robsnow.eu/shop/

image of lazy Greeks and contributed to a Greek identity crisis by drawing a dichotomy between the Greeks and other Europeans. On the other hand, some Greek media retaliated by demonizing Germans and portraying Chancellor Angela Merkel in a Nazi uniform and this led to a media war. Thanks to the intense media coverage of the crisis, Greece became the focus of international attention (if not always in a good way) and has demonstrated the world's connectivity.

Conclusion

Throughout the post-junta period there has been a symbiotic relationship between the media and political power, marked by the transition from a state monopoly to the coexistence of a number of media outlets, often operating as political pressure groups. Though the introduction of television in Greece was delayed by three decades by comparison to other European countries, thanks to EU regulations, private television broadcasting arrived earlier in Greece than in many places and simultaneously with countries such as Germany, Spain or Sweden. Deregulation has allowed market forces to prevail in terms of the reallocation of audience share and power among media players, though public service broadcasting – in the full sense of the term – has not yet been fully developed. Deregulation may have democratized the media and removed them to some extent from political interference, yet it led to a kind of 'event TV' by turning the private channels into versions of the tabloid press. The digitization of terrestrial television, EU competition rules and issues related to media regulation and ownership were some of the challenges Greek broadcasting faced at the dawn of the twenty-first century.

The study of Greek television fiction also offers insights into Greek popular culture, the ideological role of media discourse and how Greek television serials have adopted international filmic conventions. The marketization of broadcasting, increased advertising and imports of foreign programmes have led to the commercialization of Greek culture and familiarized Greeks with shows from non-European countries (Mexico, Brazil, Turkey). News stories have been completely visualized and there has been convergence with the tabloid agenda. Greece has moved rapidly from an oral society to a culture relying on a multiplicity of televisual options and the dominance of social media with one in four Greek internet users in 2016 stating that it is their main source of news.[19]

---

[19] See the 2016 Digital News Report by the Reuters Institute for Journalism, available at https://reutersinstitute.politics.ox.ac.uk/sites/default/files/research/files/Digital%2520News%2520Rep

As the crisis continued, awareness of the role of the international media in its representation increased and brought about a restructuring of the Greek TV landscape. In the digital era and under the impact of austerity the media in Greece are in constant transition, reflecting deeper social and cultural shifts.

---

ort%25202016.pdf. The 2017 Report reveals that Greeks trust social media more than news media more than any other country in Europe, available at https://reutersinstitute.politics.ox.ac.uk/sites/default/files/Digital%20News%20Report%202017%20web_0.pdf?utm_source=digitalnewsreport.org&utm_medium=referral

8

Cinematic allegories: From history to domesticity

Cinema in Greece in its heyday in the 1950s and 1960s always lagged behind the other arts. It remained basically an entertainment medium that made no pretence of following European trends (with some exceptions, such as the neorealist films Πικρό Ψωμί/*Bitter Bread* (1951), Μαγική Πόλη/*Magic City* (1954), Συνοικία το Όνειρο/*A Neighbourhood Named the Dream* (1961) and directors such as Nikos Koundouros (1926–2017), Takis Kanellopoulos (1933–1990) and Michael Cacoyannis (1921–2011)).[1] With the fall of the junta and television entering Greek households, this tradition of popular entertainment continued on the small screen where a large segment of the Greek population still enjoyed the old films. With the restoration of democracy and with no more fear of censorship, filmmakers were keen to produce a more sophisticated and politically engaged cinema. Hence, this chapter will look at developments in film-making in the post-junta period and more specifically explore one of its hallmarks. I refer to the transition from political films, depicting Greece's recent painful past and conceptualizing history as an external, often malevolent, force, to films that placed greater emphasis on interpersonal relations by presenting characters resisting the overpowering tyranny of history and immersed in the everyday realities of Greek society. Leaving behind the grand narratives of Greek political history we have ended up with the micro-narratives of family dynamics and identity politics.

This transition epitomizes a shift from the orthodox Marxist conceptions of power to Foucauldian biopolitics and is represented at one end of the spectrum by filmmakers such as Theo Angelopoulos and Pantelis Voulgaris and at the

---

[1] Cacoyannis, who produced most of his work before or during the junta, became internationally acclaimed with his *Zorba the Greek* (1964) and his numerous stage and film adaptations of ancient Greek plays with resonances of the Greek Civil War (*Electra*, 1962), the colonels' junta (*Trojan Women*, 1971) and the Turkish invasion of Cyprus (*Iphigenia*, 1977).

other by Yorgos Lanthimos, Athina Rachel Tsangari and others. However, what *Ο Θίασος/The Travelling Players* (1975) by Angelopoulos and *Κυνόδοντας/ Dogtooth* (2009) by Lanthimos have in common is the allegorical use of the family. The former, making reference to the myth of the House of Atreus, offers a meditation on Greek history through his film, a kind of family epic and arguably the first gem of the 'New Greek Cinema'. The latter, portraying a family in crisis, alludes to a society in crisis and is the poster child of the so-called 'weird wave Greek cinema'. They punctuate the beginning and end of the *Metapolitefsi*, marking a transition from an epic vision of Greek history to a claustrophobic micro-narrative of a family confined to their house that becomes a breeding ground for violence.[2]

Though since 1974 Greek cinema has produced two internationally acclaimed filmmakers (Angelopoulos and Lanthimos), it has not enjoyed great commercial successes, losing ground to the increasing invasion of Greek homes by television. This was a new medium for Greek society and it attracted some popular filmmakers (e.g. Vasilis Georgiadis, Yannis Dalianidis, Nikos Foskolos), who went over to it in order to capture larger audiences. They even dramatized Greek novels, a trend which started in 1973 with the serialization of novels by Alexandros Papadiamantis, Angelos Terzakis, M. Karagatsis and Nikos Kazantzakis (see Chapter 7). The cross-fertilization between cinema and television, which started even before the fall of the junta and involved the migration of filmmakers from cinema to television, was reversed towards the end of the twentieth century with the content of popular comedies and other series being transposed from television to cinema.

Developments in the post-junta Greek cinema also involve the transition from the 'old' values of art and anti-commercialism to the impact of the commercial world of television and advertising, which in a way reconciled the popular and art-house cinema, and even led to their offering one another mutual support. Actor-centred and studio-based 'Old Greek Cinema' dominated Greek film culture in the 1950s and 1960s. Commercially oriented and ideologically conservative, this kind of cinema was popular with the public even beyond this period. It was succeeded by the auteur, art-oriented, largely left-wing and state funded 'New Greek Cinema' (Νέος Ελληνικός Κινηματογράφος) of the 1970s and 1980s and by the so-called 'Contemporary Greek Cinema' (Σύγχρονος Ελληνικός Κινηματογράφος) of the 1990s, which did not manage to reinvigorate

---

[2] Angelopoulos points out that in his epic films 'it is "History", with a capital "H", that takes "centre stage"' (cited in Horton 1997b: 109).

the Greek cinematic culture or make its mark (Papadimitriou 2009). In the 2000s the popular and art-house films seem to transcend their troubled relationship and coexist in an overexpanded commercial audio-visual and film-making industry. In this chapter developments in Greek cinema are explored using the above categorizations and the thematic orientation of the films. One could argue that the post-junta cinema involves three main overlapping thematic areas: political history (with the emphasis on the Civil War and post-war Greece), culture (allusions to antiquity, cultural interaction, sense of belonging, rebetiko, diaspora, adaptations of novels, literary and historical figures) and social crisis in the broadest sense of the word (migration, exclusion, gender identity, dysfunctional families).

New Greek Cinema and political history

While Greece was under a military regime, the new trends in European cinema such as the French *nouvelle vague*, the English free cinema or the developments in Eastern European cinematic schools, particularly after the Prague Spring, did not fail to reach the country and they became even better known following the collapse of the dictatorship. As mentioned above, an auteur-driven cinema, known as the 'New Greek Cinema', emerged in the early 1970s and often adopted the format of the historical film panorama to portray Greece's recent past. Following the increasing politicization of Greek society after the fall of the dictatorship and the internationalist trends of the 1960s and 1970s, this 'new' cinema was politically engaged, dealing with social problems and the painful experiences of the junta, a tendency evident in the films shown at the sixteenth Thessaloniki Film Festival in September 1975.

Though its filming started under the colonels, the four-hour epic by Theo Angelopoulos, *The Travelling Players*, became a landmark production of the post-junta period, combining an innovative style with the dramatization of Greek history in mythopoetic form. Despite the fact that the Greek government refused to nominate it as one of the country's official entries, it received the International Film Critics Award (FIPRESCI) at the Cannes Film Festival in May 1975 and enjoyed worldwide acclaim. Being the first film on the Greek Civil War, and approached from a left-wing perspective, it attracted a larger audience than almost any previous Greek film, despite rejecting mainstream conventions (rapid cuts, fast pacing, star system).

The film tells the story of a troupe of itinerant actors touring the war-torn country and performing the pastoral idyll *Golfo the Shepherdess* on makeshift stages. The filmic narrative is characterized by the notion of discontinuity, represented by the disruptions of *Golfo's* performances by the Metaxas regime police, the Greco-Italian War, a violent intrusion by German troops and gunfire from ELAS (resistance fighters) while the troupe is performing the play in front of British soldiers. Notwithstanding these interruptions the camera maintains a sense of historical continuity, implying that modern Greek history is a succession of continuities and ruptures.

The history of twentieth-century Greece is presented as a re-enactment of ancient myths and as part of a larger archetypal narrative. Although in the *Travelling Players* only Orestes is identified by name, in the script and the acting credits, the travelling players have ancient names. Like Aeschylus's *Oresteia*, where Orestes kills his mother Clytemnestra and her lover Aigisthus in order to avenge the killing of his father, Agamemnon, *The Travelling Players* becomes an allegory for the self-destructive forces in Greek history, turning a family drama into a national tragedy. The characters appear powerless, carried away by the violent and impersonal forces of history. Unlike in Aeschylus's play, in the film the cycle of violence has no end. Angelopoulos's Orestes is executed by extreme right-wing forces, whereas in the play he gets away with his crimes and is granted redemption by the gods. The endless cycle of violence at the core of the House of Atreus can easily be read into post-war Greek history.[3] Angelopoulos plays with both popular melodrama (*Golfo the Shepherdess*) and the ancient tragic myth in order to create a complex web of allusions.

Eschewing close-ups, the film adopts an austere style, notable for its languidly unfolding and elaborately choreographed tracking shots. Its long takes seem almost painted rather than filmed, fostering the critical engagement of viewers by inviting them to think anew about Greek history. History is presented in different ways in the film: as a soliloquy (with characters addressing the camera and giving a historical account), as musical and re-enactment (Chrysothemis's son carries on Orestes's tradition by taking on his role at the end and whispering his name). Like Brecht's distanciation effect (*Verfremdungseffekt*), the film does not render the audience passive observers but aims to make them aware of the swirling vortex of history. Angelopoulos produced a challenging chronicle of

---

[3] As Andrew Horton pointed out 'Angelopoulos reclaimed Greek myth from the past by making it present, and from the conservative guardians of "high culture", Greek and foreign, by making his Agamemnon a working-class refugee' (1997a: 108).

Greece's recent history, which requires an effort on the part of the spectator (particularly the non-Greek) to understand all the political, historical or mythic allusions. The director embarked on a revision of the official view of the Greek wartime resistance and the ensuing civil war, a revision which continued with the subsequent films in his 'history trilogy': *The Hunters* (1977) and *Alexander the Great* (1980).[4]

The *Travelling Players* could be considered foundational for its 'political modernism' and the way it represents post-war Greek history by rejecting earlier causal, character-centred cinematic depictions of Greek history. The film's audiences are invited to understand history not as a series of events but as the result of impersonal forces. Even his long tracking shots seem to present people caught up in the cogs of history and the foreign imperialist mechanisms at work in Greece from the Metaxas' years in late 1930s through to the early 1950s. As Alex Lykidis has argued 'the historical agency in Angelopoulos' work is reminiscent of many eastern European films made between the mid-1950s and mid-1960s' (2015: 22).

Reworking the techniques of filmmakers such as Michelangelo Antonioni, Miklós Jansco or even Andrei Tarkovsky and by alluding to ancient myth, Angelopoulos fused past and present. The film begins in the town of Aigion in 1952 and ends there in 1939, proceeding with temporal switches even in the same shot. The opening scene of the film involves a time shift as the group of players, wandering a street in Aigion in 1952, observe the preparations for a campaign speech by the former Field Marshal Papagos, now running for civilian office. As they reach the end of the street, they hear a call for a welcome rally for General Metaxas in 1939, thus blurring pre-war and post-war military regimes in the same scene. This interpolation of different time periods occurs in other scenes and Angelopoulos himself justified his manipulation of time thus: 'The past is not simply a past but the present as well. I needed to find a way of narrating in which these two temporal dimensions would co-exist' (Archimandritis 2013: 31). The transcendence of time in the *Travelling Players* shifts the emphasis to spaces ranging from silent tableaux to parades, demonstrations and street battles.[5]

Angelopoulos challenges 'travel poster' Greece by letting his camera linger on bleak wintry landscapes, run-down houses and crumbling facades. Exploding the myth of an idyllic Greece (represented in the film by the play *Golfo*), he offers

---

[4] These films 'ask us to see history not from the point of view of grandiose historical figures, as it is the case of most period films, but from the point of view of the people as a collective subject' (Koutsourakis 2018: 6).

[5] For a discussion of space and time in Angelopoulos' films, see Stathi (1999).

a journey to 'the other Greece', as he says in an interview (Fainaru 2001: 88), of violence and oppression – not of the sunny islands but of desolate villages and melancholy open spaces. The priority of landscape over character, the long takes and the taciturn characters create his distinctive poetic visual style. The dreamy topography of films like Τοπίο στην Ομίχλη/*Landscape in the Mist* (1988) with their vast plateaus resonate history, while his modernist austerity combines an interrogation of modern Greek and Balkan history with the re-enactment of ancient narratives about war, family, wandering and homecoming.[6] Blending various trends from European cinema and relying on non-linear and elliptical long takes to develop his self-conscious modernist style, Angelopoulos remains a distinctively Greek auteur.

By contrast to Angelopoulos's elegiac approach and his presentation of characters as pawns controlled by the timeless forces of history, Pantelis Voulgaris tends to view recent Greek history through the schematic 'opposition between a conservative Right and a moral Left, destined to be resolved by the overwhelming power of emotions, justice and goodness' (Mini 2016: 142). In his Πέτρινα Χρόνια/*Stone Years* (1985), he adopts a sentimental and optimistic approach with the film ending in 1974 and the protagonist Eleni returning home, freed from imprisonment. She opens a door to let the light in and reviews her life by looking at some photographs of the 'stone years'. Focusing on the dignity of the characters and based on a real story, the film presents the odyssey of a couple, who have spent most of their lives in prison, meeting only a few times during the dark period between the Greek Civil War and the end of the dictatorship. Though 'this film gave the final *coup de grâce* to the New Greek Cinema' (Karalis 2012b: 210), Voulgaris manages to blend the personal story of two political prisoners with a grand historical narrative starting after the end of the Civil War. This is a general feature of his filmic oeuvre, which includes some more personal and introvert films (Το προξενιό της Άννας/*Anna's Engagement*, Ήσυχες μέρες του Αυγούστου/*Quiet Days in August*, Όλα είναι δρόμος/*It's a Long Road*) and others with historical references and epic aspirations (*Eleftherios Venizelos*, Νύφες/*Brides* and *Stone Years*).

After the fall of the junta, Greek cinema, together with fiction, offered an 'alternative' historiography of the recent past when anti-communism was still

---

[6] There are echoes of *The Odyssey* in *Ulysses' Gaze* (1995), in *Landscape in the Mist* (1988) with the young children searching, like Telemachus, for their father, and in the last film Angelopoulos completed, *The Dust of Time* (2009), with its focus on the search for family and home. Some classicists have turned their scholarly attention to exploring the ancient allusions of his films (Létoublon 2000 and 2008; Pomeroy 2008 and 2011; and Winkler 2009: 71–5, 297–300).

strong in the country and the armed forces celebrated the last battle in the Civil War on Mt Grammos. During this highly politicized period there were a number of films dealing with the Civil War and particularly its aftermath: *Happy Day* (1976) by Pantelis Voulgaris, *Ο Άνθρωπος με το Γαρύφαλλο/The Man with the Carnation* (1980) by Nikos Tzimas, *Άρης Βελουχιώτης-Το Δίλημμα/Aris Velouchiotis – The Dilemma* (1981) by Fotos Lambrinos, *Η Κάθοδος των Εννιά /The Descent of the Nine* (1984) by Christos Siopachas, *Καλή πατρίδα σύντροφε/ Happy Homecoming, Comrade* (1986) by Lefteris Xanthopoulos, *Caravanserai* (1986) by Tasos Psaras, *Τα παιδιά της χελιδόνας/The Children of the Swallow* (1987) by Costas Vrettakos (Flitouris 2008). Most of the films focus on memory, trauma and more generally the consequences of the Civil War rather than on the events themselves. After all, war films went against the aesthetic principles of the anti-commercial New Greek Cinema.

In the post-1989 period with the alleged 'end of history', the allure of the Civil War in the area of cinema recedes, but resurfaces when Pantelis Voulgaris released his film *Ψυχή Βαθιά/A Soul So Deep* (2009), depicting the fratricidal struggle in a sentimental and non-ideological way through the story of two brothers who find themselves in rival camps.[7] Focusing on ordinary people as victims of foreign powers and promoting an approach to history from below, the film fosters national reconciliation. Yet its release came only months after the riots in Athens in December 2008 (see Chapters 3 and 9), offering support to the claim that the Civil War was revisited during the period of crisis.[8]

Traumatic pasts and national culture

The Travelling Players belongs to the early, more political period in Angelopoulos's work, while his second period, beginning with the *Ταξίδι στα Κύθηρα/ Voyage to Cythera* (1984), is more emotional and existential and disenchanted with politics (Bordwell 1997: 12; Jameson 2015: 133). In this second introspective period,

---

[7] In a heated public discussion that went on for several weeks in the mainstream press, the director was criticized for his oversimplified treatment of the Civil War.
[8] Kostis Kornetis argues that this film, together with *Δεμένη Κόκκινη Κλωστή/Tied Red Thread* (2012) by Kostas Charalambous, represents 'the transition from a cinema of reconciliation that was being promoted around 2008 to the cinema of vengeance and ultra violence that became inextricably linked to the general political reconfiguration of the country since the civil unrest of 2008 and the onset of the current economic crisis' (2014: 94–5). Pantelis Voulgaris's more recent film *Το Τελευταίο Σημείωμα/The Last Note* (2017) is a German occupation drama. The film, focusing on the tragic story of Napoleon Soukatzidis, refers to the execution of two hundred prisoners of war in Kaisariani, on 1 May 1944, in retaliation for the death of four German officers in Laconia.

history and politics gradually receded, though the traumas of the past and the melancholic meditation on history kept resurfacing. A film within a film, *Voyage to Cythera* is about exile and family reunification, a kind of 'palimpsestic text in which multiple narrative layers are superimposed upon one another' (Homer 2019: 11). In this film, which inaugurates Angelopoulos's 'trilogy of silence', Spyros returns from political exile in the Soviet Union after thirty-two years and is reunited with his wife (Katerina) and children (Alexander and Voula) along with other members of his extended family. But he is unable to connect with them after such a long separation and even leaves the family home and spends the night in a cheap hotel, after an argument with his wife. During his exile he had remarried and had two children with his second wife. Stubbornly resisting his reintegration, Spyros is the only one from his village who refuses to sell his fields to a tourist developer and ends up with another expulsion order, exiling him for a second time to the Soviet Union. A ship refuses to take him on board for his return journey, and as a result, he is left stranded on a raft in international waters. His *nostos* remains unfulfilled and he sets off on the raft on a new journey into the unknown with his aged wife.

The film also delves into the trauma of the Civil War and adumbrates the reconciliation narrative promoted by PASOK after its rise to power in 1981 (see Chapter 2). In a visit to his near-deserted village, Spyros, solemn and dignified, is approached by his erstwhile enemy who, in a gesture of reconciliation, offers him a cigarette and confesses in a trembling voice: 'They made us fight. We tore into one another. You from one side and me from the other. We both lost' (Figure 6).

The past haunts the present, and in the film the Civil War is made present through its absence. It is treated as a trauma in the sense of a struggle to come to terms with the event. From the silence of history, Angelopoulos moves to the silence of love in *Ο Μελισσοκόμος/Beekeeper* (1986) and his trilogy concludes with the silence of God in *Τοπίο στην Ομίχλη/Landscape in the Mist* (1988). In the third period, starting with *Το Μετέωρο Βήμα του Πελαργού/The Suspended Step of the Stork* (1991), his films become more esoteric and existential, meditating on borders, liminality and refugees by exploring Greek-Balkan interactions (*Το Βλέμμα του Οδυσσέα/Ulysses' Gaze*, 1995).

Despite his focus on the political history of Greece, Angelopoulos works within the Greek cultural tradition and produces a narrative of Greek identity with his allusions to antiquity, Byzantine iconography, Orthodox liturgy, Karagiozis (shadow puppet show), Spyros Perisiadis's nineteenth-century pastoral idyll *Golfo* (which also became the first Greek film in 1914), the first

Figure 6 Spyros (M. Katrakis) and Antonis (D. Papagiannopoulos), his erstwhile enemy, in the emblematic scene from *Voyage to Cythera*. Courtesy of Thodoros Angelopoulos's family.

Balkan cinematographers, the Manaki brothers, Dionysios Solomos, Yannis Tsarouchis and George Seferis. He is using a modernist style to narrate the nation and reflect on its history, thus reinforcing the argument that New Greek Cinema can 'be seen as part of the wider desire to "nationalise modernism" – the project of the "Generation of the 1930s" brought, at last to cinema' (Papadimitriou 2011: 496). Hellenism in Angelopoulos is embedded in the landscape, as, for example, the image of the marble head floating on the water with the city of Thessaloniki in the background in *Landscape in the Mist*. By the 1990s he had broadened his focus and was beginning to deal with border crossing, voyages involving quests and transnational identities in the Balkans and beyond (Horton 1997a and 1997b). He also began to use European and American actors and international partners for financing his films.

From the 1990s onward the international trend for so-called 'heritage films' emerged as a distinct genre in Greek cinema too. The nostalgic revisiting of the past coupled with cosmopolitanism brought the public back to cinemas and this continued into the first decades of the twenty-first century with box office successes such as Tasos Boulmetis's *ΠΟΛΙΤΙΚΗ Κουζίνα/A Touch of Spice* (2003),[9] the biopics by Yannis Smaragdis, *El Greco* (2007), *Ο θεός αγαπάει το χαβιάρι/God loves Caviar* (2012) and the period romantic drama *Μικρά Αγγλία/Little England* (2013) by Pantelis Voulgaris (Chalkou 2017). One

---

[9] The upper case in the title of the film avoids the use of stress and thus encourages the reading of ΠΟΛΙΤΙΚΗ as both 'political' and 'Constantinopolitan'.

could say that with these films we moved from the earlier preoccupation with the political history of Greece, as depicted in the films of Angelopoulos and Voulgaris, to its cultural history with some hints of nostalgia and ethnocentrism.

A Touch of Spice was one of the most commercially successful films in Greece and in the year of its release was the Greek box office's greatest hit (Dermentzopoulos 2015). Dealing with the departure of Greek citizens from Istanbul in 1964 as a result of the re-emerging tensions between Greece and Turkey, it deploys the historical events as background and avoids nationalistic aggression by portraying the Turkish characters rather sympathetically. The main character Fanis, a Greek professor of astrophysics with an international career, tells through flashbacks the story of his early childhood in Istanbul, the deportation of his family to Athens in the early 1960s and finally his return to Istanbul. The other central character is his grandfather, owner of a shop in Istanbul where Fanis experiences the sensual pleasures of spices and his first love with the Turkish girl Saime. Despite his promises to relocate to Greece and the family gatherings, where delicious food is prepared in anticipation of his arrival, the grandfather never leaves Istanbul. In the last part of the film, set in the present, Fanis returns to Istanbul to see his dying grandfather and meets once again with his childhood sweetheart.

The film revolves around questions of identity, trauma, memory and the sense of belonging, as one memorable phrase from the film testifies: 'The Turks chased us away as Greeks and the Greeks received us as Turks.' As food crosses national boundaries, culinary syncretism becomes a metaphor for identity and an imaginary homeland. The nostalgic tone is also dominant due to a sense of loss and Fanis's frustration at not having been able to have Istanbul as his home and Saime as his wife. Blending culinary memories, emotive spaces and interethnic romance, the film oscillates between projecting intercultural dialogue and reclaiming a traumatic (national) past.[10]

Another feature of this period is the dynamic presence of a number of women directors such as Tonia Marketaki (1942–1994) with her emblematic film *Κρυστάλλινες Νύχτες/Crystal Nights* (1992), which contrasts from a psychoanalytic perspective the economistic, male approach to history with the erotic, female approach, Frida Liappa (1948–1994), Loukia Rikaki (1961–2011), Antoinetta Angelidi, Olga Malea and others. Two films from diasporic women

---

[10] Dimitris Eleftheriotis points out that 'the film's historical mobility is a two-way vector; it revisits a traumatic past, it reclaims visual ownership of its geographical space, and it delivers an optimistic manifesto for the future of Greek cinema and society' (2012: 34).

directors have also attracted a great deal of attention by exploring Greek cultural attitudes in diaspora communities in different ways. *My Big Fat Greek Wedding* (2002) by the Greek-Canadian director Nia Vardalos became an international box office success but was criticized for its cultural stereotyping, while the subversive and sexually explicit *Head On* (1998) by the Greek-Australian Ana Kokkinos exposes the generation gap in a diaspora Greek community between the traditional values of the immigrant parents and their son, who feels oppressed by and alienated from this traditional life style. The young protagonist confronts his sexuality and his Greek background, while his parents are totally unaware of his sexual and drug taking activities.

Notwithstanding the references to Greek cultural heritage in a number of films, it should be noted here that cinema now tries to a greater extent, than any other art form in Greece, to transcend the boundaries of its national culture and filmmakers are no longer targeting an exclusively Greek audience. Since the 1990s Greek cinema has been becoming increasingly international and this is evident in the films of Angelopoulos with his engagement with European funding partners and international stars such as Marcello Mastroianni, Jeanne Moreau, Harvey Keitel and others. He even adopts the English language in his later films such as *Ulysses' Gaze* and *Η Σκόνη του Χρόνου/The Dust of Time* (2008). Similar trends can be noted in *A Touch of Spice*, a film co-financed by a Turkish company, with Greek and Turkish characters speaking Greek, Turkish and English, and more recently in Lanthimos's latest films, all foreign productions made in English. With the increasingly globalizing trends in film production and more widespread aspirations to address an international audience, the notion of a 'national cinema' is more frequently questioned as is the national orientation of some filmmakers of the New Greek Cinema (Hjort and MacKenzie 2000). From representing and promoting national culture, 'Greek cinema' has gone on to challenge the very notion of a national cinema and even studying it is placed in a broader, more comparative context (Iordanova 2006; Kourelou, Liz and Vidal 2014).

Cinema and television

The irruption of television in Greek households in the early 1970s led to profound changes in film production and the habits of Greek cinemagoers. Around the mid-1960s there were over six hundred active cinemas in Athens alone and ticket prices were still cheap. By 1980 this number had gone down to three hundred and by 1994 it had shrunk to about thirty five. In 1968 around 108 Greek films were released and the total number of tickets sold was 137.4 million while in 1973 only 44 films were made and ticket sales declined to 62.2 million (Lambrinos 2003: 221; Komninou 2001: 148, 175). Gradually upstaging cinema as the number one entertainment in Greece, television became more attractive with the introduction of colour in 1979 and the popular cinema of the 1950s and 1960s found a new medium through which to reach a mass audience. Television seems to have claimed the wider audience and enormously influenced the making of popular films.[11] Successful writers of TV comedy series, such as Michalis Reppas and Thanassis Papathanassiou, wrote and directed *Safe Sex* (1999), a spicy comedy about the sexual life of Greeks, which was co-produced by the leading TV channel MEGA and became a tremendous commercial success, bringing the public back to the cinemas.[12] Maria Chalkou points to the paradoxical relationship between cinema and television in Greece arguing that

> while in the 1970s it was television that led to a slump in film audiences, three decades later it was again television that brought them back into the cinemas. In fact a reverse shift occurred in which subject matter, creative professionals, stars, aesthetic and narrative norms moved from TV back into the domestic film industry. (2012: 246)

Comedians, writers and actors (e.g. Lakis Lazopoulos and Antonis Kafetzopoulos) transposed their huge TV success to the big screen and thus brought the public back to the cinema by recycling popular culture and comic narratives from one medium to the other. Video cassette recorders (VCR) and direct-to-video films represented a new development in the 1980s and a challenge to the popular and auteur cinema by reinforcing the contrast between high and popular culture and addressing issues of gender identities (Kassaveti 2016).[13]

The decline in cinema revenues and the absence of any active film producers left in Greece, led to the establishment of the Greek Film Centre and in a way to the nationalization of film production. This ultimately did not help the film industry because it almost monopolized film-making by determining what

---

[11] Older people were attracted to the new form of entertainment provided by the television, while cinema gained a younger and more enthusiastic audience (Lambrinos 2003: 208).

[12] The films *Safe Sex*, *A Touch of Spice* and *Λούφα και Παραλλαγή: Σειρήνες στο Αιγαίο/Loafing and Camouflage: Sirens in the Aegean* (Nikos Perakis, 2005) were the top Greek box office hits and achieved more than a million admissions. For more details on the entertainment market and film attendances, see Kokonis (2012) and Kouanis (2001).

[13] To assess the impact of home viewing one can compare the number of cinemas and tickets sold throughout Greece in the 1980s (1,100 and 43,000,000 respectively) and the 1990s (620 and 13,000,000) (Vamvakas and Panagiotopoulos 2014: 68).

would be financed and what not, with many of the films thus produced never reaching the Greek cinemas after their screening at the Thessaloniki Film Festival. The deregulation of broadcasting in 1989 led to explosive growth in privately-owned TV channels, which were able to finance a large number of comedy and drama series. Even the national broadcaster ERT managed to do this and this practice reached a peak in 2007–8 when forty domestically produced serials were released on prime-time TV (Chalkou 2012: 247). The expansion of television and the dramatic growth of the advertising market resulted in massive development of the Greek audio-visual industry. This was further promoted by the staging of the 2004 Olympic Games in Athens and the spectacles of the opening and closing ceremonies, directed by the avant-garde artist Dimitris Papaioannou.[14] Out of this new audio-visual culture, which blurred the boundaries of the artistic and the popular and brought together commercial advertising, video technology and television production, the new generation of filmmakers emerged. Digital technology, shooting on video and exchanging services (filmmakers working without pay in each other's films) reduced budget costs, offered new opportunities for the making of independent or low budget films and became an ideal form of creative expression for well-educated and skilled users of new audio-visual forms.

Crisis and the reshaping of Greek cinematic culture

From the 1990s onwards the number of films with historico-political themes decreased and those on migration increased. These films cannot be seen as an extension of earlier films on emigration such as *America America* (Kazan 1963) or *Αναπαράσταση/Reconstruction* (Angelopoulos 1970), but rather deal with new concerns: illegal migration, xenophobia and Greeks' identity anxieties. The themes range from the hardships of Albanian migrants making their way to Greece (*Απ' το χιόνι/From the Snow*, Goritsas 1993), the friendship of a left-wing teacher with three illegal Albanian migrants (*Mirupafsim/See you*, Korras and Voupouras 1997), marginalized youth from minority communities (*Από την άκρη της πόλης/From the Edge of the City*, Giannaris 1998) or the victims of sex trafficking (*Ο δρόμος προς τη Δύση/The Way to the West*, Katzourakis 2003). After 1989 Greeks rediscovered their Balkan neighbours and negotiated

---

[14] Interestingly both Lanthimos and Tsangari were part of the team that prepared the opening and closing ceremonies of the Olympic Games.

a new cultural geography through cinematic representations of border crossing, migrant labour or the trafficking of women (Calotychos 2013).

At the end of this decade as older filmmakers dominated the film awards, a clash of generations and styles seems to develop. In 1998 Angelopoulos won the first prize in the State Film Awards and Konstantinos Giannaris was unhappy at coming second. Giannaris was again dissatisfied when in 2001 his film Δεκαπενταύγουστος/*One Day in August* was entirely overlooked while Lakis Papastathis's film *Το Μόνον της Ζωής του Ταξίδιον/The Only Journey of His Life* won seven prizes and in his acceptance speech the director exclaimed, 'Long live the New Greek Cinema' (Chalkou 2012: 251). Though their box office success was rather limited, the new filmmakers had studied or worked abroad and demonstrated an international orientation. This more outward-looking approach was only intensified when the Thessaloniki Film Festival, the main annual cinematic event in Greece, went international in 1992, thus helping to introduce the Greek public to a wide range of innovative films from all over the world. In 2009 a dynamic group of first-time filmmakers formed the 'Κινηματογραφιστές στην Ομίχλη' (Filmmakers in the Mist, subsequently Filmmakers of Greece FoG), an association which brought together a growing number of directors, scriptwriters and independent producers. They boycotted the fiftieth anniversary of the Thessaloniki International Film Festival by withdrawing their films from the upcoming State Film Awards in protest against the lack of state support and demanding new film legislation in line with international standards. Their protest led to limited updating of the institutional framework of Greek cinema and the establishment of the Hellenic Film Academy (Papadimitriou 2014). That year was indeed a turning point for Greece due to the outbreak of the financial crisis and a landmark for the international visibility of Greek cinema. As Lydia Papadimitriou (2009 and 2014) points out, since 2009 there has been a surge of publications on Greek cinema in English, thus facilitating its discussion outside of Greece.

For years Greek cinema had been identified by international cinema experts with the work of Theo Angelopoulos, but the year 2009 marked the start of a new era for Greek films and a reshaping of the Greek cinematic landscape with the international success of three Greek productions: *Dogtooth* (2009) by Yorgos Lanthimos, *Ακαδημία Πλάτωνος/Plato's Academy* (2009) by Filippos Tsitos and *Στρέλλα/A Woman's Way* (2009) by Panos Koutras (see Chapters 4 and 9). A year later another acclaimed film, *Χώρα Προέλευσης/Homeland* (2010) by Syllas Tzoumerkas, intertwined the stories of a Greek family and the country's recent troubled history with each story throwing light on the other. To this list

Alexandros Avranas's film *Miss Violence* (2013) could be added. This bleak film, involving domestic violence, incest, prostitution and paedophilia, paints the portrait of a family whose apparent civility is deceptive, a family riddled with secrets as a controlling father abuses and enslaves his own children. A parable of power and dysfunctional families, *Miss Violence* can be interpreted as a postbankruptcy statement. From Angelopoulos's misty and melancholic landscapes of war-torn Greece we move to the bleak and austere landscapes of the 'weird wave cinema', which some have associated with the crisis (cf. Chalkou 2012: 245; Papadimitriou 2014: 2). Anglophone critics have used the word 'weird' to refer to the semi-absurd narratives of Lanthimos and Tsangari and Greece's changing image 'from Mediterranean holiday idyll and home of big fat weddings to fractious trouble spot' (Rose 2011) while other scholars prefer the term 'Greek New Wave Cinema' (Nikolaidou 2014; Sifaki and Stamou 2020).[15]

What these films 'seem to have in common is a "new gaze" and a "new ethos", which constitutes a clear break with the past' (Chalkou 2012: 244–5), while their international success coincided with the outbreak of the economic crisis in Greece. This 'clear break' represents a thematic shift away from history to confronting contemporary anxieties about personal identity, family, sexuality and migration. Stylistically there is a transition from the earlier realism to hybrid forms involving the fusion of genres, styles or cultural forms and exploiting new technologies. The audience for this new cinematic trend tends to be more international than domestic, while the sources of funding and the marketing methods of these films are also changing, moving away from Greek state organizations to international networks and festivals. No longer only drawing on the European cinematic tradition, as was the case with 'New Greek Cinema', the films of this new trend converse with American films and, though they do not reject the 'Old Greek Cinema', tend to reassert the pivotal role of the actors, focusing on their physicality and bodily performance. Foreign cultural references are also noticeable, sometimes even in the title as in the case of Tsangari's film *Attenberg* (2010), which refers to the mispronunciation of the name of the British broadcaster and naturalist David Attenborough. Another feature of the Greek New Wave cinema, which facilitates its communication with and appeal to international audiences, is the revisiting of genre cinema and particularly the genres of comedy (Athina Rachel Tsangari, *Chevalier*), melodrama (Panos Koutras, *Strella*), neo-noir, horror and the thriller.

---

[15] Psaras embraces the epithet 'weird' and points out that the term 'New Wave' recalls other cinematic traditions (Iranian or Japanese New Wave, French Nouvelle Vague) (2016: 27).

The filmmakers of the 2000s embarked on a bitter and occasionally humorous attack on the values of contemporary Greek society and reflected on the latent brutality in domestic relations and the growing absence of societal bonding (Karalis 2012b: 242). Abandoning the dominant tendencies of earlier Greek cinema, such as the revisiting of historical traumas, the nostalgic gaze or the fetishism of youth, they focus on the family as a problematic microcosm of Greek society by exploring domesticity and parental authority (Aleksić 2016). Their emphasis is on a dark present, the violence of urban life and the traumatic experiences of young people. As mentioned above, Angelopoulos preferred open spaces and silent plateaus; by contrast, the early new weird cinema relied on enclosed or isolated spaces (home or islands), inviting an allegorical reading and demonstrating the theatrical roots of this kind of cinema. As the crisis deepened, the new films took advantage of the opportunities for performativity afforded by the city streets, squares, ruined buildings or empty spaces (Poupou 2018).

In the Greek New Wave, politics return not as an engagement or preoccupation with political history, but through a politicization of viewing which challenges previous modes of representation and introduces characters previously excluded from films (such as LGBTQI+ characters). It engages viewers sensorily by forcing them to take a stance on extreme scenes or in the face of the brutality of the economic crisis and insisting on filming the body and its physical needs. This sensory realism is heightened by the prominence of physical and verbal violence, self-harm, extreme physicality and provocative language. The style of the Greek New Wave draws on performance, the aesthetic of the absurd and the 'new extremism' of filmmakers such as Ulrich Seidl, Michael Haneke, Catherine Breillat and Lars von Trier (Nikolaidou and Poupou 2017).

The most emblematic example of this trend is *Dogtooth*, which was premiered at Cannes in May 2009, winning top prize in *Un Certain Regard*. It also earned an Oscar nomination for the Foreign Language Film Academy Award in February 2010 and awards in other prestigious international festivals. However, the film performed poorly at the Greek box office (selling around forty thousand tickets), pointing to the discrepancy between its domestic reception and its international critical success.[16] *Dogtooth* was co-produced by the Greek Film Centre and an advertising company, Boo, which could afford to take risks with financing a

---

[16] For information on the box office performance of Greek films in the period 2000–15, see Harmbis (2016). The disturbing and formally experimental films of the New/Weird Wave were not as popular (only 11,000 admissions for *Attenberg*) as the crisis-themed film Ένας Άλλος Κόσμος/*Another World* (2015) by the star-director Christophoros Papakaliatis (700,000 admissions) or period films such as *Little England* (350,000 admissions).

film after making substantial profits from its advertising activities. Interestingly, Lanthimos himself honed his skills in advertising before moving to film-making.

Avoiding any direct reference to political developments or the crisis itself, films like *Dogtooth* point to a deeper crisis by creating a self-contained and sanitized world with the film set in a secluded and fenced-off estate with a high shrubbery-lined wall, large lawn and swimming pool. A well-off and overprotective paterfamilias does not allow his children any contact with the outside world and their confinement is justified by myths of monsters waiting outside the fence. The siblings are told that they will be allowed to venture outside the estate once they lose their first 'dogtooth' (canine), hence the title of the film. With the eldest daughter escaping the house by hiding in the boot of her father's car, the final shot is ambiguous, showing the car parked in front of the father's factory with no sign of the girl emerging from the boot.

The family in the film is an example of a control mechanism, as the three siblings are homeschooled by their parents, who apply odd pedagogic and hygiene rituals. Any insubordination is punished calmly but severely. Only Christina, a security guard at the father's factory and brought to the house by him to satisfy the sexual needs of the son, disrupts the balance of power and challenges the protected family space by being the only outsider and lending some videotapes to the elder daughter. The film has been seen as a cinematic turn from the investigation of external to internal borders and demonstrating how the external borders are internalized through family discipline and notions of purity and protection. The parallels that can be drawn between Greece's exclusionary migration policies and the proliferation of internal borders through the obsessive protection of the family space, turns the family into a microcosm of the nation.

Such a reading suggests a deterritorialization of migration by treating the enclosed and incestuous family as an allegory 'for the increasing anxieties to protect the internal borders of Europe, an exclusionary turn in response to the changing composition of European society due to the dynamics of post-Cold War migration' (Celik 2013: 219). As has already been said, the 1990s in Greek cinema are considered a period predominantly concerned with the themes of migration and borders, following the collapse of the Soviet Union and the influx of migrants and refugees. It could be argued that in *Dogtooth* the external borders have been transposed to within society and the family represents an internal border to be protected, controlled or challenged. Though the fixation with purity and hygiene ultimately leads to incest, it reinforces the 'symbolic borders' against various penetrations.

The world of *Dogtooth* is a paradigmatic case of anti-sociality, an imaginary 'revolt' within the family but not extending beyond it; anything beyond the house is a threat, while there is no such thing as society.[17] On the level of language, we see a transition from the silences of Angelopoulos's films to an attempt by the characters to escape the social constraints of language by focusing on word sounds, clichéd phrases and the use of non-verbal forms of expression (e.g. dancing). In *Dogtooth*, objects or concepts are renamed to refer to something recognizable and familiar, thus pointing to a manipulative perversion of language by the parents.

In films by Lanthimos such as *Dogtooth* and *Alps* (2011) human interaction is made to appear impersonal and the de-individuation of characters is reinforced through the absence of proper names and the emphasis on routines and predetermined modes of behaviour. Even the sex scenes are mechanical and devoid of any tenderness. These features have led to the reading of these films as thematizing disempowerment and foregrounding the authoritarian biopolitics of post-democratic societies. According to this reading, the rigidity of roles established by authority figures reflect the dominance of multinational companies and the absurd machinations of bureaucratization, whereas the interpersonal violence we see in them 'can be read as an allegory of the "systemic, anonymous" violence of global capitalism' (Lykidis 2015: 11).[18]

The family in the film has been read in different ways as an allegorical critique of a corrupt and incestuous Greek political system or as a staging of Greece's loss of sovereignty, with the father, representing neo-liberalism, oppressing his children (Greece) (Lykidis 2015).[19] Others have claimed that the economic well-being and the class identity of the family point to a sociopolitical critique of the Greek ruling class (Barotsi 2016) or that the film, with reference to Alain Badiou, signifies that 'the family has once again assumed a totally dominant ideological position, a position that the actual collapse of the nuclear family in Western societies and the challenges to heterosexual normativity have done little to upset' (Fisher 2011: 25). Despite the parental cruelty, Fisher reads *Dogtooth* 'as a satire on the sociological tendency of the young to "dwell within the family until later

---

[17] On the absence of a broader social framework from this and other films and the resulting political implications, see Spatharakis (2011). For a different view, see Papanikolaou (2018a: 160–5).

[18] Dimitris Eleftheriotis points out that the absurd nature of acts may reinforce the attraction of an allegorical reading of the family in the film, but the privileging of such readings in the Weird Wave films 'constitutes a form of critical denial of the deeply problematic and specifically Greek ways in which the family (dys)functions' (2020: 4).

[19] Athina Tsangari, associate producer of Lanthimos' film, pointed out in an interview that 'the reason our politics and economy is in such trouble is that [Greece is] run as a family. It's who you know' (quoted in Rose 2011).

and later"' (2011: 25). Approaching the film's controversial meaninglessness from a queer perspective, Psaras argues that it is a 'denunciation of a particular set of meanings, immanent in the discourses that *Dogtooth* so beautifully and, at the same time, so disturbingly invokes, attacks and dismantles: namely nationalism, patriarchy, heteronormativity' (2016: 89). In whatever way we read the role of the family in the film, power and discipline coexist in the microcosm it represents, invoking Foucauldian biopolitics rather than Marxist dialectics. Despite there being no direct link between *Dogtooth* and the Greek economic crisis, the unfolding of that crisis provided the framework for its reading and supported the argument that culture could flourish in times of austerity (Kourelou, Liz and Vidal 2014).

Conclusion

In Greek cinema the period from the end of the junta to the crisis is a period caught between the 'muses' of art and commercialization, which could be described in terms of the transition from history to domesticity epitomized by the oeuvres of the two emblematic Greek auteurs: Angelopoulos and Lanthimos. Angelopoulos may have been preoccupied with history but younger filmmakers have rejected this obsession and are focusing instead on the family, gender identity and migration, depicting a state of crisis in an enigmatic and allegorical manner. Angelopoulos's misty northern Greek landscapes have given way to the violence of urban life and the realities of a multicultural Athens. The highbrow national metaphors of Angelopoulos and his melancholic view of history are challenged by the metonymies of enclosed spaces, devoid of history and locality. Yet, the combination of grotesque realism and artifice, a feature of the filmic universe of Angelopoulos, can also be found in different ways in the films of Lanthimos, Tsangari and others. The other thing that they share is that they deconstruct the image of Greece as a holiday idyll that had been constructed by earlier films, with the new filmmakers going one step further in interrogating the notion of national cinema, trying to reach a transnational audience and reflecting on the notion of homeland.

By overcoming the preoccupation with political history (Angelopoulos, Voulgaris) and cultural memory (Boulmetis, Smaragdis, Papastathis), the new cinema of the period of the crisis is becoming increasingly transnational, performative and 'auto-ethnographic'. For Thomas Elsaesser 'auto-ethnography' involves looking from outside and is often found in national cinemas attracting world attention in periods of crisis or conflict through a kind of 'politico-voyeuristic curiosity'. According to him, when addressing international audiences, auto-ethnography runs the risk of 'promoting a sort of self-exoticization', conjuring up 'the old anthropological dilemma of the participant observer being presented with the mirror of what the "native" thinks the other, the observer, wants to see' (2005: 510). With this caveat in mind, it can be noted that Greek cinema has come a long way since 1987 when, as Greek minister of culture, Melina Mercouri concluded her foreword to the first catalogue of the Greek Film Centre (1981–6) with a plea to Greek filmmakers to resist 'universalization' and 'uniformity'.

9

Youth, feminism and sexuality: From *oikos* to *demos*

After the collapse of the dictatorship in 1974, Greece witnessed the emergence of some new sociopolitical activism or the reinvigoration of old movements, such as the youth movement, the women's and the homosexual rights movements, associated with the new freedom of expression and the legitimacy of the Left. Not surprisingly, during the junta any claims made regarding the rights of women or homosexuals had been suppressed, and it was the increasing politicization and sexual liberation of the early post-junta period that propelled these movements into the limelight and swelled their ranks. Obviously, due to censorship and repression, it was difficult for these groups to speak freely before that and when they did, in the Polytechnic uprising of November 1973, a number of young people were arrested, tortured or killed. In this chapter, I will be looking at the youth movement and the women's and homosexual rights movements in an attempt to explore their dynamics and how the architectonics of Greek cultural and sexual intimacy have changed since 1974 (Herzfeld 2008: 46).

Seen as intersecting and bringing together political and cultural discourses, anti-authoritarian activism and identity politics, these movements represented a challenge to the social fabric from the micro level of the family to the global macro level. Analysed in terms of their historical development and the legislation that was introduced to improve the status of those they sought to represent, they can offer an insight into the tectonic changes that have taken place in Greek society since the junta. More importantly youth, feminism and sexuality have been used as tropes for rereading past cultural practices and springboards for producing new cultural texts. The (re-)emergence of youth, women's and queer cultures after the junta fostered closer interaction between the social and the cultural and contributed to more nuanced, alternative and diverse readings of Greek cultural history. As social movements and cultural trends, they brought Greece into line with developments in the Western world and offered new cultural perspectives.

Social movements in the Western world had focused mainly on issues of labour and national struggles. From the 1960s onwards 'new social movements' emerged centred instead on issues such as women's liberation, youth, environmental protection etc.[1] Affected as much by their cultural as their political context, these new movements did not limit themselves to seeking material gains but rather challenged social attitudes and established views (della Porta and Diani 2006). Unlike their nineteenth-century counterparts, the 'new social movements' were not concerned with the production of material goods but with contestation in the cultural realm (self-determination, access to information, contestation of symbolic resources) (Nash 2000: 140–1). Contemporary social movements are inherently pluralistic and work on several levels in their attempts to 'break down the barriers' of the existing social system. They signify the emergence of a 'network society' and are ends in themselves rather than the means to realize some future goal, promoting the complementarity of public and private spheres rather than accepting their opposition. In Melucci's view, the struggles of the new social movements were conflicts over identity: 'to push others to recognize something which they themselves recognize; they struggle to affirm what others deny' (Melucci 1989: 46).

In the new social movements, the emphasis on individual identity is linked to new forms of collective action aimed at the democratization of everyday life by bringing together civil society and the state. The dynamic emergence of these new social movements since the 1960s fostered the argument that cultural developments in Greece after 1974 represent a continuation of the long 1960s and a manifestation of the underground appropriation of Western cultural trends and liberalization projects during the junta (Van Dyck 1998; Kornetis 2013; Kornetis et al. 2016; Papanikolaou 2018a: 236–8). This, however, invites a note of caution, given that Greece did not follow the Western sexual revolution and the contraceptive pill was not widely used in the country at that time, while the Greek social movements went unacknowledged in the international literature until the 1990s.[2] Notwithstanding these reservations, the fall of the junta could be seen as signalling the end of the long 1960s in Greece in the same

---

[1] Distinguishing between social movements and other types of social and political action (such as interest groups, political parties or religious movements), Diani defines a social movement as 'a network of informal interactions between a plurality of individuals, groups and/or organizations, engaged in a political or cultural conflict on the basis of a shared collective identity' (1992: 13).
[2] Some have even dubbed Loukianos Kelaidonis's 'beach party' at Vouliagmeni (25 July 1983) the Greek Woodstock (1969). Attended by more than seventy thousand people, this gig was different from the political concerts of the *Metapolitefsi* and still lingers in the memory of many Athenians as one of the most liberating moments of the post-dictatorship era.

way the international oil crisis of 1973–4 is thought to mark the end of the 'long 1960s' in the Western world (Marwick 1998: 7; Jameson 1984).

Social and political scientists in Greece had been primarily concerned with top-down politics and less with bottom-up social change, while the first special issue on 'Social Movements and the Social Sciences' appeared in the *Greek Political Science Review* rather belatedly in 1996 (Kornetis and Kouki 2016). Social movements involve historical investigation, cultural revisionism, legislative change, social activism and theoretical debates and thus it is impossible to cover all these aspects here in detail. I shall simply aim to show the different phases in these movements since 1974 and particularly their gradual emancipation from their affiliation to political parties.

Youth and the clash of generations

According to Eric Hobsbawm (1995: 326), youth culture became dominant in developed, mostly capitalist, market economies because it represented a concentrated mass of purchasing power and had an astonishing internationalism, blending personal and social liberation and becoming the matrix of a cultural revolution in the 1960s. Protest, blue jeans, music and song are other factors that defined the emerging youth culture, while Karl Mannheim's theory of 'generations in conflict' has been the inspiration for its study for many years. Though regarded as a state of becoming, youth invites us to include age in the factors involved in historical and cultural analysis along with race, class and gender (Heilbronner 2008). Youth cultures are seen as contesting the hegemony of a 'parent' culture and constructing their distinct identity through an eclectic combination of music, dress and other symbolic activities. Intergenerational conflict was a feature of the 1960s and particularly of May 1968, while the generation gap in Greece was made manifest in the period of the dictatorship in the poem 'Young Men of Sidon, 1970' by the left-wing poet Manolis Anagnostakis. Alluding to a poem by Cavafy with a similar title ('Young Men of Sidon AD 400'), it criticized young people for their vain radicalism, hedonism and internationalism.

The emergence of a youth culture is one way of assessing Greece's westernization and resistance to it by left-leaning youngsters. In the past the Left might have decried Western leisure trends and the sexual behaviour associated with them, but the moral panic generated by youth subcultures extended beyond the Left, with the rock 'n' roll fans of the late 1950s being described in Greece as '*tediboides*' (Teddy Boys), representing the pernicious effects of the 'Western way of life' and the mimicry of foreign 'delinquent' practices such as pool halls, dancing, magazines, cinema and others (Avdela 2008). In the 1970s rock music played a crucial role in the debates about the identity of the communist youth who often promoted Greek popular music and *rebetika* as a genuine expression and vehicle of a 'popular agonistic tradition' (Papadogiannis 2010). In short, the youth came to epitomize the anxieties about the trajectories of modernity and raised the question as to whether they were children of Marx, Coca-Cola or both.

Student movements and the study of Greek youth thrived during the post-junta period.[3] This was due to the growing democratization of Greek society, the reintroduction of student councils in secondary schools in 1975, the formation of student groups affiliated to political parties, the controversies caused by the increasing number of educational reforms and the emphasis on collective rather than individual action.[4] A sign of the changing times after the fall of junta was the publication in 1975 of the Greek translation of *The Little Red School Book* (1969) by Søren Hansen and Jesper Jensen.[5] The book served as an initiation manual for many students to taboo subjects such as sexuality, drinking and drugs but caused a global scandal once it was translated into many languages in the early 1970s and it was banned in France and Italy. Segregation by gender had been abolished in almost all Greek high schools by 1979, and a few years later (1982–3) the first socialist government showed itself particularly favourable towards young people by introducing the right to vote at 18, abolishing the student uniform and establishing the anniversary of the Polytechnic uprising (17 November) as a school holiday.

The Greek student movement since 1821 and the appearance of youth organizations became a subject for study (Lazos 1987; Liakos 1988; Giannaris 1993), indicating that youth, together with the history of women and the cities (e.g. Hermoupolis, Thessaloniki), were the new areas being explored by Greek historiography. From 1983 onwards, the General Secretariat for Youth, re-established by the PASOK government, funded a research and publishing

---

[3] Astrinakis (1991), Karamanolakis et al. (2010), Avdela (2013), Katsapis (2013), Kornetis (2013) and Papadogiannis (2015).

[4] Political youth organizations opposed the so-called 'intensification of studies' and the implementation of Law 815, introduced in August 1978, aiming to reform higher education in Greece. This opposition led to widespread occupation of university premises by students and to the government withdrawing Law 815 on 4 January 1980. Recalling her involvement in the student movement of Rigas Feraios, Angela Kastrinaki points out that during the early years of the *Metapolitefsi* 'the I had to disappear in front of the we' and 'the individual was understood as just a unit in a group' (2014: 28, 241–2).

[5] The writings of intellectuals, such as the Marxist Herbert Marcuse (1898–1979) and the psychoanalyst Wilhelm Reich (1897–1957), were also popular among the youth at that time.

project, *The Historical Archive of Greek Youth*, which organized three international symposia (1984, 1987 and 1997) and produced a number of monographs. The aim of the project was to study the history of Greek youth by deploying social, demographic, educational and cultural approaches.[6] This shows that young people were one of the priorities of the post-junta Greek governments, and particularly of PASOK, which tried to seduce youngsters with the introduction in 1996 of the 'Panehellenic Student Symposium' and the 'Parliament of the Ephebes'. Yet, despite this growing interest in youth culture, Greece relied on reverse intergenerational support. Older people with their pensions supported the younger generation rather than the other way around with the public purse contributing more to the state pension fund in Greece than in any other EU country. Post-junta society was not youth-centred but focused more on the elderly, favouring pensioners, and this explains why 17.5 per cent of GDP even today goes on pensions.[7] Attempts to regulate their behaviour or people treating their culture as a cause of moral concern made young people feel they were living in a society that favoured older generations, and this feeling intensified during the crisis.

The intense involvement of the young in politics during and just after the junta was followed by a period of disillusionment and distancing from politics on their part. Apart from the politically committed youth groups there were other youth subcultures (e.g. punks (Kolovos 2015)) that had a rather ephemeral character and promoted their own mythical figures, such as the rock musicians Pavlos Sidiropoulos (1948–1990) and Nicholas Asimos (1949–1988), the filmmaker and writer Nikos Nikolaidis (1939–2007) or the actor and poet Katerina Gogou (1940–1993). The word 'αμφισβήτηση' (contestation) became increasingly popular, while the marginal and the irreverent were glorified by filmmakers such as Nikos Zervos, the publisher of countercultural magazines Leonidas Christakis (1928–2009), the musician and stand-up comedian Tzimis Panousis and others. Breaking away from canons of decorum, these subcultures assumed an antagonistic character and a distinctive countercultural flavour, with the year 1980 marking the beginning of punk rock in Greece and the promotion of anti-establishment ideas and practices (Kitis 2015: 8).[8] Savvopoulos's early

---

[6] The project's website is http://www.eie.gr/nhrf/institutes/inr/structure/section_c3-en.html.
[7] Alberto Nardelli, 'Unsustainable futures? The Greek pensions dilemma explained', *The Guardian*, 15 June 2015, https://www.theguardian.com/business/2015/jun/15/ unsustainable-futures-greece-pensions-dilemma-explained-financial-crisis-default-eurozone.
[8] The 'anarchists' or 'anti-authoritarian' *chóros*, a loose affiliation of groups, collectives and self-managed community spaces, had its origins in both the non-parliamentary Left and youth subcultures. It shifted political activity from factories and universities to the streets and lifestyles and attracted more attention following the events of December 2008 (Kitis 2015).

music also appealed to the youth counterculture, mixing, as it did, Greek folk music or *rebetika* with rock, thus hybridizing Greek culture and destabilizing the Greek tradition.

In the post-junta period and in the wake of the Polytechnic events, a number of older and younger writers began to deal with young people in their novels as a category representing both hope and challenge in their transition from allegiance to party politics to narcissistic self-indulgence. Among the works by younger writers the novel by Christos Chomenidis, *Το σοφό παιδί/ The Wise Kid* (1993) stands out. Charting the narrator's rite of passage from childhood to early adulthood and his move from the village of Papingo in Epirus to Athens, it became a bestseller. Written in 1990, when the author was just 24, the novel combines a racy narrative with youthful irony and could be considered emblematic of the irreverent youth culture of the early period of the *Metapolitefsi* (including the work of other young 'tongue-in-cheek' writers who thematized youth in their novels, such as Vangelis Raptopoulos, Petros Tatsopoulos, Christos Vakalopoulos). The proliferation of literary texts about youth after 1974 continues even into the twenty-first century. For example, Amanda Michalopoulou's novel *Γιατί σκότωσα την καλύτερή μου φίλη/Why I Killed My Best Friend* (2003) could also be viewed as a chronicle of the post-junta period seen from the perspective of two female students, Maria and Anna, growing up in the era of punk rock, the dominance of PASOK and the material excesses of the 1990s. Maria, from a conservative family, becomes a political activist while Anna, whose parents were exiled during the junta, enjoys a wealthy and shallow lifestyle as an adult. The novel engages critically with the notion of Europeanization in the run-up to the 2004 Olympics and the ineffectiveness of left-wing activism (Katsan 2019: 120–2).

The younger generation, who grew up in the post-dictatorship period with increased material prosperity, better education and improved living standards than previous generations, have often been perceived as self-centred consumers without a distinct political identity. According to surveys among young people between 18 and 29 years old, 43.5 per cent had a strong interest in politics in 1988 but this had gone down to 24.5 per cent by 2006. In the same age group, politics was associated primarily with mistrust: 28.3 per cent (women) and 27.3% per cent (men) in 1988 and 53.7 per cent (women) and 54.4 per cent (men) in 2006 (Pantelidou Malouta 2015: 13–14). They did not care about institutionalized politics and instead practised the 'politics of youthful anti-politics'. Unless we interpret it as a sign of a different kind of politics, this downward trend seems to be inconsistent with the large-scale school occupations in 1990–1 (in which the former prime minister Alexis Tsipras was involved as a student) and 1998–9 (Sklavenitis 2016). The highly competitive system of university entrance exams and the realization that obtaining a university degree would not necessarily lead to stable employment caused feelings of insecurity and frustration among young people. Therefore, sit-ins became a standard form of opposition in Greek schools at the end of the twentieth century, and their aim was to cancel reforms rather than suggest alternatives.

Until 1980 the only rock concert given in Athens by a world-famous band was that by the Rolling Stones just a few days before the 1967 coup. Subsequently, the number of rock concerts in Athens increased and attracted many young people who often clashed with the police. After 1980 the anti-conventional youth lifestyle, often involving concert-venue, football and street violence, was not easily pigeonholed under the existing political categories, and this widened the generation gap, causing anxiety about the political orientation of this new, but still male-orientated, youth culture. Moreover, the spread of youth slang in the 1980s, deemed by older people as impoverished or vulgar language, contributed to the gap between the generations (Androutsopoulos 1998; see also Chapter 5). Yet, it has been claimed that from the late 1980s onwards the youth movement toned down its opposition to the older generation and instead tried to build intergenerational solidarity in opposing reforms (pension and educational systems), while school sit-ins often had the moral support of parents and teachers (Panagiotopoulos 2018: 176–7). Young people who were not affiliated to political organizations followed multiple trajectories and displayed various tastes ranging from foreign popular music to football. On the other hand, the youth wings of the political parties (particularly of the Left) continued with their annual festivals and often linked leisure and sexuality, treating the former as conducive to sexual emancipation or drug use. Interestingly, the pro-Soviet communist youth denounced the views of the philosopher and political theorist Herbert Marcuse for encouraging the substitution of class conflict with generational conflict.

The increasing emancipation of young people since 1974 has led to the rise and decline of symbols, marking the transition from celebrating the Polytechnic uprising against the junta to the indictment of the so-called 'generation of the Polytechnic' as responsible for the recent crisis. The antagonism of the 1980s surrounding the appropriation of the aura of the 'generation of the Polytechnic' gave way to demythologization and disillusionment (Lambrinou 2015). The mythical generation of the Polytechnic, the symbol of the *Metapolitefsi*, has ended up being challenged by the digital generation and the unemployed youth of the crisis. We are witnessing a process involving mythologization, canonization and questioning as well as the end of a heroic genealogy and mythology (the celebrated generation of Resistance, the Lambrakides' generation of the 1960s and the generation of the Polytechnic) encapsulated in the slogan 'EAM- ELAS- Polytechnio'. Since the student revolt at Athens Polytechnic against the junta in November 1973, a number of countercultural groups and discourses have emerged, making their presence felt first through activism and later though squatting (primarily around the Exarcheia district in Athens), the media (e.g. Athens Indymedia) and social networks or posters.

A turning point in this process was the assassination of a fifteen-year-old student, Alexis Grigoropoulos, by police in December 2008 and the rebellious outburst which followed, bringing the dissatisfaction and indignation of the younger generation to the forefront of the Greek public sphere.[9] Their distrust of the political system and their questioning of the state institutions marked the rise of alternative modes of political engagement and of articulating public discourse. December 2008 and its aftermath has been seen as a game changer and made Greece an international case study in times of crisis bringing together activists and theorists. The novelty of the December insurrection lies in the fact that a new subject appeared in the public realm, the immigrant protester, opening up new spaces of citizenship from below. The immigrants did not join the protests as bearers of their 'ethnic' identities but as claimants of citizenship outside its national legal form (Kalyvas 2010). From being a peripheral case, Greece became an international paradigm alongside the unrest in the Paris suburbs in 2005, the *Indignados* movement in Spain, Occupy in the United States and the Arab Spring in the Middle East and North Africa. Therefore, it has been claimed that the worst riots Greece has experienced since the end of its Civil War was a transnational and not just a Greek event (Figure 7).

The December unrest offered an opportunity to debate the culture of the *Metapolitefsi* and reflect on its possible causes. No other recent event has triggered such a debate and engendered such a range of intellectual responses.[10] Some have treated it as a by-product of a political culture of nihilism and permissiveness, a senseless eruption of violence without political or ideological justification, while others saw it as a social movement and a manifestation of

---

[9] It should be noted that in 1985 another 15-year-old student, Michalis Kaltezas, had also been shot dead by a policeman.

[10] See the contributions in Economides and Monastiriotis (2009), special issues of the periodicals *Synchrona Themata* (no. 103, October–December 2008) and *Nea Estia* (no. 1819, February 2009) and Balampanidis (2009). Alexandra Halkia offers a gendered reading of the December events as a contest of masculinities (Apostolelli and Halkia 2012: 244).

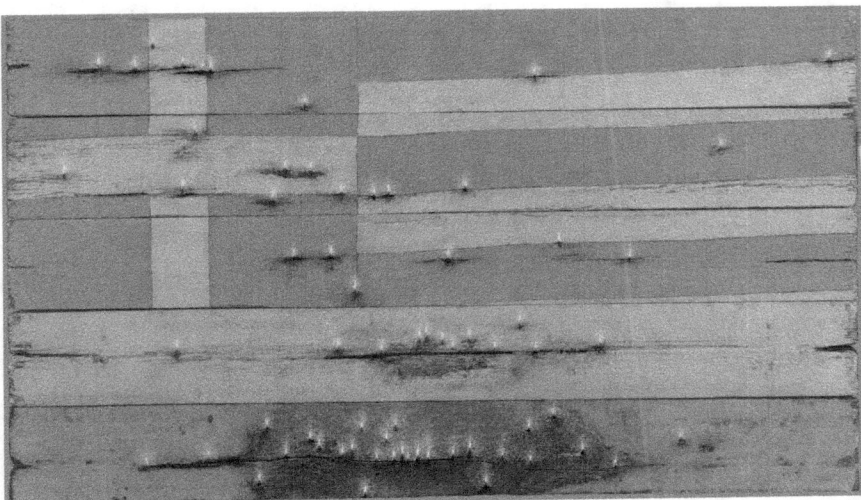

Figure 7 '*National Memory I*', a painting by Christos Bokoros made after the events of December 2008. Courtesy of the artist.

radicalism.[11] The debate centred on the following questions: Was it a symptom of a culture of disobedience and the failure of Greek society to regulate itself or a manifestation of rising social tensions and youth disenchantment with prevailing neoliberal policies and a failing education system? Were the December events a spontaneous eruption, an 'event' in Alain Badiou's terms, or a youth movement with a national and transnational genealogy and the culmination of an underground process? Riots or revolt? Answers to these questions were divided according to whether the emphasis was placed on the cultural or the social causes.

It could be said that December 2008 was a rite of passage, marking a transition from a student movement affiliated to political parties to a youth movement questioning the existing political system and relying on self-organization, new technologies and social media. In an attempt to integrate the domestic with the transnational, a number of graffiti and leaflets were written (and reproduced in French and English), something quite unprecedented.[12] A new kind of political activism involving street action and social media rejected the past practices of

---

[11] For opposing views on the events of December 2008, see Kalyvas (2008) and Sotiris (2010), Johnston and Seferiades (2012). For a review of the Greek intellectual responses to the events, see Sotiris (2013).

[12] Andreas Kalyvas has argued that 'by all accounts, the December protests were more militant, oppositional, and destructive than the better organized and disciplined pre-dictatorial struggles' (2010: 353).

political parties and trade unions and encouraged young people to take things into their own hands.[13] Graffiti and street art became like weapons with which they could express what they felt about the society in which they lived. Facing various challenges, such as limited job prospects, low income and frustrated expectations, they were drawn into activism and nihilism, feeling that their generation of risk and precariousness had replaced the old proletariats. Caught between consumerism and precarity, this generation, marginalized by the financial squeeze, is a deconstructive generation, attacking established forms of authority and cultural symbols (Smith 2015). The main outlets for its energy and creativity are seeking employment abroad, political activism or unconventional art forms.

The film by Argyris Papadimitropoulos and Jan Vogel, *Wasted Youth* (2011), inspired by the murder of Alexis Grigoropoulos in 2008, is a sort of docu-fiction blending youth culture with the impact of the financial crisis and epitomizing the clash of the generations. Set in Athens, over one sweltering summer's day, it juxtaposes two parallel stories of unrelated individuals to emphasize the lack of dialogue within Athenian society and particularly the lack of communication between generations. The first story focuses on Haris, a 16-year-old teenager, who spends his day skateboarding aimlessly around Athens with his friends. Representing a form of freedom and independence, skateboarding offers the opportunity to teenagers to move freely through the city and claim public open spaces in contrast to the closed spaces inhabited by adults. As a youngster, with no real sense of purpose and a carefree lifestyle, Haris clashes with his bullying father while his mother is seriously ill in hospital, unable to support her son. The second story features the life of Vassilis, a middle-aged police officer, who is frustrated with his dead-end job and lives with his family in a cramped apartment. He seems depressed and on the verge of exploding at any moment, chastising his teenage daughter for wearing headphones at the dinner table. Interestingly, we are not aware of his occupation until we have watched two-thirds of the film. The film reaches an unexpected climax and the two concurrent stories converge just before the end when Vassilis's patrol partner fires a fatal shot at Haris. The directors claim in their note:

---

[13] It has been claimed that Golden Dawn's appeal to a section of the Greek youth cannot simply be attributed to their anger over the crisis but their support for a fascist political agenda should also be understood in terms of a deeper ideological affinity with the party's xenophobic discourse and earlier manifestations of dissatisfaction with the functioning of representative democracy, which have been building over the previous two or three decades (Koronaiou et al. 2015).

The film is indeed a portrait of the city on the verge of a nervous breakdown. It is also about the real existence of adolescence with the vivacity and the energy that silently burns in it. It is also a film about a young man who struggles to do what all young men struggle to do, without knowing that maybe their future will be wasted – and as it happens it is wasted indeed.[14]

A portrait of a dystopian metropolis and a kind of urban movie, the film could be seen as a metaphor for a country suffering from economic implosion and failing its teenagers. The dysfunctional families in the film create an oppressive and suffocating environment for the youngsters. Dealing with adolescent rites of passage, youth culture and simmering family tensions, *Wasted Youth* builds on a trend seen in earlier films with similar themes such as Konstantinos Giannaris's *Από την άκρη της πόλης/At the Edge of the City* (1998) and the more recent *Κυνόδοντας/Dogtooth* (2009) by Yorgos Lanthimos, *Στρέλλα/A Woman's Way* (2009) by Panos Koutras or *Attenberg* (2010) by Athena Rachel Tsangari or American independent films, such as the emblematic *Kids* (1995) by Larry Clark and the suggestive *Elephant* (2003) by Gus Van Sant (Mylonaki 2013: 171). Compared to the other recent Greek films mentioned above, *Wasted Youth* is more explicitly connected with the psychological and existential effects of the crisis, pointing to a profound intergenerational crisis. Youth might be presented as frivolous, disoriented or unwilling to take any serious responsibilities, yet the film seems to celebrate youth's anarchic energy and wasted exuberance.

It could be said that after the events of December 2008, Greek youth returned to the political activism of the early post-junta period in a more challenging and globally informed way. This return also involved a demythologization of the past and a generational rift, because the young people felt victims not only of the crisis but also of the long-standing privileging of the older generation in Greek society. Though institutional changes and social developments have supported youth culture since 1974, Greek society has not lost its age bias. The crisis, which has hit young people particularly hard and forced them to leave the country to find work, perpetuated this bias and increased youth frustration. The post-war gilded generations failing young people is not just a Greek phenomenon and redress is now being demanded across Europe (particularly after the Covid-19 pandemic). The fact that there is no equivalent Greek word to 'gerontocracy' in respect of the youth is telling, while Greece is fast becoming an ageing society

---

[14] Jim Papamichos, 'Wasted Youth', *Myfilm* [on line], 6 January 2011, https://www.myfilm.gr/8328.

due to demographic decline, partly a consequence of the crisis (see Introduction, note 6).

Feminism, politics and culture

Feminist history tends to be categorized in terms of waves. The first wave was mainly concerned with women's right to vote. In the second wave (of the 1960s to 1980s), the emphasis shifted to issues of equality and sexual liberation, whereas in the third wave (from the 1990s onwards) the focus has been on sexual harassment, violence and intersectionality (demonstrating how race, ethnicity, gender and religion are all significant factors when discussing feminism). Feminism in Greece has more or less followed this pattern and the emergence of a women's movement can be traced back to the late nineteenth century, though it was restricted to a small number of educated, city-dwelling women. The Greek feminist cause was bolstered by improvements in the educational attainment of women and their access to full suffrage in 1952, more than a century after men (with Lina Tsaldari becoming the first female government minister in 1956).[15] Any feminist activity was stifled during the dictatorship and the Panhellenic Union of Greek Women (founded in 1964) was suppressed. It made a vigorous comeback after the fall of the military dictatorship and contact with similar, and more well-established, movements in Western Europe and the United States. In a period when most other European countries continued to manifest a trend towards increasing female integration into the wage economy, paradoxically Greece registered a decline, with the rate only starting to rise again in the 1980s.

Anthropologists have also pointed to the 'domestic model of gender' and have argued that gender attributes were linked to domestic kinship roles. Womanhood meant nurturing, cooking, cleaning, while manhood meant providing for the household, representing or defending kinship loyalties. The sexes were represented as being in a relationship of complementarity, mutual dependence and ideal equality (Loizos and Papataxiarchis 1991: 7–8). The supremacy of marriage, family and kinship networks shaped the position of women until the 1980s. For years marriage remained the ideal for Greek society, closely related to social recognition and personal fulfilment with its cultural acceptance attested by the low divorce and cohabitation rates as well as the

---

[15] Female suffrage in Greece could be seen as part of the international post-war democratization process.

small number of children born outside wedlock. The family's image and social prestige rested to a large extent on the woman's ability to organize the household, maintain family cohesion and successfully perform the fetishized role of 'good housekeeper'.

The pride associated with this role was thought to give women a sense of accomplishment and acted as a strong incentive for them to comply with its expectations. Their role in the family did not necessarily suggest a sense of submissiveness but it carried relative power. Women entered paid employment as long as this did not pose a threat to their role in the family and their traditional status. Though in the 1980s the decline seen in previous decades in the number of women in the labour force was reversed, the figures for unemployed women fluctuated and were significantly higher than in all other EEC countries. Women's unpaid labour 'provided essential services in lieu of the social infrastructure that the state refused to create' (Stamiris 1986: 103). Women classified as unpaid family members constituted 36 per cent of the female work force in 1981 but dropped to 31 per cent in 1989 compared to Spain's 12 per cent and Ireland's 3.7 per cent. The reasons for the high proportion of women in unpaid employment lie, according to Nota Kyriazis, 'in the economic structure, the significant role of the family in Greek society, and the traditional attitudes regarding women's appropriate roles' (1995: 273). While the labour market was gradually changing in Greece and the family continued to retain its traditional importance, three women's organizations emerged after 1974 as what were essentially appendages to the political parties of the Left.

The 'Democratic Women's Movement' (KDG) was formed in 1975 and was tied to the Greek Communist Party-Interior (KKE-Interior), the 'Federation of Greek Women' (OGE) associated with the Greek Communist Party (KKE) was set up the following year together with the 'Union of Greek Women' (EGE), a feminist organization affiliated to the socialist party PASOK and led by the American-born wife of its leader, Margaret Papandreou.[16] Feminism in Greece did not develop as a grass-roots movement and at a time of heightened anti-Americanism it was associated with undesirable influence from the United States and was generally perceived 'as yet another import of "decadent" cultural imperialism' (Stamiris 1986: 108). Women who were members of the political parties and the affiliated women's organizations faced the difficult task of maintaining loyalty to the party and the feminist cause. Political parties were considered effective means of spreading feminist ideas while the primacy

---

[16] The right-wing New Democracy party rejected the idea of an autonomous women's organization.

of safeguarding democracy underpinned feminist activities after 1974. The coexistence of politics and feminism, either in the form of mutual support or of autonomous pathways, was often debated in the women's organizations, causing tension in their ranks. Women's organizations or movements were not necessarily feminist.

The 'Women's Liberation Movement' (KAG) could be seen as an exception to this trend. Formed in 1975, its members were either not affiliated to political parties or came from the ranks of fringe groups on the Left. Some of them, having lived outside Greece during the junta and been in touch with European and American movements, argued that there were similar conditions in Greece for the development of such a movement. Its structure was rather loose and non-hierarchical. During its four-year lifespan (1975–9) KAG focused particularly on the issues of abortion and contraception, promoting them in terms of a woman's choice to have control over her body and not within the usual parameters of family planning. For this purpose, they organized an exhibition in Athens (9–24 July 1976), which had a tremendous impact, and launched a campaign focusing on sexuality rather than motherhood (Sklaveniti 2013). As the UN 'Decade for Women' (1975–85) came to a close and a new abortion law was passed in May 1985, the heyday of Greek feminist movements was almost over, but some feminists kept fighting and resisting their absorption into what they called 'state feminism'. In the 1980s there was simmering tension in Greece between the women's movements supported by the political parties and the autonomous feminist movements. The latter pointed to the omission of Eleni Varikas's contribution on Greek feminists from the Greek translation of the special issue on 'La Grèce en mouvement' of the French journal *Les Temps Modernes* in 1985 and their exclusion from the article on the women's movement in Greece by Eleni Stamiris, a member of PASOK, published in the *New Left Review of Books* in 1986 (Sklaveniti 2018: 78).

The Left treated gender inequities as part of the wider sociopolitical change required after the fall of junta and such an approach did not favour autonomous movements, since gender inequality was seen as an inevitable part of the capitalist system. Following Friedrich Engels and August Bebel's *Women under Socialism* (1904), it was believed by some that the women's struggle could be perceived as part of the wider working-class struggle for equality and 'the women's issue' could effectively be addressed within a socialist society by combating capitalism (Karamanou 2003: 276). The relationship between feminism and the Left was rather strained, ranging from outright hostility on the part of the prudish, pro-Soviet communists to cautious acceptance by other male left-wingers, who

Figure 8 Women's Rights Demonstration in Athens (1981). Banner reads: 'I don't belong to my father, I don't belong to my husband, I want to be myself'. Courtesy of Athina Lekkakou.

started reflecting on what might constitute non-sexist male behaviour.[17] Political activism within the boundaries of the political parties was perceived by women as a more effective way of promoting feminist concerns since gender equality was considered a product of the abolition of class exploitation. The slogan of most feminists during this period was 'There can be no women's liberation without social liberation, no social liberation without women's liberation', and for political parties women's issues provided a platform for mobilizing women and a mechanism through which to ensure their political involvement. On the other hand, some second-wave feminists criticized left-wing parties and their youth organizations for being overly attached to the patriarchal status quo (Figure 8).[18]

In short, two competing approaches to feminism emerged in the early post-junta period. One saw it as a political movement equating social liberation

---

[17] Articles in *Odigitis*, the periodical of the communist youth movement (KNE), lambasted the feminist slogan 'the personal is political', presenting it as a vehicle for individualistic preoccupations and bourgeois desires.

[18] Without rejecting motherhood, second-wave feminist groups maintained that women should decide whether and when coitus should lead to procreation. Alexandra Halkias (2004) shows how nationalism, gender and sexuality came together in Greece in the 1990s by exploring the paradox of the high incidence of abortion in a country where the low birth rate was considered a national crisis. The demographic discourse seems to sexualize the nation-building process and penalize having an abortion, which has been legal in Greece since 1986.

with women's emancipation and evoking the progressive gender politics of the Resistance, while for the other it was an autonomous struggle for individual freedom and female subjectivity ('the personal is political'), echoing the spirit of May 1968. The first approach seems to have prevailed and thus feminism in Greece emerged in step with party politics rather than as the sexual revolution it was in the rest of the Western world.

In 1975 the new Greek constitution introduced equality for men and women for the first time and equal pay, while Greece's entry into the European Community and PASOK's coming to power in 1981 brought a plethora of legislative changes in women's status.[19] Family Law was revised in the early 1980s and both spouses then became jointly responsible for family decisions. The dowry system was abolished, married women could keep their maiden name, divorce by mutual consent was institutionalized and children born out of wedlock had the same rights as all other children.[20] Adultery also ceased to be a criminal offence. Until 1982 a woman could not set up her own business without the consent of her husband. The status of rural women was improved, paid maternity leave of twelve weeks was introduced, rape was made a statutory offence and the right of women to have an abortion during the first twelve weeks of pregnancy was established.[21] In 1985 the General Secretariat for Equality (an upgrading of the Council for Equality formed in 1982) was established as a state agency for the promotion of equality, and school books were rewritten with the help of women's organizations. As a result, the 1980s were a period of significant change in the area of gender equality, employment rights and discrimination in the workplace, making Greece arguably one of the most advanced countries in Europe regarding women's rights at that time. Though female voters seem to have rewarded PASOK in the subsequent elections for improving their status, these reforms raised the question as to whether the empowerment of women could be achieved simply through legislation (Pollis 1992b).

Small autonomous feminist groups sprang up in the universities and elsewhere and a number of feminist books and magazines were published. The most influential magazine was Σκούπα για το Γυναικείο Ζήτημα/Broom

---

[19] In the 1970s, and as part of the equality debate, there was discussion about compulsory national service for women (originally floated as a junta initiative), but by 1979 this argument had subsided in line with the diminishing nationalist fervour (Poulos 2009: 167–71).

[20] In the large post-war tide of emigration (that amounted to almost a million migrants by the early 1970s) the number of women emigrating because of the dowry system had increased dramatically (Stamiris 1986: 104).

[21] As a result of the gender equality legislation of the 1980s, Greek women were allowed *jure sanguinis* to pass their nationality on to their children (Law 1438/1984) for the first time in Greek history (Christopoulos 2019: 115).

for Women's Issue (five issues, 1979–81), followed by *Δίνη*/Whirlpool (1986–97, nine issues and a one-off volume in 2005 (Michailidou and Halkia 2005)), *Κατίνα: φεμινιστικό περιοδικό/Katina: Feminist Journal* (1987–91, six issues) and others. In October 1983 the first bookshop for women opened (closing in 1990), and in the same year a group for the promotion of women's studies was set up at the University of Thessaloniki (Repoussi 2003: 140–1). Before the mid-1990s, courses on women's and gender history were rarely offered in Greek universities. But from then on there has been a distinct increase in the production of this kind of research, while EU funding, through the so-called EPEAEK programmes, has been contributing to the development of such courses since 2003.[22] Though the first conference in Greece on 'Gender in history: Assessments and paradigms' (12 November 2011, University of Athens) took place rather belatedly, the turn to gender history was evident in the paradigm shift from political to social history, from facts to problems or from 'structures' and 'mechanisms' to social subjects and agents. Gender studies facilitated the passage from a sociological to an anthropological and cultural approach to the study of Greek society. New areas of research opened up such as the gendered content of citizenship, female labour and education, feminist urbanism and the rise of bourgeois values, the healthy body and sport, and sexuality and performing identities (Fournaraki and Yannitsiotis 2013; Avdela 2010).[23] In the 1990s many feminist groups in Greece lost momentum and their magazines ceased publication. Some feminists of the 1970s and 1980s got new positions or access to European institutions and contributed to the preparation and implementation of directives or guidelines on discrimination at a European level.[24] Women's rights were no longer seen as a national issue and became a European one with new transnational concerns emerging, such as sex-trafficking and the exploitation of migrant women.

In 1985 the Greek Parliament had thirteen women MPs out of a total of three hundred deputies. In the elections of April 2000 there was a marked increase in the number of female MPs (thirty-one out of three hundred, that is 10.3 per cent compared to 6.3 per cent of the previous parliament). In the elections of June

---

[22] An EU directive from 2000 has been instrumental in supporting such programmes/courses by specifying that 10 per cent of the budget for education coming from the Third Community Support Framework (2000–6) was to be spent on promoting 'Gender and Equality'.

[23] The creation in 2007 of the Greek National Committee of the International Federation for Research in Women's History has encouraged the study of gender in modern Greek historiography (Papadogiannis 2017: 77).

[24] The 2019 Gender Equality Index from the European Institute for Gender Equality shows that Greece has one of the lowest scores in Europe on gender equality (with less than 52 points) with the top scorer Sweden scoring 83.6 points. https://eige.europa.eu/news/gender-equality-index-2019-still-far-finish-line.

2012, this number went up to sixty-three, in the elections of January 2015 it went up again to sixty-eight but in the September elections of the same year it went down to fifty-four. In the elections of May/July 2019, sixty-one MPs (out of three hundred) and five MEPs (out of twenty-one) were women. At local level just one woman has been elected regional governor in the country's thirteen regions, and out of 332 mayors only 19 have been female. Underrepresentation of women in the parliament and in high-level decision-making provoked a debate about the introduction of a quota for women in parliamentary and local elections. In 2001 a law was passed that effectively required one-third of the candidates for the regional and local elections to be women (extended in 2008 to parliamentary elections). This quota was raised to 40 per cent in 2018 and 2019, respectively. Though the law was couched in gender neutral terms (the ratios applied to both male and female candidates), there were complaints that these measures were insulting to women, because they implied they could not get elected without the help of quotas.[25] Interestingly, surveys indicate that in 2006 young women were less interested in politics (43.9 per cent) than in 1988 (15.4 per cent) (Pantelidou-Malouta 2010: 456, 461).

Despite the fact that women were underrepresented in the political decision-making process for many years, since the 1980s they have made their mark in the area of culture and more particularly in writing fiction.[26] Novels such as Maro Douka's *Η Αρχαία Σκουριά/Fool's Gold* (1979) and Alki Zei's *Η Αρραβωνιαστικιά του Αχιλλέα/Achilles Fiancée* (1987) highlight self-discovery rather than political involvement by shifting the emphasis away from the historical reality towards the formation of personal identity. These narratives together with others contributed to the re-evaluation of the personal and a rethinking of the separation between individual and public history. The events narrated by Myrsini in *Fool's Gold* begin the summer before the military dictatorship came to power in April 1967 and continue until the fall of that regime in 1974. *Achilles Fiancée* covers a much longer period, from the German occupation of Greece to the dictatorship. In both novels the female narrators embark on a quest for self-identity, bringing together the postmodern 'decentring' of subjectivity with an affirmation of the female self. The novels illustrate the transition from the male

---

[25] Interestingly Greek women appear more left-wing than the men. According to statistics, in the elections of June 2012 45.4 per cent of young women (18–24 year-olds) in Athens voted for SYRIZA compared to 20.5 per cent of men. The neo-Nazi party Golden Dawn (Χρυσή Αυγή) appears to be more attractive to men, with 11.6 per cent of the same age group (18–24) voting for it in the January 2015 elections compared to 7.4 per cent of women (Pantelidou-Malouta 2015: 23, 35).

[26] It should be noted that in 1975 on the occasion of International Women's Year, Ersi Lange published an anthology of Greek women writers (*Ελληνίδες πεζογράφοι*, Athens: Synhroni Epohi).

version of the *Bildungsroman* to a female one, conceptualizing female identity as both a goal and a recoverable entity (Tziovas 2003b). They also show how the female protagonists grow out of their dependency on their male partners and how the private female space can be invaded by political events, to some extent replicating the ways in which feminism in Greece interacted with politics after 1974. Feminism in Greek fiction tends to manifest itself by pointing either to history as a matter of linear progression and public engagement or to a kind of romantic individualism, looking back to some Edenic past.

In addition to fiction, women's life stories from the 1940s highlighted the political significance of gender-specific ways of remembering. The publication of these autobiographical narratives started slowly after 1974, with the legalization of the Communist Party, and took off in the 1980s, transcending patriarchal silences and the concept of the war(s) as something predominantly masculine. According to Tasoula Vervenioti (2008), immediately after 1974 women who had experienced the turbulent decade of the 1940s started writing and publishing. Their narratives of exile and prison memoirs written by women proliferated in the 1980s and from the 1990s on women's stories started engaging with a previously untouched subject, their involvement in the Democratic Army of Greece (DSE).

In the 1980s and 1990s a number of studies were published in English on both women and men and, in turn, prepared the ground for similar studies in Greece. For example, the first issue of the *Journal of Modern Greek Studies* (May 1983) contained papers from the Modern Greek Studies Association's (USA) symposium on 'Women and men in Greece: A society in transition' and in the same year Deborah Tannen published her book on Lilika Nakos (1983), aspiring 'to open the way for in-depth studies of women's contributions to modern Greek prose'. Anthropologists also began to study gender and masculinity, primarily in rural Greece, while more attention was paid to women's writing.[27] The revival of the feminist movement in post-junta Greece might not have produced iconic feminist texts (like Simone De Beauvoir's *The Second Sex*, 1949, or Germaine Greer's *Female Eunuch*, 1970), but it encouraged women to discuss whether women's poetry existed (Frantzi et al. 1990) or revisit Greek cultural history and rehabilitate unduly neglected female voices (Kontogianni 2008). Challenging the oppositions between private/women and public/men, feminists revisited the life stories of those women as told in works such as the autobiography of Elisavet Moutzan-Martinengou, who endeavoured to question the confinement

---

[27] Loizos and Papataxiarchis (1991), Dubisch (1986) and Van Dyck (1998).

of women to the private sphere (Avdela and Papageorgiou 1979; Varika 1989). The history of feminism in Greece and Europe also received scholarly attention and anthologies of women's writing from earlier periods were published (Varika and Sklaveniti 1981; Avdela and Psara (1985); Varika 1987).[28]

Since the 1980s there has been a transition at international level from women's to gender studies and a move to transcend old taxonomies (male vs female, homosexual vs heterosexual), facilitated by Foucault's dismantling of traditional views on sexuality (Foucault 1978). From the politics of an emancipatory movement aiming to improve the social and institutional standing of women, feminism moved on to the probing of fluid identities and examining the way gender worked as a social and historical rather than biological category. Rather than recovering the historical experiences of women and men as evidence of gender difference, the focus shifted onto how that difference was produced discursively and how gender identities were disseminated in various ways over time (Morgan 2006: 13). This shift from a history of subjects (namely women) to a history of relations (gender) undoubtedly had an impact on Greek academic studies (Papadogiannis 2017).

With its emphasis on 'women's rights', early feminism has been seen as contributing to the reification of gender difference rather than to its dissolution. It attracted criticism from anti-essentialist feminists who adopted Judith Butler's argument that 'women' do not exist outside of performances, which bring identity into practice. Supplementing Foucault with a Derridean logic of difference, Butler's work (1990 and 1993) has been influential in both feminist and queer theory by challenging the very identities on which the older movements were based. Her theory contributed to a transition from innate tendencies to performances, from a discourse on rights to the disruption of all fixed identities and from binarisms to the way the term queer defies definition. For Halperin queer represents '*whatever* is at odds with the normal, the legitimate, the dominant. *There is nothing in particular to which it necessarily refers*. It is an identity without an essence [which] demarcates not a positivity but a positionality vis-à-vis the normative' (1995: 62; 2003). Regarded as both an asset and a drawback, this terminological indeterminacy of 'queer' enables a critique of the so-called 'liberation movements', be they gay, lesbian or feminist,

---

[28] A recent exhibition and colloquium on Greek feminism considered 1974–1990 to have been its heyday (Vaiou and Psara 2018). See also a personal account of the feminist movement by Bobolou (2008).

for being willing to surrender their revolutionary potential in exchange for social integration (Schoene 2006: 286).²⁹

Sexuality and queer culture

Discussion of the post-junta period with its emphasis on the transition to democracy does not often include the LGBTQI+ movements and their liberation politics. It is only recently that their activities have been revisited and their history has started to be pieced together. Did the fall of the military regime entail the relaxing of sexual repression in Greece? Was the Greek public sphere prepared for such movements? Did the efforts to consolidate democratic institutions in Greece sidestep the defence of human rights? Did the political parties, particularly of the Left, pay enough attention to issues of gender identity and equality in the 1970s?

For a number of Western writers and artists, Greece, particularly after the Second World War, became synonymous with sexual freedom. Combining a classicizing with an orientalizing topography, it attracted a number of well-known homosexuals (such as the American poet James Merrill, 1926–1995). Male homosexuality was decriminalized in Greece in 1951 (lesbians were not mentioned or acknowledged in the Greek criminal code), yet traditional values remained securely entrenched.³⁰ While technically Greece was among the first states to decriminalize same-sex relationships; this was not a sign of broad social acceptance but due to homosexuality being treated as a medical condition (Riedel 2010: 233). Even more than a quarter of a century after its decriminalization, a survey in 1977 found that 79.9 per cent of those surveyed considered sex between men a criminal offence (Daskalakis et al. 1983: 258). In the 1950s and 1960s sexuality in Greece was treated as a 'natural' act aimed either at reproduction or satisfying men's 'biological' needs (Yannakopoulos 2016: 175), and this contributed to the fact that homosexuality was considered a moral danger. Greek popular films of that period also contributed to the stereotyped image of gay men by presenting them as 'effeminate', restricted to

---

[29] On the synergies of queer and feminist theories and their shared understanding of the logic of domination, see Rudy (2000) and Marinucci (2010).

[30] In Sweden homosexuality was decriminalized in 1944, whereas in Britain and Germany this occurred later, in 1967 and 1969, respectively, and in Romania it was as late as 1996 under pressure from Brussels. By contrast Hungary and Czechoslovakia had decriminalized same-sex relations between consenting adults in 1961 while in Poland homosexuality had never been illegal (Herzog 2011:168–9, 182–5). Thus, there were differing attitudes towards homosexuality across Europe.

secondary roles and mere caricatures of 'real' men (Hadjikyriacou 2013: 90–1). Broadly speaking homosexuality in Greece was perceived as a sexual practice and not an identity.

As objects of desire for middle-class gays, working-class men, who offered their muscular bodies for sex in exchange for material goods, became icons of 'authentic' masculinity. The exaltation of their 'tough' beauty was often thought of as the outcome of a life beset by hardships and this reinforced the stereotype that material deprivation promotes 'natural' masculinity and encouraged the interpretation of gender difference as class difference. This working-class masculinity of the 1950s and 1960s, deemed 'authentic' by comparison with the overweight bodies of the more affluent, gradually gave way to a focus on the adornment of the body, which included wearing fancy clothes and using cosmetics. Perfumes were signs of bourgeois elegance and 'effeminacy' and therefore the beautification of the male body was perceived by older homosexuals as a sign of compromised masculinity and the ascendance of 'Western' gay culture (Yannakopoulos 2016: 177, 182). Only military uniforms, as in some Tsarouchis paintings, were considered 'masculine' accessories and an erotic fetish.

Social mobility and improved living standards had an impact on patterns of sexual behaviour and this led in the 1990s to the replacement of working-class young men (*tekná*) as sexual partners by young immigrants arriving in Greece at that time from the Balkans and elsewhere.[31] Labour lost its masculine sexual glamour for Greeks and consumerism led to a commodification of the male body and the commercialization of gay culture. Traditionally, masculinity was understood in terms of a man's ability to live up to the standards set for his gender. It was linked to hard work and performances associated with beauty care, fashion trends or provocative lifestyles were deemed incompatible with the identities of a man as a fighter or provider.[32] Economically dependent women went unchallenged by society, but unemployed men were often seen as weak and effeminate. Thus, the high levels of unemployment in Greece during the crisis represented an additional blow to the male ego and drove older unemployed men to despair. They not only felt robbed of an income to provide for their families but also divested of their masculinity.

Female chastity, on the other hand, even after the junta was still under surveillance and women, especially the unmarried ones, were not normally

---

[31] This new sex economy is captured in Koumandareas's collection of stories *Η μυρωδιά τους με κάνει να κλαίω/ Their Smell Makes Me Want to Cry* (1996) and particularly the story 'The Romanian Kid'.
[32] The first magazines intended for a male audience were published in the 1980s: the Greek edition of *Playboy* (1985) followed by *Status* (1988).

allowed to go out with men unaccompanied. The taboo of the loss of virginity was gradually replaced by an emphasis on tender and serious relationships and this shift in sentiment enabled young women to have premarital sexual relationships, although the use of the contraceptive pill, associated with the sexual revolution elsewhere, was not widespread in Greece. In 1991, 33 per cent of the female students of the University of Athens reported that they had had sexual relations before adulthood, while the figure was only 17 per cent in 1978 (Close 2002: 221). Sexual predation, identified earlier with the 'kamaki' (casual Casanovas), gave way in the 1990s to a 'softer', more 'well-mannered' masculinity. Perceived as a sign of sexual deprivation and a feature of an impoverished past that Greece had left behind, sexual aggression was now predominantly associated with young immigrants.

From the 1970s onwards, Western conceptualizations of sexual identity and homosexuality impacted on Greek society, and earlier gendered categories such as *andras* and *adelfi/poustis/toioutos* coexisted with modern distinctions, 'homosexuals/gays' and 'heterosexuals/straights'. Sexual identities were increasingly conceptualized in terms of choice of sexual partners, while the neologism *sexoualikotita*/sexuality entered Greek discourse and identity politics. According to Faubion the word for same-sex sexuality (ομοφυλοφιλία) had no currency in everyday spoken Greek prior to the 1980s (1993: 217).[33] Male sexual encounters could take place in almost any public space (parks, squares, cinemas, public lavatories) but, once television and video rentals became widespread in the 1980s, the focus shifted from the public to the private space and transformed the home into a place of consumerist and personal pleasure. This privatization of sexual pleasure was just part of wider social changes. Cinemas near Omonia Square in Athens no longer attracted young working-class men, since hardcore porn movies were available on video cassettes. Also, the all-male cafes (kafeneia) were replaced in urban areas by places of mixed, heterosexual sociability such as cafeterias or discos (popular in the 1970s and 1980s), and by the end of the millennium gay culture in Greece (and particularly in Athens) had become vibrant with a proliferation of gay bars and even designated gay neighbourhoods (e.g. Gazi). The privatization of affection was complete with the shift from male homosociality to the homosexual couple (Yannakopoulos 2010: 268). Exploring

---

[33] The term 'queer' started to be used in the early 1990s. In her introduction to the special issue of *Differences* (vol. 5, Summer 1991) Teresa De Lauretis justifies the juxtaposition in the title page of 'Queer theory' and 'Lesbian and gay sexualities' in this way: 'The term "queer", juxtaposed to the "lesbian and gay" of the subtitle, is intended to mark a certain critical distance from the latter, by now established and often convenient, formula' (iv). In the Greek context the term 'queer' appears in May 2009 in the title of a colloquium at Panteion University.

the development of a queer culture in Greece offers a useful perspective on the transitions and new identities emerging during the period from junta to crisis, which may help us assess the truth of the claim that Greece 'is one of Europe's most socially conservative societies'.[34]

During the dictatorship, the ethnographer Elias Petropoulos (1928–2003) published his book *Kaliarda* (1971), a collection of slang words used by homosexuals (Apostolelli and Halkia 2012: 79–91). This first public acknowledgment of a queer subculture in Greece received a hostile response from the military regime and cost its author a prison sentence. After the restoration of democracy in 1974, the dictionary became a bestseller together with his other provocative books which combined autobiography, fiction and a recording of Greek underground lifestyles and sexual geographies. Best known for his work on the *rebetika* songs of the urban underworld, the so-called Greek blues, Petropoulos spent time in prison for defying the authorities and in 1975 fled to Paris where he remained until his death. The junta was a period of repression for homosexuals while at the same time it offered 'new opportunities for the public display of homosexual identity' (Papanikolaou 2014b: 162).

Soon after the junta's fall, in 1977, the *Liberation Movement of Homosexual Greece* (AKOE) was formed by a group of young homosexuals who had studied in France and Italy and were in touch with the Gay Liberation movements there and particularly the Italian gay journal *Fuori*.[35] A year earlier Loukas Theodorakopoulos (1925–2013), subsequently a leading figure in AKOE, published an autobiographical book entitled Καιάδας: Χρονικό μιας πολιορκίας/ *Kaiadas: Chronicle of a Siege* in which he gives an account of the persecution of homosexuals by the military regime and includes an interview ('The French May 1968 and the homosexual revolution') with the French writer and queer theorist Guy Hocquenghem (1946–1988), who had been involved in the events of May 1968 in France (Papanikolaou 2013). This book was a watershed for the gay community because it linked older left-wing gay activists (such as Theodorakopoulos) with younger ones (such as the director Andreas Velissaropoulos and the poet Andreas Angelakis).

These were the people who were involved in the publication of the magazine *ΑΜΦΙ/AMFI* (1978–90) with its playful title alluding both to political contestation (αμφισβήτηση) and sexuality (αμφιφυλοφιλία) (Mais 2015: 19;

---

[34] https://www.theguardian.com/world/2017/oct/10/greece-passes-gender-change-law.
[35] The cultural assumptions about 'gay liberation' made by those who were living abroad during the junta occasionally differed from those made by people who had remained in Greece.

Tsambrounis 2008).[36] In November 1980 the magazine was taken to court for indecency but acquitted. Brought about by the publication of an erotic poem by Nikos Spanias, illustrated with an image of Hermes by Praxiteles, the court case provoked an international wave of protest and solidarity. By publishing translations and interviews of leading intellectuals such as Félix Guattari and Michel Foucault, the magazine introduced Greek readers to the discussions that had been going on about gender and sexuality in the West and this perhaps led to the periodical's subtitle being changed from 'the liberation of homosexuals' to the 'liberation of homosexual desire', thus shifting the emphasis away from the desiring subject. In November 1982 the magazine organized a conference on 'Sexualities and politics' with speakers including Félix Guattari, Konstantinos Tsoukalas and Yorgos Veltsos, and in 1984 it published a special issue (nos 16–17) on Cavafy. But still the Left in Greece was not ready to embrace the homosexual movement and support its aims. It should be noted here that the majority on the Left, with the exception of the small Eurocommunist party (Communist Party of the Interior) and its youth branch 'Rigas Feraios', were reserved, if not hostile, towards homosexuality and the newly emergent gay movement (AKOE). The puritanical Communist Party and its youth movement still promoted the stable heterosexual couple as the model of 'normal' and 'healthy' sexual relationships (Papadogiannis 2015: 252–75).

Counter to the expectations raised by the restoration of democracy, the legislation concerning (homo)sexual conduct became stricter. The Karamanlis government's declared intention to pass a law controlling illegal sexual activity and screening sex workers for venereal diseases led to a demonstration in January 1981. But only a few homosexuals participated in this demonstration without masks covering their faces.[37] Coming out was still not easy in Greece and only well-known writers such as Kostas Tachtsis (1927–1988), who actually clashed with AKOE, were able to do so. The rise of PASOK to power, raising hopes of legislation more favourable to homosexuals, and the threat of HIV/AIDS led to AKOE's decline, while the emblematic gay film Άγγελος/Angel (1982) divided the editorial board of AMFI. It has been argued that the homosexual movement was

---

[36] Other periodicals include Κοντροσόλ στο Χάος (1986–92, five issues) edited by Alexis Bistikas, Dimitris Papaioannou and Pavlos Avouris, Το κράξιμο (1981–94, fourteen issues) edited by Paola Revenioti, a trans woman, Λάβρυς – meaning 'lesbian' in kaliarda – (1982–3, three issues) published by the Autonomous Group of Homosexual Women formed around 1979, Μαντάμ Γκου (1995–7, five issues) and Η νταλίκα (2009–16, nine issues) (Kantsa 2018; Apostolelli and Halkia 2012: 17–18, 39–41).

[37] See the interview with Loukas Theodorakopoulos, Lifo, 2 February 2013, https://www.lifo.gr/team/gayandlesbian/35779.

verging on introversion and crisis around the mid-1980s when in 1985 a leading member of AKOE Andreas Velissaropoulos died of AIDS. The internalization of repression still kept the personal and the political separate, and the homosexual movement seems not to have been in a position at that stage to expand beyond Athens and Thessaloniki or to have clear aims. AKOE lost momentum in the early 1980s and by spring of 1987 had in effect collapsed. Only one issue of *AMFI* was published in 1983 (compared to the three issues published in 1980) while the monthly newspaper *Lamda* ceased publication in 1981 (Riedel 2010: 238). For a transitional period, Gregory Vallianatos assumed the publication of *AMFI* and from 1988 it was taken over by EOK (Greek Homosexual Community), created by some former members of AKOE and which worked more like an NGO than a pressure group (Mais 2015: 22).

The late development of the homosexual movement in Greece played a role in social attitudes towards the AIDS epidemic (Plexoussaki 2000). The response to AIDS in Greece came primarily from the medical profession and women's social organizations and not from organizations like the Gay Men's Health Crisis in the United States. In Greece AIDS did not provoke public debate as in other countries and was treated as an essentially foreign disease, a perception reinforced by the fact that the first victim of the disease was a Zambian student who died in Athens in 1983 (Riedel 2010: 240). It was treated as a private matter and not a public issue. Only individual cases, such as Alexis Bistikas (1964–1995), Billy Bo (1954–1987), Alexandros Iolas (1907–1987) and Mairi Papagiannidou (1965–2012), attracted some attention. Even the most celebrated performance dedicated to AIDS, the *Ρέκβιεμ για το τέλος του Έρωτα* /*Requiem for the End of Eros* (1995) with choreography by Dimitris Papaioannou and music by Yorgos Koumentakis, failed to provoke a debate about gay culture or AIDS. Towards the end of the 1980s and in the 1990s Greece entered a conservative period, and this is evident in the attack on the leading musician Manos Chatzidakis by the newspaper *Avriani*, one of the popular papers at that time with a wider circulation and lower price than other newspapers.

At a concert, in front of an unsuspecting audience of several thousands, who had come to hear his music and Nana Mouskouri perform at the Panathenian Stadium in Athens on 7 September 1987, Manos Chatzidakis publicly denounced the vulgarity of *Avriani* and called for its closure. The next day the newspaper responded with an article calling him a neo-Nazi and making a scurrilous attack on his sexual preferences. It also invited anyone who had ever had an affair with him to report their experiences to the newspaper. Two days later *Avriani* published another scathing article ('The psychological AIDS of a corrupting pervert'), calling on politicians and the public to condemn Chatzidakis and defend the freedom of the press. Many politicians then responded to the call of this powerful newspaper, which supported the socialist PASOK, and defended media pluralism without addressing the issue of homosexuality. A year later, in July 1988 Chatzidakis sent a letter to the newspapers *Kathimerini* and *Avgi* criticizing a message issued by the then President Christos Sartzetakis on the occasion of the restoration of democracy in 1974. He called again for the shutting down of the newspaper and was again attacked as a homosexual who had 'destroyed' many young people with his perversion.[38] It is remarkable that this dispute did not trigger off a discussion about discrimination against homosexuals in Greece. Instead, it was seen as an issue of press freedom and a political stand-off between the 'right-wing' elitist Chatzidakis and a newspaper supposedly conveying popular public opinion. This controversy can be seen as symptomatic of Greek attitudes to homosexuality in the late 1980s and indicates how party politics often obscured human rights and gender issues.

Around the same time the poet and critic Dinos Christianopoulos rejected the description 'homosexual poet'. Instead, he claimed to be an erotic poet and this raised questions about the representation of homoeroticism in Greek literature (1988: 44 and 1999: 131–2). Outwardly heterosexual poets such as Yannis Ritsos have been included in the *History of Gay Literature* and some of his poems have been read as homoerotic (Woods 1992 and 1998; Tziovas 2014b) while Tachtsis's writings and Ioannou's *Omonoia 1980* have been revisited from this perspective (Mackridge 1991; Robinson 1997a, 1997b and 2001). It is interesting that most of these approaches came from outside Greece and this is the case with the controversial issue of the *Journal of the Hellenic Diaspora* on Cavafy in 1983. Its editorial stated, 'Let it finally be said: Cavafy is neither "perverse" nor "obsessed" nor even "erotic". Cavafy is gay. Cavafy articulates a specifically homosexual strategy of liberation and historical consciousness.'[39] This statement caused uproar, because for the first time Cavafy was called gay and not an erotic poet, highlighting the reluctance of Greek critics to acknowledge the queerness of Cavafy's poetry. Things gradually changed and the unearthing in 2005 of the forgotten 'first Greek lesbian novel' *Ερωμένη της/Her Lover* (1929) did not spark any debate or controversy, only inquiries about the true identity of the author, given that the novel was published under the pseudonym Dora

[38] For more details, see the musician's official website http://www.hadjidakis.gr/the-battle-against-avriani/, the blog of Nikos Sarantakos https://sarantakos.wordpress.com/2014/06/16/hatzidakis/ and his entry in Petsini and Christopoulos (2018: 528–30).

[39] 'Statement', *Journal of the Hellenic Diaspora*, vol. 10, nos 1–2, Spring–Summer 1983, p. 6.

Rozetti. A year later Eleni Bakopoulou, an activist in the feminist and lesbian movement during the 1970s and 1980s, revealed that the author of the novel was Nelli Kaloglopoulou-Bogiatzoglou (1908–1989) and thus ended the speculation about the first lesbian Greek novelist.

Though unearthing lesbian texts and 'gay identities' in the Greek past or writing the history of modern Greek (homo)sexuality has been critiqued as running the risk of creating a 'whitewashed' history of gay emergence and undermining the ability of queer politics to address contemporary intersectional demands (Papanikolaou 2018b: 176), it still offers useful rereadings and insights into Greek cultural history. It also maps out the transition from the latent or timid homoeroticism (the closet) of earlier writers (Nikos-Alexis Aslanoglou, Dinos Christianopoulos, Menis Koumandareas, Yorgos Ioannou, Pavlos Matessis) and artists (Karolos Koun, Minos Volanakis) to contemporary subversive aesthetics and queer performativity, such as the collective theatre performance by the feminist director and US-educated Christiana Lambrinidis *Lesbian Blues* (1998), the first experimental performance that ended the invisibility of lesbians in Greece (Pakis 2013). Yet compared to the 'vocal' 1980s, the 1990s can be seen as a decade of 'going quiet' or transition for the homosexual movement in Greece (Kantza 2018: 69), preparing the ground for the increased visibility of the LGBTQI+ groups and queer culture in the twenty-first century.

The most emblematic film of the new Greek queer culture, transcending the country's patriarchal and homophobic past, is Panos Koutras's *Στρέλλα/A Woman's Way* (2009). A contemporary version of an ancient tragedy, a reversal of the Oedipus myth, it blends realism and dreaming by alluding to Pasolini, Almodóvar and the classic film *Stella* (1955) by Cacoyannis. George is released from prison after fifteen years for a murder he committed in his small Greek village. He spends his first night out in a cheap hotel in Athens. There he meets Strella, a young transsexual sex worker. They spend the night together, but the past is catching up with George and Strella. She falls in love with the father who once killed her uncle for seducing her. George realizes that Strella is his missing son, something she knew all along. After the initial shock and distancing, the odd couple has to come to terms with the ultimate taboo of incest. The film ends with a New Year's party with a number of guests invited to Strella's small apartment as members of a newly created queer family. This last festive scene could be seen either as normalizing or as articulating a new queer kinship built upon the decimation of the nuclear family and envisaging a new kind of extended family, not based on blood ties but on love (Butler and Athanasiou 2013: 62). The spatial and temporal ambiguity of the last shot, as George opens a window to look outside at Athens, decontextualizes the story and points to a queer utopia. In Koutras's queer melodrama patriarchy, femininity and Greekness are re-enacted and/or renegotiated along with long-established national myths from the archetypal Oedipus myth to that of the sacred nuclear family (Psaras 2016). Oedipus is redeemed, the Symbolic order collapses and a queer utopia emerges by reframing perceptions and resisting fixity.

After a period of quiescence, following the suspension of the publication of *AMFI* in 1989, the homosexual movement in Greece received a boost with the formation in 2003 of the *Gay and Lesbian Community of Greece* (OLKE) and its application to become a legally recognized entity (Yannakopoulos 2010: 272–3). The formation of queer groups in Greece was not so much related to anti-HIV politics as in other countries such as Spain or the United States. They emerged as part of the anti-authoritarian and squatting activism in the country's large towns and cities and as a form of resistance to 'the way austerity reinforces gender binaries and heteronormative domination in all aspects of social life' (Eleftheriadis 2015: 1037). The group Queericulum Vitae (QV), formed in Athens in 2004 (folded 2015), was a pioneer of such queer politics in Greece, together with other collectivities or publishers (Roz Kafeneio, Polychromos Planitis, Flesh Machine and others). Queer groups distanced themselves from the traditional demands of the gay movement (right to same-sex marriage, adoption) and focused on the construction of identity rather than its celebration. With the rise of the neo-Nazi party Golden Dawn and the denouncing of non-heteronormative subjects as the 'shame' of the nation, queer groups pointed to their exclusion from society as the nation's 'others' and to an increase in 'sexual nationalism'. The antifascist framing of queer discourse became more visible following the violent demonstrations by neo-Nazis and religious fundamentalists against the play *Corpus Christi* by Terence McNally, deemed 'blasphemous' on account of its homoerotic references, during its premiere in Athens in October 2012.

In the twenty-first century three areas attracted particular attention: same-sex partnerships and transgender rights, the representation of homosexuality in the media and pride parades. These three areas can be used to monitor institutional changes and resistance in Greek society and assess whether public opinion had followed suit. In June 2008, local people on the island of Lesvos went to court to reclaim the name Lesbian, which they claimed had been 'usurped' after 1924 when, according to the *Oxford English Dictionary*, it was still being used exclusively to describe a native of the island.[40] The same month, the mayor of

---

[40] https://www.theguardian.com/world/2008/jun/10/gayrights.greece.

the Aegean island of Tilos, Anastasios Aliferis, married two same-sex couples, two lesbians and two gay men, citing a loophole in Greek civil law, which at that time did not stipulate the gender of those wishing to get married.[41] The marriage was condemned by the Orthodox Church, which in the past had also opposed the introduction of civil marriage, and eventually in May 2009 the authorities managed to annul these marriages. However, in December 2016 we get a different picture, because according to a survey 50.4 per cent of Greeks were in favour of same-sex marriages compared to 36.3 per cent in April 2015 before civil partnerships had been extended to same-sex couples.[42] Since the 1990s the issue of same-sex marriage had become a contested issue among LGBTQI+ organizations with some groups expressing reservations as to whether marriage constituted an emancipatory act and others stridently demanding a right to it in light of the crucial role of marriage in Greek society (Kantza 2014). If marriage afforded them greater visibility, it also compelled homosexuals to comply with the terms of heteronormativity.

In December 2015, civil partnerships (the σύμφωνο συμβίωσης, i.e. 'cohabitation agreement' in Greek) were legalized for same-sex couples, without, however, all the legal protections and rights available to heterosexual married couples. Same-sex civil partnership and marriage provoked a debate in Greece and invited comparisons with other EU countries. It should be noted that the Netherlands offered full civil marriage rights to same-sex couples in 2001, Belgium followed in 2003 and Spain in 2005, but the UK (excluding Northern Ireland) only legalized same-sex marriage some years later in 2014. By 2017 transgender people in Greece were no longer required to undergo sterilization in order to change their legal gender and their identity documents,[43] and in May 2018, the Greek Parliament passed a law granting same-sex couples the right to foster children. Same-sex marriage is not currently legal in Greece, even though some officials of the SYRIZA government were in favour of it and had proposed legalization.

The Greek National Council for Radio and Television (NCRTV/ESR) also played an important role in monitoring the representation of homosexuality in the Greek media and often clashed with the LGBTQI+ community. In 2003 it imposed a fine of €100,000 on the MEGA channel for showing two men kissing in Christophoros Papakaliatis's television series 'Close your eyes' (Κλείσε

---

[41] http://news.bbc.co.uk/1/hi/world/europe/7432949.stm.
[42] https://www.dianeosis.org/en/2017/04/greeks-believe-in-2017/.
[43] https://www.theguardian.com/world/2017/oct/10/greece-passes-gender-change-law.

τα μάτια). Three years later the Supreme Court overturned this decision and cancelled the fine. However, the same channel was fined again in 2010 for showing the film *Straight Story* (2006), in which being homosexual is depicted as 'normal' and heterosexuality 'not normal'. On 15 October 2012, Greek National Television (ERT) aired the pilot of the British television series *Downtown Abbey*, cutting out a scene depicting two men kissing. On the other hand, the council did not fine programmes with homophobic comments and only approved the showing of Athens Pride 2018 on television in a late-night spot (after 22.30).

Though a first attempt to organize a gay pride event in Greece was made by AKOE in June 1980 in Athens, it was not until June 2005 that the first Athens Pride parade took place. Since then one has been held there every year, and has been followed by similar events in Thessaloniki, Patras and Crete. In Thessaloniki the first annual pride event took place in 2012 and two years later it featured as part of the programme of the European Youth Capital. This event was very successful and attracted around ten thousand people despite opposition from the Church and other groups. With the support of the former Mayor Yannis Boutaris, Thessaloniki was trying to shake off its image as a conservative and homophobic city by holding these pride events. In spite of the strengthening of gender hierarchies and an increase in violent homophobic incidents, 'in the early 2000s, queer culture seemed to be ... everywhere in Greece' (Papanikolaou and Kolocotroni 2018: 146).

The growing visibility of queer culture led to discontent with the commercialization of the pride parades and the advertising of the Greek islands as the ideal destination for same-sex weddings. Recently there has been criticism that LGBTQI+ communities have become NGOs and that the pride parade in Athens being endorsed by the Municipality of Athens and Foreign Embassies has turned it into a commercialized fiesta (Mais 2015: 22). The recent changes in legislation, films such as *Strella*, studies on queer cinema (Kyriakos 2017; special session on the history of the Greek queer cinema in Thessaloniki Film Festival, 2018), irreverent queer representations of Greekness in theatre and performance (Dimitris Dimitriadis, Nova Melancholia), Athens Museum of Queer Arts, queer linguistics (Canakis 2015) and a queer rereading of Cavafy (Papanikolaou 2014a) might point to greater queer visibility, but it has been pointed out that Greece is still trying to challenge its widespread homophobia, unlike the English-speaking countries where the queer movement revised and radicalized gay aesthetics and politics (Papanikolaou 2018a: 366). Notwithstanding claims that austerity brought out aspects of a Greek patriarchal culture and gendered racialized violence in the context of an 'affective economy of hostility' (Carastathis 2015), an Athenian homosexual topography has emerged and a public space has been claimed for non-normative sexuality.[44] According to a 2018 report by ILGA Europe, which assesses LGBTQI+ rights in European countries, Greece achieved the greatest improvements among the forty-nine countries in the legal status of LGBTQI+ people between 2014 and 2018, with an overall score of 52 per cent.[45] Social issues, such as enabling citizens to determine their own gender identity, have turned out to be the most reliable markers for determining the divisions between Left and Right and Greece's alignment with other EU countries.

Conclusion

In the early post-junta period social movements developed under the auspices of the political parties of the Left, but either did not succeed in becoming autonomous (feminist or youth movements) or were ignored by the political establishment (homosexual movement). As the grip of the traditional political system was loosened or questioned and social structures changed with the increase in individual autonomy and the waning of the importance of the family, these movements acquired more autonomy and demanded greater legal recognition and protection following the pattern of the growing impact of similar movements in the West. In line with international trends, the trajectories of those movements in post-junta Greece involved transitions from macro to micro level and a continuous process of emancipation from political control towards increasing visibility and autonomy. These transitions were not always one-way processes (from *oikos* to *demos*) since they displayed both signs of extroversion (e.g. greater visibility of women or queer culture) and an emphasis on privacy (a non-existent concept earlier in Greece) and introvert lifestyles (increasing home entertainment, privatization of pleasure). The negotiation of space (public and private, creation and contestation) also becomes central in these transitional processes.

Gender politics is an area on which the Left in Greece has left its mark and developed a clear dividing line between it and the conservative parties. Immense strides were made in eliminating gender differences and establishing LGBTQI+

---

[44] See also the supplement of the newspaper *Η Εφημερίδα των Συντακτών* (8 June 2019) on queer culture in Greece under the telling title 'Αόρατη Ιστορία/Invisible history' and the special issue on 'Queer Athens', *Lifo*, no. 608, 6 June 2019.

[45] ILGA – Europe Annual Review of the Human Rights Situation of Lesbian, Gay, Bisexual, Trans and Intersex People in Europe https://rainbow-europe.org.

rights, at least at an institutional level, whenever left-wing parties were in power. However, legislation is not always sufficient to change traditional attitudes and established cultural norms, while legislative changes are not easily translated to changes in the economic structures and the public sphere. The 1980s could be seen as the decade of women, when their status was improved and their cultural presence was established, while during the first decades of the twentieth-first century LGBTQI+ rights were institutionalized and queer culture gained momentum. I would venture to say that in the case of the women's movement there was more of a top-down approach, whereas the LGBTQI+ movement was more of a grass-roots movement. All these groups brought Greece closer to Western Europe and the United States and facilitated a cultural dialogue focusing on gender, identity, intimacy and biopolitics. They also had a considerable impact on Greek culture either through music and street art (youth), women's fiction and queer cinema or by reversing the orientation of Greek culture away from dated heteronormative discourses and an Apollonian Greekness. The (hi)stories of youth, women and sexuality vividly portray the cultural transitions and social tensions in Greek society since the fall of the junta.

10

The rediscoveries of Greece: From the ancient ruins to the ruins of crisis

Greece has been rediscovered in different periods and various ways in the past; and by rediscovery, I mean the renewal of international (particularly Western) interest in the country. We can talk about a 'rediscovery' of Greece during the crisis in the sense of the world media spotlight being turned on the country in an attempt to understand what had gone wrong, reassess its economy and its European aspirations or revisit its symbolic role in the world arising out of its classical heritage. All these things, together with the severity of the crisis, made Greece the centre of world attention, inviting us to reflect on how the image of Greece was constructed in the period of crisis by placing it in a wider historical context.

There have been two opposing approaches to Greece since the end of the eighteenth century: as a vaunted spiritual ancestor of Europe on the one hand and as a despised cultural backwater of that same Europe on the other. An imaginary and idealized construction of Greece (mostly classical) coexisted with a critical and pragmatic approach to modern Greece; Greece and its myth collided with the endless capacity of the Greeks to disappoint.[1] The projection of both ancient and modern Greece on the same screen caused confusion but also invited comparison. As we have seen in the first chapter, this dualist approach, or two-fold colonial gesture, has been translated into models of anthropological analysis such as honour and shame or models of self-presentation: Hellenic and Romeic. It might be helpful to review briefly the Western (re)discoveries of Greece and examine how they prioritize these approaches or combine them

---

[1] C. M. Woodhouse described the attitudes of some philhellenes in this way: 'They loved the Greece of their dreams: the land, the language, the antiquities, but not the people. If only, they thought, the people could be more like the British scholars and gentlemen; or failing that, as too much to be hoped, if only they were more like their own ancestors: or better still, if only they were not there at all' (1969: 38–9).

in different ways. This will help us to put the rediscovery of Greece by the international media during the crisis into context.

The first romantic rediscovery of Greece during the late eighteenth and early nineteenth centuries favoured the imaginary and idealistic approach and was based mostly on textual rather than material evidence since very few travellers ventured beyond Italy and continued their grand tour to the East. When more Western travellers started visiting the Greek world or followed the example of James Stuart and Nicholas Revett in trying to match textual information from ancient sources with monuments, topographical traces or archaeological findings on the ground, then fascination with the classical past was combined with a colonial desire for the acquisition of classical artefacts. This, in turn, highlighted the discrepancy between the glorification of ancient Greece in the Western imagination and the irrational 'superstitions' of local people who failed to appreciate their ancient heritage. The inability of the indigenous population to draw a clear separation between past and present, and the confusion over the value of antiquity, was evoked to justify in part accounts for the material colonization of Greece by the looting of its antiquities.

The story of the 'Ceres or Demeter from Eleusis' is an interesting case in point. The statue was removed in 1801 and transferred to Cambridge by Edward Clarke who had found it 'in the midst of a heap of dung, buried as high as the neck'. The inhabitants of the small village then situated among the ruins of Eleusis 'still regarded this *Statue* with a high degree of superstitious veneration'.

> They attributed to its presence the fertility of their land; and it was for this reason that they heaped around it the manure intended for their fields. They believed that the loss of it would be followed by no less a calamity than the failure of their annual harvests. (Clarke 1814: 772)

Though Clarke secured a permit from the local Ottoman governor to remove the statue, the local people resisted this move because they regarded it as protecting their fields. They even treated it as a Christian icon by placing a votive lamp in front of it on Christian feast days.

The naïve beliefs or prejudices of the ordinary folk were often castigated by Western travellers, who pointed out that the logic of conservation was alien to the indigenous population (Hamilakis 2007: 64–74 and 2008). Linear and unidirectional temporality, fundamental to Western modernity, was contrasted with the native temporal (con)fusion, as displayed in the veneration of the statue from Eleusis as a Christian icon. In this way, a gap developed between the modern

West and pre-modern Greece, which allowed the former to appropriate classical Greece and treat modern Greeks as unworthy guardians of their heritage.

This gap narrows in the second rediscovery of Greece as a historical continuum and embraced by scholars from J. C. Lawson, *Modern Greek Folklore and Ancient Greek Religion: A Study in Survivals* (1910), to George Thompson, 'The continuity of Hellenism' (1971), and Margaret Alexiou, *The Ritual Lament in Greek Tradition* (1974, revised and reprinted in 2002). Nelly's photographs are an example of how Greeks deployed this approach. She juxtaposed shepherds and village girls with ancient statues in order to prove Hellenic racial continuity. The aim of the photographs was to demonstrate, through visual similarity, that the racial continuity was beyond doubt. Probably familiar with Leni Riefenstahl's work, she presented portraits of contemporary Greeks whose features matched those found on ancient Greek busts, and thus her idealizing gaze produced a Greece which served Western Aryan, particularly German, racial ideals and satisfied the Greek longing for continuity (Damaskos 2008; Panayotopoulos 2009).

The third rediscovery of Greece occurs during the 1940s and 1950s when the war and the Greek resistance to the Axis forces turned Europe's attention towards the country. This rediscovery was driven not by a fascination with antiquity but by an interest in modern literature, landscape and material pleasures. The architects of this new philhellenism, Henry Miller and Lawrence Durrell, no longer compared modern Greeks to their ancient ancestors.[2] Idealism and survivalism seem to have given way to existentialism and to a more pragmatic and pleasure-seeking appreciation of modern Greek culture. The shift of focus from classical antiquity to the exuberance of modern Greek life was signalled by an article of Lawrence Durrell's, 'Hellene and Philhellene', published anonymously in *The Times Literary Supplement* in 1949 (Durrell 1949).

In this article the classical bias of the earlier travellers, who were keen to dismiss contemporary Greeks and search for the idealized Hellas, is supplanted by a different kind of idealization of the Greek landscape and the radiance of its light in the midst of war and the aftermath of a civil conflict. Instead of the textual investigation of ruins and an imaginary Hellas, there is a transition to an anthropological appreciation of Greece and its orientalist pleasures. The sacred *topos* of ruins is rediscovered as a modern Dionysian place, an exotic land for tourists and a sensual paradise for intellectuals. In this rediscovery of Greece

---

[2] Robert Kaplan noted that 'Durrell and Miller were selling Greece in almost the same way that the hippie movement would later sell California and India as a place to escape from the world and get in touch with your inner self' (1993: 251).

exoticism, sensuality and existentialism converge and construct the touristic image of Greece over the post-war decades. It should be pointed out that in this rediscovery of Greece the role of antiquity is played down and exoticism is highlighted (Tziovas 2018).

Greece is represented as a place for foreigners to find themselves. This might be something that can be tracked back to Lord Byron but it becomes more popular after the Second World War (the English boss in the film *Zorba the Greek* (1964), Leonard Cohen, the itinerant student in John Fowles's novel *The Magus* (1965), the film *Shirley Valentine* (1989)) and extends to the film *Mamma Mia* (2008)). Though the word 'Greece' is only mentioned once in the film, the setting is all-important. Those sweeping vistas, whitewashed houses and narrow charming streets are a shortcut to all that a Greek island represents in the Western imagination.[3] The *Mamma Mia* approach privileges Greece as a place of self-discovery and silences or ignores the natives. It is the Western travellers, artists, writers or filmmakers who speak on their behalf turning them into subaltern or colonial subjects.

Though during the dictatorship there was renewed interest in Greece and outside support for the restoration of democracy, it cannot be claimed that the country was approached in a new way. It is not until the crisis that we find another focus on Greece that could be considered a kind of rediscovery. As I said above, the first rediscovery of Greece relied more on an imaginary and idealistic approach, the second on a historical approach promoting the ideal of continuity, the third tended to be more pragmatic and material, praising the landscape and light of Greece and led to the construction of the Zorba stereotype. Often these approaches overlapped or fused, but I am trying to disentangle them here for analytical purposes in order to understand how the crisis reactivated both the idealistic and critical attitudes to Greece and offered a mixture of idealism, stereotypes and exoticism.

The idealism in this case is not abstract and historical as in the earlier rediscoveries but political. Some Westerners have praised Greece as a bastion of resistance to neo-liberalism and the technocracies of post-democracy. Particularly before and after the referendum of 5 July 2015, the global significance of the Greek crisis has been highlighted and articles appeared with headings such as 'We are all (or should be) Greeks now'.[4] The celebrated writer of *Trainspotting*,

---

[3] Elena Nicolaou, 'Once you notice this about *Mamma Mia*, you can't unsee it', *Refinery 29*, 2018, https://www.refinery29.uk/2018/07/205020/mamma-mia-erases-greek-local-characters.
[4] Murray Dobbin 'We are all (or should be) Greeks now', *Canadian Dimension*, 13 July 2015, https://canadiandimension.com/articles/view/we-are-all-or-should-be-greeks-now.

Irvine Welsh, congratulated the Greeks on the result of the referendum and sent the following twitter message on the same night: 'The world will hopefully find out over the next few years, just how much we owe the beautiful, courageous people of Greece.'[5] He projected his anti-conformist fantasies onto the Greeks as the ones who would change Europe and challenge capitalism, while he himself was enjoying a wealthy lifestyle between Europe and Miami. Crisis-hit Greece was presented by outsiders as both a utopia of resistance (a kind of anti-capitalist Arcadia) and a dystopian failed state, cited by the former British prime minister David Cameron as a cautionary example of what happens to countries that lose their credibility.

Greeks writing in English or other languages promoted the perception of Greece as 'a test case for the new phase of neo-liberal correction in the wake of the economic and financial crises' or reminded international audiences that 'the Greeks must fight for all of us' as in Shelley's times.[6] Shelley's declaration was resurrected 'as a battle cry of an international movement against austerity and in support of the Greek people' (Hanink 2017: 247). Like the European philhellenes who were called to support the Greek War of Independence during the early nineteenth century, as a more general struggle between civilization and barbarism, contemporary Europeans were invited to support the Greek resistance to the widespread onslaught of anti-democratic austerity forces. As Étienne Balibar has observed, from being a peripheral country Greece has become a focal point that epitomizes the problems facing the continent: 'If Europe is for us first of all the name of an *unresolved political problem*, Greece is one of its centers, not because of the mythical origins of our civilization, symbolized by the Acropolis of Athens, but because of the current problems concentrated here' (2004: 2).

A kind of idealization also reinforced an understanding of reciprocal debt: Europe owes Greece its very foundations and Greece owes Europe its bailout. Johanna Hanink used the notion of the symbolic debt as a red thread in her book *The Classical Debt* (2017) to chart the fraught triangular relationship between the West, classical antiquity and modern Greece. She used the example of the French film director Jean-Luc Godard who argued that the 'Greeks gave us logic. We owe them for that ... We use this word millions of times, to make

---

[5] See his interview to Panagiotis Menegos on 7 July 2015, http://popaganda.gr/irvine-welsh-greferendum/.
[6] Costas Douzinas, 'Greeks must fight the neoliberal EU', *The Guardian*, 4 February 2010, https://www.theguardian.com/commentisfree/2010/feb/04/greece-eu-fiscal-policy-protest. See also Yanis Varoufakis (2013).

our most important decisions. It's about time we started paying for it'. He even suggested that each time we use the word 'therefore', we should each pay ten euros to Greece to avoid the Parthenon being sold to the Germans (2017: 241). This kind of conflation of the current Greek monetary debt with the abstract classical debt seems to ignore the complexities of the crisis and the relationship between ancient and modern Greece.

Like the nineteenth-century Western travellers who visited the country, foreign journalists have flocked to Athens to report history in the making. CNN and its leading broadcaster Richard Quest reported live from Athens on the night of 30 June/1 July 2015 with a clock ticking the countdown to financial calamity. More recently another reporter presented Athens as rising again as an exotic cultural capital: 'The city has endured crisis and chaos, and yet is now emerging from the wreckage as one of Europe's most vibrant and significant cultural capitals.'[7] Even the term 'Greek weird cinema', coined by a British critic, has been seen as a label 'that exoticizes Greek cinema as an-Other national cinema' (Kourelou, Liz and Vidal 2014: 141) and fetishizes the deprivation of the crisis. Anthropological interest in the country has also revived with a growing emphasis on the visual representation of the crisis, discrediting the postcard image of Greece.

The rediscovery of Greece during the crisis makes frequent use of the stereotypes, whether those developed after the third rediscovery of Greece that are modelled on Zorba and depict Greeks as feckless, lazy or profligate or the ones based on the contrast between ancient and modern Greece. A characteristic example of the former is the cover of the German periodical *Der Spiegel* (no. 29, 11 July 2015) with the headline 'Our Greeks: An approach to a strange people' (Unsere Griechen: Annäherung an ein seltsames Volk), showing a German tourist trying to dance *syrtaki* with a Greek in traditional dress on a Greek island (Figure 9). Arguably, he is paying for his fun and making the Greek man dance, just as in some nineteenth-century caricatures Africans were shown as creatures that danced for their paymasters. Interestingly, the German is holding his wallet full of money to his chest trying to protect it from the exuberant Zorba.

As for the contrast between ancient and modern Greece, one can argue that it has become a dominant trope in the international media's reporting and comment on the Greek crisis. The imaginative force of Greek mythology has been repeatedly deployed to describe the trials and tribulations of the Greek people.

---

[7] Charly Wilder, 'Athens, rising', *New York Times*, 18 June 2018, https://www.nytimes.com/2018/06/18/travel/athens-after-the-economic-crisis.html.

Figure 9 The cover of the periodical *Der Spiegel* (11 July 2015), © DER SPIEGEL 29/2015.

Antiquity has been a constant point of reference, either in stereotypical headlines such as 'Greek tragedy', 'Greeks caught between Scylla and Charybdis', 'Greeks bearing gifts', 'Odyssey without end' or in images and cartoons.[8] The iconology

---

[8] 'From Hercules to Hemingway, Greece's debt tragedy gets scholarly – and silly', *France 24*, 6 December 2015, https://www.france24.com/en/20150611-hercules-hemingway-sisyphus-kafka-greece-debt-tragedy.

of the crisis often relied on the juxtaposition of ancient and modern figures or monuments (Tziovas 2017). Unlike the juxtaposition of images in Nelly's photographs to demonstrate continuity, it is now used to show the incongruity between ancient and modern Greece and imply that modern Greeks do not deserve their ancient heritage. Western academics have also offered an 'ancient Greek solution for [the] debt crisis', thus reaffirming the usefulness of ancient wisdom as opposed to modern folly,[9] while we have been reminded of the myths of Sisyphus or the Minotaur by the former Greek finance minister Yanis Varoufakis, who has become the darling of the Western media.[10] Ancient metaphors play well with Western audiences, pointing to both ruptures and continuities between past and present or highlighting the cultural ambivalence of modern Greece as both intrinsic to and yet not quite belonging to Europe.

Whereas antiquity was central to the idealistic and historical rediscoveries of the country, it has gradually come to serve the stereotypical approach. Such stereotypes have often sustained the perception of Greece as exotic, but during the crisis the subtext of the stereotypical use of antiquity was to allude to the inadequacy of modern Greeks, not only as regards looking after the state's finances but also their ancient heritage. In turn, there were cartoons and articles suggesting ancient monuments or cultural artefacts be sold off to pay off the debt. While on many occasions ancient and modern Greece are sharply distinguished (and incidentally Greek language is the only living European language defined as 'modern'), in moments of crisis their connection resurfaces to serve as an implicitly unfavourable contrast for the Greece of today.

Despite the frequent references to antiquity in the international media, the ruins of the crisis have upstaged the ancient ones on the ground and 'a flowering of street art and graffiti has given the city an edgier look'.[11] Like the earlier travellers, who visited Greece to discover and record the ancient ruins, contemporary visitors are attracted by these new 'ruins'. Angry and witty street art, including a giant portrait of a fierce-looking owl, the emblem of Athens

---

[9] Josiah Ober, 'Ancient Greece's answer to the financial crisis', *Daily Beast*, 13 July 2015, https://www.thedailybeast.com/ancient-greeces-answer-to-the-financial-crisis and Armand D'Angour, 'Ancient Greek solution for debt crisis', *BBC*, 6 June 2012, https://www.bbc.com/news/business-18255039.

[10] See the interview with Yanis Varoufakis in *Le Monde* (Allain Salles, Après la victoire de Syriza, Athènes veut «arrêter d'imiter Sisyphe», 2 February 2015, https://www.lemonde.fr/economie/article/2015/02/02/athenes-veut-arreter-d-imiter-sisyphe_4567736_3234.html and his book *The Global Minotaur* (Varoufakis 2011a).

[11] 'How angry street art is making Athens hip', *The Economist*, 30 September 2017, https://www.economist.com/europe/2017/09/30/how-angry-street-art-is-making-athens-hip.

since antiquity, has transformed the city into a culturescape and a spectacle for tourists. The crisis, according to *The Economist*, has made Greece cheaper for holidaymakers and this has even encouraged crisis tourism and the treatment of Greece as a colonial spectacle. The best example of such exploitation is an advert posted in March 2018 in *The Guardian* online which was subsequently withdrawn, offering a holiday to Greece for seven nights (£2,500 per person) in order to explore the impact of the financial and refugee crises in the country. The trip, which was 'exclusively designed for Guardian readers', was intended, according to the newspaper's website, to give travellers 'the chance to meet local families and discover how their lives have been affected by the financial crisis'. Social media users criticized the newspaper for 'insulting' Greeks and 'making money out of misery' or promoting 'poverty porn'.[12]

By focusing on Greece as myth and not the Greeks, exoticism is not only a colourful or unusual image constructed by others but its existence can also be attested in the reactions of the locals who feel exoticized. No significant reaction by Greeks against the earlier rediscoveries of Greece is recorded. Instead, they often subscribed to the views of the outsiders or followed their approach. It was only during the recent crisis that we have seen for the first time some resistance to the cultural rediscovery of Greece and the aestheticization of the crisis.[13] The postcolonial consideration of Greece as a Western fantasy or imaginary construction should take into account first local challenges and instances of native resistance to this fantasy and secondly the darker side of this construction which separates the ancient ideal from the belatedly modern by ignoring or devaluing the latter. Both the rediscovery and idealization of Greece in the early nineteenth century and its post-Second World War presentation as a tourist paradise always involved a process that separated and protected the classical and the ideal from contamination by the modern and the real. In other words, two discourses about and images of Greece co-exist and vie with each other: the idealistic philhellenic version and the critical anti-modern Greek one. The construction of Greece as an imaginary or exotic land coexists with a critical

---

[12] The Chinese activist Ai Weiwei planned to set up a studio and a refugee memorial on the island of Lesvos to highlight the plight of refugees. He received similar criticism and has been described as the Santa Claus of the refugees.

[13] It has been argued that Greece sells to the outside world only as an exotic or suffering country. A Greece not in ruins does not fit Western narratives and therefore the romantic image of the ancient ruins has to be completed by the modern ones (Ilias Kanellis, 'Ο φοκλορισμός της ερειπωμένης Ελλάδας' and Christos Chomenidis 'Ως πότε ηρωικοί και πένθιμοι;' *Ta Nea*, 10–11 August 2019).

attitude towards the modern country, carefully disassociating it from the ancient ideal.[14]

The Greek crisis has generated international interest, inviting interpretation and mediation from agents with different perspectives and agendas. It seems to have encouraged an interplay of resistance and victimhood, empathy and blame, anti-capitalism and exoticism, often leading to a clash between the way outsiders read the cultural manifestations of the crisis and how insiders react to this reading. This clash has raised the following questions: Do outsiders adopt a monolithic and narrow reading of Greek culture in crisis? Do they promote the concept of 'crisis art' based on the colonial expectation that in peripheral countries art reflects reality realistically or engages with it allegorically, whereas in metropolitan cultures it transcends it imaginatively or invents it aesthetically? Should the focus be on the representation of crisis or on a crisis of representation? These questions have been raised in connection with poetry anthologies on the crisis and particularly *Austerity Measures* edited by Karen van Dyck (2016).

She aspired to show the multilingualism and the multiculturalism of contemporary Greek poets and to register the dynamics of Greek society in conditions of austerity. In its publicity blurb the anthology claims that it offers 'the best of the writing to emerge from the remarkable creative ferment of Greece's decade of crisis'. Greek critics welcomed the greater visibility afforded to the contemporary poetry of their country by a leading global publisher, but they were wary of the commodification of the dystopia of crisis and the endorsement by Yanis Varoufakis. The anthology was criticized in Greece for exploiting and selling the crisis; it was treated as a colonial gesture to which the natives responded with the insecurity of the colonized:

> How could one not think this way, though, seeing how desperately we need the approving glance of the 'other' and the worth we think their approval bestows on us. It is enough for us that they bothered with us, that we were on the receiving end of their generosity. Then, unanimously, the incorruptible and unbiased mass media leading the way, we pour out hymns of praise and the hearts of the nation beat as one, often for works which, if produced by a local, we would have entirely ignored, if not vehemently condemned.

> This is a collective insecurity syndrome which reveals that we are not standing firmly on our own feet and require the acceptance and approval of foreigners to

---

[14] Dimitris P. Sotiropoulos, 'Νόου σπηκ ήνγκλις και οι σύγχρονοι Ζορμπάδες', *I Kathimerini*, 22 May 2018, http://www.kathimerini.gr/964751/article/politismos/vivlio/nooy-sphk-hngklis-kai-oi-sygxronoi-zormpades.

feel we are worth something. It is precisely this stance which demonstrates that we are caught in a net we have woven from our innermost selves, imprisoned within ourselves, waiting for outsiders to set us free.[15]

Van Dyck has been criticized for describing an Athens 'taken out of a postmodern Dantean inferno' and producing a Baudrillardian tableau with wild exotic animals living in Greece which foreign readers can enjoy from the tranquillity of their sitting room.[16] This criticism by the editorial team of a poetry magazine in Athens was based on the following comments made by van Dyck in an article in *The Guardian* promoting her anthology:

> Broken promises and corruption on all sides breed unfounded accusations and fatalism. Hardly anyone keeps money in the bank anymore. News of murders and robberies shares equal airtime with ads for hi-tech security systems. ...
> Poetry, though, is one thing there is more of. Much more. Poets writing graffiti on walls, poets reading in public squares, theatres and empty lots, poets performing in slams, chanting slogans, and singing songs at rallies, poets blogging and posting on the internet, poets teaming up with artists and musicians, teaching workshops to school children and migrants.[17]

The Greek edition of the anthology has also been criticized for casting an outwardly compassionate gaze on contemporary Greek poetry while concealing a sense of cultural hegemony under political correctness. Having been crafted merely to satisfy the international interest on the crisis, the selection criteria employed by van Dyck have been challenged as not literary (Garantoudis 2018). The anthology seems not to engage with the question of how the crisis is represented in literature. Does it invite a realistic mode of narrative or does it demand new tropes, signalling a crisis of representation? (Kargiotis 2017). Answers to these questions are not straightforward, but the critical reception of the anthology suggests that the crisis caused a clash of literary expectations between outsiders and insiders, with the former privileging the experience of crisis and the latter aesthetic resistance. Van Dyck treats poetry as a cultural event while its Greek critics see it as an aesthetic canon. The anthology *Austerity Measures* is not the only example of foreigners clashing with the natives for

---

[15] Editorial, 'Metra gia tsarouchia (ή όταν η κρίση πουλάει)', *Athens Review of Books*, no 75, June 2016. See also Lambrini Kouzeli, 'Η ποίηση της λιτότητας', *To Vima*, 12 June 2016 and Kostas Voulgaris, 'Όταν η κρίση πουλάει ποιήματα', *Avgi*, 9 October 2016.
[16] Editorial, 'Το πολιτικό (ως στάση) στην ποίηση (ως πράξη)', *[φρμκ] Farmako*, 11, Spring–Summer 2018, pp. 6–10.
[17] Karen van Dyck, 'The new Greek poetry', *The Guardian*, 25 March 2016, https://www.theguardian.com/books/2016/mar/25/new-greek-poetry-karen-van-dyck.

ignoring the local cultural production and trying to 'sell' the crisis to an international audience, adopting a colonial posture.

Documenta 14, Germany's prestigious contemporary art event, which was divided between Athens (8 April–16 July 2017) and Kassel (10 June–17 September 1917), did not escape similar criticisms. As we have seen earlier rediscoveries of Greece by Westerners have focused on its ancient heritage at the expense of contemporary culture or they have read the latter in connection with or in opposition to the ancient one. Documenta 14 tried to reverse this trend and create curiosity in Athens as a place where contemporary art could also be enjoyed. As the meeting point of the economic and migration crises, Athens was chosen as a venue because it reflected the social and cultural dilemmas that have troubled Europe. Examining issues such as mass migration, displacement and the search for identity, more than 160 artists showcased new works over more than forty locations throughout the city.[18] Featuring the financial crisis, along with Greece's political turmoil and social struggles the documenta 14 exhibition and its theme 'Learning from Athens' aspired to make the periphery the new cultural centre, adopting the 'South as a State of Mind'. According to its artistic director Adam Szymczyk:

> The city lies in this part of Europe which seems to constitute a paradigmatic model for often violent oppositions and fragile hopes and fears, which cannot be dismissed as an internal problem of Greece or of any other vulnerable modern democracy. Athens generally embodies the uncertain future of the western European democracy in a world which experiences in a dramatic way the loss of stable reference points. The so called 'Greek crisis' makes Athens perhaps the most productive site to think about the future, now.[19]

However, such statements were not sufficient to forestall criticism about 'crisis tourism' in which the troubled city was to serve as a striking backdrop for the international art elite. While curators and artists hoped that the exhibition would reinvigorate the Athenian artistic scene and the city's mayor, Yorgos Kaminis, maintained that documenta was fantastic for tourism, critics complained that it smacked of cultural imperialism.[20] The title 'Learning from Athens' presupposed

---

[18] 'DOCUMENTA 14 "Learning from Athens"', https://whyathens.com/events/documenta-14-athens/.
[19] Dimitris Politakis, 'documenta 14: Τι θα μας μάθει η Αθήνα το 2017', *Popaganda*, 15 Οκτωβρίου 2014, http://popaganda.gr/documenta-14-ti-tha-mas-mathi-athina-2017/.
[20] It should be noted that documenta 14 worked only with cash-strapped Greek public institutions and supported them, particularly the National Museum of Contemporary Art (EMST). This has been recognized as one of the contributions of the exhibition despite the lukewarm response of the Athenian public and the deficit of €7 million for the Athenian part of the operation. See Dorian Batycka, 'Cultural diplomacy and artwashing at documenta in Athens', *Hyperallergic*, 12 June 2017, https://hyperallergic.com/384199/cultural-diplomacy-and-artwashing-at-documenta-

the distance and the difference of the learning subject without disclosing its identity. At the same time the city acquired status as a source of knowledge and in turn the power to share it. But there were pressing questions: Who is the learning subject? What can wealthy northern Europe really learn from a city that's struggling to stay afloat? What happens when the event is over? And what purpose does art serve in times of crisis?[21]

Yanis Varoufakis, one of the exhibition's critics, called it 'a gimmick' to exploit the tragedy in Greece.[22] He even compared it to trips to the Greek island of Makronisos, where political dissidents were exiled during the 1940s and 1950s, or Brazil's 'favela tours':

> There are tourist trips now to Makronisos, which even offer an inmate's menu. I have no doubt that there is a lot of demand for this type of tourism, where you get embedded into the context of others' suffering. In Brazil they also have 'favela tours', as I think they call them, in which tourists experience 'life in the favela'. This is not too different from how most Greeks see Documenta 14.[23]

The exhibition did not escape critiques about colonizing or exoticizing the natives, judging from the graffiti on walls in Athens castigating the spectacle as 'Crapumenta 14' or conveying the opposition of local people: 'I refuse to exoticize myself to increase your cultural capital. Signed: The People.' The slogan 'Learning from Capitalism' and the stencil 'Dear Documenta 14: It must be nice to critique capitalism with a 38 (70?) million Euro budget. Sincerely. Oi 18ageneis' appeared on the campus of the Athens School of Fine Arts, a documenta venue (Figure 10). Along with the question posed by the artist Thierry Geoffroy, 'Is Documenta the botox of late capitalism?', this kind of graffiti reinforced the argument put forward by critics that the exhibition amounted to

---

in-athens/, Selana Vronti, 'Ερωτήματα, απαντήσεις για την d14 της Αθήνας', *Kathimerini*, 9 July 2017 and the various contributions in the newspaper *Avgi* (17 and 24 July 2017).

[21] 'Learning from Athens – documenta 14', https://www.dw.com/en/learning-from-athens-documenta-14/a-37750140. Critically observing and engaging with aspects of documenta's presence in Athens social anthropologist Eleana Yalouri of Panteion University and Elpida Rikou, an instructor at the Athens School of Fine Arts, developed a research project called 'Learning from documenta'.

[22] He also said about the exhibition: 'It's like rich Americans taking a tour in a poor African country, doing a safari, going on a humanitarian tourism crusade.' An interview with Yanis Varoufakis by Leon Kahane, 'Doing documenta in Athens is like rich Americans taking a tour in a poor African country', *Spike Art Magazine*, 7 October 2015, https://www.spikeartmagazine.com/articles/doing-documenta-athens-rich-americans-taking-tour-poor-african-country.

[23] '"We come bearing gifts" – Iliana Fokianaki and Yanis Varoufakis on documenta 14 Athens', https://conversations.e-flux.com/t/we-come-bearing-gifts-iliana-fokianaki-and-yanis-varoufakis-on-documenta-14-athens/6666.

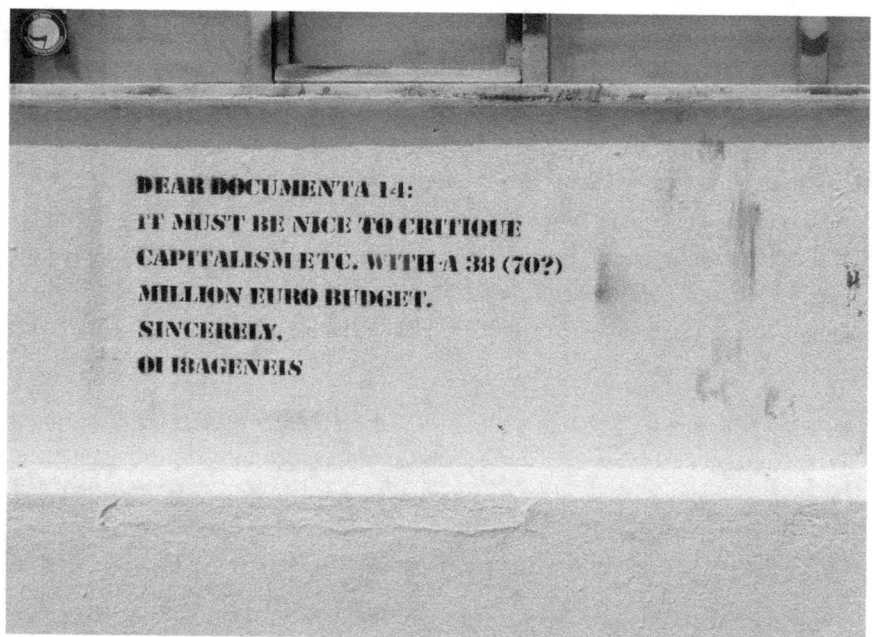

Figure 10 A stencil on the campus of the Athens School of Fine Arts, courtesy of Julia Tulke.

the worst kind of crisis tourism.[24] The organizers also faced criticism for offering precarious employment schemes and for not adequately showcasing the local artistic production.

With reference to the exhibition, the journalist Maria Katsounaki argued that, in the eyes of foreigners, the crisis remained hostage to a one-sided and dated approach, being presented 'as a TV drama, peppered with elements of disaster, conspiracy theories, stories of violence and anarchy'.[25] And an American art historian also commented: 'Simply walking around the graffiti-filled Exarcheia neighborhood of Athens, with its many self-organized community spaces and political meeting grounds – an area associated with radical leftists and anarchists – felt closer to the Greek state of emergency than nearly anything in

---

[24] Helena Smith, '"Crapumenta!" … Anger in Athens as the blue lambs of Documenta hit town', *The Guardian*, 14 May 2017, https://www.theguardian.com/artanddesign/2017/may/14/documenta-14-athens-german-art-extravaganza.

[25] Maria Katsounaki, 'Από την πλευρά του Τόνι Νέγκρι', *I Kathimerini*, 7 September 2016, http://www.kathimerini.gr/873801/opinion/epikairothta/politikh/apo-thn-pleyra-toy-toni-negkri, 'Η τέχνη της κρίσης, η κρίση της τέχνης', *I Kathimerini*, 11 September 2016, http://www.kathimerini.gr/874299/opinion/epikairothta/politikh/h-texnh-ths-krishs-h-krish-ths-texnhs.

the exhibition'.²⁶ Following a similar line, a Greek art critic, writing in English, claimed that 'Documenta 14 has a lot to think about how (and if) it challenges colonial and orientalist mechanisms (especially when using the anti-colonial element as a flag)' and raised the question of whether 'texts like Preciado's "Qui la dette grecque réchauffe-t-elle?" in *Libération* present the most vivid exoticisation of the Athenian landscape as the place par excellence for fantasising the creation of resistance towards the international collapse of democracy, dignity and the welfare state'.²⁷ Focusing on corporeality and affect and arousing a good deal of discussion, documenta 14 was more than an exhibition; it functioned as a 'performative action' that aimed to challenge the status quo. What is interesting here is not so much its contribution to the Athenian art scene as the perception of it both inside and outside of Greece as merely paying lip service to radical politics while practising cultural colonialism. Though it tried to challenge Western anthropological epistemologies or to explore post-identitarian body politics, the exhibition did not present forward-looking art of political engagement.

The major published document of the exhibition, *The documenta 14 Reader* (2017), came out too late for the Greek part of the project and has been criticized for not having a single Athenian writing from Athens. Cultural arbiters, like Adam Szymczyk, have been described as making sure they had 'Athens to themselves, unadulterated by any Athenians, either by not visiting it (following the example of nearly all Romantic writers and artists) or by reducing its inhabitants to non-speaking roles (as do all foreign movies filmed in the city)'.²⁸ Here the analogies with the earlier rediscoveries of Greece and the construction of an imaginary Athens by those early travellers (like Gibbon), who never visited it, and Greece as a state of mind are striking. Documenta colonized Athens in its attempt to decolonize it by focusing on the process of othering. Aspiring to redefine the other, it ended up deterritorializing it and reconfirming the status of Greece as an artistic periphery. This angered a number of Greeks who perceived the organizers more as colonizers than connoisseurs.²⁹

---

²⁶ T. J. Demos, 'Learning from documenta 14: Athens, post-democracy, and decolonisation', *Third Text*, http://thirdtext.org/demos-documenta.

²⁷ Despina Zefkili, ' "Exercises of Freedom": Documenta 14', *Third Text*, February 2017, http://thirdtext.org/exercises-freedom-documenta14.

²⁸ Vassilis Lambropoulos, 'Are there any Greeks in this publication? (2)', 15 August 2017, https://poetrypiano.wordpress.com/2017/08/16/are-there-any-greeks-in-this-book-2/.

²⁹ See 'Connoisseurs or colonists? Documenta's controversial stay in Athens', *The Economist*, 6 April 2017, https://www.economist.com/books-and-arts/2017/04/06/documentas-controversial-stay-in-athens?zid=307&ah=5e80419d1bc9821ebe173f4f0f060a07. Dimitris Plantzos was also critical of the exhibition: 'I do believe that the show, succumbing as it did to its own narcissism, failed to discuss the tensions, the controversies, the frustrations, and the prevalent sense of defeat associated with the "Greek crisis", simply because it seemed to take advantage of them rather than engaging with them' (2019: 473).

The defenders of documenta 14, on the other hand, argued that the exhibition once again addressed the question of 'political art' and had avoided reducing Athens to an idealized primordial space. It demonstrated that Europe and its institutions could not be treated in a monolithic manner and that the Greek criticism levelled against the exhibition was so obsessed by domestic political preconceptions that it had failed to look at the exhibition per se. Highlighting the city's vibrancy and state of emergency, the exhibition 'served as a kind of double mirror with which we could see the cultural relation of Greece with Europe and the world, but also the reverse: that of Europe with Greece'.[30] This involved a dual role for Athens in terms of proximity and distance, that is to say an ambivalent presentation of Athens as being at the core of European identity and at the same time remote from it. In this way Athens emerged as a metonymy not only for the Greek crisis, but also for global dystopia.

Over the last ten years a crisis 'space' has been constructed and invested with an outsider's horizon of expectations. Though it is difficult to argue that there has been a sublimation or manipulative handling of suffering like the mediated spectacles of televised wars (e.g. the Iraq War), the international mediation of the Greek crisis has involved an element of aestheticization and the politics of pity with emotions and ethical dispositions evoked in the public sphere (Boltanski 1999). This aestheticization of crisis involved its spectacularization, transforming the human suffering into a phantasmagoric *tableau vivant* (Baudrillard 1995). The crisis has been marketed and mediated by outsiders as a cultural product and capital, turning the subjects of the crisis into narrative objects. For the outside world contemporary Greek culture seems not to have existed outside the master narrative of crisis; it had been acquiring significance due to the crisis and was produced by the crisis. Greece, in turn, has been invested with agonistic potential, inviting outsiders to live out their revolutionary fantasies in the Disneyland of crisis.

---

[30] Theophilos Tramboulis and Yorgos Tzirtzilakis, 'When crisis becomes form: Athens as a paradigm', *Stedelijk Studies*, 6, 2018, https://stedelijkstudies.com/wp-content/uploads/2018/04/Stedelijk-Studies-6-When-Crisis-Becomes-Form-Tramboulis-Tzirtzilakis.pdf.

Conclusion

What constitutes the most distinctive feature of the culture of the *Metapolitefsi*? I would argue that it is the prominent role of identity in various forms resulting from the major shift seen in this period from politics to culture, involving the disentanglement of group identities from political affiliations and the move from a battle for political power to a clash for cultural hegemony. This does not mean that culture has been divested of politics, but some debates and contests have been transferred from the realm of party politics to the broader cultural domain. Now the focus is more likely to be on issues such as identity, otherness, sexuality, heritage and memory with socio-political debates being turned into culture wars. Moreover, the ascendancy of the anthropological and biopolitical conception of culture as a way of life, in contrast to its humanist perception as heritage and spirituality, has promoted the association of culture with identity and in turn the prominence of identity politics as in other Western countries. As I have shown in individual chapters, the identity issues of the post-junta period have been accentuated by transitions from homogeneity to diversity or ambivalent tensions (between private and public, high and low, marginal and mainstream, centripetal and centrifugal). The promotion and questioning of modernization have also contributed to identity dilemmas by (re)activating cultural dualisms or querying the priority of politics over culture.

After 1974 Greece opened up to the world and renegotiated its position and its image by looking not only towards the West but also eastward and engaging with its forgotten Balkan and Ottoman pasts. EU membership, the redrawing of the map of the Balkans, the end of the Cold War, migration and globalization led to earlier political divisions being overridden by ambitious visions regarding the cultural role of Greece and the revival of religious alliances. The growth of tourism, heritage issues (the Macedonian question, the Parthenon sculptures), membership of the eurozone, the Olympic Games of 2004 and the financial crisis attracted the attention of the outside world and raised questions about nation branding. To judge by the impressive number of translations of foreign literature, the desire to export Greek culture abroad or the increasing cosmopolitanism of Greek novels, the *Metapolitefsi* experienced unprecedented cultural extroversion and saw a revaluation of the role of the Greek diaspora. The commercialization of culture and literature created additional concerns and called attention to the cultural rifts between aesthetic and consumer culture, shifting the emphasis from the producers to the end users.

The common denominator in the fundamental questions that preoccupied Greeks during the post-junta period (how the nation is defined; who owns the past; and how the past is remembered) (addressed in Chapter 3) is the quest for identity. The notion of the cultural continuity of the Greek nation was increasingly challenged by scholars who acknowledged the plurality of cultural traditions (ancient, Byzantine, Ottoman, Venetian) and shifted the focus to the invention, construction and negotiation of the past, thus contributing to a widening gap between historians and the general public, that still held to traditional views. As a result of this critical engagement with the past and its perceived loss of stability, questions were posed about identity more intensely than ever before. The role of fiction in revisiting the archives of the past and turning them into a battleground of memories was also instrumental in this process.

There was also increasing concern about language and identity with the old language question being superseded by anxieties about the decline of linguistic standards, the introduction of the monotonic system, the invasion of English, Latinization and teenage slang. While in the past language had been a less important factor than religion in defining national identity, in the post-junta years language and national identity became ever more closely entwined. Treating Greek as a monument to be safeguarded, language debates turned into crusades to 'save' or 'protect' Greek, and any threats to the language were perceived as challenges to the national identity.

With Greek culture losing its oral character and being rapidly exposed to visual challenges and digital technologies, the deregulation of the Greek media and the importation of foreign TV shows did not simply contribute to cultural pluralism; they also raised issues of cultural consumption and identity. Fictional stories on television, for instance, made fun of Greek behavioural patterns, prompting introspection while during the crisis foreign media contributed to a Greek identity crisis by contrasting Greeks to other Europeans. In the post-junta period, television and cinema coexisted in a symbiotic and antagonistic relationship, with the former claiming a wider audience and the latter aspiring to transcend the boundaries of national culture by exploring new social issues, engaging with transnational audiences or deconstructing the image of Greece as a holiday idyll. The thematic shift in contemporary Greek cinema away from the grand narratives of political history to concerns about identity, sexuality and family dynamics coincided with similar transitions in social movements. These movements were emancipated from narrow political affiliations by claiming new or autonomous identities (youth, women), while homosexuality began to be perceived as an identity and no longer just a sexual practice. This fostered yet another transition, from a discourse on rights to the disruption of all fixed identities, and queer culture gained in visibility and contributed to growing cultural diversity and changing identity politics.

Another sign of the increasing preoccupation with identities has been the emphasis on Greekness and its definition. The politically driven ethnocentrism of the post-Civil War era gave way to a cultural ethnocentrism and debates about the aesthetics of Hellenism or the role of the Generation of the 1930s in promoting Greekness. The certainties associated with the essentialist notion of national consciousness have been called into question by the constructionist and relativist concept of identity. Or in Stuart Hall's words 'identities are about questions of using the resources of history, language and culture in the process of becoming rather than being ... not the so-called return to roots but a coming-to-terms-with our 'routes'' (Hall 1996: 4). From a broader perspective the theory that Greece was a European cultural construct and that the West exercised a kind of cultural colonialism or crypto-colonialism over the country added another dimension to the identity debates of the period.

After the end of the Civil War, Greece faced a series of challenges. In the 1950s and 1960s, it was the challenge of rebuilding the country after the devastation of the war, resulting in an unprecedented urbanization; in the 1970s and 1980s, it was the redistribution of power and wealth with the concomitant rise of consumer culture; and since the early 1990s, it has been the negotiation of the country's position in the world order, following the end of the Cold War, and as a result of further EU integration, migration and globalization. This has brought to the fore issues of identity, cultural repositioning and national rebranding and could lead to the argument that it is the preoccupation with identities that has stolen the limelight and which defines the post-junta period as a whole. Starting with political euphoria and ending in an economic debacle, the *Metapolitefsi* may have become politically synonymous with democratization and reconciliation, yet culturally, it signifies an age of identities marked by competing narratives: the reformist and forward-looking one of the modernizers, the critically retrospective and melancholically reflective one of the Left and the anti-Western one, harking back to a lost communitarianism, of the neo-Orthodox intellectuals. One could claim that, if politics helps to divide the period from the junta to the crisis into phases, culture and identity draw it together, acting as its overarching metaphors.

References

Adorno, T. W. (1991), 'Culture industry reconsidered', in J. M. Bernstein (ed.), *The Culture Industry: Selected Essays on Mass Culture*, 85–92, London: Routledge.

Aggestam, L. (2008), 'Introduction: Ethical power Europe?', *International Affairs*, 84 (1): 1–11.

Aitaki, G. (2018a), 'The academic study of Greek television: Mapping a scattered field', *Critical Studies in Television*, 13 (2): 244–53.

Aitaki, G. (2018b), ' "All good people have debts": Framing the Greek crisis in television fiction', in M. Patrona (ed.), *Crisis and the Media: Narratives of Crisis across Cultural Settings and Media Genres*, 107–26, Amsterdam: John Benjamins.

Aitaki, G. (2019), 'Television fiction as a window into a nation's past: *The Arbitraries* and the concept of the Neohellene', in T. Stauning Willert and G. Katsan (eds), *Retelling the Past in Contemporary Greek Literature, Film, and Popular Culture*, 151–64, Lanham, MD: Lexington.

Aleksić, T. (2016), 'Sex, violence, dogs and the impossibility of escape: Why contemporary Greek film is so focused on family', *Journal of Greek Media & Culture*, 2 (2): 155–71.

Alivizatos, N. C. (1986), *Κράτος και Ραδιοτηλεόραση*, Athens: Sakkoulas.

Alivizatos, N. C. (1999), 'A new role for the Greek Church?', *Journal of Modern Greek Studies*, 17 (1): 23–40.

Alivizatos, N. C. (2003), 'The contribution of modern Greece to today's European identity', *MGSA Bulletin*, 35:19–24.

Alivizatos, N. C. (2011), *Το σύνταγμα και οι εχθροί του στη νεοελληνική ιστορία, 1800–2010*, Athens: Polis.

Alivizatos, N. C. (2015), 'Για μια περιοδολόγηση της μεταπολίτευσης', in M. Avgeridis, E. Gazi and K. Kornetis (eds), *Μεταπολίτευση: Η Ελλάδα στο μεταίχμιο δύο αιώνων*, 432–4, Athens: Themelio.

Allardt, E. (2005), 'Europe's multiple modernity', in E. Ben-Rafael and Y. Sternberg (eds), *Comparing Modernities: Pluralism versus Homogeneity, Essays in Homage to Shmuel N. Eisenstadt*, 483–99, Leiden: Brill.

Amanatidis, V. (2001), 'Η ποιητική «γενιά» του 90: προσέγγιση – χωρίς παραδείγματα – σε μια αφανή γενιά', *Entefktirio*, 53: 49–52.

Ambatzopoulou, F. (1993), *Το Ολοκαύτωμα στις μαρτυρίες των Ελλήνων Εβραίων*, Thessaloniki: Paratiritis.

Ambatzopoulou, F. (1995), *Η λογοτεχνία ως μαρτυρία: Έλληνες πεζογράφοι για τη γενοκτονία των Εβραίων*, Thessaloniki: Paratiritis.

Ambatzopoulou, F. (1998), *Ο άλλος εν διωγμώ: Η εικόνα του Εβραίου στη λογοτεχνία – Ζητήματα ιστορίας και μυθοπλασίας*, Athens: Themelio.

Anagnostopoulos, V. D. (1993), *Μοναχικές Αναγνώσεις: Το ιδιωτικό όραμα και η ποίηση – Ανθολογία*, Athens: Vivliogonia.

Anastasakis, O., K. Nicolaidis and K. Öktem, eds (2009), *In the Long Shadow of Europe: Greeks and Turks in the Age of Post-nationalism*, Leiden: Martinus Nijhoff.

Anastasiadis, A. (2011), 'Trauma - memory – narration: Greek Civil War novels of the 1980s and 1990s', *Byzantine and Modern Greek Studies*, 35 (1): 92–108.

Andreou, S., M. Fotiadis and K. Kotsakis (1996), 'Review of Aegean prehistory V: The Neolithic and Bronze Age of Northern Greece', *American Journal of Archaeology*, 100 (3): 537–97.

Andriakaina, E. (2016), 'Public history and Greek identity: The 1821 revolution as metaphor for the "Greek Crisis"', in A. Novak-Imaani and J. El-Burki (eds), *Defining Identity and the Changing Scope of Culture in the Digital Age*, 56–79, Hershey, PA: IGI-Global.

Androusou, A., and N. Askouni, eds (2011), *Πολιτισμική ετερότητα και ανθρώπινα δικαιώματα*, Athens: Metaihmio.

Androutsopoulos, J. K. (1998), 'Γλώσσα των νέων και γλωσσική αγορά της νεανικής κουλτούρας', in *Μελέτες για την ελληνική γλώσσα: Πρακτικά της 18ης Ετήσιας Συνάντησης του Τομέα Γλωσσολογίας της Φιλοσοφικής Σχολής του Α.Π.Θ.*, 41–55, Thessaloniki: Kyriakidis.

Androutsopoulos, J. K. (1999), 'Από τα φραγκοχιώτικα στα greeklish', *Το Vima*, 5 September.

Androutsopoulos, J. K. (2009), '"Greeklish": Transliteration practice and discourse in the context of computer-mediated digraphia', in A. Georgakopoulou and M. Silk (eds), *Standard Languages and Language Standards: Greek, Past and Present*, 221–49, Farnham: Ashgate.

Angelou, A. (1997), *Το Κρυφό Σχολειό*, Athens: Estia.

Angouri, J., and R. Wodak (2014), '"They became big in the shadow of the crisis": The Greek success story and the rise of the far Right', *Discourse and Society*, 25 (4): 540–65.

Antoniou, G. (2007), 'The lost Atlantis of objectivity: The revisionist struggles between the academic and public spheres', *History and Theory*, 46 (4): 92–112.

Antoniou, G. (2013), 'Οι γιορτές μίσους και οι πόλεμοι της δημόσιας μνήμης (1950–2000): από το τραύμα των ηττημένων στο τραύμα των νικητών', in N. Demertzis, E. Paschaloudi and G. Antoniou (eds), *Εμφύλιος: Πολιτισμικό Τραύμα*, 215–49, Athens: Alexandreia.

Antoniou, G., and N. Marantzidis (2003), 'The Greek Civil War historiography, 1945–2001: Toward a new paradigm', *Columbia Journal of Historiography*, 1. [no longer available in printed or online form].

Antoniou, G., and N. Marantzidis (2008), 'Το επίμονο παρελθόν', in G. Antoniou and N. Marantzidis (eds), *Η Εποχή της Σύγχυσης: η δεκαετία του '40 και η ιστοριογραφία*, 11–52, Athens: Estia.

Antoniou, G., and A. Dirk Moses, eds (2018), *The Holocaust in Greece*, Cambridge: Cambridge University Press.

Apostolelli, A., and A. Halkia, eds (2012), *Σώμα, Φύλο, Σεξουαλικότητα: ΛΟΑΤΚ Πολιτικές στην Ελλάδα*, Athens: Plethron.

Apostolidou, V. (2003), *Λογοτεχνία και Ιστορία στη μεταπολεμική αριστερά: η παρέμβαση του Δημήτρη Χατζή 1947–1981*, Athens: Polis.

Apostolidou, V. (2010), *Τραύμα και Μνήμη: Η πεζογραφία των πολιτικών προσφύγων*, Athens: Polis.

Archimandritis, Y. (2013), *Θόδωρος Αγγελόπουλος: Με γυμνή φωνή*, Athens: Patakis.

Argyriou, A. (1979), *Η ελληνική ποίηση: Ανθολογία-Γραμματολογία*, Athens: Sokolis.

Argyriou, A. (1996), 'Ο μοντερνισμός στην ελληνική λογοτεχνία: οι αφετηρίες, οι αρχές και η διάρκειά του', in *Μοντερνισμός: Η ώρα της αποτίμησης*, 243–78, Athens: Etaireia Spoudon Neoellenikou Politismou kai Genikis Paideias.

Argyriou, A., A. Kotzias, K. Kouloufakos, S. Plaskovitis and S. Tsirkas (1973), 'Η νεοελληνική πραγματικότητα και η πεζογραφία μας', *Synecheia*, 4: 172–9.

Argyriou, A., A. Ziras, A. Kotzias and K. Kouloufakos (1976/7), 'Το οδυνηρό πέρασμα στην πολιτικοποίηση', *Diavazo*, 5–6: 62–83.

Aristinos, Y. (2007), *Νάρκισσος και Ιανός: Η νεωτερική πεζογραφία στην Ελλάδα*, Athens: Mesogeios.

Ashcroft, B., G. Griffiths and H. Tiffin (2007), *Post-Colonial Studies: The Key Concepts*, London: Routledge.

Assmann, J. (1998), *Moses the Egyptian: The Memory of Egypt in Western Monotheism*, Cambridge, MA: Harvard University Press.

Astrinakis, A. E. (1991), *Νεανικές Υποκουλτούρες*, Athens: Papazisis.

Athanasiadis, H. (2015), *Τα αποσυρθέντα βιβλία: Έθνος και σχολική Ιστορία στην Ελλάδα, 1858–2008*, Athens: Alexandreia.

Avdela, E. (2000), 'The teaching of history in Greece', *Journal of Modern Greek Studies*, 18 (2): 239–53.

Avdela, E. (2008), '"Corrupting and uncontrollable activities": Moral panic about youth in post-Civil-War Greece', *Journal of Contemporary History*, 43 (1): 25–44.

Avdela, E. (2010), 'Η ιστορία του φύλου στην Ελλάδα: Από τη διαταραχή στην ενσωμάτωση', in V. Kantsa, V. Moutafi and E. Papataxiarchis (eds), *Φύλο και κοινωνικές επιστήμες στη σύγχρονη Ελλάδα*, 89–117, Athens: Alexandreia.

Avdela, E. (2013), *Νέοι εν κινδύνω*, Athens: Polis.

Avdela, E., and G. Papageorgiou (1979), 'Πίσω από τις τζελουτζίες: Η Αυτοβιογραφία της Ελισάβετ Μαρτινέγκου', *Skoupa*, 2: 26.

Avdela, E., and A.Psara, eds (1985), *Ο φεμινισμός στην Ελλάδα του μεσοπολέμου: Μια ανθολογία*, Athens: Gnosi.

Avgeridis, M. (2017), 'Debating the Greek 1940s: Histories and memories of a conflicting past since the end of the Second World War', *Historein*, 16 (1–2): 8–46.
Avgeridis, M., E. Gazi and K.Kornetis, eds (2015), *Μεταπολίτευση: Η Ελλάδα στο μεταίχμιο δύο αιώνων*, Athens: Themelio.
Babiniotis, G. (1992), *Η γλώσσα της Μακεδονίας: Η αρχαία Μακεδονική και η ψευδώνυμη γλώσσα των Σκοπίων*, Athens: Olkos.
Babiniotis, G. (1998), 'Ο διωγμός των λέξεων', *To Vima*, 31 May.
Babiniotis, G. (1999), 'Τι γλώσσα μιλάμε', *To Vima*, 5 December.
Babiniotis, G. (2001), 'Ένας ανύπαρκτος εχθρός', *To Vima*, 28 January.
Baerentzen, L., J. O. Iatrides and O. L. Smith, eds (1987), *Studies in the History of the Greek Civil War 1945–1949*, Copenhagen: Museum Tusculanum Press.
Balampanidis, I. (2009), 'Προσεγγίσεις του "Δεκέμβρη": Ερμηνευτικές και Μεθοδολογικές Προκείμενες', *Synchrona Themata*, 105, April–June: 8–13.
Balampanidis, I. (2019), 'The abduction of Europa: Europeanism and Euroscepticism in Greece, 1974–2015', in M. E. Cavallaro and K. Kornetis (eds), *Rethinking Democratisation in Spain Greece and Portugal*, 91–121, New York: Palgrave Macmillan.
Balibar, É. (2004), *We, the People of Europe? Reflections on Transnational Citizenship*, trans. J. Swenson, Princeton, NJ: Princeton University Press.
Baltsiotis, L. (1997), 'Η πολυγλωσσία στην Ελλάδα', *Synchrona Themata*, 63: 89–95.
Baltsiotis, L. (2013), 'Ποιον ωφελεί η αναδιάταξη της θέσης των Ποντίων: Γενοκτονία, πολιτική και ιστορία', *Chronos*, 6, http://chronosmag.eu/index.php/index.php/lplss-p-fl-ex-ths-p.html.
Baltsiotis, L. (2016), 'Από την κρατική λογοκρισία στην αυτολογοκρισία: Η περίπτωση της ετερότητας στην Ελλάδα', in P. Petsini and D. Christopoulos (eds), *Η Λογοκρισία στην Ελλάδα*, 245–51, Athens: Rosa Luxemburg Foundation.
Bampilis, T. (2013), *Greek Whisky: The Localization of a Global Commodity*, Oxford: Berghahn.
Barotsi, R. (2016), 'Whose crisis? *Dogtooth* and the invisible middle class', *Journal of Greek Media & Culture*, 2 (2): 173–86.
Baudrillard, J. (1995), *The Gulf War Did Not Take Place*, trans. P. Patton, Bloomington: Indiana University Press.
Bauman, Z. (1991), *Modernity and Ambivalence*, Cambridge: Polity.
Beard, M. (2002), *The Parthenon*, London: Profile Books.
Beaton, R. (1999), *An Introduction to Modern Greek Literature*, Oxford: Clarendon Press.
Beaton, R. (2019), *Greece: Biography of a Modern Nation*, London: Allen Lane.
Beck, U., A. Giddens and S. Lash (1994), *Reflexive Modernization: Politics, Tradition and Aesthetics in the Modern Social Order*, Cambridge: Polity Press.
Beck, U., W. Bonss and C. Lau (2003), 'The theory of reflexive modernization: Problematic, hypotheses and research programme', *Theory, Culture & Society*, 20 (2): 1–33.

Bernal, J. M. (2007), 'Spelling and script debates in interwar Greece', *Byzantine and Modern Greek Studies*, 31: 170–90.
Bhabha, H. K. ed. (1990), *Nation and Narration*, London: Routledge.
Bhabha, H. K. (1994), *The Location of Culture*. London: Routledge.
Bickes, H., T. Otten and L. C. Weymann (2014), 'The financial crisis in the German and English press: Metaphorical structures in the media coverage on Greece, Spain and Italy', *Discourse and Society*, 25 (4): 424–45. doi: 10.1177/0957926514536956.
Bien, P., P. Constantine, E. Keeley and K. van Dyck, eds (2004), *A Century of Greek Poetry 1900–2000*, River Vale, NJ: Kosmos.
Billig, M. (1995), *Banal Nationalism*, London: Sage.
Bjelić, D. I., and O. Savić (2002), *Balkan as Metaphor: Between Globalization and Fragmentation*, Cambridge: MIT Press.
Bobolou, L. (2008), *Φεμινισμός εσωτερικού χώρου: Ιστορίες γυναικών – Χρονικό μιας πορείας στο φεμινιστικό κίνημα (1979–2005)*, Athens: Koukida.
Boltanski, L. (1999), *Distant Suffering: Morality Media and Politics*, trans. G. Burchell, Cambridge: Cambridge University Press.
Bordwell, D. (1997), 'Modernism, minimalism, melancholy: Angelopoulos and visual style', in A. Horton (ed.), *The Last Modernist: The Films of Theo Angelopoulos*, 11–26, Trowbridge: Flicks Books.
Bourdieu, P. (1986), *Distinction: A Social Critique of the Judgement of Taste*, trans. R. Nice, London: Routledge.
Bourdieu, P. (2003), *Language and Symbolic Power*, ed. J. B. Thompson, Cambridge: Polity.
Brown, K. S., and Y. Hamilakis, eds (2003), *The Usable Past: Greek Metahistories*, Lanham, MD: Lexington Books.
Burke, P. (2001), 'History of events and the revival of narrative', in P. Burke (ed.), *New Perspectives on Historical Writing*, 2nd edn, 283–300, Cambridge: Polity.
Butler, J. (1990), *Gender Trouble: Feminism and the Subversion of Identity*, London: Routledge.
Butler, J. (1993), *Bodies that Matter: On the Discursive Limits of Sex*, London: Routledge.
Butler, J., and A. Athanasiou (2013), *Dispossession: The Performative in the Political*, Cambridge: Polity.
Calotychos, V. (2003), *Modern Greece: A Cultural Poetics*, Oxford: Berg.
Calotychos, V. (2013), *The Balkan Prospect: Identity, Culture, and Politics in Greece after 1989*, New York: Palgrave Macmillan.
Cameron, D. (2012), *Verbal Hygiene*, London: Routledge.
Cameron, D., and D. Kulick (2003), *Language and Sexuality*, Cambridge: Cambridge University Press.
Canakis, C. (2015), 'The desire for identity and the identity of desire: Language, gender and sexuality in the Greek context', *Gender and Language*, 9 (1): 59–81.

Canakis, C., V. Kantsa and K. Yannakopoulos, eds (2010), *Language and Sexuality (through and) beyond Gender*, Newcastle upon Tyne: Cambridge Scholars.

Capelos, T., and T. Exadaktylos (2015), '"The good, the bad and the ugly": Stereotypes, prejudices and emotions on [sic] Greek media representation of the EU financial crisis', in G. Karyotis and R. Gerodimos (eds), *The Politics of Extreme Austerity: Greece in the Eurozone Crisis*, 46–68, London: Palgrave Macmillan.

Carastathis, A. (2015), 'The politics of austerity and the affective economy of hostility: Racialised gendered violence and crises of belonging in Greece', *Feminist Review*, 109 (1): 73–95.

Cavallaro, M. E., and K. Kornetis, eds (2019), *Rethinking Democratisation in Spain, Greece and Portugal*, New York: Palgrave Macmillan.

Celik, A. I. (2013), 'Family as internal border in *Dogtooth*', in R. Merivirta, K. Ahonen, H. Mulari and R. Mähkä (eds), *Frontiers of Screen History: Imagining European Borders in Cinema, 1945–2010*, 219–33, Bristol: Intellect.

Chadi, A., and M. Krapf (2017), 'The Protestant fiscal ethic: Religious confession and euro skepticism in Germany', *Economic Inquiry*, 55 (4): 1813–32.

Chakrabarty, D. (2000), *Provincializing Europe: Postcolonial Thought and Historical Difference*, Princeton, NJ: Princeton University Press.

Chalkou, M. (2012), 'A new cinema of "emancipation": Tendencies of independence in Greek cinema of the 2000s', *Interactions: Studies in Communication & Culture*, 3 (2): 243–61.

Chalkou, M. (2017), 'Μνήμη, νοσταλγία και κοσμοπολιτισμός: ταινίες πολιτισμικής και ιστορικής κληρονομιάς (heritage films) στον ελληνικό κινηματογράφο', in M. Paradeisi and A. Nikolaidou (eds), *Από τον πρώιμο στον σύγχρονο ελληνικό κινηματογράφο*, 261–81, Athens: Gutenberg.

Chambers, J. K. (2003), *Sociolinguistic Theory: Linguistic Variation and Its Social Significance*, Oxford: Blackwell.

Charalambis, D., L. Maratou-Alipranti and A. Hadjiyanni, eds (2004), *Recent Social Trends in Greece 1960–2000*, Québec: McGill-Queen's University Press.

Chartoulari, M. (2015), 'The representation of the Other in recent Greek fiction', in N. Lemos and E. Yannakakis (eds), *Critical Times, Critical Thoughts*, 63–91, Newcastle upon Tyne: Cambridge Scholars.

Checkel, J. T., and P. J. Katzenstein (2009), 'The politicization of European identities', in J. T. Checkel and P. J. Katzenstein (eds), *European Identity*, 1–28, Cambridge: Cambridge University Press.

Chilcote R. H., S. Hadjiyannis, F. Lopez, D. Nataf and El. Sammis (1990), *Transitions from Dictatorship to Democracy: Comparative Studies of Spain, Portugal and Greece*, New York: Crane Russak.

Christianopoulos, D. (1988), 'Ο δε υπομείνας εις τέλος …' (interview with Ch. Zafeiris), *Paratiritis*, 6–7: 37–48.

Christianopoulos, D. (1999), *Δοκίμια*, Paiania: Bilieto.

Christidis, A. F. (1998), 'Βαρύ έλλειμμα κοινωνικής ανοχής', *I Kathimerini*, 31 May.
Christidis, A. F. (1999), *Γλώσσα, Πολιτική, Πολιτισμός*, Athens: Polis.
Christidis A. F., ed. (2001), *Ιστορία της Ελληνικής Γλώσσας*, Thessaloniki: Kentro Ellinikis Glossas-Institouto Neoellenikon Spoudon.
Christopoulos, D., ed. (1999), *Νομικά ζητήματα θρησκευτικής ετερότητας στην Ελλάδα*, Athens: Kritiki.
Christopoulos, D. (2006), 'Greece', in R. Bauböck et al. (eds), *Acquisition and Loss of Nationality: Policies and Trends in 15 European States*, Vol. 2, 255–90, Amsterdam: Amsterdam University Press.
Christopoulos, D. (2009), 'Defining the changing boundaries of Greek nationality', in D. Tziovas (ed.), *Greek Diaspora and Migration since 1700: Society, Politics and Culture*, 111–23, Farnham: Ashgate.
Christopoulos, D. (2017), 'An unexpected reform in the maelstrom of the crisis: Greek nationality in the times of the memoranda (2010–2015)', *Citizenship Studies*, 21 (40): 483–94.
Christopoulos, D. (2019), *Ποιος είναι Έλληνας; Δύο αιώνες ιθαγένεια*, Athens: Vivliorama.
Clarke, D. E. (1814), *Travels in Various Countries of Europe Asia and Africa. Part II: Greece, Egypt and the Holy Land*, section II, London: Printed for T. Cadell and W. Davies.
Clements B., Nanou K. and S. Verney (2014), ' "We no longer love you, but we don't want to leave you": The Eurozone crisis and popular Euroscepticism in Greece', *Journal of European Integration*, 36 (3): 247–65.
Clogg, R. (1992/2002), *A Concise History of Greece*, 2nd edn, Cambridge: Cambridge University Press.
Clogg, R. (1993), *Greece 1981–89: The Populist Decade*, New York: St. Martin's Press.
Clogg, R., ed. (2002), *Minorities in Greece: Aspects of a Plural Society*, London: Hurst.
Close, D. H. (2002), *Greece since 1945: Politics, Economy and Society*, London: Longman.
Close, D. H. (2004), 'The road to reconciliation? The Greek Civil War and the politics of memory in the 1980s', in P. Carabott and Th. D. Sfikas (eds), *The Greek Civil War: Essays on a Conflict of Exceptionalism and Silences*, 257–78, Aldershot: Ashgate.
Cole, J. (2017), 'Personhood, relational ontology, and the trinitarian politics of eastern orthodox thinker Christos Yannaras', *Political Theology*, doi: 10.1080/1462317X.2017.1291127.
Collard, A. (1990), 'The experience of civil war in the mountain villages of central Greece', in M. Sarafis and M. Eve (eds), *Background to Contemporary Greece*, Vol. 2, 223–54, London: Merlin.
Collard, A. (1993), 'Διερευνώντας την «κοινωνική μνήμη» στον ελλαδικό χώρο', in E. Papataxiarchis and T. Paradellis (eds), *Ανθρωπολογία και παρελθόν: Συμβολές στην κοινωνική ιστορία της νεότερης Ελλάδας*, 357–89, Athens: Alexandreia.

Confino, A. (2011), 'History and memory', in A. Schneider and D. Wolf (eds), *The Oxford History of Historical Writing*, Vol. 5, 36–51, Oxford: Oxford University Press.

Curthoys, A., and J. Docker (2005), *Is history fiction?*, Ann Arbor: University of Michigan Press.

Dalakoglou, D. (2013), '"From the bottom of the Aegean Sea" to Golden Dawn: Security, xenophobia, and the politics of hate in Greece', *Studies in Ethnicity and Nationalism*, 13 (3): 514–22.

Damaskos, D. (2008), 'The uses of antiquity in photographs by Nelly: Imported modernism and home-grown ancestor worship in inter-war Greece', in D. Damaskos and D. Plantzos (eds), *A Singular Antiquity: Archaeology and Hellenic Identity in Twentieth-Century Greece*, 321–36, Athens: Mouseio Benaki.

Danforth, L. M. (1984), 'The ideological context of the search for continuities in Greek culture', *Journal of Modern Greek Studies*, 2 (1): 53–85.

Danforth, L. M. (1995), *The Macedonian Conflict: Ethnic Nationalism in a Transnational World*, Princeton, NJ: Princeton University Press.

Danforth, L. M. (2010), 'Ancient Macedonia, Alexander the Great and the Star or Sun of Vergina: National symbols and the conflict between Greece and the Republic of Macedonia', in J. Roisman and I. Worthington (eds), *A Companion to Ancient Macedonia*, 572–98, Oxford: Blackwell.

Danopoulos, C. P. (2014), 'The cultural roots of corruption in Greece', *Mediterranean Quarterly*, 25 (2): 105–30.

Daskalakis, I., A. Avdritou, P. Papadopoulou, P. Pappas, I. Perandzaki and D. Tsabarli (1983), *Απονομή της Ποινικής Δικαιοσύνης στην Ελλάδα*, Athens: National Centre for Social Research.

Daskalov, R. (1997), 'Ideas about, and reactions to modernization in the Balkans', *East European Quarterly*, 31 (2): 141–80.

Davies, N. (1997), *Europe: A History*, London: Pimlico.

Delanty, G. (1995), *Inventing Europe: Idea, Identity, Reality*, London: Macmillan.

Della Porta, D., and M. Diani (2006), *Social Movements: An Introduction*, Oxford: Blackwell.

Demacopoulos, G. E., and A. Papanikolaou (2013), 'Orthodox naming of the Other: A postcolonial approach', in G. E. Demacopoulos and A. Papanikolaou (eds), *Orthodox Constructions of the West*, 1–22, New York: Fordham University Press.

Demertzis, N. (1997), 'Greece', in R. Eatwell (ed.), *European Political Cultures: Conflict or Convergence?*, 107–21, London: Routledge.

Demertzis, N. (2011), 'The drama of the Greek Civil War trauma', in R. Eyerman, J. C. Alexander and E. B. Breese (eds), *Narrating Trauma*, 133–61, Boulder, CO: Paradigm.

Demertzis, N., S. Papathanassopoulos and A. Armenakis (1999), 'Media and nationalism: The Macedonian Question', *Harvard International Journal of Press/Politics*, 4: 26–50.

Dermentzopoulos, Ch. A. (2015), *Η επινόηση του τόπου: Νοσταλγία και μνήμη στην Πολίτικη Κουζίνα*, Patra: Opportuna.
Derrida, J. (1981), *Positions*, trans. A. Bass, Chicago: University of Chicago Press.
Derrida, J. (1994), *Specters of Marx*, trans. P. Kamuf, London: Routledge.
Dertilis, G. B. (2016), *Επτά πόλεμοι, τέσσερις εμφύλιοι, Επτά πτωχεύσεις 1821-2016*, Athens: Polis.
Diamandouros, N. P. (1993), 'Politics and culture in Greece, 1974-91', in R. Clogg (ed.), *Greece, 1981-89: The Populist Decade*, 1-25, New York: St. Martin's Press.
Diamandouros, N. P. (1994), 'Cultural dualism and political change in postauthoritarian Greece', Estudios = Working papers/Instituto Juan March de Estudios e Investigaciones, Centro de Estudios Avanzados en Ciencias Sociales 50, Madrid: Instituto Juan March de Estudios e Investigaciones.
Diamandouros, N. P. (2000), *Πολιτισμικός δυισμός και πολιτική αλλαγή στην Ελλάδα της Μεταπολίτευσης*, Athens: Alexandreia.
Diamandouros, N. P. (2013), 'Postscript: Cultural dualism revisited', in A. Triandafyllidou, R. Gropas and H. Kouki (eds), *The Greek Crisis and European Modernity*, 208-32, Basingstoke: Palgrave Macmillan.
Diani, M. (1992), 'The concept of social movement', *Sociological Review*, 40 (1); 1-25.
Dimaras, A. (1973 and 1974), *Η μεταρρύθμιση που δεν έγινε (Τεκμήρια ιστορίας)*, vol. 1 and 2, Athens: Ermis.
Dimitroulia, T. (2012), 'Νέοι ποιητές στα τέλη του 20ου και στις αρχές του 21ου αιώνα', in A. Kastrinaki, A. Politis and D. Tziovas (eds), *Για μια ιστορία της ελληνικής λογοτεχνίας του εικοστού αιώνα*, 402-18, Herakleio: Panepistimiakes Ekdoseis Kritis and Mouseio Benaki.
Dimitroulia, T., E. Kotzia, L. Pantaleon, Y. Perantonakis and V. Hatzivasileiou (2009), 'Μεταπολιτευτική Πεζογραφία: Μια προσπάθεια χαρτογράφησης τάσεων και δυναμικών' (discussion), *K*, 18: 44-71.
Dimou, N. (2011), 'Η Ευρώπη "μας"', *Lifo*, 28 November, http://www.lifo.gr/mag/columns/4427.
Dimou, N. (2013), *On the Unhappiness of Being Greek*, Winchester: Zero Books.
Dimou, N. (2014), 'Ανήκομεν εις την Δύσιν;', *I Kathimerini*, 9 March.
Douzinas, C. (2013), *Philosophy and Resistance in the Crisis*, Cambridge: Polity.
Doxiadis, A., and M. Matsaganis (2012), *National Populism and Xenophobia in Greece*, London: Counterpoint, https://counterpoint.uk.com/wp-content/uploads/2017/04/507_CP_RRadical_Greece_web-1.pdf.
Dragona, Th. (2014), 'The vicissitudes of identity in a divided society: The case of the Muslim minority in Western Thrace', in K. Featherstone (ed.), *Europe in Modern Greek History*, 135-52, London: Hurst.
Dubisch, J., ed. (1986), *Gender and Power in Rural Greece*, Princeton, NJ: Princeton University Press.

Durrell, L. (1949), 'Hellene and Philhellene', *Times Literary Supplement*, 13 May. The article was translated and published in the *Anglo-Greek Review* ('Έλληνες και Φιλέλληνες', 4/5, July–August 1949: 188–91).

Eagleton, T. (2000), *The Idea of Culture*, Oxford: Blackwell.

Echtler, I. (2013), 'Η ελληνική δημοσιονομική κρίση στο γερμανικό τύπο', in Y. Pleios (ed.), *Η κρίση και τα ΜΜΕ*, 181–226, Athens: Papazisis.

Economides, S. (2005), 'The Europeanisation of Greek foreign policy', *West European Politics*, 28 (2): 471–91.

Economides, S. (2014), 'The relevance of "Europe" to Greek foreign policy', in K. Featherstone (ed.), *Europe in Modern Greek History*, 61–76, London: Hurst.

Economides, S., ed. (2017), *Greece: Modernisation and Europe 20 Years On*, London: Hellenic Observatory, LSE.

Economides, S., and V. Monastiriotis, eds (2009), *The Return of Street Politics? Essays on the December Riots in Greece*, London: Hellenic Observatory, LSE.

Eisenstadt, S. N. (2000), 'Multiple modernities', *Daedalus*, 129 (1): 1–29.

Eisenstadt, S. N. (2003), *Comparative Civilizations and Multiple Modernities*, London: Brill.

Eleftheriadis, K. (2015), 'Queer responses to austerity: Insights from Greece of crisis', *ACME: An International E-Journal for Critical Geographies*, 14 (4): 1032–57.

Eleftheriotis, D. (2012), 'A touch of spice: Mobility and popularity', in L. Papadimitriou and Y. Tzioumakis (eds), *Greek Cinema: Texts, Histories, Identities*, 17–36, Bristol: Intellect.

Eleftheriotis, D. (2020), 'Introspective cosmopolitanism: The family in the Greek Weird Wave', *Journal of Greek Media & Culture*, 6 (1): 3–27.

Ellis, J. (1992), *Visible Fictions: Cinema, Television, Video*, London: Routledge.

Elsaesser, T. (2005), *European Cinema: Face to Face with Hollywood*, Amsterdam: Amsterdam University Press.

Elytis, O. (1999), 'Things public and private', in *Carte Blanche: Selected Writings*, trans. D. Connolly, 65–73, Amsterdam: Harwood Academic.

Embirikos, L., et al., eds (2001), *Γλωσσική ετερότητα στην Ελλάδα*, Athens: Alexandreia.

Epistimoniko Symposio (1997), *Ιστορική Πραγματικότητα και Νεοελληνική Πεζογραφία (1945–1995)*, Athens: Etaireia Spoudon Neoellenikou Politismou kai Genikis Paideias.

Epistimoniko Symposio (2003), *Το παρόν του παρελθόντος: Ιστορία, Λαογραφία, Κοινωνική Ανθρωπολογία*, Athens: Etaireia Spoudon Neoellenikou Politimsou kai Genikis Paideias.

Eudes, D. (1970), *Les Kapetanios: La Guerre Civile Grecque, 1943–1949*, Paris: Fayard.

Exertzoglou, H. (2002), 'Ιστορία και ιστοριογραφία: ένα σχόλιο', *I Avgi*, 1 December.

Fainaru, D. (2001), *Theo Angelopoulos: Interviews*, Jackson: University Press of Mississippi.

Fais, M., ed. (1999), *Ξένος, ο άλλος μου εαυτός*, Athens: Patakis.

Faubion, J. D. (1993), *Modern Greek Lessons: A Primer in Historical Constructivism*, Princeton, NJ: Princeton University Press.

Featherstone, K. (1998), '"Europeanisation" and the centre periphery: The case of Greece in the 1990s', *South European Politics and Society*, 3 (1): 23–39.

Featherstone, K. (2014), 'Introduction', in K. Featherstone (ed.), *Europe in Modern Greek History*, 1–16, London: Hurst.

Featherstone, K., and D. Papadimitriou (2008), *The Limits of Europeanization: Reform Capacity and Policy Conflict in Greece*. Basingstoke: Palgrave Macmillan.

Featherstone, K., and S. Verney (1990), 'Greece', in J. Lodge (ed.), *The 1989 Election of the European Parliament*, 90–106, London: Macmillan.

Ferguson, C. A. (1959), 'Diglossia', *Word*, 15: 325–40.

Filippou, F. (2015), 'Crime fiction during the crisis', in N. Lemos and E. Yannakakis (eds), *Critical Times, Critical Thoughts: Contemporary Greek Writers Discuss Facts and Fiction*, 144–59, Newcastle upon Tyne: Cambridge Scholars.

Finlay, G. (1836), *The Hellenic Kingdom and the Greek Nation*, London: J. Murray.

Fisher, M. (2011), 'The family syndrome', *Film Quarterly*, 64 (4): 22–7.

Fleischer, H. (2014), 'Οι Έλληνες απέναντι στους «'Άλλους». Εθνικά στερεότυπα και λεξικογραφικές ερμηνείες ταυτότητας', in *Τα Βαλκάνια: Εκσυγχρονισμός, Ταυτότητες, Ιδέες*, Herakleio: Herakleio: Panepistimiakes Ekdoseis Kritis and ISM-ITE, 371–98.

Fleischer, H., and N. Svoronos, eds (1989), *Η Ελλάδα 1936–1944: Δικτατορία-Κατοχή-Αντίσταση*, Athens: Morfotiko Instituto ATE.

Fleming, K. E. (2000), 'Orientalism, the Balkans, and Balkan historiography', *American Historical Review*, 105 (4): 1218–33.

Fleming, K. E. (2008), *Greece: A Jewish History*, Princeton, NJ: Princeton University Press.

Flitouris, L. (2008), 'Ο εμφύλιος στο «σέλιλοϊντ»: Ιστορία και μνήμη', in R. Van Boeschoten, T. Vervenioti, E. Voutira, V. Dalkavoukis and K. Bada (eds), *Μνήμες και λήθη του ελληνικού εμφυλίου πολέμου*, 387–404, Thessaloniki: Epikentro.

Fokas, E. (2000), 'Greek Orthodoxy and European identity', in A. Mitsos and E. Mossialos (eds), *Contemporary Greece and Europe*, 275–300, Aldershot: Ashgate.

Fokas, E. (2008), 'A new role for the church? Reassessing the place of religion in the Greek public sphere', Hellenic Observatory Papers on Greece and Southeast Europe, GreeSE Paper no. 17.

Fokas, E. (2013), 'Religion in the Greek public sphere: Debating Europe's influence', in G. E. Demacopoulos and A. Papanikolaou (eds), *Orthodox Constructions of the West*, 181–92, New York: Fordham University Press.

Foucault, M. (1976/8), *The History of Sexuality*, 3 Vols, trans R. Hurley, Vol. I: *The Will to Knowledge*, London: Penguin.

Fournaraki, E., and Y. Yannitsiotis (2013), 'Three decades of women's and gender history in Greece: An account', *Aspasia: The International Yearbook of Central, Eastern and South Eastern European Women's and Gender History*, 7: 162–73.

Frangoudaki, A. (1977), Εκπαιδευτική μεταρρύθμιση και φιλελεύθεροι διανοούμενοι: Άγονοι αγώνες και ιδεολογικα αδιέξοδα στο μεσοπόλεμο, Athens: Kedros.

Frangoudaki, A. (1978), Ο εκπαιδευτικός δημοτικισμός και ο γλωσσικός συμβιβασμός του 1911, Ioannina: University of Ioannina.

Frangoudaki, A. (1992), 'Diglossia and the present language situation in Greece: A sociological approach to the interpretation of diglossia and some hypotheses on today's linguistic reality', Language in Society, 21 (3): 365–81.

Frangoudaki, A. (1997), 'The metalinguistic prophecy on the decline of the Greek language: Its social function as the expression of a crisis in Greek national identity', International Journal of the Sociology of Language, 126: 63–82.

Frangoudaki, A. (2001), 'Γλωσσική πολιτική στην Ευρωπαϊκή Ένωση', Ta Nea, 20 November.

Frangoudaki, A., and C. Keyder, eds (2007), Ways to Modernity in Greece and Turkey: Encounters with Europe, 1850–1950, London: I.B. Tauris.

Frantzi, A., K. Angelaki-Rooke, R. Galanaki, A. Papadaki and P. Pampoudi (1990), Υπάρχει, λοιπόν, γυναικεία ποίηση;, Athens: Etaireia Spoudon Neoellenikou Politismou kai Genikis Paideias.

Fukuyama, F. (2012), 'The two Europes', American Interest, 8 May. http://www.the-american-interest.com/2012/05/08/the-two-europes/.

Fytili, M. (2013), 'Η «ιδεολογική ηγεμονία της Αριστεράς» στην εποχή της κρίσης', http://www.alterthess.gr/content/i-ideologiki-igemonia-tis-aristeras-stin-epohi-tis-krisistis-magdas-fytili.

Gadamer, H. G. (1989), Truth and Method, London: Sheed & Ward.

Gallaher, B. (2009), 'Christos Yannaras, Orthodoxy and the West: Hellenic Self-Identity in the Modern Age' (Review), Logos: A Journal of Eastern Christian Studies, 50 (3–4): 537–42.

Gallant, T. W. (2001/16), Modern Greece: From the War of Independence to the Present, London: Bloomsbury.

Garantoudis, E. (1991), 'Για το σύγχρονο ελληνικό ελεύθερο στίχο', Poiisi, 1: 105–40.

Garantoudis, E. (2008), Η Ελληνική Ποίηση του 20ου αιώνα, Athens: Metaihmio.

Garantoudis, E. (2014), 'Το επικοινωνιακό φαινόμενο Κική Δημουλά', Athens Review of Books, 52: 50–4.

Garantoudis, E. (2018), 'Η ελληνική ποίηση στον καιρό του Varoufakis με τον τρόπο της Van Dyck', Athens Review of Books, 94: 20–2.

Gazi, E. (2003), 'Περί μεταμοντερνισμού και ιστοριογραφίας', O Politis, 107: 18–21.

Georgakopoulou, A., and K. Giaxoglou (2018), 'Emplotment in the social mediatization of the economy: The poly-storying of economist Yanis Varoufakis', Language & Internet, 16, article 6 (urn:nbn:de:0009-7-47918).

Germanacos, N. C. (1973), 'An interview with three Greek prose writers (May, 1972): Stratis Tsirkas, Thanassis Valtinos, George Ioannou', Boundary 2, 1 (2): 266–313.

Gerstenblith, P. (2001), 'The public interest in the restitution of cultural objects', *Connecticut Journal of International Law*, 16 (2): 197–245.

Giannaris, Y. (1993), *Φοιτητικά Κινήματα και Ελληνική Παιδεία*, vols 1 and 2, Athens: Pontiki.

Giannopoulou, E., and Th. Tramboulis (2012–13), 'Οι συγγραφείς ως οργανικοί διανοούμενοι: από την ηθογραφία στην ηθικολογία', *Unfollow*, 12, 13, 14, 16, (December–April).

Goldsworthy, V. (1998), *Inventing Ruritania: The Imperialism of the Imagination*, New Haven, CT: Yale University Press.

González-Vaquerizo, H. (2017), '"Visit Greece and live your myth": The use of classical antiquity by the Greek National Tourism Organization', in F. Carlà-Uhnik, M. Carcía Morcillo and C. Walde (eds), Advertising Antiquity, *Thersites* 6: 241–303.

Gorner, P. (2000), *Twentieth-Century German Philosophy*, Oxford: Oxford University Press.

Gourgouris, S. (1996), *Dream Nation: Enlightenment, Colonization and the Institution of Modern Greece*, Stanford: Stanford University Press.

Goutsos, D. (2009), 'Competing ideologies and post-diglossia Greek: Analysing the discourse of contemporary "Myth-Breakers"', in A. Georgakopoulou and M. Silk (eds), *Standard Languages and Language Standards: Greek, Past and Present*, 321–37, Farnham: Ashgate.

Goutsos, D., and O. Hatzidaki, eds (2017a), *Greece in Crisis: Combining Critical Discourse and Corpus Linguistics Perspectives*, Amsterdam: John Benjamins.

Goutsos, D., and O. Hatzidaki (2017b), 'Discourses and counter-discourses of the Greek crisis: A critical linguistic perspective', in D. Tziovas (ed.), *Greece in Crisis: The Cultural Politics of Austerity*, 282–99, London: I.B. Tauris.

Grigoriadis, I. N. (2011), 'Redefining the nation: Shifting boundaries of the "Other" in Greece and Turkey', *Middle Eastern Studies*, 47 (1), 167–82.

Grigoriadis, I. N. (2012), *Instilling Religion in Greek and Turkish Nationalism: A 'Sacred Synthesis'*, Basingstoke: Palgrave Macmillan.

Gropas, R., and A. Triandafyllidou (2005), 'Migration in Greece at a glance', ELIAMEP, https://www.eliamep.gr/wp-content/uploads/en/2008/10/migration.pdf.

Guha, R., and G. C. Spivak (1988), *Selected Subaltern Studies*, Oxford: Oxford University Press.

Habermas, J. (2006), 'Religion in the public sphere', *European Journal of Philosophy*, 14 (1): 1–25.

Hadjikyriacou, A. (2013), *Masculinity and Gender in Greek Cinema, 1949–1967*, New York: Bloomsbury.

Halkias, A. (2004), *The Empty Cradle of Democracy: Sex, Abortion and Nationalism in Modern Greece*, Durham, NC: Duke University Press.

Hall, S. (1996), 'Introduction: Who needs "Identities"?' in S. Hall and P. Du Gay (eds), *Questions of Cultural Identity*, 1–17, London: SAGE.

Hallin, D. C., and P. Mancini (2004), *Comparing Media Systems: Three Models of Media and Politics*, Cambridge: Cambridge University Press.

Halperin, D. (1995), *Saint Foucault: Towards a Gay Hagiography*, New York: Oxford University Press.

Halperin, D. (2003), 'The normalization of queer theory', *Journal of Homosexuality*, 45 (2–3): 339–43.

Hamilakis, Y. (2007), *The Nation and Its Ruins: Antiquity, Archaeology, and National Imagination in Greece*, Oxford: Oxford University Press.

Hamilakis, Y. (2008), 'Decolonizing Greek archaeology: Indigenous archaeologies, modernist archaeology and the postcolonial critique', in D. Damaskos and D. Plantzos (eds), *A Singular Antiquity: Archaeology and Hellenic Identity in Twentieth-Century Greece*, 273–84, Athens: Mouseio Benaki.

Handler, R. (1991), 'Who owns the past? History, cultural property, and the logic of possessive individualism', in B. Williams (ed), *The Politics of Culture*, 63–74, Washington: Smithsonian Institution.

Hanink, J. (2017), *The Classical Debt: Greek Antiquity in an Era of Austerity*, Cambridge, MA: Belknap Press of Harvard University Press.

Harcourt, A. (2002), 'Engineering Europeanization: The role of the European institutions in shaping national media regulations', *Journal of European Public Policy*, 9 (5): 736–55.

Haris, Y. H. (2001a), 'Welcome to Hellas!', *Τα Νέα*, 13 April reprinted in his 2003 book *Η Γλώσσα, τα Λάθη και τα Πάθη*, 283–87, Athens: Polis.

Haris, Y. H., ed. (2001b), *Δέκα Μύθοι για την Ελληνική Γλώσσα*, Athens: Patakis.

Harmbis, A. (2016), 'Η τιμή του ελληνικού σινεμά', *I Kathimerini*, 6 March.

Harvey, D. (2010), *The Enigma of Capital and the Crises of Capitalism*, London: Profile Books.

Hatsios, Y. (1998), 'Απαγόρευση του … «Βούλγαρου». Και με φυλακή απειλεί η δικαστική απόφαση τον Γ. Μπαμπινιώτη για την ερμηνεία στο λεξικό του', *Ta Nea*, 14 July.

Hatzis, D. (2005), *Το Πρόσωπο του Νέου Ελληνισμού: Διαλέξεις και Δοκίμια*, Athens: Rodakio.

Hatzivasileiou, V. (2010), 'Ο Εμφύλιος στοιχειώνει το μυθιστόρημα', *Eleftherotypia*, 30 October, http://www.enet.gr/?i=news.el.article&id=218349.

Hatzivasileiou, V. (2018), *Η Κίνηση του Εκκρεμούς: Άτομο και Κοινωνία στη νεότερη ελληνική πεζογραφία: 1974–2017*, Athens: Polis.

Heilbronner, O. (2008), 'From a culture *for* youth to a culture *of* youth: Recent trends in the historiography of western youth culture', *Contemporary European History*, 17 (4): 575–91.

Heraclides, A. (2012), '"What will become of us without barbarians?": The enduring Greek-Turkish rivalry as an identity-based conflict', *Southeast European and Black Sea Studies*, 12 (1): 115–34.

Herzfeld, M. (1982/6), *Ours Once More: Folklore, Ideology, and the Making of Modern Greece*, New York: Pella.

Herzfeld, M. (1987), *Anthropology through the Looking-Glass: Critical Ethnography in the Margins of Europe*, Cambridge: Cambridge University Press.

Herzfeld, M. (2002), 'The absent presence: Discourses of crypto-colonialism', *South Atlantic Quarterly*, 101 (4): 899–926.

Herzfeld, M. (2008), 'Archaeological etymologies: Monumentality and domesticity in twentieth-century Greece', in D. Damaskos and D. Plantzos (eds), *A Singular Antiquity: Archaeology and Hellenic Identity in Twentieth-Century Greece*, 43–54, Athens: Benaki Museum.

Herzog, D. (2011), *Sexuality in Europe: A Twentieth-Century History*, Cambridge: Cambridge University Press.

Hirsch, M. (2012), *The Generation of Postmemory: Writing and Visual Culture after the Holocaust*, New York: Columbia University Press.

Hirschon, R. (1999), 'Identity and the Greek state: Some conceptual issues and paradoxes', in R. Clogg (ed.), *The Greek Diaspora in the Twentieth Century*, 158–80, London: Macmillan.

Hirschon, R. (2014), 'Cultural mismatches: Greek concepts of time, personal identity and authority in the context of Europe', in K. Featherstone (ed.), *Europe in Modern Greek History*, 153–69, London: Hurst.

Hjort, M., and S. MacKenzie (2000), *Cinema and Nation*, London: Routledge.

Hobsbawm, E. (1995), *The Age of Extremes: The Short Twentieth Century 1914–1991*, London: Abacus.

Hodgkin, K., and S. Radstone, eds (2003), *Contested Pasts: The Politics of Memory*, London: Routledge.

Hokwerda, H., ed. (2003), *Constructions of the Greek Past: Identity and Historical Consciousness from Antiquity to the Present*, Groningen: Egbert Forsten.

Holton, D. (2002), 'Modern Greek: Towards a standard language or a new diglossia?', in M. C. Jones and E. Esch (eds), *Language Change: The Interplay of Internal, External and Extra-Linguistic Factors*, 169–79, New York: Mouton de Gruyter.

Homer, S. (2019), 'History as trauma and the possibility of the future: Theo Angelopoulos' *Voyage to Cythera*', *Journal of Greek Media & Culture*, 5 (1): 3–19.

Hooghe, L. (2007), 'What drives Euroscepticism?', *European Union Politics*, 8 (1): 5–12.

Horrocks, G. (1997), *Greek: A History of the Language and its Speakers*, London: Longman.

Horton, A. (1997a), *Theo Angelopoulos: A Cinema of Contemplation*, Princeton, NJ: Princeton University Press.

Horton, A. (1997b), *The Last Modernist: The Films of Theo Angelopoulos*, Trowbridge: Flicks Books.

Howard, M. M. (2012), *The Politics of Citizenship*, Cambridge: Cambridge University Press.

Huntington, S. P. (1993), 'The clash of civilizations?', *Foreign Affairs*, 72 (3): 22–49.

Huntington, S. P. (2002), *The Clash of Civilizations*, London: Simon & Schuster.
Hutcheon, L. (1988), *A Poetics of Postmodernism: History, Theory, Fiction*, London: Routledge.
Hutcheon, L. (2003), *The Politics of Postmodernism*, London: Routledge.
Iatrides, J., ed. (1981), *Greece in the 1940s: A Nation in Crisis*, Hanover: University Press of New England.
Ioakimidis, P. C. (2000), 'The Europeanisation of Greece's foreign policy: Progress and problems', in A. Mitsos and E. Mossialos (eds), *Contemporary Greece and Europe*, 350–72, Aldershot: Ashgate.
Ioakimidis, P. C. (2001), 'The Europeanization of Greece: An overall assessment', in K. Featherstone and G. Kazamias (eds), *Europeanization and the Southern Periphery*, 73–94, London: Frank Cass.
Ioakimidis, P. C. (2011), 'Κρίση και Ελληνικός Εξαιρετισμός', *Athens Review of Books*, 15: 21–2.
Iordanidou, A. (2000), 'Σύγκριση και αξιολόγηση των τεσσάρων λεξικών', *I Kathimerini*, 5 November.
Iordanidou, A., and J. Androutsopoulos (2001), 'Youth slang in modern Greek', in A. Georgakopoulou and M. Spanaki (eds), *A Reader in Greek Sociolinguistics: Studies in Modern Greek Language, Culture and Communication*, 285–302, Oxford: Peter Lang.
Iordanova, D. (2006), *Cinema of the Balkans*, London: Wallflower.
Jameson, F. (1984), 'Periodizing the 60s', *Social Text*, 9/10: 178–209.
Jameson, F. (1998), *The Cultural Turn: Selected Writings on the Postmodern, 1983–1998*, London: Verso.
Jameson, F. (2015), 'Angelopoulos and collective narrative', in F. Jameson, *Ancients and the Postmoderns*, 131–48, London: Verso.
Jeffreys, M. (1995), 'Macedonia is Australian', *Modern Greek Studies (Australia and New Zealand)*, 3: 83–96.
Jeffreys, M. (1997), 'The Australian dimension of the Macedonian Question', *Kambos: Cambridge Papers in Modern Greek*, 5: 47–62.
Jenkins, T. (2016), *Keeping their Marbles*, Oxford: Oxford University Press.
Johnston, H., and S. Seferiades (2012), 'The Greek December, 2008', in H. Johnston and S. Seferiades (eds), *Violent Protest, Contentious Politics, and the Neoliberal State*, 147–92, Farnham: Ashgate.
Jordheim, H., and E. Wigen (2018), 'Conceptual synchronisation: From progress to crisis', *Millennium: Journal of International Studies*, 46 (3): 421–39.
Judt, T. (2010), *Postwar: A History of Europe since 1945*, London: Vintage.
Juko, S. (2010), 'Have the media made the Greek crisis worse? An inquiry into the credit crisis of the state', *Economic Sociology*, 12 (1): 28–41.
Jusdanis, G. (1987), 'Is postmodernism possible outside the "West"? The case of Greece', *Byzantine and Modern Greek Studies*, 11: 69–92.
Jusdanis, G. (1991), *Belated Modernity and Aesthetic Culture: Inventing National Literature*, Minneapolis: University of Minnesota Press.

Kalaitzidis, P. (2003), 'Ορθοδοξία και Νεοελληνική Ταυτότητα', *Indiktos*, 17: 44–94.
Kalaitzidis, P. (2004), 'Ορθοδοξία και Πολυπολιτισμικότητα', *Synaxi*, 91: 93–7.
Kalaitzidis, P. (2009), 'Η ανακάλυψη της ελληνικότητας και ο θεολογικός αντιδυτικισμός', in P. Kaliatzidis, Th. N. Papathanasiou and Th. Ambatzidis (eds), *Αναταράξεις στη Μεταπολεμική Θεολογία – Η «Θεολογία του '60»*, 429–514, Athens: Indiktos.
Kalaitzidis, P. (2010), 'Orthodoxy and Hellenism in contemporary Greece', *St Vladimir Theological Quarterly*, 54 (3–4): 365–420.
Kalaitzidis, P. (2013), 'The image of the West in contemporary Greek theology', in G. E. Demacopoulos and A. Papanikolaou (eds), *Orthodox Constructions of the West*, 142–60, New York: Fordham University Press.
Kallinis, Y. (2001), *Ο μοντερνισμός ενός κοσμοπολίτη: Στοιχεία και τεχνικές του μοντερνισμού στο μεσοπολεμικό μυθιστόρημα του Κοσμά Πολίτη*, Thessaloniki: University Studio Press.
Kallivretakis, L. (2017), *Δικτατορία και Μεταπολίτευση*, Athens: Themelio.
Kalpadakis, G., and D. A. Sotiropoulos (2007). 'Europeanism and nationalist populism: The Europeanization of Greek civil society and foreign policy', *Études Helléniques/Hellenic Studies*, 15 (1): 43–66.
Kalyvas, A. (2010), 'An anomaly? Some reflections on the Greek December 2008', *Constellations*, 17 (2): 351–65.
Kalyvas, S. N. (2000), 'Red terror: Leftist violence during the Occupation', in M. Mazower (ed.), *After the War Was Over: Reconstructing the Family, Nation and State in Greece, 1943–1960*, 142–83, Princeton, NJ: Princeton University Press.
Kalyvas, S. N. (2003), 'Εμφύλιος πόλεμος (1943–1949): το τέλος των μύθων και η στροφή προς το μαζικό επίπεδο', *Epistimi kai Koinonia*, 11: 37–70.
Kalyvas, S. N (2008), 'Why Athens is burning', *International Herald Tribune*, 11 December.
Kalyvas, S. N (2015), *Modern Greece: What Everyone Needs to Know?*, Oxford: Oxford University Press.
Kalyvas, S. N. (2016), *Πού είμαστε και πού πάμε; Διατρέχοντας την κρίση (2009–2016) και ατενίζοντας το μέλλον*, Athens: Metaihmio.
Kalyvas, S., and N. Marantzidis (2004), 'Νέες τάσεις στη μελέτη του Εμφυλίου Πολέμου', *Ta Nea-Vivliodromio*, 20–1 March.
Kalyvas, S., and N. Marantzidis (2015), *Εμφύλια πάθη: 23 ερωτήσεις και απαντήσεις για τον Εμφύλιο*, Athens: Metaihmio.
Kalyvas, S., G. Pagoulatos and H. Tsoukas, eds (2012), *From Stagnation to Forced Adjustment: Reforms in Greece, 1974–2010*, London: Hurst.
Kambris, A. (2000), 'Η μονοτονία του μονοτονικού συστήματος', *To Vima*, 19 March.
Kanarakis, G. (2012), 'The Greek diaspora in a globalised world', *Modern Greek Studies (Australia and New Zealand)*, 293–302, special issue: Thinking Diversely: Hellenism and the Challenge of Globalisation, https://openjournals.library.sydney.edu.au/index.php/MGST/article/view/11455.

Kantsa, V. (2014), 'The price of marriage: Same-sex sexualities and citizenship in Greece', *Sexualities*, 17 (7): 818–36.

Kantsa, V. (2018), 'Αντηχήσεις από τρία Ελληνικά λεσβιακά περιοδικά: *Η Λάβρυς, Μαντάμ Γκου, Η Νταλίκα*', in D. Vaiou and A. Psara (eds), *Εννοιολογήσεις και πρακτικές του φεμινισμού: Μεταπολίτευση και «μετά»*, 63–72, Athens: Idryma tis Voulis ton Ellinon.

Kaplan, R. D. (1993), *Balkan Ghosts: A Journey through History*, New York: St. Martin's Press.

Kaplan, R. D. (2012), *The Revenge of Geography: What the Map Tells Us about Coming Conflicts and the Battle Against Fate*, New York: Random House.

Kaplani, G. (2009), *A Short Border Handbook*, London: Portobello (original Greek: *Μικρό ημερολόγιο συνόρων*, Livanis 2006, second edition Epikentro 2018).

Karabelias, Y. (1996), 'Ποια Ευρώπη;', *Ardin*, 2, May, https://ardin-rixi.gr/archives/194599.

Karalis, V. (2012a), 'In search of neo-Hellenic culture: Confronting the ambiguities of modernity in an ancient land', *Interactions: Studies in Communication & Culture*, 3 (2): 129–45.

Karalis, V. (2012b), *A History of the Greek Cinema*, New York: Continuum.

Karamanolakis, V. (2019), *Ανεπιθύμητο παρελθόν: Οι φάκελοι κοινωνικών φρονημάτων στον 20ο αι. και η καταστροφή τους*, Athens: Themelio.

Karamanolakis, V., E. Olympitou and I. Papathanasiou, eds (2010), *Η Ελληνική Νεολαία στον 20ο αιώνα: Πολιτικές διαδρομές, κοινωνικές πρακτικές και πολιτιστικές εκφράσεις*, Athens: Themelio.

Karamanou, A. (2003), 'The changing role of women in Greece', in Th. A. Couloumbis, Th. Kariotis and F. Bellou (eds), *Greece in the Twentieth Century*, 274–93, London: Frank Cass.

Karamouzi, E. (2014), *Greece, the EEC and the Cold War, 1974–1979*, New York: Palgrave Macmillan.

Karantzola, E. (1998), 'Λεξικογραφικά ιδεολογήματα', *Anti*, 662: 26–8.

Karavidas, K. (2015), 'Αναζητήσεις της λαϊκότητας: ιδεολογικές διασταυρώσεις και απομακρύνσεις στο *Αντί* και τον *Πολίτη*', in M. Avgeridis, E. Gazi and K. Kornetis (eds), *Μεταπολίτευση: Η Ελλάδα στο μεταίχμιο δύο αιώνων*, 302–16, Athens: Themelio.

Kargiotis, D. (2017), 'Κρίση αναπαράστασης, κρίση εκπροσώπησης', *Athens Review of Books*, 83: 58–62 (reprinted in his book *Γεωγραφίες της μετάφρασης: Χώροι, κανόνες, ιδεολογίες*, 77–96, Athens: Kapa Ekdotiki 2017).

Kassaveti, U. H. (2016), 'Audio-visual consumption in the Greek VHS era: Social mobility, privatization and the VCR audiences in the 1980s', in K. Kornetis, E. Kotsovili and N. Papadogiannis (eds), *Consumption and Gender in Southern Europe since the Long 1960s*, 241–56, London: Bloomsbury.

Kassimeris, G. (2001), *Europe's Last Red Terrorists: The Revolutionary Organisation, 17 November*, London: Hurst.

Kassimeris, G. (2013), 'Greece: The persistence of political terrorism', *International Affairs*, 89 (1):131–42.

Kassis, K. D. (1983), *Το ελληνικό λαϊκό μυθιστόρημα (1840–1940): Μυθιστορήματα και μελέτες σε λαϊκά φυλλάδια*, Athens.

Kassos, V. (1989), 'Ιδιωτικό όραμα και ποιητική συμφωνία στη γενιά του 1980', in *Ασφυξία του βλέμματος: σύγχρονη ελληνική ποίηση και ιδεολογία*, 76–83, Athens: Nea Synora.

Kastrinaki, A. (2005), *Η λογοτεχνία στην ταραγμένη δεκαετία 1940–1950*, Athens: Polis.

Kastrinaki, A. (2014), *Και βέβαια αλλάζει!*, Athens: Kichli.

Katsan, G. (2019), 'The anxieties of history: Greek fiction in crisis', in T. Stauning Willert and G. Katsan (eds), *Retelling the Past in Contemporary Greek Literature, Film, and Popular Culture*, 117–32, Lanham, MD: Lexington.

Katsapis, K. (2013), *Το πρόβλημα 'νεολαία', μοντέρνοι νέοι, παράδοση και αμφισβήτηση στη μεταπολεμική Ελλάδα 1964–1974*, Athens: Aprovleptes Ekdoseis.

Katsikis, I., and D. Spyropoulos (1999), *Το αλφαβητάρι της γλώσσας των νέων*, Athens: Diavlos.

Katsoulis, I (2017), 'Η Νεοελληνική κοινωνία: «μεταξύ» εκσυγχρονισμού και παράδοσης', *Books' Journal*, 73: 14–23.

Kazazis, I. N. (1998), 'Λεξικογραφικό ατόπημα', *I Kathimerini*, 31 May.

Kechriotis, V. (2013), 'History as a public claim and the role of the historian: Two recent debates regarding the Ottoman past in Greece and Bulgaria', in E. Ginio and K. Kaser (eds), *Ottoman Legacies in the Contemporary Mediterranean: The Balkans and the Middle East*, 287–309, Jerusalem: European Forum at the Hebrew University.

Kefalas, I. (1987), *Η γενιά του ιδιωτικού οράματος: νέες εμφανίσεις στην ποίηση*, Athens: Tethrippon.

Kessareas, E. (2015), 'Orthodox theological currents in modern Greece after 1974: Ongoing tensions between reform and conservatism', *Journal of Modern Greek Studies*, 33 (2): 237–68.

Kessareas, E. (2018), 'The Greek debt crisis as theodicy: Religious fundamentalism and socio-political conservatism', *Sociological Review*, 66 (1): 122–37.

Kitis, E. D. (2015), 'The anti-authoritarian *Chóros*: A space for youth socialization and radicalization in Greece (1974–2010)', *Journal for the Study of Radicalism*, 9 (1): 1–36.

Kitromilides, P. M. (1989), '"Imagined communities" and the origins of the national question in the Balkans', *European History Quarterly*, 19: 149–94.

Kitromilides, P. M. (1994), Review of Jean-Baptiste Duroselle, *Europe: A History of Its Peoples* (trans. R. Mayne), London: Viking 1990, *European History Quarterly*, 24: 123–7.

Kitromilides, P. M. (1996a), *Νεοελληνικός Διαφωτισμός: Οι πολιτικές και κοινωνικές ιδέες*, Athens: MIET.

Kitromilides, P. M. (1996b), '"Balkan mentality": History, legend, imagination', *Nations and Nationalism*, 2 (2): 163-91.

Kitromilides, P. M. (1999), 'The Greek cultural presence in the Balkans', in V. Coufoudakis, H. J. Psomiades and A. Gerolymatos (eds), *Greece and the New Balkans: Challenges and Opportunities*, 193-209, New York: Pella.

Kitromilides, P. M. (2013), *Enlightenment and Revolution: The Making of Modern Greece*, Cambridge, MA: Harvard University Press.

Kokonis, M. (2012), 'Is there such a thing as a Greek blockbuster? The revival of contemporary Greek cinema', in L. Papadimitriou and Y. Tzioumakis (eds), *Greek Cinema: Texts, Histories, Identities*, 37-53, Bristol: Intellect.

Koliopoulos, J. S., and Th. M. Veremis, (2010), *Modern Greece: A History since 1821*, Oxford: Wiley-Blackwell.

Kolovos, Y. (2015), *'Κοινωνικά απόβλητα': Η ιστορία της πανκ σκηνής στην Αθήνα 1979-2015*, Athens: Aprovleptes Ekdoseis.

Komninou, M. (2001), *Από την Αγορά στο Θέαμα*, Athens: Papazisis.

Kondylis, P. (1991/2011), *Οι αιτίες της παρακμής της σύγχρονης Ελλάδας: Η καχεξία του αστικού στοιχείου στη νεοελληνική κοινωνία και ιδεολογία*, Athens: Themelio.

Kontochristou, M., ed. (2007), *Ταυτότητα και ΜΜΕ στη σύγχρονη Ελλάδα*, Athens: Papazisis.

Kontochristou, M., and G. Terzis (2007), 'The Greek media landscape', in G. Terzis (ed), *European Media Governance: National and Regional Dimension*, 225-37, Bristol: Intellect.

Kontogianni, V. (2008), *Λόγος Γυναικών, Πρακτικά Διεθνούς Συνεδρίου*, Athens: ELIA.

Kopidakis, M. Z. (1999), *Ιστορία της Ελληνικής Γλώσσας*, Athens: ELIA/MIET.

Kornetis, K. (2010), 'No more heroes? Rejection and reverberation of the past in the 2008 events in Greece', *Journal of Modern Greek Studies*, 28 (2): 173-97.

Kornetis, K. (2013), *Children of the Dictatorship: Student Resistance, Cultural Politics, and the 'Long 1960s' in Greece*, New York: Berghahn Books.

Kornetis, K. (2014), 'From reconciliation to vengeance: The Greek Civil War on screen in Pantelis Voulgaris' *A Soul So Deep* and Kostas Charalambous' *Tied Red Thread*', *Filmicon: Journal of Greek Film Studies*, 2: 93-116.

Kornetis, K. (2015), 'The end of a parable? Unsettling the transitology model in the age of crisis', *Historein*, 15 (1): 5-12.

Kornetis, K., and H. Kouki (2016), 'From the centre to the periphery and back to the centre: Social movements affecting social movement theory in the case of Greece', in O. Fillieule and G. Accornero (eds), *Social Movement Studies in Europe: The State of the Art*, 371-87, New York: Berghahn.

Kornetis, K., E. Kotsovili and N. Papadogiannis, eds (2016), *Consumption and Gender in Southern Europe since the Long 1960s*, London: Bloomsbury.

Koronaiou, A. et al. (2015), 'Golden Dawn, austerity and young people: The rise of fascist extremism among young people in contemporary Greek society', *Sociological Review*, 63 (S2): 231–49.

Korovesis, P. (1978), 'Το τέλος της μικρής μας λογοτεχνίας', *To Dentro*, 1: 26–31.

Koselleck, R. (1988), *Critique and Crisis: Enlightenment and the Pathogenesis of Modern Society*, Cambridge, MA: Berg.

Koselleck, R. (2006), 'Crisis', *Journal of the History of Ideas*, 67 (2): 357–400.

Koselleck, R. (2018), *Sediments of Time: On Possible Histories*, trans. and ed. S. Franzel and S. L. Hoffman, Stanford: Stanford University Press.

Kostavara, A., ed. (2002), *Η Γεωμετρία μιας αθέατης γενιάς: Ανθολογία της γενιάς του '90*, Athens: Mandragoras.

Kostis, K. (2018), *History's Spoiled Children: The Formation of the Modern Greek State*, trans. J. Moe, London: Hurst.

Kotsakis, K. (1998), 'The past is ours: Images of Greek Macedonia', in L. Meskell (ed.), *Archaeology Under Fire: Nationalism, Politics and Heritage in the Eastern Mediterranean and Middle East*, 44–67, London: Routledge.

Kotzia, E. (2000), 'Ελληνική πεζογραφία 1930–1999: ηθικά προστάγματα ή ευζωία', *Vivliothiki (Eleftherotypia)*, 118, 1 September: 9–10.

Kotzia, E. (2009), 'Πεζογραφία 1974–2004', *I Kathimerini*, 7 June.

Kotzia, E. (2012), 'Το ευπώλητο μυθιστόρημα και η ιδέα της λογοτεχνικότητας, 1985–2010', in A. Kastrinaki, A. Politis and D. Tziovas (eds), *Για μια ιστορία της ελληνικής λογοτεχνίας του εικοστού αιώνα*, 379–86, Herakleio: Panepistimiakes Ekdoseis Kritis and Mouseio Benaki.

Kotzia, E., and V. Hatzivasileiou (2003), 'Η Ελληνική Λογοτεχνία: 1974–2000', in V. Panayotopoulos (ed.), *Ιστορία του Νέου Ελληνισμού 1770–2000*, vol. 10, 183–200, Athens: Ellenika Grammata.

Kotzias, A. (1987), *Ιαγουάρος*, Athens: Kedros (English translation by H. E. Criton, *The Jaguar*, 1991).

Kouanis, P. (2001), *Η κινηματογραφική αγορά στην Ελλάδα 1944–1999*, Athens: Finatec.

Korma, L. (2017), 'The historiography of the Greek diaspora and migration in the twentieth century', *Historein* 16 (1–2), 47–73.

Koulouri, Ch., ed. (2002), *Clio in the Balkans: The Politics of History Education*, Thessaloniki: Center for Democracy and Reconciliation in Southeast Europe.

Kourelou, O., M. Liz and B. Vidal (2014), 'Crisis and creativity: The new cinemas of Portugal, Greece and Spain', *New Cinemas: Journal of Contemporary Film*, 12 (1 and 2): 133–51.

Kourtovik, D. (2002), *Η θέα πέρα από τον ακάλυπτο: κριτικές και δοκίμια (1992–2002)*, Athens: Estia.

Koutsikou, D., ed. (1984), *Κάτι το «ωραίον»: μια περιήγηση στη νεοελληνική κακογουστιά/Kitsch – made in Greece*, Athens: Friends of *Anti* magazine.

Koutsogiannis, D., and B. Mitsikopoulou (2003), 'Greeklish and Greekness: Trends and discourses of "glocalness"', *Journal of Computer-Mediated Communication*, 9 (1), available at https://doi.org/10.1111/j.1083-6101.2003.tb00358.x.

Koutsombolis, D. (2005), 'Ο Τύπος για το λεξικό Μπαμπινιώτη', *Glossa*, 60: 61–73.

Koutsou, D. (2004), 'Ο διάλογος για τα αρχαία ελληνικά στην εφημερίδα Ελευθεροτυπία', *Glossa*, 59: 75–83.

Koutsourakis, A. (2018), *The Cinema of Theo Angelopoulos*, Edinburgh: Edinburgh University Press.

Koutsourelis, K. (2008), 'Η επιστροφή του μέτρου: Για την αναβίωση των παραδοσιακών μορφών στη σύγχρονη ποίηση', *Planodion*, 44: 860–65.

Koutsourelis, K. (2012), 'Πώς η ποίηση από τέχνη έγινε χόμπι', *I Kathimerini*, 9 December.

Koutsourelis, K. (2013a), 'Το διαζύγιο ποιητών-κοινού', *I Kathimerini*, 22–3 June.

Koutsourelis, K. (2013b), 'Μιχάλης Γκανάς, Ποιήματα 1978–2012', *Book Press Online*, 4 December, https://bookpress.gr/kritikes/poiisi/3536-ganas-poiimata.

Koutsourelis, K. (2019), *Η τέχνη που αυτοκτονεί: Για το αδιέξοδο της ποίησης του καιρού μας*, Athens: Mikri Arktos.

Kouzeli, L. (2014), 'Η μόδα του πολυτονικού: ύφος και όχι γλώσσα', *To Vima*, 13 July.

Kremmydas, V. (2002), '6 μέρες ιστοριογραφίας: έτσι κλείσαμε', *I Avgi*, 17 November.

Kremmydas, V. (2004), 'Απολογιζόμαστε και χαιρετούμε', in P. M. Kitromilides and T. E. Sklavenitis (eds), *Historiography of Modern and Contemporary Greece 1833–2002*, vol. 2, 735–40, Athens: Institute for Neohellenic Research.

Kriaras, E. (1997), 'Το μονοτονικό και οι «βραχονησίδες»', *Ta Nea*, 26 July.

Kriaras, E. (1999), 'Ο αγώνας (ο γλωσσικός) συνεχίζεται (ή πρέπει ...)', *Ta Nea*, 3 November.

Kriaras, E. (2000), 'Γιατί χρειάζεται το μονοτονικό', *Ta Nea*, 9 April.

Kriesi, H. (2009), 'Rejoinder to Liesbet Hooghe and Gary Marks', *British Journal of Political Science*, 39 (1): 221–4.

Kristeva, J. (1999), 'Le poids mystérieux de l'orthodoxie', *Le Monde*, 18 April.

Kristeva, J. (2000), *Crisis of the European Subject*, trans. S. Fairfield, New York: Other Press.

Kyriakos, K. (2017), *Επιθυμίες και Πολιτική: Η queer ιστορία του ελληνικού κινηματογράφου (1924–2016)*, Athens: Aigokeros.

Kyriazis, N. (1995), 'Feminism and the status of women in Greece', in D. Constas and Th. G. Stavrou (eds), *Greece Prepares for the Twenty-First Century*, 267–301, Washington, DC: Woodrow Wilson Centre Press and Johns Hopkins University Press.

Labrianidis, L., and M. Pratsinakis (2017), 'Crisis brain drain: Short-term pain/long-term gain?', in D. Tziovas (ed.), *Greece in Crisis: The Cultural Politics of Austerity*, 87–106, London: I.B. Tauris.

Lambrinos, F. (2003), 'Ελληνικός κινηματογράφος: Από τη μεταπολίτευση στο τέλος του 20ού αιώνα', in V. Panayotopoulos (ed.), *Ιστορία του Νέου Ελληνισμού 1770–2000*, vol. 10, 201–26, Athens: Ellinika Grammata.

Lambrinou, K. (2015), 'Η "Γενιά του Πολυτεχνείου" στο καλειδοσκόπιο της Μεταπολίτευσης', in M. Avgeridis, E. Gazi and K. Kornetis (eds), *Μεταπολίτευση: Η Ελλάδα στο μεταίχμιο δύο αιώνων*, 152–68, Athens: Themelio.

Lambropoulos, V. (1988), *Literature as National Institution: Studies in the Politics of Modern Greek Criticism*, Princeton, NJ: Princeton University Press.

Lambropoulos, V. (1997), 'Modern Greek studies in the age of ethnography', *Journal of Modern Greek Studies*, 15 (2): 197–208.

Lambropoulos, V. (2016a), 'Review of Theodoros Chiotis and Dinos Siotis anthologies', *Journal of Modern Greek Studies*, 34 (2): 404–8.

Lambropoulos, V. (2016b), 'Left melancholy in the Greek poetry generation of the 2000s', *Journal of Modern Greek Studies, Occasional Paper 10*, https://www.scribd.com/document/320277344/Vassilis-Lambropoulos#fullscreen&from_embed.

Lavdas, K. (1997), *The Europeanisation of Greece: Interest Politics and the Crises of Integration*, London: Macmillan.

Layoun, M. N., ed. (1990), *Modernism in Greece? Essays on the Critical and Literary Margins of a Movement*, New York: Pella.

Lazos, C. D. (1987), *Ελληνικό φοιτητικό κίνημα 1821–1973*, Athens: Gnosi.

Leconte, C. (2010), *Understanding Euroscepticism*, New York: Palgrave Macmillan.

Le Goff, J. (1992), *History and Memory*, trans. Steven Rendall and Elizabeth Claman, New York: Columbia University Press.

Lemos, N., and E. Yannakakis, eds (2015), *Critical Times, Critical Thoughts: Contemporary Greek Writers Discuss Facts and Fiction*, Newcastle upon Tyne: Cambridge Scholars.

Létoublon, F. (2000), 'Η Οδύσσεια του Αγγελόπουλου', in I. Stathi (ed.), *Βλέμματα στον κόσμο του Θόδωρου Αγγελόπουλου*, 31–41, Thessaloniki: Festival Kinimatografou Thessalonikis.

Létoublon, F. (2008), 'Theo Angelopoulos in the underworld', in B. Graziosi and E. Greenwood (eds), *Homer in the Twentieth Century: Between World Literature and the Western Canon*, 210–77, Oxford: Oxford University Press.

Liakos, A. (1988), *Η εμφάνιση των νεανικών οργανώσεων – Το παράδειγμα της Θεσσαλονίκης*, Athens: Lotos.

Liakos, A. (2001a), 'Αδικαιολόγητες ανησυχίες', *To Vima*, 28 January.

Liakos, A. (2001b), 'Η Νεοελληνική Ιστοριογραφία το τελευταίο τέταρτο του εικοστού αιώνα', *Synchrona Themata*, 76/77: 72–91.

Liakos, A. (2003a), 'Αντάρτες και συμμορίτες στα ακαδημαϊκά αμφιθέατρα', in H. Fleischer (ed.), *Η Ελλάδα '36-'49: Από τη Δικτατορία στον Εμφύλιο*, 25–36, Athens: Kastaniotis.

Liakos, A. (2003b), 'Μεταμοντερνισμός, Ιστοριογραφία και Αριστερά', *O Politis*, 107: 12–17.

Liakos, A. (2004a), 'Το ζήτημα της «συνέχειας» στη νεοελληνική ιστοριογραφία', in P. M. Kitromilides and T. Sklavenitis (eds), *Δ' Διεθνές Συνέδριο Ιστορίας: Ιστοριογραφία της νεότερης και σύγχρονης Ελλάδας, 1833–2002*, vol. 1, 53–65, Athens: Institute for Neohellenic Research.

Liakos, A. (2004b), 'Modern Greek historiography (1974–2000). The era of tradition from dictatorship to democracy', in U. Brunbauer (ed.), *(Re)Writing History. Historiography in Southeast Europe after Socialism*, 351–78, Münster: LIT Verlag.

Liakos, A. (2008/9), 'History wars – notes from the field', *International Society for History Didactics Yearbook*, 57–74.

Liakos, A. (2014), *Η επιστροφή της κοκκινοσκουφίτσας*, Athens: Nefeli.

Liakos, A. (2019), *Ο ελληνικός 20ός αιώνας*, Athens: Polis.

Liakos, A., and H. Kouki (2015), 'Narrating the story of a failed national transition: Discourses on the Greek crisis, 2010–2014', *Historein*, 15 (1): 49–61.

Lialiouti, Z. (2015), 'Ο αντιαμερικανισμός και το εθνικό αφήγημα της Μεταπολίτευσης 1974–1985: ανορθολογικά στοιχεία, ορθολογικές χρήσεις', in M. Avgeridis, E. Gazi and K. Kornetis (eds), *Μεταπολίτευση: Η Ελλάδα στο μεταίχμιο δύο αιώνων*, 197–210, Athens: Themelio.

Lialiouti, Z. (2016), *Ο αντιαμερικανισμός στην Ελλάδα (1947–1989)*, Athens: Asini.

Lialiouti, Z., and G. Bithymitris (2013), 'The Nazis strike again: The concept of "the German enemy", party strategies, and mass perceptions through the prism of the Greek economic crisis', in C. Karner and B. Mertens (eds), *The Use and Abuse of Memory: Interpreting World War II in Contemporary European Politics*, 155–72, New Brusnwick, NJ: Transaction.

Linz J., A. Stepan and R. Gunther (1995), 'Democratic transition and consolidation in Southern Europe, with reflections on Latin America and Eastern Europe', in R. Gunther, N. P. Diamandouros and H. J. Puhle (eds), *The Politics of Democratic Consolidation: Southern Europe in Comparative Perspective*, 77–123, Baltimore, MD: Johns Hopkins University Press.

Loizos, P., and E. Papataxiarchis, eds (1991), *Gender and Kinship in Modern Greece*, Princeton, NJ: Princeton University Press.

Lorenz, C. (2014), 'Blurred lines: History, memory and the experience of time', *International Journal for History, Culture and Modernity*, 2 (1): 43–62.

Lykidis, A. (2015), 'Crisis of sovereignty in recent Greek cinema', *Journal of Greek Media & Culture*, 1 (1): 9–27.

Lytra, V., ed. (2014), *When Greeks and Turks Meet: Interdisciplinary Perspectives on the Relationship since 1923*, Farnham: Ashgate.

Mackridge, P. (1991), 'The protean self of Costas Tahtsis', *European Gay Review*, 6/7: 172–98.

Mackridge, P. (2000), 'Ο ελληνικός δημόσιος λόγος μετά τη διγλωσσία/Le Discours public en Grèce après l'abolition de la diglossia', in *Η ελληνική γλώσσα και οι διάλεκτοί της/La Langue grecque et ses dialectes*, 65–8 and 133–6, Athens: Kentro Ellinikis Glossas.

Mackridge, P. (2008), 'Cultural difference as national identity in modern Greece', in Katerina Zacharia (ed.), *Hellenisms: Culture, Identity, and Ethnicity from Antiquity to Modernity*, 297–319, Aldershot: Ashgate.

Mackridge, P. (2009a), *Language and National Identity in Greece, 1766–1976*, Oxford: Oxford University Press.

Mackridge, P. (2009b), 'Mothers and daughters, roots and branches: Modern Greek perceptions of the relationship between the ancient and modern languages', in A. Georgakopoulou and M. Silk (eds), *Standard Languages and Language Standards: Greek, Past and Present*, 259–76, Farnham: Ashgate.

Mackridge, P. (2016), ' "Omileite …anglika?" English influences in contemporary Greek', in U. Moennig (ed.), '*…ὡς ἀθύρματα παῖδας*' Festschrift für Hans Eideneier, 465–76, Berlin: Edition Romiosini/CeMoG, Freie Universität Berlin.

Mackridge, P., and E. Yannakakis, eds (2004), *Contemporary Greek Fiction in a United Europe: From Local History to the Global Individual*, Oxford: Legenda.

Madianou, M. (2005), *Mediating the Nation: News, Audiences and the Politics of Identity*, London: UCL Press.

Mais, H. (2015), 'Το Απελευθερωτικό Κίνημα Ομοφυλοφίλων Ελλάδας (ΑΚΟΕ): Έμφυλες αντιστάσεις στην Μεταπολιτευτική Ελλάδα', *Entropia*, 5: 18–23.

Makrides, V. N. (1998), 'Byzantium in contemporary Greece: The neo-orthodox current of ideas', in D. Ricks and P. Magdalino (eds), *Byzantium and the Modern Greek identity*, 141–53, Aldershot: Ashgate.

Manitakis, A. (2000), *Οι σχέσεις της εκκλησίας με το κράτος-έθνος στη σκιά των ταυτοτήτων*, Athens: Nefeli.

Marangudakis, M. (2019), *The Greek Crisis and Its Cultural Origins: A Study in the Theory of Multiple Modernities*, Cham, Switzerland: Palgrave Macmillan.

Marantzidis, N., and G. Antoniou (2004), 'The Axis occupation and Civil War: Changing trends in Greek historiography, 1941–2002', *Journal of Peace Research*, 41 (2): 223–31.

Margaritis, Y. (2000–1), *Ιστορία του Ελληνικού Εμφυλίου Πολέμου 1946–1949*, vols 1 and 2, Athens: Vivliorama.

Margaritis, Y. (2002), 'Η δεκαετία του 1940–1950: Μια ιστοριογραφική πρόκληση', *O Politis*, 104: 28–34.

Margellou Inglessi, C. (2014), 'Δημόσιοι καιροί και ιδιωτικές ακαιρίες', *Books' Journal*, 46 (September), http://booksjournal.gr/διάλογος/item/576-δημόσιοι-καιροί-και-ιδιωτικές-ακαιρίες.

Marinucci, M. (2010), *Feminism Is Queer: The Intimate Connection between Queer and Feminist Theory*, London: Zed Books.

Maronitis, D. N. (1999), 'Από την εμπάθεια στην απάθεια', *To Vima*, 24 October.

Martinidis, P. (1982), Συνηγορία της παραλογοτεχνίας, Athens: Polytypo.
Marwick, A. (1998), *The Sixties: Cultural Revolution in Britain, France, Italy and the United States, c. 1958–c.1974*, Oxford: Oxford University Press.
Mavrogordatos, G. Th. (1983), *Stillborn Republic: Social Coalitions and Party Strategies in Greece 1922–1936*, Berkeley: University California Press.
Mavrogordatos, G. Th. (1999), 'Η "ρεβάνς" των ηττημένων', *To Vima*, 17 October.
Mavrogordatos, G. Th. (2003), 'Orthodoxy and nationalism in the Greek case', *West European Politics*, 26 (1): 117–36.
Mazower, M. (2004), *Salonica, City of Ghosts: Christians, Muslims and Jews 1430–1950*, London: HarperCollins.
Melucci, A. (1989), *Nomads of the Present: Social Movements and Individual Needs in Contemproary Society*, J. Keane and P. Mier (eds), London: Hutchinson Radius.
Merdjanova, I. (2000), 'In search of identity: Nationalism and religion in Eastern Europe', *Religion, State & Society*, 28 (3): 233–62.
Mergel, T. (2012), 'Modernization', European History Online (EGO), published by the Leibniz Institute of European History (IEG), Mainz, http://www.ieg-ego.eu/mergelt-2011-en.
Meselidis, S. (2010), 'Teachers, history wars and teaching history grade 6 in Greece', in J. Zajda (ed.), *Globalisation, Ideology and Education Policy Reforms*, 39–48, Cham, Switzerland: Springer Science.
Michailidou, A. (2017), '"The Germans are back": Euroscepticism and anti-Germanism in crisis-stricken Greece', *National Identities*, 19 (1): 91–108.
Michailidou, M., and A.Halkia, eds (2005), Η παραγωγή του κοινωνικού σώματος, Athens: Katarti & Dini.
Miles, S. (1998), *Consumerism: As a Way of Life*, London: Sage.
Millas, H. (1991), 'History textbooks in Greece and Turkey', *History Workshop Journal*, 31 (1): 21–33.
Millas, I. (2001), Εικόνες Ελλήνων και Τούρκων: σχολικά βιβλία, ιστοριογραφία, λογοτεχνία και εθνικά στερεότυπα, Athens: Alexandreia.
Millas, I. (2006), 'Tourkokratia: History and the image of Turks in Greek literature', *South European Society & Politics*, 11 (1): 47–60.
Milton, G. (2009), *Paradise Lost: Smyrna 1922 – the Destruction of Islam's City of Tolerance*, London: Sceptre.
Mini, P. (2016), 'The historical panorama in post-1974 Greek cinema: *The Travelling Players, Stone Years, Crystal Nights, The Weeping Meadow*', *Journal of Greek Media & Culture*, 2 (2): 133–53.
Mishkova, D. (2008), 'Symbolic geographies and visions of identity: A Balkan perspective', *European Journal of Social Theory*, 11 (2): 237–56.
Mitralexis, S. (2017), 'Studying contemporary Greek neo-orientalism: The case of the "underdog culture" narrative', *Horyzonty Polityki/Horizons of Politics*, 8 (25): 125–49.

Mitralexis, S. (2019), '"A luscious anarchism in all of this": Revisiting the 1980s and 1990s Greek "Neo-Orthodox" current of ideas', *Journal of Modern Greek Studies*, 37 (2): 295–326.

Mitsopoulos, M., and Th. Pelagidis (2012), 'The 2010 Greek economic crisis and the conditionality programme', in S. Kalyvas, G. Pagoulatos and H. Tsoukas (eds), *From Stagnation to Forced Adjustment: Reforms in Greece, 1974–2010*, 211–45, London: Hurst.

Morgan, S. (2006), *The Feminist History Reader*, New York: Routledge.

Morton, S. (2007), *Gayatri Spivak: Ethics, Subalternity and the Critique of Postcolonial Reason*, Cambridge: Polity.

Moschonas, S. A. (2004), 'Relativism in language ideology: On Greece's latest language issues', *Journal of Modern Greek Studies*, 22 (2): 173–206.

Moskov, C. (1972/4), *Η Εθνική και Κοινωνική Συνείδηση στην Ελλάδα 1830–1909: Ιδεολογία του μεταπρατικού χώρου*, Athens.

Moskov, C. (1980), *Δοκίμια, Ι*, Athens: Exantas.

Moullas, P. (2007), *Ο χώρος του εφήμερου: Στοιχεία για την παραλογοτεχνία του 19ου αιώνα*, Athens: Sokolis.

Mouzelis, N. (1978), *Modern Greece: Facets of Underdevelopment*, London: Macmillan.

Mouzelis, N. (1995), 'Greece in the twenty-first Century: Institutions and political culture', in D. Constas and Th. G. Stavrou (eds), *Greece Prepares for the Twenty-first Century*, 17–34, Washington, DC: Woodrow Wilson Centre Press and Johns Hopkins University Press.

Mouzelis, N. (1996), 'The concept of modernization: Its relevance for Greece', *Journal of Modern Greek Studies*, 14 (2): 215–27.

Mylonaki, A. (2013), 'Wasted youth by Argyris Papadimitropoulos and Jan Vogel (2011)', *Filmicon: Journal of Greek Film Studies*, 1: 167–74.

Mylonas, Y. (2012), 'Media and the economic crisis of the EU: The "culturalization" of a systemic crisis and Bild-Zeitung's framing of Greece', *TripleC: Cognition, Communication, Co-operation*, 10 (2): 646–71.

Mylonas, Y. (2014), 'Crisis, austerity and opposition in mainstream media discourses of Greece', *Critical Discourse Studies*, 11 (3): 305–21. doi: 10.1080/17405904.2014.915862.

Nash, K. (2000), *Contemporary Political Sociology: Globalization, Politics, and Power*, Oxford: Blackwell.

Neils, J., ed. (2005), *The Parthenon: From Antiquity to the Present*, Cambridge: Cambridge University Press.

Nelsen, B. F., and J. L. Guth (2015), *Religion and the Struggle for the European Union: Confessional Culture and the Limits of Integration*, Washington, DC: Georgetown University Press.

Nguyen, V. T. (2016), *Nothing Ever Dies: Vietnam and the Memory of War*, Cambridge, MA: Harvard University Press.

Nikolaidou, A. (2014), 'The performative aesthetics of the "Greek New Wave"', *Filmicon: Journal of Greek Film Studies*, 2: 20–44.

Nikolaidou, A., and A. Poupou (2017), 'Κάποιες post-weird σκέψεις για το νέο κύμα του ελληνικού κινηματογράφου/Post-weird notes on the New Wave of Greek cinema', *Non-Catalogue*, 88–105, Thessaloniki: 58th Thessaloniki International Film Festival.

Nikolakopoulos, I. (2013), 'Τα διλήμματα της Μεταπολίτευσης: μεταξύ συνέχειας και ρήξης', *Archiotaxio*, 15: 6–13.

Nikolakopoulos, I. (2015), 'Συνέχειες και ρήξεις: Ο αμφίσημος όρος Μεταπολίτευση', in M. Avgeridis, E. Gazi and K. Kornetis (eds), *Μεταπολίτευση: Η Ελλάδα στο μεταίχμιο δύο αιώνων*, 429–31, Athens: Themelio.

Nikolopoulou, M. (2008a), 'Ο «τριακονταετής πόλεμος»: η πεζογραφία με θέμα τον Εμφύλιο και η διαχείριση της μνήμης στο πεδίο της αφήγησης (1946–1974)', in G. Antoniou and N. Marantzidis (eds), *Η Εποχή της Σύγχυσης: η δεκαετία του '40 και η ιστοριογραφία*, 419–93, Athens: Estia.

Nikolopoulou, M. (2008b), '*Ιαγουάρος* του Αλέξανδρου Κοτζιά: ένα σχόλιο για τη λειτουργία της μνήμης του εμφυλίου στη δεκαετία του 1980', in R. van Boeschoten, T. Vervenioti, E. Voutira, V. Dalkavoukis and K. Bada (eds), *Μνήμες και Λήθη του Ελληνικού Εμφυλίου Πολέμου*, 373–85, Thessaloniki: Epikentro.

Özkırımlı, U., and S. A. Sofos (2008), *Tormented by History: Nationalism in Greece and Turkey*, London: Hurst.

Pagoulatos, G., and X. A. Yataganas (2010), 'Europe othered, Europe enlisted, Europe possessed: Greek public intellectuals and the European Union', in J. Lacroix and K. Nicolaidis (eds), *European Stories: Intellectual Debates on Europe in National Contexts*, 183–202, Oxford: Oxford University Press.

Pakis, E. (2013), 'Playing in the dark: Staging *Lesbian Blues*, questioning gendered belonging', *Journal of Modern Greek Studies*, 31 (2): 217–47.

Paloma Aguilar, F. (2002), *Memory and Amnesia: The Role of the Spanish Civil War in the Transition to Democracy*, Oxford: Berghahn.

Panagiotakis, N. M. (1993), *Origini della letteratura neogreca: atti del secondo congresso internationale 'Neograeca Medii Aevi'* (Venezia, 7–10 Novembre 1991), Venice: Elleniko Instituto Venetias.

Panagiotopoulos, P. (2018), 'Οικογενειακή μηχανική: μια κοινωνιολογία της διαγενεακής συναίνεσης στη μεταπολίτευση', in K. Spanou and D. A. Sotiropoulos (eds), *Κουλτούρα, Ιστορία, Δημοκρατία*, 170–91, Athens: Papadopoulos.

Panagiotopoulos, P., and V. Vamvakas (2014), 'Acrobats on a rope: Greek society between contemporary European demands and archaic cultural reflexes', in B. Temel (ed.), *The Great Catalyst: European Union Project and Lessons from Greece and Turkey*, 113–34, Lanham, MD: Lexington.

Panagiotopoulos, V., ed. (2003), *Ιστορία του Νέου Ελληνισμού 1770–2000 – Η Ελλάδα της ομαλότητας, 1974–2000*, vol. 10, Athens: Ellinika Grammata.

Panayotopoulos, N. (2009), 'On Greek photography: Eurocentrism, cultural colonialism and the construction of mythic Classical Greece', *Third Text*, 23 (2): 181–94.

Pantelidou-Malouta, M. (2010), 'Αλλαγές στις πολιτικές αντιλήψεις των νέων γυναικών στο τέλος του 20ού αιώνα', in V. Karamanolakis, E. Olympitou and I. Papathanasiou (eds), *Η Ελληνική Νεολαία στον 20ό αιώνα: Πολιτικές διαδρομές, κοινωνικές πρακτικές και πολιτιστικές εκφράσεις*, 453–63, Athens: Themelio.

Pantelidou-Malouta, M. (2015), 'Η νεολαία επιστρέφει: ελληνική πολιτική κουλτούρα και μεταβαλλόμενα πρότυπα πολιτικότητας των νέων στην κρίση', *Ellliniki Epitheorisi Politikis Epistimis*, 43: 5–46.

Papadimitriou, L. (2009), 'Greek film studies today: In search of identity', *Kampos: Cambridge Papers in Modern Greek*, 17: 49–78.

Papadimitriou, L. (2011), 'The national and the transnational in contemporary Greek cinema', *New Review of Film and Television Studies*, 9 (4): 493–512.

Papadimitriou, L. (2012), 'Music, dance and cultural identity in the Greek film musical', in L. Papadimitriou and Y. Tzioumakis (eds), *Greek Cinema: Texts, Histories, Identities*, 147–66, Bristol: Intellect.

Papadimitriou, L. (2014), 'Locating contemporary Greek film cultures: Past, present, future and the crisis', *Filmicon: Journal of Greek Film Studies*, 2: 1–18.

Papadimitriou, N., and A. Anagnostopoulos, eds (2017), *Το Παρελθόν στο Παρόν: Μνήμη, ιστορία και αρχαιότητα στη σύγχρονη Ελλάδα*, Athens: Kastaniotis.

Papadogiannis, N. (2010), 'Η πολλαπλή υποδοχή της ροκ μουσικής από τις κομμουνιστικές οργανώσεις νεολαίας στην Ελλάδα στα τέλη της δεκαετίας του 1970', in V. Karamanolakis, E. Olympitou and I. Papathanasiou (eds), *Η Ελληνική Νεολαία στον 20ό αιώνα: Πολιτικές διαδρομές, κοινωνικές πρακτικές και πολιτιστικές εκφράσεις*, 318–44, Athens: Themelio.

Papadogiannis, N. (2015), *Militant Around the Clock? Left-Wing Youth Politics, Leisure, and Sexuality in Post-Dictatorship Greece 1974–1981*, Oxford: Berghahn.

Papadogiannis, N. (2017), 'Gender in modern Greek historiography', *Historein*, 16 (1–2): 74–101.

Papageorgiou, K. G., and V. Hatzivasileiou (2007–2013), *Ανθολογία της ελληνικής ποίησης (20ος Αιώνα)*, vols 1–4, Athens: Kotinos.

Papagiorgis, K. (1997), *Αλέξανδρος Αδαμαντίου Εμμανουήλ*, Athens: Kastaniotis.

Papailias, P. (2005), *Genres of Recollection: Archival Poetics and Modern Greece*, New York: Palgrave Macmillan.

Papandreou, A. (1973), *Democracy at Gunpoint: The Greek front*, Harmondsworth: Penguin.

Papanikolaou, D. (2007), *Singing Poets: Literature and Popular Music in France and Greece*, Oxford: Legenda.

Papanikolaou, D. (2013), 'Η απόφαση της λησμονιάς: Το ΑΚΟΕ, τα μεταδικτατορικά κινήματα και η αφασία της δημόσιας σφαίρας', *Archeiotaxio*, 15: 84–7.

Papanikolaou, D. (2014a), *"Σαν κ' εμένα καμωμένοι": Ο ομοφυλόφιλος Καβάφης και η ποιητική της σεξουαλικότητας*, Athens: Patakis.

Papanikolaou, D. (2014b), 'Mapping/unmapping: The making of queer Athens', in M. Cook and J. V. Evans (eds), *Queer Cities, Queer Cultures: Europe since 1945*, 151–70, London: Bloomsbury.

Papanikolaou, D. (2018a), *Κάτι τρέχει με την οικογένεια: έθνος, πόθος και συγγένεια την εποχή της κρίσης*, Athens: Patakis.

Papanikolaou, D. (2018b), 'Critically queer and haunted: Greek identity, crisis-scapes and doing queer history in the present', *Journal of Greek Media & Culture*, 4 (2): 167–86.

Papanikolaou, D., and V. Kolocotroni (2018), 'New queer Greece: Performance, politics and identity in crisis', *Journal of Greek Media & Culture*, 4 (2): 143–50.

Papargyriou, E. (2011), *Reading Games in the Greek Novel*, Oxford: Legenda.

Papataxiarchis, E., ed. (2006), *Περιπέτειες της ετερότητας: Η παραγωγή της πολιτισμικής διαφοράς στη σημερινή Ελλάδα*, Athens: Alexandreia.

Papathanassopoulos, S. (1997), 'The politics and the effects of the deregulation of Greek television', *European Journal of Communication*, 12 (3): 351–68.

Papathanassopoulos, S. (2001), 'The decline of newspapers: The case of the Greek press', *Journalism Studies*, 2 (1): 109–23.

Papathanassopoulos, S. (2002), 'Τα … παράδοξα των ελληνικών εφημερίδων', *I Kathimerini*, 2 June.

Papathanassopoulos, S. (2010), 'The "state" of "public" broadcasting in Greece', in P. Iosifidis (ed.), *Reinventing Public Service Communication: European Broadcasters and Beyond*, 222–33, Bristol: Palgrave Macmillan.

Papathanassopoulos, S. (2015), 'European media views of the Greek crisis', in S. Schifferes and R. Roberts (eds), *The Media and Financial Crises: Comparative and Historical Perspectives*, 103–18, London: Routledge.

Papathanassopoulos, S. (2019), *Greece-Media Landscape*, European Journalism Centre, available at https://medialandscapes.org/country/pdf/greece.

Pappas, T. S. (2014), *Populism and Crisis Politics in Greece*, Basingstoke: Palgrave Macmillan.

Paraschos, M. (1995), 'The Greek media face the twenty-first century: Will the Adam Smith complex replace the Oedipus Complex?', in D. Constas and Th. G. Stavrou (eds), *Greece Prepares for the Twenty-First Century*, 253–66, Washington, DC: Woodrow Wilson Centre Press and Johns Hopkins University Press.

Paratiritis, (1997), '"Γλωσσικώς ορθά!"', *I Kathimerini*, 20 August.

Parker, H. N. (2011), 'Toward a definition of popular culture', *History and Theory*, 50: 147–70.

Paschalidis, G. (2005), 'Η Ελληνική Τηλεόραση', in N. Vernikos et al. (eds), *Πολιτιστικές Βιομηχανίες: Διαδικασίες, Υπηρεσίες και Αγαθά*, 173–200, Athens: Kritiki.

Paschalidis, G. (2018), 'Το χαμένο παράδειγμα της ελληνικής τηλεόρασης', in V. Vamvakas and G. Paschalidis (eds), *50 Χρόνια Ελληνική Τηλεόραση*, 9–41, Thessaloniki: Epikentro.

Passas, A. G., D. P. Sotiropoulos, A. Triantafyllopoulou and Th. N. Tsekos, eds (2016), *Οι θεσμοί στην Ελλάδα της μεταπολίτευσης: Αποτίμηση μιας αντιφατικής περιόδου*, Athens: Papazisis.

Patrikiou, A. (2017), 'On the historiography of the language question in post-1974 Greece', *Historein*, 16: 102–19.

Payne, D. P. (2003), 'The clash of civilizations: The Church of Greece, the European Union and the question of human rights', *Religion, State & Society*, 31 (3): 261–71.

Petsini, P., and D. Christopoulos (2018), *Λεξικό Λογοκρισίας στην Ελλάδα*, Athens: Kastaniotis.

Pettifer, J. (1993/2000), *The Greeks: The Land and the People since the War*, London: Penguin.

Phillis, P. (2017), 'The Albanian in the room: Revisiting Greek hospitality in *From the Snow* and *Plato's Academy*', in T. Kazakopoulou and M. Fotiou (eds), *Contemporary Greek Film Cultures from 1990 to the Present*, 231–59, Oxford: Peter Lang.

Plakoudas, S. (2016), 'The debt crisis and Greece's changing political discourse', *Byzantine and Modern Greek Studies*, 40 (9): 307–14.

Plantzos, D. (2008), 'Archaeology and Hellenic identity, 1896–2004: The frustrated vision', in D. Damaskos and D. Plantzos (eds), *A Singular Antiquity: Archaeology and Hellenic Identity in Twentieth-Century Greece*, 11–30, Athens: Benaki Museum.

Plantzos, D. (2019), 'We owe ourselves to debt: Classical Greece, Athens in crisis, and the body as battlefield', *Social Science Information*, 58 (3): 469–92.

Plexoussaki, E. (2000), 'Η διαχείριση της ετερότητας: αφηγήσεις για το AIDS', in R. Kaftantzoglou and M. Petronoti (eds), *Όρια και Περιθώρια: Εντάξεις και Αποκλεισμοί*, 109–29, Athens: National Centre for Social Research.

Politou-Marmarinou, E., and S. Denissi, eds (2000), *Identity and Alterity in Literature, 18th–20th c.*, Conference Proceedings of the Greek General and Comparative Literature Association, Athens: Domos.

Pollis, A. (1992a), 'Greek national identity: Religious minorities, rights, and European norms', *Journal of Modern Greek Studies*, 10 (2): 171–96.

Pollis, A. (1992b), 'Gender and social change in Greece: The role of women', in Th. C. Kariotis (ed.), *The Greek Socialist Experiment: Papandreou's Greece 1981–1989*, 279–303, New York: Pella.

Pollis, A. (1993), 'Eastern orthodoxy and Human Rights', *Human Rights Quarterly*, 15 (2): 339–56.

Pomeroy, A. (2008), *Then It Was Destroyed by the Volcano: The Ancient World in Film and on Television*, London: Duckworth.

Pomeroy, A. (2011), 'The sense of epiphany in Theo Angelopoulos', *Ulysses' Gaze*, *Classical Receptions Journal*, 3 (2): 213–26

Popp, S. (2008/9), 'National textbook controversies in a globalizing world', *Yearbook of the International Society for History Didactics*, 29/30: 109–22.

Poulos, M. (2009), *Arms and the Woman: Just Warriors and Greek Feminist Identity*, New York: Columbia University Press.

Poupou, A. (2018), 'The poetics of space in the films of the New Wave of contemporary Greek cinema', *Parabasis*, 16 (1): 295–313.

Pournara, M. (2011), 'Ο Εμφύλιος στοιχειώνει την πολιτική ζωή ακόμη', *I Kathimerini*, 3 April.

Pratsinakis, M., P. Hatziprokopiou, D. Grammatikas and L. Labrianidis (2017), 'Crisis and the resurgence of emigration from Greece: Trends, representations, and the multiplicity of migrant trajectories', in B. Glorius and J. Domínguez-Mujica (eds), *European Mobility in Times of Crisis. The New Context of European South-North Migration*, 75–102, Bielefeld: Transcript.

Pretenderis, I. K. (1996), *Η Δεύτερη Μεταπολίτευση*, Athens: Polis.

Prevelakis, N. (2012), 'Theologies as alternative national histories: Christos Yannaras and John Romanides', Harvard Center for Hellenic Studies, https://chs.harvard.edu/CHS/article/display/4889.

Proguidis, L. (1997), *La Conquête du Roman: De Papadiamantis à Boccace*, Paris: Les Belles Lettres (Greek translation *Η κατάκτηση του μυθιστορήματος*, Athens: Estia 1998).

Proguidis, L. (2002), *Ο Παπαδιαμάντης και η Δύση*, Athens: Estia.

Psaras, M. (2016), *The Queer Greek Weird Wave*, Cham, Switzerland: Palgrave Macmillan.

Radstone, S. (2000), 'Screening trauma: *Forrest Gump*, film and memory', in S. Radstone (ed.), *Memory and Methodology*, 79–107, Oxford: Berg.

Radstone, S., and K. Hodgkin (2007), 'Regimes of memory: An introduction', in S. Radstone and K. Hodgkin (eds), *Memory Culture: Memory, Subjectivity and Recognition*, 1–22, New Brunswick: Transaction.

Raftopoulos, D. (1999), 'Μεταπτώσεις της Νεοτερικότητας 1960-'75-'90...', *Anti*, 688: 27–31.

Rakopoulos, Th. (2014), 'Resonance of solidarity: Meanings of a local concept in anti-austerity Greece', *Journal of Modern Greek Studies*, 32 (2): 313–37.

Ramfos, S. (2000/11), *Ο Καημός του Ενός*, Athens: Armos (trans. N. Russell, *Yearning for the One*, Brookline MA: Holy Cross Orthodox Press).

Ramfos, S. (2012), *Time Out: Η ελληνική αίσθησι του χρόνου*, Athens: Armos.

Repoussi, M. (2003), 'Ο Χώρος των Γυναικών: Πολιτικά κόμματα, γυναικείες οργανώσεις και ομάδες', in Vasilis Panayotopoulos (ed.), *Ιστορία του Νέου Ελληνισμού 1770–2000*, vol.. 10, 121–44, Athens: Ellenika Grammata.

Repoussi, M. (2007), 'Politics questions history education: Debates on Greek history textbooks', *Yearbook of the International Society for History Didactics*, 2006/7, 99–110.

Repoussi, M. (2009), 'Battles over the national past of Greeks: The Greek history textbook controversy 2006–2007', *Geschichte für heute. Zeitschrift für historisch-politische Bildung*, 56–63.

Repoussi, M. (2011), 'History education in Greece', in E. Erdmann and W. Hasberg (eds), *Facing, Mapping, Bridging Diversity: Foundation of a European Discourse on History Education*, 329–70, Erlangen: Wochenschau Verlag.

Repoussi, M., Ch. Andreadou, A. Ploutachidis and A. Tsivas (2006), *Στα Νεότερα και Σύγχρονα Χρόνια*, Ministry of Education and Religion Affairs, Pedagogical Institute, Athens: Organisation for Schoolbooks Publishing.

Ricks, D. (2009), 'Orthographic standardization of the Modern Greek classics: Gain and loss', in A. Georgakopoulou and M. Silk (eds), *Standard Languages and Language Standards: Greek, Past and Present*, 131–47, Farnham: Ashgate.

Ricoeur, P. (2004), *Memory, History, Forgetting*, trans. K. Blamey and D. Pellauer, Chicago: University of Chicago Press.

Riedel, B. (2010), 'The movement that was not? Gay men and AIDS in urban Greece, 1950–1993', in D. A. Feldman (ed.), *AIDS, Culture, and Gay Men*, 231–49, Gainesville: University Press of Florida.

Robertson, R. (1995), 'Glocalization: Time-space and homogeneity-heterogeneity', in M. Featherstone, S. Lash and R. Robertson (eds), *Global Modernities*, 25–44, London: Sage.

Robinson, C. (1997a), 'Social, sexual and textual transgression: Kostas Tahtsis and Michel Tremblay, a comparison', in D. Tziovas (ed.), *Greek Modernism and Beyond*, 205–14, Lanham, MD: Rowman & Littlefield.

Robinson, C. (1997b), 'Gender, sexuality and narration in Kostas Tachtsis: A reading of *Τα ρέστα*', *Kambos: Cambridge Papers in Modern Greek*, 5: 63–80.

Robinson, C. (2001), 'Yorgos Ioannou: Fragmentation in life and art', *Kambos: Cambridge Papers in Modern Greek*, 9: 83–100.

Roitman, J. (2013), *Anti-Crisis*, Durham, NC: Duke University Press.

Romaine, S. (1984), *The Language of Children and Adolescents*, Oxford: Blackwell.

Rose, S. (2011), 'Attenberg, Dogtooth and the weird wave of Greek cinema', *The Guardian*, 27 August.

Roudometof, V. (1999), 'Nationalism, globalization, eastern orthodoxy: "unthinking" the "clash of civilizations" in Southeastern Europe', *European Journal of Social Theory*, 2 (2): 233–47.

Roudometof, V. (2001), *Nationalism, Globalization and Orthodoxy: The Social Origins of Ethnic Conflict in the Balkans*, Westport CT: Greenwood Press.

Roudometof, V. (2011), 'Eastern Orthodox Christianity and the uses of the past in contemporary Greece', *Religions*, 2: 95–113.

Roudometof V., and V. N. Makrides (2010), *Orthodox Christianity in 21st Century Greece*, Farnham: Ashgate.

Rozakis, Ch. L. (1996), 'The international protection of minorities in Greece', in K. Featherstone and K. Ifantis (eds), *Greece in a Changing Europe: Between European Integration and Balkan Disintegration?*, 95–116, Manchester: Manchester University Press.

Rudy, K. (2000), 'Queer theory and feminism', *Women's Studies: An Interdisciplinary Journal*, 29 (2): 195–216.
Sarafis, M., ed. (1980), *Greece: From Resistance to Civil War*, Nottingham: Spokesman.
Sarafis, M., and M. Eve, eds (1990), *Background to Contemporary Greece*, vols 1 and 2, London: Merlin Press.
Sarantakos, N. (2013), 'Η γλώσσα στη Μεταπολίτευση', *Archeiotaxio*, 15: 48–51.
Schmidt, V. H. (2006), 'Multiple modernities or varieties of modernity?', *Current Sociology*, 54 (10): 77–97.
Schoene, B. (2006), 'Queer politics, queer theory, and the future of "identity": spiralling out of culture', in E. Rooney (ed), *The Cambridge Companion to Feminist Literary Theory*, 283–302, Cambridge: Cambridge University Press.
Sella-Mazi, E. (1997), 'Διγλωσσία και ολιγότερο ομιλούμενες γλώσσες στην Ελλάδα', in K. Tsitselikis and D. Christopoulos (eds), *Το Μειονοτικό Φαινόμενο στην Ελλάδα*, 349–413, Athens: Kritiki.
Sevastakis, N. (2004), *Κοινότοπη Χώρα: Όψεις του δημόσιου χώρου και αντινομίες αξιών στη σημερινή Ελλάδα*, Athens: Savvalas.
Sevastakis, N., and Y. Stavrakakis (2012), *Λαϊκισμός, Αντιλαϊκισμός και Κρίση*, Athens: Nefeli.
Sifaki, E., and A. Stamou (2020), 'Film criticism and the legitimization of a New Wave in contemporary Greek cinema', *Journal of Greek Media & Culture*, 6 (1): 29–49.
Simopoulos, K. (1990), *Ξενοκρατία, μισελληνισμός και υποτέλεια*, Athens.
Sjöberg, E. (2011), 'The past in peril: Greek history textbook controversy and the Macedonian crisis', *Education Inquiry*, 2 (1): 93–107.
Sjöberg, E. (2017), *The Making of the Greek Genocide: Contested Memories of the Ottoman Greek Catastrophe*, Oxford: Berghahn Books.
Skamnakis, A. (2018), 'Accelerating a freefall? The impact of the post-2008 economic crisis on Greek media and journalism', *Journal of Greek Media and Culture*, 4(1): 9–25.
Sklaveniti, K. (2013), 'Αντισύλληψη, έκτρωση, σεξουαλικότητα: μια φεμινιστική έκθεση του 1976', *Archeiotaxio*, 15: 76–83.
Sklaveniti, K. (2018), 'Αυτόνομες φεμινιστικές ομάδες της Μεταπολίτευσης: δύο τρία πράγματα που ξέρω γι' αυτές', in D. Vaiou and A. Psara (eds), *Εννοιολογήσεις και πρακτικές του φεμινισμού: Μεταπολίτευση και «μετά»*, 73–79, Athens: Idryma tis Voulis ton Ellinon.
Sklavenitis, D. (2016), *«Κάτσε καλά, Γεράσιμε...»: Μαθητικό κίνημα και καταλήψεις 1974–2000*, Athens: Asini.
Slater, D. (1997), *Consumer Culture and Modernity*, Cambridge: Polity.
Smith, A. D. (2000), *Myths and Memories of the Nation*, Oxford: Oxford University Press.
Smith, H. (2015), 'Young, gifted and Greek: Generation G – the world's biggest brain drain', *The Guardian*, 19 January, https://www.theguardian.com/world/2015/jan/19/young-talented-greek-generation-g-worlds-biggest-brain-drain.

Sotiris, P. (2010), 'Rebels with a cause: The December 2008 Greek Youth Movement as the condensation of deeper social and political contradictions', *International Journal of Urban and Regional Research*, 34 (1): 203–9.

Sotiris, P. (2013), 'Reading revolt as deviance: Greek intellectuals and the December 2008 revolt of Greek youth', *Interface: A journal for and about Social Movements*, 5 (2): 47–77.

Spatharakis, K. (2011), 'Η οικογενειακή αλληγορία και η αναζήτηση του πολιτικού', *Levga*, 1: 26–9.

Spivak, G. C. (1998), 'Can the subaltern speak?', in G. Nelson and L. Grossberg (eds), *Marxism and the Interpretation of Culture*, 271–313, Urbana: University of Illinois Press.

Spyropoulou, A., and Th.Tsimpouki, eds (2002), *Σύγχρονη Ελληνική Πεζογραφία: Διεθνείς προσανατολισμοί και διασταυρώσεις*, Athens: Alexandreia.

Stamiris, E. (1986), 'The women's movement in Greece', *New Left Review*, 158: 98–112.

Stamou, E. (2014), *Η επέλαση του ροζ*, Athens: Gutenberg.

Stangos, A. (1991), 'The Greek press: Its function, ownership and relations with the government', in S. Vryonis (ed.), *Greece on the Road to Democracy: From the Junta to PASOK, 1974–1986*, 274–84, New Rochelle, NY: A.D. Caratzas.

Stathi, I. (1999), *Χώρος και Χρόνος στον κινηματογράφο του Θόδωρου Αγγελόπουλου*, Athens: Aigokeros.

Stavrakakis, Y. (2002), 'Religious populism and political culture: The Greek case', *South European Society & Politics*, 7 (3): 29–52.

Stavridi-Patrikiou, R. (1976), *Δημοτικισμός και κοινωνικό πρόβλημα*, Athens: Ermis.

Stefanidis, I. D. (2007), *Stirring the Greek Nation: Political Culture, Irredentism and Anti-Americanism in Post-War Greece, 1945–1967*, Aldershot: Ashgate.

Svoronos, N. G. (1976), *Επισκόπηση της νεοελληνικής ιστορίας*. Athens: Themelio (trans. of Histoire de la Grèce moderne, Paris: Presses Universitaires de France 1953, 1964 2e éd.).

Swingewood, A. (1998), *Cultural Theory and the Problem of Modernity*, London: Macmillan.

Tabaki, A., and O. Polycandrioti, eds (2016), *Ελληνικότητα και ετερότητα: Πολιτισμικές διαμεσολαβήσεις και 'εθνικός χαρακτήρας' στον 19ο αιώνα*, vols 1 and 2, Athens: University of Athens and National Research Institute.

Tachopoulos, Y. (2012), *Θεσσαλονίκη, Μαζάουερ και τα φαντάσματα του Οθωμανισμού*, Athens: Enallaktikes Ekdoseis.

Tamm, M. (2008), 'History as cultural memory: Mnemohistory and the construction of the Estonian nation', *Journal of Baltic Studies*, 39 (4): 499–516.

Tamm, M. (2013), 'Beyond history and memory: New perspectives in memory studies', *History Compass*, 11 (6): 458–73.

Tamm, M., and L. Olivier, eds (2019), *Rethinking Historical Time*, London: Bloomsbury.

Tannen, D. (1983), *Lilika Nakos*, Boston: Twayne.
Theodoropoulos, T., P. Mandravelis, P. Markaris and V. Papavasileiou (2010), *Υπό το μηδέν: Τέσσερα σχόλια για την κρίση*, Athens: Okeanida.
Theodossopoulos, D., ed. (2007), *When Greeks Think About Turks: The View from Anthropology*, London: Routledge.
Theodossopoulou, M. (2003), 'Της ποιήσεως', *I Epochi*, 9 February.
Theotokas, N. (2002a), 'Η αριστερά απέναντι στην ιστορία της', *I Avgi*, 10 March.
Theotokas, N. (2002b), 'Μεταμοντερνισμός και Ιστοριογραφία: περί αλήθειας και αληθειών στην ιστορία', *O Politis*, 106: 24–35.
Theotokas, N. (2003), 'Ο εκλεκτικισμός ως "θεωρία"', *O Politis*, 108: 21–5.
Thompson, G. (1971), 'The continuity of Hellenism', *Greece and Rome*, 18 (1): 18–29.
Todorova, M. (1997), *Imagining the Balkans*, Oxford: Oxford University Press.
Tonnet, H. (1993), *Histoire du grec moderne: la formation d'une langue*, Paris: L'Asiathèque.
Topali, M. (2005), 'Οι δύο όψεις μιας δημοφιλούς ποίησης', *Poiese*, 26: 246–9.
Traverso, Enzo (2017), *Left-Wing Melancholia: Marxism, History, and Memory*, New York: Columbia University Press.
Trianadafyllidou, A. (2014), 'European influences in Greece's migration policies: Between "hard" impact and "soft" influence', in K. Featherstone (ed.), *Europe in Modern Greek History*, 116–34, London: Hurst.
Triandafyllidou A., and M. Maroufof (2008), *Immigration towards Greece at the Eve of the 21st Century: A Critical Assessment*, Athens: ELIAMEP, http://www.eliamep.gr/wp-content/uploads/en/2009/02/immigration-towards-greece-at-the-eve-of-the-21st-century-a-critical-assessment.pdf.
Triandafyllidou, A., and R. Gropas (2009), 'Constructing difference: The mosque debates in Greece', *Journal of Ethnic and Migration Studies*, 35 (6): 957–75.
Triandafyllidou, A., R. Gropas and H.Kouki, eds (2013), *The Greek Crisis and European Modernity*, Basingstoke: Palgrave Macmillan.
Trpeski, D. (2013), 'Nationalism and the use of cultural heritage: A few post-socialist Macedonian examples', in V. C. De Munck and L. Risteski (eds), *Macedonia: The Political, Social, Economic and Cultural Foundations of a Balkan State*, 89–108, London: I.B. Tauris.
Tsakalotos, E. (2008), 'Modernization and centre-left dilemmas in Greece: The revenge of the underdogs', GreeSE Paper no. 13, Hellenic Observatory Papers on Greece and Southeast Europe, http://eprints.lse.ac.uk/5567/1/GreeSE_No13.pdf.
Tsambrounis, D., ed. (2008), *Η ιστορία του λεσβιακού-γκέι-αμφί και τρανς κινήματος στην Ελλάδα: μια πρώτη αποτίμηση*, Athens: Futura and Athens Pride.
Tseronis, A., and A. Iordanidou (2009), 'Modern Greek dictionaries and the ideology of standardization', in A. Georgakopoulou and M. Silk (eds), *Standard Languages and Language Standards: Greek, Past and Present*, 167–85, Farnham: Ashgate.

Tsibiridou, F., and N. Palantzas, eds (2013), *Myths of the Other in the Balkans: Representations, Social Practices, Performances*, Thessaloniki (eBook ISBN978-960-8096-05-9).

Tsimas, P. (2014), *Ο φερετζές και το πηλήκιο: Το πολιτικό μυθιστόρημα της ελληνικής τηλεόρασης*, Athens: Metaihmio.

Tsitselikis, K. (2006), 'Citizenship in Greece: Present challenges for future change', in D. Kalekin-Fishman and P. Pitkänen (eds), *Multiple Citizenship as a Challenge to European Nation-States*, 145–70, Rotterdam: Sense.

Tsoukalas, K. (1977), *Εξάρτηση και Αναπαραγωγή: Ο κοινωνικός ρόλος των εκπαιδευτικών μηχανισμών στην Ελλάδα (1830–1922)*, Athens: Themelio.

Tsoukalas, K. (1983), 'Παράδοση και Εκσυχρονισμός: Μερικά γενικότερα ερωτήματα', in D. G. Tsaousis (ed.), *Ελληνισμός-Ελληνικότητα: Ιδεολογικοί και βιωματικοί άξονες της νεοελληνικής κοινωνίας*, 37–48, Athens: Estia.

Tziovas, D., ed. (1997), *Greek Modernism and Beyond*, Lanham, MD: Rowman & Littlefield.

Tziovas, D. (2001), 'Beyond the Acropolis: Rethinking neohellenism', *Journal of Modern Greek Studies*, 19 (2): 189–220.

Tziovas, D., ed. (2003a), *Greece and the Balkans: Identities, Perceptions and Cultural Encounters since the Enlightenment*, Aldershot: Ashgate.

Tziovas, D. (2003b), *The Other Self: Selfhood and Society in Modern Greek Fiction* Lanham, MD: Lexington Books.

Tziovas, D. (2004), 'Centrifugal topographies, cultural allegories and metafictional strategies in Greek fiction since 1974', in P. Mackridge and E. Yannakakis (eds), *Contemporary Greek Fiction in a United Europe: From Local History to the Global Individual*, 24–49, Oxford: Legenda.

Tziovas, D. (2008), 'Reconfiguring the past: Antiquity and Greekness', in D. Damaskos and D. Plantzos (eds), *A Singular Antiquity: Archaeology and Hellenic Identity in Twentieth-Century Greece*, 278–98, Athens: Benaki Museum.

Tziovas, D., ed. (2009), *Greek Diaspora and Migration since 1700: Society, Politics and Culture*, Farnham: Ashgate.

Tziovas, D. (2011), *Ο μύθος της Γενιάς του Τριάντα: νεοτερικότητα, ελληνικότητα και πολιτισμική ιδεολογία*, Athens: Polis.

Tziovas, D., ed. (2014a), *Re-imagining the Past: Antiquity and Modern Greek Culture*, Oxford: Oxford University Press.

Tziovas, D. (2014b), 'The wound of history: Ritsos and the reception of Philoctetes', in D. Tziovas (ed.), *Re-imagining the Past: Greek Antiquity and Modern Greek Culture*, 297–317, Oxford: Oxford University Press.

Tziovas, D. (2014c), 'Παράδοση ή Κανόνας;', in *Κουλτούρα και λογοτεχνία: Πολιτισμικές διαθλάσεις και χρονότοποι ιδεών*, 201–15, Athens: Polis.

Tziovas, D. (2017), 'Narratives of the Greek crisis and the politics of the past', in D. Tziovas (ed.), *Greece in Crisis: The Cultural Politics of Austerity*, 19–64, London: I.B. Tauris.

Tziovas, D. (2018), 'Between propaganda and modernism: The Anglo-Greek review and the rediscovery of Greece', in P. Mackridge and D. Ricks (eds), *The British Council and Anglo-Greek Literary Interactions 1945-1955*, 123-54, London: Routledge.

Tzogopoulos, G. (2013), *The Greek Crisis in the Media: Stereotyping in the International Press*, Farnham: Ashgate.

Vaiou, D., and A. Psara, eds (2018), *Εννοιολογήσεις και πρακτικές του φεμινισμού: Μεταπολίτευση και "μετά"*, Athens: Idryma tis Voulis ton Ellinon.

Valaoritis, N., and Th. Maskaleris (2003), *An Anthology of Modern Greek Poetry*, Jersey City: Talisman House.

Valoukos, S. (1998), *Η Ελληνική Τηλεόραση (1967-1998)*, Athens: Aigokeros.

Valoukos, S. (2018), *Ιστορία της Ελληνικής Τηλεόρασης (1960-2-18)*, Athens: Aigokeros/ Etaireia Ellinon Skinotheton.

Valtinos, Th. (1995/2009), 'Πέρα από την πραγματικότητα', in Th. Valtinos (ed.), *Κρασί και Νύφες*, 151-63, Athens: Estia.

Vamvakas, V. (2014), 'Αλλαγή. Ατομικισμός και καταναλωτική κουλτούρα', in V. Vamvakas (ed.), *Ο λόγος της κρίσης: Πόλωση, βία, αναστοχασμός στην πολιτική και δημοφιλή κουλτούρα*, 255-66, Thessaloniki: Epikentro.

Vamvakas, V. (2018), 'Η ύστερη μεταπολίτευση με τη ματιά των τηλεθεατών στις ελληνικές σειρές', in V. Vamvakas and G. Paschalidis (eds), *50 Χρόνια Ελληνική Τηλεόραση*, 213-31, Thessaloniki: Epikentro.

Vamvakas, V., and P. Panagiotopoulos, eds (2014), *Η Ελλάδα στη Δεκαετία του '80: Κοινωνικό, πολιτικό και πολιτισμικό λεξικό*, Athens: Epikentro.

Vamvakas, V., and A. Gazi, eds (2017), *Αμερικανικές σειρές στην ελληνική τηλεόραση. Δημοφιλής κουλτούρα και ψυχοκοινωνική δυναμική*, Athens: Papazisis.

Van Boeschoten, R. (2000), 'The impossible return: Coping with separation and the reconstruction of memory in the wake of the Civil War', in M. Mazower (ed.), *After the War Was Over: Reconstructing the Family, Nation and State in Greece, 1943-1960*, 122-41, Princeton, NJ: Princeton University Press.

Van Dyck, K. (1998), *Kassandra and the Censors: Greek Poetry since 1967*, Ithaca, NY: Cornell University Press.

Van Dyck, K., ed. (2016), *Austerity Measures: The New Greek Poetry*, London: Penguin.

Varika, E. (1987), *Η εξέγερση των κυριών. Η γένεση μιας φεμινιστικής συνείδησης στην Ελλάδα (1833-1907)*, Athens: Emboriki Trapeza tis Ellados.

Varika, E. (1989), 'Les "longues robes de l'esclavage": stratégies privées et publiques dans le journal d'une recluse', *Les Cahiers du CEDREF*, 1: 123-33.

Varika, E., and K. Sklaveniti (1981), *Η εξέγερση αρχίζει από παλιά: Σελίδες από τα πρώτα βήματα του γυναικείου κινήματος, Εκδοτική ομάδα γυναικών*, Athens: Gnosi.

Varon-Vassard, O. (2008), 'Η γενοκτονία των Ελλήνων Εβραίων (1943-1944) και η αποτύπωση της: μαρτυρίες, λογοτεχνία και ιστοριογραφία', in G. Antoniou and

N. Marantzidis (eds), *Η Εποχή της Σύγχυσης: η δεκαετία του '40 και η ιστοριογραφία*, 289–343, Athens: Estia.

Varon-Vassard, O. (2013), *Η ανάδυση μιας δύσκολης μνήμης: κείμενα για τη γενοκτονία των Εβραίων*, Athens: Estia.

Varon-Vassard, O. (2019), 'The emergence and construction of the memory of the Shoah in Greece (1945–2015): From oblivion to memory', *Historein* 18 (1), https://doi.org/10.12681/historein.14399.

Varoufakis, Y. (2011a), *The Global Minotaur: America, the True Origins of the Financial Crisis and the Future of the World Economy*, London: Zed Books.

Varoufakis, Y. (2011b), *Κρίσης Λεξιλόγιο*, Athens: Potamos.

Varoufakis, Y. (2013), 'We are all Greeks now! The crisis in Greece in its European and global context', in A. Triandafyllidou, R. Gropas and H. Kouki (eds), *The Greek Crisis and European Modernity*, 44–58, New York: Palgrave.

Vasilopoulou, S. (2013), 'Continuity and change in the study of Euroscepticism: Plus ça change?', *Journal of Common Market Studies*, 51 (1): 153–68.

Vayenas, N., ed. (1991), *Νεοελληνικά Μετρικά*, Herakleio: Panepistimiakes Ekdoseis Kritis.

Vayenas, N. (1997), 'Hellenocentrism and the literary generation of the thirties', in D. Tziovas (ed.), *Greek Modernism and Beyond*, 43–8, Lanham, MD: Rowman & Littlefield.

Vayenas, N. (1999), 'Η λογοτεχνική αντίσταση στη δημοτική', *To Vima*, 31 January.

Vayenas, N. (2001), 'Η επαναμάγευση του ποιητικού λόγου', *To Vima*, 11 March.

Vayenas, N. (2005), 'Οι περιπέτειες της ελληνικής συνείδησης', *To Vima*, 23 January.

Vayenas, N. (2013), *Σημειώσεις από την αρχή του αιώνα*, Athens: Polis.

Vayenas, N., T. Kagialis and M. Pieris (1997), *Μοντερνισμός και ελληνικότητα*, Herakleio: Panepistimiakes Ekdoseis Kritis.

Veloudis, Y. (1992), *Ψηφίδες: Για μια θεωρία της λογοτεχνίας*, Athens: Gnosi.

Venturas, L. (2009), '"Deterritorializing" the nation: The Greek state and "ecumenical Hellenism"', in D. Tziovas (ed.), *Greek Diaspora and Migration since 1700: Society, Politics and Culture*, 125–40, Farnham: Ashgate.

Veremis, Th. (2011), 'Όταν η κατακερματισμένη κοινωνία συναντά τον λαϊκισμό', 9 December, http://www.protagon.gr/?i=protagon.el.article&id=10772.

Vernardakis, Ch. (2011), *Πολιτικά κόμματα, εκλογές και κομματικό σύστημα: Οι μετασχηματισμοί της πολιτικής αντιπροσώπευσης 1990–2010*, Athens: Sakkoulas.

Verney, S. (1993), 'From the "special relationship" to Europeanism: PASOK and the European Community 1981–89', in R. Clogg (ed.), *Greece 1981–89: The Populist Decade*, 131–53, Basingstoke: Macmillan.

Verney, S. (2015), 'Waking the "sleeping giant" or expressing domestic dissent? Mainstreaming Euroscepticism in crisis-stricken Greece', *International Political Science Review*, 36 (3): 279–95.

Verney, S., and S. Michalaki (2014), 'Greece', in N. Conti (ed.), *Party Attitudes towards the EU in the Member States: Parties for Europe, Parties against Europe*, 133–57, New York: Routledge.

Vervenioti, T. (2002), 'Προφορική ιστορία και έρευνα για τον ελληνικό εμφύλιο: η πολιτική συγκυρία, ο ερευνητής και ο αφηγητής', *Epitheorisi Koinonikon Erevnon*, 107: 157–81.

Vervenioti, T. (2008), 'Γραφές γυναικών για τον ελληνικό εμφύλιο: Οι συλλογικές μνήμες και η αμνησία', in G. Antoniou and N. Marantzidis (eds), *Η Εποχή της Σύγχυσης: η δεκαετία του '40 και η ιστοριογραφία*, 345–83, Athens: Estia.

Vidos, K. (2014), '45 χρόνια ελληνική τηλεόραση: τα σίριαλ της ζωής μας', *To Vima (tv+celebrities)*, 28 December.

Vlasidis, V., and S. Karekla (2018), 'Η εκκλησία στην TV: Θρησκευτικές εκπομπές και εκκλησιαστικά δίκτυα στην ελληνική τηλεόραση', in V. Vamvakas and G. Paschalidis (eds), *50 Χρόνια Ελληνική Τηλεόραση*, 319–33, Thessaloniki: Epikentro.

Vlastaris, Y. (2018), *Λεξικό χωρίς γραβάτα*, Athens: Armos.

Voglis, P. (2008), 'Οι μνήμες της δεκαετίας του 1940 ως αντικείμενο ιστορικής ανάλυσης: μεθοδολογικές προτάσεις', in R. van Boeschoten, T. Vervenioti, E. Voutira, V. Dalkavoukis and K. Bada (eds), *Μνήμες και Λήθη του Ελληνικού Εμφυλίου Πολέμου*, 61–80, Thessaloniki: Epikentro.

Voglis, P. (2011), 'Να τελειώνουμε με τη μεταπολίτευση', *Avgi tis Kyriakis/Enthemata*, 6 March.

Voglis, P., and I. Nioutsikos (2017), 'The Greek historiography of the 1940s: A Reassessment', *Südosteuropa*, 65 (2): 316–33.

Voulgaris, K. (2017), *Η Μεταμυθοπλασία στη Νεοελληνική Πεζογραφία*, Athens: Vivliorama.

Voulgaris, Y. (2001), *Η Ελλάδα της Μεταπολίτευσης 1974–1990*, Athens: Themelio.

Voulgaris, Y. (2013), *Η Μεταπολιτευτική Ελλάδα 1974–2009*, Athens: Polis.

Voulgaris, Y. (2019), *Ελλάδα: Μια χώρα παραδόξως νεωτερική*, Athens: Polis.

Vouri, S. (2010 [¹1992]), *Εκπαίδευση και εθνικισμός στα Βαλκάνια: Η περίπτωση της βορειοδυτικής Μακεδονίας (1870–1904)*, Athens: Gutenberg.

Voutsaki, S. (2002), 'The "Greekness" of Greek prehistory: An investigation of the debate 1876–1900', *Pharos: Journal of the Netherlands Institute in Athens*, 10: 105–21.

Voutsaki S. (2017), 'The Hellenization of the prehistoric past: The search for Greek identity in the work of Christos Tsountas', in S. Voutsaki and P. Cartledge (eds), *Ancient Monuments and Modern Identities: A Critical History of Archaeology in 19th and 20th Century Greece*, 130–47, London: Routledge.

Vovou, I. (2010), 'Στοιχεία για μια μετα-ιστορία της ελληνικής τηλεόρασης: Το μέσο, η πολιτική και ο θεσμός', in I. Vovou (ed.), *Ο κόσμος της τηλεόρασης: Θεωρητικές προσεγγίσεις, ανάλυση προγραμμάτων και ελληνική πραγματικότητα*, 93–140, Athens: Irodotos.

White, H. (1978), *Tropics of Discourse: Essays in Cultural Criticism*, Baltimore, MD: Johns Hopkins University Press.

White, H. (1987), *The Content of the Form: Narrative Discourse and Historical Representation*, Baltimore, MD: Johns Hopkins University Press.

Willert, T. S. (2019a), *The New Ottoman Greece in History and Fiction*, New York: Palgrave Macmillan.

Willert, T. S. (2019b), 'Getting intimate with the unwanted past: New approaches to the Ottoman legacy in Greek Fiction', in T. S. Willert and G. Katsan (eds), *Retelling the Past in Contemporary Greek Literature, Film, and Popular Culture*, 13–27, Lanham, MD: Lexington.

Willert, T. S. and G.Katsan, eds (2019), *Retelling the Past in Contemporary Greek Literature, Film, and Popular Culture*, Lanham, MD: Lexington.

Williams, R. (1989), *Resources of Hope: Culture, Democracy, Socialism*, London: Verso.

Winkler, M. M. (2009), *Cinema and the Classical Texts*, Cambridge: Cambridge University Press.

Woodhouse, C. M. (1969), *The Philhellenes*, London: Hodder & Stoughton.

Woods, G. (1992), 'The internal exile of Yannis Ritsos', *European Gay Review*, 8–9: 88–98.

Woods, G. (1998), *A History of Gay Literature: The Male Tradition*, New Haven, CT: Yale University Press.

Xenakis, S. (2013), 'Normative hybridity in contemporary Greece: Beyond "modernizers" and "underdogs" in socio-political discourse and practice', *Journal of Modern Greek Studies*, 31 (2): 171–92.

Xydakis, N. G. (2001), 'Οι μηχανές μιλούν πολλά ελληνικά', *I Kathimerini*, 14 January.

Xydakis, N. G. (2014), 'Πόσο Ευρωπαίοι είναι οι Έλληνες;', *I Kathimerini*, 9 February.

Yannakopoulos, K. (2010), 'Cultural meanings of loneliness: Kinship, sexuality and (homo)sexual identity in contemporary Greece', *Journal of Mediterranean Studies*, 18 (2): 265–82.

Yannakopoulos, K. (2016), '"Naked piazza": Male (homo)sexualities, masculinities and consumer cultures in Greece since the 1960s', in K. Kornetis, E. Kotsovili and N. Papadogiannis (eds), *Consumption and Gender in Southern Europe since the long 1960s*, 173–89, London: Bloomsbury.

Yannaras, Ch. (1997), *Πολιτισμός, το κεντρικό πρόβλημα της πολιτικής*, Athens: Indiktos.

Yannaras, Ch. (2006), *Orthodoxy and the West*, trans. P. Chamberas and N. Russell, Brookline, MA: Holly Cross Orthodox Press (original Greek *Ορθοδοξία και Δύση στη νεώτερη Ελλάδα*, 1992).

Yannaras, Ch. (2014), *Finis Graeciae*, Thessaloniki: Ianos.

Yannopoulou, E., and Th. Tramboulis (2012–13), 'Οι συγγραφείς ως οργανικοί διανοούμενοι: από την ηθογραφία στην ηθικολογία', *Unfollow*, 12, 13, 14 (December–April).

Zacharia, K., ed. (2008), *Hellenisms: Culture, Identity, and Ethnicity from Antiquity to Modernity*, Aldershot: Ashgate.

Zachariadis, N. (1953), *Συλλογή Έργων*, Publication of the Central Committee of KKE.

Zaharopoulos, Th. (2002), 'Perceived foreign influence and television viewing in Greece', in M. G. Elasmar (ed.), *The Impact of International Television: A Paradigm Shift*, 39–56, London: Routledge.

Zenakos, A., and H. Natsis (2017), 'Ιδεολογική ηγεμονία της Αριστεράς', *I Avgi*, 15–16 April, http://www.avgi.gr/article/10808/8074246/-ideologike-egemonia-tes-aristeras-.

Zestanakis, P. (2016), 'Revisiting the Greek 1980s through the prism of the crisis', in K. Kornetis, Ei. Kotsovili and N. Papadogiannis (eds), *Consumption and Gender in Southern Europe since the Long 1960s*, 257–74, London: Bloomsbury.

Zizioulas, J. D. (1985a), 'Ευρωπαϊκό πνεύμα και ελληνική Ορθοδοξία', *Efthyni*, 163 and 167: 329–33, 569–73.

Zizioulas, J. D. (1985b), *Being as Communion: Studies in Personhood and the Church*, Crestwood, NY: St Vladimir's Seminary Press.

Zorba, M. (2014), *Πολιτική του Πολιτισμού: Ευρώπη και Ελλάδα στο δεύτερο μισό του 20^{ου} αιώνα*, Athens: Patakis.

Zoumboulakis, S. (2013), 'The Orthodox Church in Greece today', in A. Triandafyllidou, R. Gropas and H. Kouki (eds), *The Greek Crisis and European Modernity*, 132–51, Basingstoke: Palgrave Macmillan.

Index

Acropolis 41, 73 n.5, 237
Adorno, Theodor W. 171
Aeschylus (*Oresteia*) 182
aesthetic populism 32, 36
aestheticism 32
Aggestam, Lisbeth 46
Agouridis, Savvas 56
AIDS 224
Aitaki, Georgia 165 n.4, 172, 175
Ai Weiwei 241, n.12
Almodóvar, Pedro 226
Aleksić, Tatiana 194
Alexakis, Orestis 147
Alexakis, Vasilis 153
Alexandrou, Aris 85, 86, 87, 149, 151
Alexiou, Margaret 235
Aliferis, Anastasios 228
Alivizatos, N. C. 2 n.2, 24 n.13, 59 n.16, 93, 112, 162
Allardt, Erik 12
Althusserian Marxism, 164
Amanatidis, Vasilis 145
Ambatzopoulou, Fragkiski 107
American way of life 32, 45n.4
Anagnostakis, Manolis 147, 154, 201
Anagnostopoulos, Aris 69 n.2,
Anagnostopoulos, V. D. 147 n.5
Anastasakis, Othon 102 n.9
Anastasiadis, Athanasios 87
Ancient/Classical Greece 10, 66, 128, 233–4, 240 n. 9
Anderson, Barry 71
Andreou, Stelios 68
Andriakaina, Eleni 23 n.10
Andronikos, Manolis 68, 69, 72
Androusou, Alexandra 96 n.3
Androutsopoulos, J. K. 133, 138 n.10, 205
Angelidi, Antoinetta 188
Angelopoulos, Theo 39, 179, 180–4, 186–9, 191, 192, 194, 197
Angelou, Alkis 103
Anglo-Saxon academic system 106

Angouri, Jo 140
Antetokounmpo, Giannis 99
Anti 15 n. 12, 33
anti-Americanism 45–7, 64
anti-authoritarian culture 3
anti-clericalism 112
anti-commercialism 180
anti-communism 1, 46, 79, 113, 184–5
Anti-Defamation League (ADL) 108
anti-Europeanism 8, 44
anti-fascism 1
anti-Semitism 107–11
anti-systemic forces 26
anti-Westernism 21, 51–60, 64, 113
Antonioni, Michelangelo 183
Antoniou, Giorgos 76, 79, 80, 80 n. 11, 81 n.14, 107 n.12, 108 n.18
Apostolelli, Anna 206 n.10, 222, 223 n.36
Apostolidis, Renos 157
Apostolidou, Venetia 67, 86
Aquinas, Thomas 54
Archimandritis, Yiorgos 183
Argyriou, Alexandros 143 n.1, 155, 156 n.13
Aristinos, Yorgos 138, 158
Armed Forces Information Services (YENED) 163
Armenakis, Antonis 166 n.6
Arnold, Matthew 30
Asdrachas, Spyros 105
Ashcroft, Bill 23
Asimos, Nicholas 203
Askouni, Nelli 96 n.3
Aslanoglou, Nikos-Alexis 226
Assmann, Jan 83
Asteriou, Christos 153
Astrinakis, Antonis E. 202 n.3
Athanasiadis, Haris 104
Athanasiou, Athena 226
Augustinian scholasticism 54
authoritarianism 26
auto-ethnography 197–8

Avdela, Efi 104, 202, 215, 218
Avgeridis, Manos 2 n.2, 18 n.15, 77 n.7
Avouris, Pavlos 223n. 36
Avranas, Alexandros 193
Avrianismos (Chatzidakis) 35
Axelos, Kostas 156
Axioti, Melpo 155, 157
Axiotis, Diamantis 152

Babiniotis, Georgios 127, 128, 129, 130, 131, 132, 135 n.12, 137
Badiou, Alain, 196, 207
Baerentzen, Lars 79 n.10
Bakopoulou, Eleni 226
Balampanidis, Yannis 61, 206 n.10
Balibar, Étienne 237
Balkanism 49
Baltsiotis, Lambros 94, 109
Bampilis, Tryfon 36
Baran, Paul A. 6
Barotsi, Rosa 196
Batycka, Dorian 244 n.20
Baudrillard, Jean 243, 248
Bauman, Zygmunt 12
Beard, Mary 73
Beaton, Roderick 15 n.15, 18 n.15, 96, 143
Bebel, August 212
Beck, Ulrich 12
Benjamin, Walter 30
Beratis, Yannis 157
Bernal, Josep M. 133
Bernal, Martin 59 n.16
Bhabha, Homi K. 27, 54, 65, 96
Bickes, Hans 175 n.18
Bien, Peter 148 n.8
Billig, Michael 173
binarisms 11, 55, 218
biopolitics 15, 179, 196, 197, 231
Bistikas, Alexis 223n. 36, 224
Bithymitris, Giorgos 62 n.19
Bjelić, Dušan I. 49 n.6
Bloom, Harold 154 n.12
Bo, Billy 224
Bobolou, Lilika 218 n.28
Boltanski, Luc 248
Bonss, Wolfgang 12
Bordwell, David 185
Boulmetis, Tasos 187, 197
Bourdieu, Pierre 39, 125

Boutaris, Yannis 103, 229
brain drain 117, 121–2
Brecht, Bertolt 182
Breillat, Catherine 194
broadcasting deregulation 162–7
Brown, K.S. 69 n.2
Burke, Peter 85
Butler, Judith 218, 226
Byron, Lord 236

Cacoyannis, Michael 179, 226
Calderon, Petro de la Barca 147
Calotychos, Vangelis 22, 49 n.7, 96, 101, 192
Cameron, David 237
Cameron, Deborah 131, 140 n.26,
Canakis, Costas 140 n.26, 229
Cannes Film Festival 181
Capelos, Tereza 63 n.20
Carastathis, Anna 229
Catholicism 52, 59
Castoriadis, Cornelius 156
Cavafy, C.P. 37, 143, 201, 223, 225, 229
Cavallaro, Maria Elena 15
Celik, A. Ipek 195
centralized education systems 103
Centre for Educational Research and Training 126
Centre for the Greek Language 129, 131
Cervantes, Miguel de 51
Chadi, Adrian 60
Chakrabatry, Dipesh 10 n.11, 12
Chalkou, Maria 187, 190, 191, 192, 193
Chambers, J. K. 138 n.20
Charalambidis, Michalis 109
Charalambis, Dimitris 35 n.29
Charitopoulos, Dionysis 80n. 12
Charter of Fundamental Rights 59
Chartoulari, Mikela 152
Chatzidakis, Manos 35, 224–5
Chatzinis, Yannis 155
Checkel, Jeffrey T. 44
Chilcote Ronald H., S. 15
Childe, Gordon 69
Chiotis, Theodoros 148
Charalambous, Kostas 185 n.8
Chomenidis, Christos 204, 241 n. 13
Chourmouzios, Aimilios 155
Christakis, Leonidas 203

Index

Christian Orthodox 28 n.21
Christianopoulos, Dinos 225, 226
Christidis A.F.130, 131, 131 n.9
Christidis, Minas 164
Christopoulos, Dimitris 96 n.3, 98, 99, 100, 110 n.21, 115 n.23, 171 n.16, 214 n.21, 225 n.38
Chrysopoulos, Christos 73 n.5, 153
cinematic allegories
   cinema and television 189–91
   national culture 185–9
   new Greek cinema and political history 181–5
civil partnerships 228
Clark, Larry 209
Clarke, D. E. 234
clientelistic system 24
Clogg, Richard 3, 18 n.15, 96 n.3
Close, David 18 n. 15, 76, 78, 79 n.9, 221
Cohen, Leonard 236
Cold War 6, 11, 13, 46, 49, 52, 58, 64, 77, 84, 98, 118, 109, 159, 195, 249, 251
Cole, Jonathan 54
Collard, Anne 78
colony of debt 27 n.19
Confino, Alon 14, 83, 89, 91
Communist Party (KKE) 1, 47, 66, 77, 79, 80, 82, 104, 127, 154, 166, 211, 217, 223
Communist Party of the Interior 47, 223
Communist Youth (KNE) 45 n.4, 205, 213 n. 17
communitarianism 56
complacent isolationism 145
consumerism 19 n.1, 30–41
consumerist culture 33, 35
Contemporary Greek Cinema 180
Contemporary Social History Archives (ASKI) 80
continuous perennialism 102
cosmopolitanism 51, 61, 151, 152, 187, 250
cosmopolitan memory 108
Costa-Gavras 73 n.5
crypto-colony 13, 49, 251
cultural decentralization 26
cultural dualism 8, 9, 11, 13, 19–30
cultural politics, 15
culture 31
   anti-authoritarian 3
   consumerist 33, 35
   folk 33
   Greek cinematic 181, 191–7
   humanist 31, 35. 40, 249
   individual-centred 22
   national 30, 42, 60, 70, 93, 97, 185–9, 250
   popular 31–36, 38–41, 66, 135, 158, 172–3, 177, 190
   postcolonial 27
   of poverty 144 n.3
   power of television 170–3
   queer 219–31, 251
   reformist 21
   religious divide 51–60
   underdog 23–6, 36, 42
   Western 16, 59
Curthoys, Ann 85

Dacey, Philip 147
Dalakoglou, Dimitris 101
Dalianidis, Yannis 180
Damaskos, Dimitris 235
Danforth, Loring M. 71, 72, 74
D'Angour, Armand 240 n.9
Danopoulos, Constantine P. 5 n.8
Daskalakis, Ilias 219
Daskalov, Roumen 10 n.11
Davvetas, Nikos 89
Davies, Norman 52
Dawkins, Richard 111
De Beauvoir, Simone 217
December events 2008 3, 90, 185, 2006–8
decentralization, cultural 26
Demos, T. J. 247 n. 26
Delanty, Gerard 5
De Lauretis, Teresa 221 n.33
Della Porta, Donatella 200
Demacopoulos, George E. 55
Demertzis, Nicholas 25 n.17, 68 n.1, 80, 166 n.6
Democratic Women's Movement (KDG) 211
demotic (language) 27, 36, 125, 126, 127, 128, 129, 130, 132, 133, 138, 139, 140, 154
demoticism 126
Denissi, Sophia 96 n.3

dependency theory 6–8, 11–2
Dermentzopoulos, Christos A. 188
Derrida, Jacques 24, 84
Dertilis, G. B. 17
Diamandouros, N. P. 20, 21, 22, 29, 30
Diamantopoulou, Anna 135
Diani, Mario 200, 200 n. 1
diaspora 21, 71, 72, 117–122, 133, 155, 166, 181, 189, 250
diglossia 125, 128, 132, 133, 140, 141
Dimaras, Alexis 9, 126
Dimaras, K. Th. 105
Dimitrakaki, Angela 152, 153 n. 11
Dimitras, Panagiotis 107 n.15
Dimitriadis, Dimitris 229
Dimitriou, Sotiris 132
Dimitroulia, Titika 145 n.4, 148 n.8, 150, 158
Dimou, Nikos 9, 53
Dimoula, Kiki 40
Dinas, Elias 108 n.18
diversity 6, 11–5, 17, 18, 23, 30, 35, 41, 42, 50, 56, 69, 71, 89, 93, 94, 96, 97, 114, 125, 132, 136, 140, 145, 148, 150, 151, 154, 155, 160, 162, 249, 251
Dobbin, Murray 236 n.4
Docker, John 85
documenta 14 244–8
Doufexi-Pope, Aliki 37 n.31
Douka, Maro 102, 103, 149, 151, 152, 216
Doukas, Yannis 147
Douzinas, Costas 29, 237 n. 6
dowry system 214
Doxiadis, Aristos 25 n.16
Dragona, Thalia 115
Dragoumis, Ion 56
dualism
  cultural 8, 9, 11, 13, 19–30
  political 21–2
Dubisch, Jill 217 n.27
Duroselle, Jean-Baptiste 51
Durrell, Lawrence 235

Eagleton, Terry 15, 31
Eastern nationalism 57
Echtler, Ilia 175 n.18
Economides, Spyros 8, 44, 45, 206 n.10
ecumenical Hellenism 120
Ecumenical Patriarchate 60 n. 17, 139

EEC/EU 4, 7, 8, 10, 13, 21, 25, 27, 29, 41, 43–5, 49–50, 52–3, 58–64, 69, 74, 100, 106, 115, 119–21, 135–6, 161, 164, 167, 170 n. 170, 172, 177, 203, 215, 228, 230, 249, 251
egalitarianism 21, 93
Eisenstadt, S. N. 12
Eleftheriotis, Dimitris 188 n.10, 196 n. 18
Eleftheriadis, Konstantinos 227
Eleftheriou, Manos 40
Eliot, T. S. 30
Elisaf, Moses 108 n.19
Ellinikos Glossikos Omilos 127
Ellinismos. *see* Hellenism
Ellis, John 173
Elsaesser, Thomas 197
Elytis, Odysseus 56, 127, 143, 158
Embirikos, Leonidas 94
Empeirikos, Andreas 154
Engels, Friedrich 212
English language 106, 135, 189, 250
Engonopoulos, Nikos 154
Enlightenment 51, 57, 60 n. 17, 103, 106, 126, 129
Eudes, Dominique 79
Eurocentrism 23
European Court of Human Rights 112, 115
European identity 13, 52, 53, 59, 62, 248
Europeanization 2, 8, 9, 11, 13, 14, 16, 42–5, 50, 53, 58, 204
euroscepticism 11, 43, 44 n.1, 45–7, 61, 63
  to integration 47–51
Evans, Arthur 69
Eve, Martin 18 n. 15
Exadaktylos, Theofanis 63 n.20
Exertzoglou, Haris 106

Fainaru, Dan 184
Fais, Michel 96 n.3, 152
Fallmerayer, Jakob 49, 70
Faubion, James D. 221
Featherstone, Kevin 43, 44, 45, 49
Federation of Greek Women (OGE) 211
feminism 210–18
  state 212
feminist magazines 214–5
Ferguson, Charles 125, 125 n.1
Ferris, Kostas 171

Filintas, Menos 133
Filippou, Filippos 39
Filis, Nikos 110
Filmmakers in the Mist 192
Finlay, George 93
Fisher, Mark 196
Fleischer, Hagen 79 n.10, 132
Fleming, K. E. 49 n.7, 96 n.3
Flitouris, Lampros 185
Florovsky, George 54
Fokas, Effie 59, 60, 112
Fokianaki, Iliana 245 n.23
folk culture 33
Foreign Language Film Academy Award 194
Foskolos, Nikos 180
Fotiadis, Michael 68
Foucault, Michel 218, 223
Fournaraki, Eleni 215
Fowles, John 236
Frangoudaki, Anna 102 n.9, 126, 128, 129, 135
Frantzi, Andia 217
Fukuyama, Francis 96
Fytili, Magda 81

Gage, Nicholas 84 n.16
Gadamer, Hans-Georg 83
Galanaki, Rhea 143, 151
Gallaher, Brandon 55
Gallant, Thomas W. 9 n.10, 18 n. 15
Ganas, Michalis 40, 147
Garantoudis, Evripidis 40 n.40, 147 n. 6, 148 n. 8, 243
Gatsos, Nikos 40
Gay and Lesbian Community of Greece (OLKE) 227
gay pride 229
Gazi, Efi 2 n.2, 18 n.15, 106, 171
Gellner, Ernest 21, 71
General Secretariat for Equality 214
General Secretariat for Greeks Abroad 118
General Secretariat for Youth 202
Generation of the 1930s 54 n.11, 132, 155, 157, 187, 251
genocides 107–11
Geoffroy, Thierry 245
Georgakopoulou, Alexandra 176
Georgiadis, Vassilis 171, 180

Georgousopoulos, Kostas 40 n.39
German legal system 24
Germanacos, N. C. 143 n. 1
Gerstenblith, Patty 74
Ghosh, Palash 62 n.18
Giannaris, Konstantinos 191, 192, 209
Giannaris, Yorgos 202
Giannopoulou, Efi 39
Giaxoglou, Korina 176
Gibbon, Edward 247
Giddens, Anthony 12
Gkoritsas Sotiris 39
global capitalism 196
global Hellenism 120
globalization 2, 4, 32, 50, 63, 74, 97, 104, 105, 114, 133, 136, 150, 161–2, 170, 249, 251
Godard, Jean-Luc 237
Gogou, Katerina 203
Golden Dawn, 61, 104, 108, 208 n.13, 216 n.25, 227
Goldsworthy, Vesna 49 n.6
Gondikakis, Vassileios 57
González-Vaquerizo, Helena 75
Gorner, Paul 83
Gourgouris, Stathis 10, 49 n. 7
Gourogiannis, Vasilis 73n.5, 151
Goutsos, Dionysis 132 n. 10, 140
Grammatikas, Dimitris 122
Greek Church 28, 59, 104, 108, 115–6, 139, 167 n7
Greek cinematic culture 191–7
Greek Civil War 26 n. 18, 71, 76–90, 95, 99, 112, 117, 159, 179 n.1, 181, 183–6, 206, 251
Greek collaborationist Security Battalions 4 n.7
Greek crisis 4, 5, 21 n. 6, 140, 148, 173, 175, 176, 236, 238, 242, 244, 248
Greek Cypriot literature 155
Greek ethos 29
Greek exceptionalism 4, 74, 105
Greek Film Centre 27, 190, 194, 198
Greek Homosexual Community (EOK) 224
Greek identity 135, 157, 159, 170–3, 177, 186, 250
Greek kitsch 33
Greek law on proselytism 112

Greeklish 133–4
Greek National Tourist Organization 74
Greek new wave cinema 193, 194
Greek neo-orientalism 20 n.4
Greek postmodernism 157, 159
Greek press 168–170
Greek Radio and Television (ERT) 3, 163–64, 171, 174, 191
Greek school system 99
Greek Semiotic Society 156
Greek-Turkish Friendship Committee 102
Greer, Germaine 217
Grigoriadis, Ioannis N. 95, 102 n.9
Grigoriadis, Theodoros 17, n 14, 151
Grigoropoulos, Alexis 90, 206, 208
Gropas, Ruby 114, 118
Guha, Ranajit 23 n.11
Guattari, Félix 223
Guth, James L. 52

Habermas, Jürgen 111
Hadjikyriakos-Ghikas, Nikos 127
Hadjikyriacou, Achilleas 220
Halbwachs, Maurice 83
Halkia(s), Alexandra 206 n.10, 213 n. 18, 215, 222, 223n. 36
Hall, Stuart 251
Hallin, Daniel C. 161, 168 n.10
Halo, Thea 110
Halperin, David 218
Hamilakis, Yannis 69, 69 n.2, 234
Handler, Richard 74
Hanink, Johanna 74, 237
Hansen, Søren 202
Harcourt, Alison 161
Haris, Yannis H. 132 n.10, 135 n.12
Harmbis, Aimilios 194 n.16
Harvey, David 5
Hatsios, Yorgos 130
Hatzidaki, Ourania 140
Hatziiosif, Christos 84 n. 15, 106
Hatziprokopiou, Panos 122
Hatzis, Dimitris 33 n. 26, 66, 67, 149
Hatzivasileiou, Vangelis 16, 39, 84, 89 n.17, 148 n.8, 149, 153, 158
Hatzopoulos, Nikos 147
Hatzopoulos, Takis 171
Hebdige, Dick 35
Heidegger, Martin 54
Heilbronner, Oded 201
Heimonas, Yorgos 127
Hellenic Film Academy 192
Hellenic image 20. *see* Romeic self-image
Hellenism 22 n.7, 27 n. 20, 55, 56, 65, 67, 69, 70, 75–6, 113, 118, 121 n. 33, 187, 235, 251
 ecumenical 120
 ethnocentrism 57
 global 120
Heraclides, Alexis 102
heritage films 187
Herzfeld, Michael 20, 49 n7, 199
Herzog, Dagmar 219 n. 30
Hirsch, Marianne 89
Hirschon, Renée 10, 22 n.9, 136
Hislop, Victoria 172
history teaching 102–4
Hjort, Mette 189
Hobsbawm, Eric 201
Hocquenghem, Guy 222
Hodgkin, Katharine 84, 86
Hokwerda, Hero 69 n.2
Holocaust 89, 107, 108, 111
Holton, David 125, 130
Homer, Sean 186
homoeroticism 225, 226
Hooghe, Liesbet 50
Hope, Kerin 122, n. 34
Horrocks, Geoffrey 130
Horton, Andrew 180 n.2, 182 n.3, 187
Houkli, Maria 139 n.25
Houzouri, Elena 152
Howard, Marc Morjé 99
humanism 30–41
humanist culture 31, 35, 40, 249
Huntington, Samuel P. 58, 59, 123
Hutcheon, Linda 158
hybridization/hybridity 12, 17, 20, 22, 27, 29, 39, 40, 140, 153

Iatrides, John O. 5, 79 n.10
identity cards 28, 60, 115
identity politics 15, 31, 50, 179, 199, 221, 249, 251
Iliou, Filippos 105
Iliou, Maria 103
individual-centred culture 22
individualism 2, 6 n.9, 31, 55, 57
 Western 53, 56

institutional reforms 41, 64
intercultural education 119
International Film Critics Award
  (FIPRESCI) 181
intra-European Orientalism 13
inverted syncretism 26 n.17
Ioakimidis, Panagiotis C. 5 n.8, 25 n.14,
  43, 50
Ioannidis, Panayotis 148 n. 9
Ioannou, Yorgos 225, 226
Iollas, Alexandros 224
Iordanidou, Anna 130 n.7, 138 n.20
Iordanova, Dina 189
Islamic fundamentalism 114
Islamic (Sharia) law 114

Jameson, Fredric 14, 185, 201
Janscó, Miklós 183
Jauss, David 147
Jeffreys Michael 72
Jenkins, Tiffany 73
Jensen, Jasper 202
Johnston, Hank 207 n.11
Jordheim, Helge 16
Judt, Tony 46 n.5, 47
Juko, Sonja 175 n.18
Junker, Jean-Claude 62
Jusdanis, Gregory 10, 156

Kachtitsis, Nikos 157
Kafetzopoulos, Antonis 190
Kahane, Leon 245 n.22
Kalaitzidis, Pantelis 54 n.11 and 12, 55,
  57, 117
Kalas, Nicolas 157
Kaliarda (Petropoulos) 222
Kallinis, Yiorgos 157
Kallivretakis, Leonidas 1 n.1
Kaliorais, Yannis 132
Kaloglopoulou-Bogiatzoglou, Nelli 226
Kalokyris, Dimitris 138
Kalpadakis, George 44 n2
Kalpouzos, Yannis 102-3
Kaltezas, Michalis 206 n. 9
Kalyvas, Andreas 206, 207 n12
Kalyvas, Stathis 3, 18 n15, 24, 58 n. 15,
  81-2, 207 11n
Kambris, Antonis 127 n.5
Kaminis, Yorgos 244

Kanarakis, George 120
Kanelli, Liana 139 n.25
Kanellis, Ilias 241 n.13
Kanellopoulos, Takis 179
Kantsa, Venetia 140 n.26, 223 n.36,
  226, 228
Kaplan, Rober D. 52, 58, 64, 235 n.2
Kaplani, Gazmend 99
Kapodistrias, Ioannis 21
Kapsalis, Dionysis 147
Karabelias, Yorgos 26, 56
Karagatsis, M. 157, 171, 180
Karagiorgas, Sakis 53 n.10
Karagiozis 186
Karakasidou Anastasia N. 70 n.3
Karalis, Vrasidas 32 n.25, 184, 194
Karamanlis, Konstantinos 46, 113, 163
  n.2, 223
Karamanolakis, Vangelis 80, 202 n.3,
Karamanou, Anna 212
Karamouzi, Eirini 46
Karantzola, Eleni 132
Karavidas, Konstantinos 56
Karavidas, Kostas 33 n.26
Karekla, Sofia 167 n.7
Kargiotis, Dimitris 243
Karnezis, Panos 153 n.11
Karthaios, Kostas 133
Kassaveti, Ursula-Helen 190
Kassimeris, George 3
Kassis, K. D. 38
Kassos, Vangelis 147 n.5
Kastrinaki, Angela 76, 202 n.4
katharevousa 125, 126 n.3, 127, 128, 129,
  133, 138, 140, 154
Katsan, Gerasimus 69 n.2, 204
Katsapis, Kostas 202 n.3
Katsounaki, Maria 246
Katzenstein, Peter J. 44
Katzourakis, Kyriakos 191
Kazantzakis, Nikos 158, 171, 180
Kazazis, I. N. 131
Kechriotis, Vangelis 104
Kefalas, Ilias 147 n. 5
Keitel, Harvey 189
Kelaidonis, Loukianos 200 n.2
Kemal, Mustafa (Attatürk) 109
Kessareas, Efstathios 6 n.9, 56
Keyder, Caglar 102

Kitis, E. Dimitris 203, 203 n.8
Kitromilides, Paschalis M. 9, 52, 94, 97 n.5
Kitsikis, Dimitris 26
Klik (Click) 35
Kokkinos, Ana 189
Kokonis, Michalis 190 n.12
Koliopoulos, John S. 18 n.15, 21, 24 n.15
Kolliakou, Dimitra 153 n.11
Kolocotroni, Vasiliki 229
Kolokotronis, Theodoros 29 n.23
Kolovos, Yannis 203
Komnenos, Alexios 152
Komninou, Maria 190
Kondylis, Panagiotis 9, 40 n.37
Konstantas, Grigorios 155
Kontochristou, Maria 166 n.6, 169 n.12
Kontogianni, Vassiliki 217
Kontogiorgis, Yorgos 26
Kopidakis, M. Z. 130
Korais, Adamantios 20, 29 n.23, 44, 51
Korma, Lena 120 n.29
Kornetis, Kostis 2 n.2, 15, 18 n.15, 26 n.18, 90, 185 n.8, 200, 201, 202 n. 3
Koronaiou, Alexandra 208 n.13
Korras, Yorgos 191
Kotsias, Tilemachos 152
Koropoulis, Yorgos 147
Korovesis, Periklis 149
Koselleck, Reinhart 5, 16
Koskotas, George, 168 n. 9
Kosmidis, Spyros 108 n.18
Kostavara, Angeliki 145
Kostis, Kostas 18 15n, 25 15n
Kotsakis, Kostas 68, 69
Kotzia, Elisavet 38, 144, 145, 149, 150, 158 n.15
Kotzias, Alexandros 36–7, 85, 87, 88
Kouanis, Panos 190 n. 12
Kouki, Hara 3, 201
Koulouri, Christina 102
Koun, Karolos 226
Koumandareas, Menis 220 n.3, 226
Koundouros, Nikos 179
Kourelou, Olga 189, 197, 238
Kourtovik, Dimosthenis 145, 152
Koutras, Panos 192, 193, 209, 226, 227
Koutroumbousis, Panos 45
Koutsikou, Daphne 33, 34

Koutsogiannis, Dimitris 133
Koutsou, Dimitra 138 n.19
Koutsourakis, Angelos 183 n.4
Koutsourelis, Kostas 40, 145, 147
Kouzeli, Lambrini 243 n.15
Kranaki, Mimika 153
Krapf, Matthias 60
Kremmydas, Vasilis 106
Kriaras, Emmanouil 127 n.5, 128, 130, 130 n.7
Kriesi, Hanspeter 50
Kritiotis, Stavros 152 n. 11
Kristeva, Julia 59
Küçük, Ferhat 109 n.20
Kulick, Don 140 n.26
Kyriakos, Konstantinos 229
Kyriazis, Nota 211

Labrianidis, Lois 122
Lacanian psychoanalysis 164
Lagios, Ilias 147
Laikos Orthodoxos Synagermos (LAOS) 44, 114, 166
Lambrinidis, Christiana 226
Lambrinos, Fotos 185, 190
Lambrinou, Katerina 205
Lambropoulos, Vassilis 96 n.3, 148, 157, 247 n.28
Lange, Ersi 215 n.26
language of Skopje 137
language politics 132–40
language question 1, 36, 125, 126, 128, 129,132, 133, 136, 140, 154, 250
language reform of 1976 27, 126
Lanthimos, Yorgos 180, 191n. 14, 192, 193, 195, 196, 197, 209
Latinization 127, 133, 139, 250
Lavdas, Kostas 43
Lawson J. C. 235
Layoun, Mary N. 156
Lazopoulos, Lakis 190
Lazos, C. D. 202
Leavis, F. R. 30
Leconte, Cécile 44 n.1
Le Goff, Jacques 103
Leigh Fermor, Patrick 20
Leivaditis, Tasos 40
Lemos, Natasha 96 n.3
Létoublon, Françoise 184 n.6

Index

Liakos, Antonis 2, 3, 3 n.3, 15, 18 n. 15, 29, 68 n.1, 69, 79–80 n.10, 105, 106, 135 n.12, 202
Lialiouti, Zinovia 45, 62 n.19
Liappa, Frida 188
liberalism 21, 60, 93
Liberation Movement of Homosexual Greece (AKOE) 222
liberation movements 218
Linz, Juan J. 15
Loizos, Peter 210, 217 n. 27
long 1960s 200–1
Lorenz, Chris 16
Lossky, Vladimir 54
Louganis, Greg 99 n.7
Loules, Vassilis 107
Lykidis, Alex 183, 196
Lytra, Vally 102 n.9

Macedonian question 70–4, 136, 249
MacKenzie, Scott 189
Mackridge, Peter 73, 97, 128, 129, 130, 133, 136, 141, 150, 154, 225
MacNally, Terence 227
Madianou, Mirca 166 n.5
Malea, Olga 188
Manaki brothers 187
Mais, Hristos 222, 224, 229
Makrides, Vasilios N.54, 60 n.17
Makryannis 54 n.10
Mancini, Paolo 161, 168 n.10
Manitakis, Antonis 115 n.23
Manthoulis, Roviros 80 n,12, 171
Marangopolous, Aris 139
Marangudakis, Manussos 5 n.8
Marantzidis, Nikos 76, 79, 80, 82
Marcuse, Herbert 202 n. 5, 205
Margaritis, Yorgos 82, 106
Margellou Inglessi, Cecile 40 n.40
Marinucci, Mimi 219 n.29
Maris, Yannis 39
Markaris, Petros 39
Marketaki, Tonia 188
Maronitis, D. N. 128, 131 n.9, 155
Martinidis, Petros 38 n.35
Marwick, Arthur 201
Marx, Karl 202
masculinity 220
Maskaleris, Thanasis 148 n.8

mass media 29, 63, 90, 170
Mastroianni, Marcello 189
materialism 6 n.9, 30, 56
Matessis, Pavlos 226
Matsaganis, Manos 25 n.16
Mavrogordatos, George T. 23 n.12, 26 n.18, 114 n.22
Mavrokordatos, Alexandros 21, 29 n.23
Mazower, Mark 103
media populism 63
Meimaris, Spyros 45
melancholy, left-wing 30, 148
Melucci, Alberto 200
Menegos, Panagiotis 237 n.5
Mercouri, Melina 26, 33, 73, 198
Merdjanova, Ina 57
Mergel, Thomas 12
Merkel, Angela 63
Merrill, James 219
Meselidis, Stilianos 104
Metallinos, Georgios 57, 59
Metapolitefsi 1–20, 40 n.18, 41, 42, 80–81, 100, 143, 145 n. 4, 156, 158, 180, 200 n. 2, 202 n. 4, 204–6, 249–51
Metaxas, Ioannis 66, 98, 162, 182, 183
Metropolitan Chrysanthos 109
Metropolitan of Nafpaktos Hierotheos 57
Michailidis, Michalis 37 n.31
Michailidou Asimina 62 n. 19
Michailidou, Martha 215
Michalaki, Sofia 50
Michalopoulou, Amanda 204
Miles, Steven 19 n.1
Milios, Yannis 53 n.10
Millas, Hercules 96 n.3, 101
Miller Henry 235
Milton, Giles 103
Ministry for Press and Mass Media 165
Mishkova, Diana 49 n.6
Missios, Chronis 38 n.36
Mitralexis, Sotiris 20 n.4, 54 n. 10
Mitsikopoulou, Bessie 133
Mitsopoulos, Michael 5 n.8
Mitsotakis, Konstantinos 172
mnemohistory 65, 83, 87, 90
modernity 8–13, 15, 16, 17, 22, 23, 36, 39, 51, 55–6, 59, 60 n. 17, 65–6, 68,

96, 102, 111, 113, 150, 155, 160, 162, 202, 234
modernization 6–13, 17, 19–30, 41–2, 44–5, 50, 53, 57, 62, 63, 114, 126, 136, 139, 156–7, 162, 249
Modinos, Michalis 153
Monastiriotis, Vassilis 206 n.10
monoculturalism 93, 97
monophonic media 161
monotonic system 27–8, 126–7, 139 n 24, 250
Moreau, Jeanne 189
Morgan, Sue 218
Morton, Stephen 23 n.11
Moschonas, Spiros A. 129
Moses, A. Dirk 107 n.12
Moskov, Costis 8, 26, 53, 56
Moullas, Panagiotis 38
Mouskouri, Nana 224
Moutzan-Martinengou, Elisavet 217
Mouzelis, Nicos 7, 9, 21 n.5
multiculturalism 57, 71, 96, 103, 117, 122–3, 242
My Number One (Paparizou) 75
Mylonaki, Angeliki 209
Mylonas, Yiannis 5, 175, 175 n.17
Myrivilis, Stratis 157, 172

narcissistic consumerism 35
narcissistic individualism 35
Nash, Kate 200
National Book Centre (EKEBI) 14, 38
National Council for Radio and Television (NCRT/ESR), 164, 167, 228
National Foundation of Radio and Television (EIRT) 163
national identity 7, 8, 23, 43, 50, 59, 71–2, 98–9, 105, 111, 115, 123, 128, 136, 158, 173, 250
Nationalism 29, 50, 56–7, 61, 67–9, 71, 72 n.4, 74, 102, 105, 112–4, 123, 137, 166 n.6, 173, 197, 213 n.18, 227
national romanticism 56
Natsis, Hristos 81
Nazism 45, 62 n.19
Negrepontis, Yannis 127
Neils, Jennifer 73
Nellas, Panagiotis 53
Nelsen, Brent F. 52

neoliberal eclecticism 106
neo-liberalism 29, 196, 236
neo-Orthodox intellectuals 53–4, 56, 64, 113
network society 200
New Democracy (ND) 46, 47, 49, 61, 170 n. 13, 172, 211 n.16
New Greek Cinema 180, 181, 184, 185, 187, 189, 192, 193
Nguyen, Viet Thanh 83
Nicolaou, Elena 236 n.3
Nikolaidis, Aristotelis 127
Nikolaidis, Nikos 203
Nikolaidou, Afroditi 193, 194
Nikolaidou, Sophia, 89, 89 n.17, 159
Nikolakopoulos, Ilias 16
Nikolopoulou, Maria 85, 87
Nioutsikos, Ioannis 78
Nollas, Dimitris 138 n. 22, 149, 152
Nova Melancholia 229

Ober, Josiah 240 n.9
Oikonomou, Christos 152
Old Greek Cinema 180, 193
Olivier, Laurent 16
Olympic Games, 2004 17, 39, 66, 74, 103, 191, 249
omogenia 117, 120
organic community 30
Organization for Economic Co-operation and Development (OECD) 7, 120, 121 n. 31
Organization for Security and Co-operation in Europe (OSCE) 95, 96
Orthodox communalism 57
Orthodoxy 111–17
Orwell, George 65
Ovid 147

Pagoulatos, George 18 n.15, 49
Pakis, Elisavet 226
Palaiologos, Grigorios 154
Palaiologos, Yannis 122 n.34
Palantzas, Nikitas 96 n.3
Paloma Aguilar, Fernández 76 n.6
Panagiotakis, N. M. 67
Panagiotopoulos, Panayis 3, 29, 33 n.27, 38 n.36, 190 n.13, 205

Panagiotopoulos, Vasilis 18 n.15,
    84 n.15, 105
Panayotopoulos, Nikos 235
Panhellenic Socialist Movement (PASOK)
    20 n.4, 25 n.15, 36, 46–50, 61, 76,
    78–9, 88, 95, 109, 172, 186, 202–4,
    211–2, 214, 223, 225
Panou, Yannis 152
Panselinos, Alexis 149, 152–3
Pantaleon, Lina 145
Pantelidou-Malouta, Maro 204, 216,
    216 n.25
Papadiamantis, Alexandros 51, 138, 154,
    171, 180
Papadimitriou, Dimitris 44
Papadimitriou, Lydia 20, 181, 187,
    192, 193
Papadimitriou, Nikos 69 n.2
Papadimitropoulos, Argyris 208
Papadogiannis, Nikolaos 33 n.26, 35, 202,
    202 n.3, 215 n.23, 218, 223
Papadopoulou, Maria 164
Papagelis, Theodoros, 147
Papageorgiou, Georgia 218
Papageorgiou, K. G. 148 n.8
Papagiannidou, Mairi 224
Papagiorgis, Kostis 51
Papagos, Alexandros 183
Papailias, Penelope 87
Papaioannou, Dimitris 191, 223n. 36, 224
Papakaliatis, Christophoros 194 n.16, 228
Papamichos, Jim 209 n.14
Papandreou, Andreas 21 n.6, 33, 36, 43,
    111, 172
Papandreou, Margaret 211
Papanikolaou, Aristotle 55
Papanikolaou, Dimitris 40 n.38, 196 n.17,
    200, 222, 226, 229
Papargyriou, Eleni 157 n.14
Paparrigopoulos, Konstantinos 67, 105
Papastathis, Lakis 171, 192, 197
Papataxiarchis, Evthymios 96 n.3, 210,
    217 n.27
Papathanassiou, Thanassis 56
Papathanassopoulos, Stylianos 162–64,
    166 n.6, 168, 169, 175 n.18
Papathanasopoulou, Maira 38 n.35
Pappas, Takis S 2–3
paralogotechnia 37–8

Paraschos, Manolis 165, 168
Parker, Holt, N. 36
parochialism 22
Parthenon 22, 73, 238
    sculptures 22, 70–4, 249
Paschalidis, Grigoris 163–65, 167 n.8, 172
Pasolini, Pier Paolo 226
Passas, Argyris G. 18 n.15
Patrikalakos, David 62 n.18
Patrikiou, Alexandra 137 n.18
patriotism 1, 77–8, 151
Payne, Daniel P. 58, 113
Pelagidis, Theodoros 5 n.8
Pentzikis, N. G. 157
Perantonakis, Yorgos 145
Perisiadis, Spyros 186
Perks, Nikos 190 n.12
Petropoulos, Elias 222
Petsini, Pinelopi. 110 n.21, 171 n.16,
    225 n.38
Pettifer, James 18 n.15
Philippidis, Daniel 155
Phillis, Philip 99 n.6
Pikionis, Dimitris 33
Plakoudas, Spyros 62 n.19
Plantzos, Dimitris 69, 247 n.29,
Plexoussaki, Efi 224
Politakis, Dimitris 244 n.19
political youth organizations 202 n.4
Politis, Kosmas 157, 171
Politis, O 15, n. 12, 33
Politopoulou, Marlena 89
Politou-Marmarinou, Eleni 96 n.3
Pollis, Adamantia 112, 214
Polycandrioti, Ourania 96 n.3
polyphonic media 161
polytonic system 126–7
Pomaks 132, 136
Pomeroy, Arthur 184 n.6
Pontic Greeks 109, 110, 118, 130
Popp, Susanne 103
popular culture 31–36, 38–41, 66, 135,
    158, 172–3, 177, 190
populism 3, 11, 21 n. 6, 36, 44
    aesthetic 32, 36
    in literature 37 n.33
    media 63
    nationalist 44 n.2
postcolonial cultures 27

postcolonial theory 23, 96
postmodernism 32, 68, 105, 106, 156–9
Poulantzas, Nikos 156
Poulios, Lefteris 43
Poulos, Margaret 214
Poupou, Anna 194
Pournara, Margarita 84
Pratsinakis, Manolis 122
Preciado, Paul B. 247
Pretenderis, I. K. 2
Prevelakis, Nicolas 54 n.12, 56
Proguidis, Lakis 51
Promotion of Greek Language (Organization) 137
protectionism 14, 74, 132–41
Psara, Angelika 218, 218 n.18
Psaras, Marios 193 n.15, 197, 227
Psaras, Tasos 185
Psychopedis, Kosmas 106
Pyromaglou, Komninos 77 n.7

queer culture 219–31, 251
Queericulum Vitae 227
Quest, Richard 238

Rabelais, François 51
Radstone, Susannah 84, 86, 89
Raftopoulos, Dimitris 149
Rakopoulos, Theodoros 41
Ramfos, Stelios 9, 22 n.9, 53
Raptopoulos, Vangelis 204
Rasoulis, Manolis 26
rebetika 26, 35, 40, 202, 204, 222
Reform of the Education of Muslim Minority Children 115
reformist culture 21
Regling, Klaus 4 n.5
Reich, Wilhelm 202 n.5
Repoussi, Maria 70, 104, 105, 215
Reppas, Michalis 190
Revett, Nicholas 234
Ricks, David 139 n.24
Ricoeur, Paul 82
Riedel, Brian 219, 224
Riefenstahl, Leni 235
Rhigas Velestinlis 29 n.23
Rikaki, Loukia 188
Rikou, Elpida 245 n.21
Ritsos, Yannis 143, 154, 225

Robertson, Roland 140
Robinson, Christopher 225
Roidis, Emmanouil 138, 154
Roitman, Janet 5
Romanides J.S. 54
Romaine, Suzanne 138 n.20
Roman Catholicism 59
Romas, Dionysus 171
Romeic self-image 20
Rolling Stones 205
Rose, Steve 193, 196 n.19
Roudometof, Victor 59, 60 n.17, 97 n.5, 111, 115
Rozakis, Christos L 94
Rozetti, Dora 225–6
Rudy, Kathy 219 n.29
Ruskin, John 30

Saltiel, Leon 108 n.18
Sarafis, Marion 18 n.15, 79 n.10
Sarantakos, Nikos 127, 225 n.38
Sartzetakis, Christos 139, 225
Savić, Obrad 49 n.6
Savvopoulos, Dionysis 40 n.38, 53, 56 n.13
Schäuble, Wolfgang, 63
Schmidt, Volker H. 12
Schoene, Berthold 219
segmentary society 21
Scholiastis, O 15 n. 12, 33, 53
Seferiades, Seraphim 207 n. 11
Seferis, George 37, 51, 132, 143, 158, 187
Seidl, Ulrich 194
Sella-Mazi, Eleni 94 n.1
semi-colony 49
Seraphim, Archibishop 113–14
Sevastakis, Nikolas 36, 56
sexuality 219–22
Shelley, Percy Bysshe 237
Sidiropoulos, Pavlos 203
Simitis, Costas 20 n.4, 44, 50, 115
Simopoulos, Kyriakos 100
Siopachas, Christos 185
Sjöberg, Erik 103, 109, 110
Skamnakis, Antonis 174
Skarimbas, Yannis 154, 157
Skassis, Thomas 89
Skiadas, Aristoxenos 127
Sklaveniti, Kostoula 212, 218
Sklavenitis, Dimitris 205

Skyladika 35
Slater, Don 31
Slavophones 95
Smaragdis, Yannis 187, 197
Smith, Anthony D. 67, 102, 208
Smith, Helena 246 n.24
Smith, Ole L. 79 n.10
social media 59 n.16, 104, 122, 140, 170, 173, 177–8 n.19, 207, 241
social movements 11, 15, 199–201, 230, 251
Sofos, Spyros A. 102 n.9
Solomos, Dionysios 137 n.17, 138, 153, 158, 187
Sotiris, Panagiotis 207 n.5
Sotiropoulos, Dimitris A. 44 n.2
Sotiropoulos, Dimitris P. 242 n.14
Soviet communism 57
Soviet Union 47, 98, 110, 118, 119, 186, 195
Spanias, Nikos 223
Spatharakis, Kostas 196 n.17
spiritual geography 59
Spivak, G. C. 23 n.11
Spyropoulos, D. 138 n.21
Spyropoulou, Angeliki 144
Stamiris, Eleni 211, 212, 214 n.20
Stamou, Anastasia 193
Stamou, Eva 38 n.35
standardization 125, 128, 131, 132
Stangos, Angelos 168, 169
state feminism 212
State Film Awards 192
Stathi, Irini 183 n.5
Stavrakakis, Yannis 28 n.21, 36
Stavrianos, Leften 104 n.11
Stavridi-Patrikiou, Rena 126
Stefani, Eva 73 n.5
Stefanidis, Ioannis D. 26 n.17, 45
Stefanou, Pagona 81
Stuart, James 234
subaltern 23, 236
Svoronos, Nikos G. 27 n.20, 67, 79 n.10, 105
Sweezy, Paul 6
Swingewood, Alan 31
Szymczyk, Adam 244

Tabaki, Anna, 96 n.3
Tachopoulos, Yannis 103
Tachtsis, Kostas 132, 223, 225
Tamm, Marek, 16, 83
Tannen, Deborah 217
Tarkovsky, Andrei 183
Tatsopoulos, Petros 37 n.31, 204
Terzakis, Angelos 132, 157, 171, 180
The Historical Archive of Greek Youth 203
Themelis, Nikos 29 n.23, 153
Theodorakopoulos, Loukas 222, 223 n.37
Theodoropoulos, Takis 51 n.8, 144 n.3
Theodossopoulos, Dimitris 101
Theodossopoulou, Mari 148
Theotokas, Nikos 106
Theotokas, Yorgos 132, 157
Thessaloniki Film Festival 181, 191, 192, 229
third space of enunciation 27
Thompson, George 235
Todorova, Maria 49 n.6
Tonnet, Henri 130
Topali, Maria 40 n.39
Tsambrounis Dimitris 223
Tsarouchis, Yannis 187
Tsenai, Odysseas (Odhise Qenaj) 98
traditionalism 11
Tramboulis, Theofilos 39, 156, 248 n.30
Transition(s), 1, 3, 13–18, 31, 35, 41, 68, 76n.6, 81, 83–4, 87–90, 93, 97, 106, 110, 111, 123, 128, 133, 151, 160, 172, 177–80, 193, 197, 204–5, 207, 216–9, 222, 226, 230–1, 235, 249, 251
Traverso, Enzo 30
Travlantonis, Antonis 171
Treaty of Lausanne 109
Trier, Lars von 194
Triantafyllidis Foundation 129, 130
Triantafyllidis, Manolis 126, 132
Triandafyllidou, Anna 11, 22, 62 n.18, 114, 118
Triantafyllou, Soti 153
Trikoupis, Charilaos 21
Tritsis, Antonis 113–4, 138
Troika 4, 25, 61, 63, 176
Trpeski, Davorin 72 n.4
Tsakalotos, Euclid 20 n.4
Tsaknias, Spyros 155
Tsaldari, Lina 210
Tsangari, Athina Rachel 180, 191 n. 14, 193, 196 n.19, 197, 209

Tseronis, Assimakis 130 n.7
Tsibiridou, Fotini 96 n.3
Tsimas, Pavlos 162, 165, 171 n.16
Tsimpouki, Theodora 144
Tsipras, Alexis 28 n.22, 205
Tsirkas, Stratis 37, 149
Tsitos, Filippos 99 n.6, 192
Tsitselikis, Konstantinos 98, 119
Tsountas, Christos 69
Tsoukalas, Konstantinos 7, 8, 223
Tsoukas, Haridimos 18 n.15
Tzimas, Nikos 185
Tziovas, Dimitris 6, 22 n.8–9, 63, 66, 69 n. 2, 97 n. 5, 100, 120, 150, 154, 156, 157, 217, 225, 236, 240
Tzirtzilakis, Yorgos 248 n.30
Tzogopoulos, George 174, 175 n.18
Tzoumerkas, Syllas 192

UEFA European Championship, 2004 74–5
underdog culture 23–6, 36, 42
uniform education system 23
Union of Greek Women (EGE) 210, 211
universalism 31, 57

Vaiou, Dina 218 n.28
Vakalopoulos, Christos 164, 204
Valaoritis, Nanos 148 n.8
Valoukos, Stathis 167, 172, 174
Valtinos, Thanassis 85–7, 150, 152, 158, 159
Vamvakas, Vasilis 3, 29, 31, 33 n.27, 38 n.36, 171, 173, 190 n.13
Van Boeschoten, Riki 82
Van Dyck, Karen 148, 200, 217 n.27, 242, 243
Van Sant, Gus 209
Vardalos, Nia 189
Varika, Eleni 212, 218
Varikas, Vasos. 155
Varon-Vassard, Odette 107, 107 n.12
Varoufakis, Yanis 62, 140, 175, 176, 237 n.6, 240, 242, 245
Vasilopoulou, Sofia 44 n.1
Vayenas, Nasos 37 n.33, 67, 68 n.1, 147, 154, 157
Velouchiotis, Aris 78, 80 n.12
Veloudis, Yorgos 36 n.30, 68 n.1

Veltsos, Yorgos 223
Venezis, Ilias 171
Venizelos, Eleftherios 21
Venturas, Lina 118
Veremis, Thanos M.18 n.15, 21, 24 n.13
Vernardakis, Christoforos 2 n.2
Verney, Susannah 46, 49, 50, 61, 64
Vervenioti, Tasoula 77, 80, 81, 217
Vidal, Belén 189, 197, 238
Vidos, Kosmas 17
Vitti, Mario 155
Vizyinos, Yeorgios 154
Vlachs/Aromanians 131–2, 136
Vlasidis, Vlasis 167 n.7
Vlastaris, Yannis 140
Vletsas, Spyros 63 n.20
Vogel, Jan 208
Voglis, Polymeris 2, 76, 78, 79, 81
Volanakis, Minos 226
Voulgaris, Kostas 158, 243 n. 15
Voulgaris, Pantelis 179, 184, 185, 187–8, 197
Voulgaris, Yannis 2, 8, 13, 18 n.15, 24 n. 13, 50, 78
Voupouras, Christos 191
Vouri, Sofia 102
Voutiras, Dimosthenis 157
Voutsaki, Sofia 68, 69
Vovou, Ioanna 162, 171
Vrettakos, Costas 185
Vronti, Selana 245 n.20

Weber, Max 60
weird wave Greek cinema 180, 193, 194 n.16, 196 n.18, 23
Western culture 16, 59
Western imperialism 46
Western individualism 53
Western legalism 55
Western nihilism 57
Western rationalism 56
White, Hayden 85
Wigen, Einar 16
Wilder, Charly 238 n.7
Willert, Trine Stauning 69 n.2, 103
Williams, Raymond 30
Winkler, M.M. 184 n.6
Wodak, Ruth 140

Women's Liberation Movement (KAG) 212
Woodhouse, C. M. 77, 233 n.1
Woods, Gregory 225
World Council of Hellenism Abroad 118

Xanthopoulos, Lefteris 185
Xanthoulis, Yannis 38 n.36
Xenakis, Sappho 22 n.8
Xenopoulos, Grigorios 171
Xydakis, Nikos 26
Xydakis, Nikos G. 53, 135 n.12

Yalouri, Eleana 245 n.21
Yannakakis, Eleni 96 n. 3, 97, 150, 153 n. 11
Yannakopoulos, Kostas 140 n.26, 219, 220, 221, 227
Yannaras, Christos 26, 53–57, 59 n.16, 113
Yannitsiotis, Yannis 215
Yannopoulos, Periklis 33
Yannopoulou, Efi 156

Yataganas, Xenophon A. 49
Yofyllis, Fotos 133
youth 201–10
youth culture 201, 203–5, 208, 209
youth slang 138, 205

Zacharia, Katerina 69
Zahariadis, Nikos 66
Zaharopoulos, Thimios 168, 171
Zefkili, Despina 247 n.27
Zei, Alki 144, 216
Zenakos, Avgoustinos 81
Zervos, Nikos 203
Zestanakis, Panagiotis 3
Ziras, Alexis 155
Zizioulas, I.D. 57, 113
Zolotas, Xenophon 137 n.16
Zorba, Myrsini 33
Zorba the Greek (Cacoyannis) 20, 41, 179 n.1, 236, 238
Zoumboulakis, Stavros 108, 116
Zouraris, Kostas 26, 53

www.ingramcontent.com/pod-product-compliance
Lightning Source LLC
Chambersburg PA
CBHW052150300426
44115CB00011B/1597